RIGHTLY DIVIDING
THE
BOOK OF REVELATION

RIGHTLY DIVIDING
THE
BOOK OF
REVELATION

J. E. BECKER

WINEPRESS WP PUBLISHING

ISBN 1-57921-497-5
Library of Congress Catalog Card Number: 2002111635

AUTHOR'S NOTE
TO READERS

This book is about teaching the Book of Revelation to Christians, not to sensationalize any personal predictions about the future. These are the last words of Jesus to His Church; thus they are of utmost importance. It is not a book for mere curiosity seekers but to help Christians come to a fuller knowledge of God's plans for our future. It is not for "babes in Christ" but for those able to chew "strong meat." Therefore, I make no apology for the depths it takes to reveal this vision and its meaning. It is my hope that pastors and teachers will take what has been uncovered and build beyond where I have gone, breaking it down so all may come to maturity in Christ, "unto the measure of the stature of the fulness of Christ" (Eph. 4:13). The overcomers' rewards promised to the Sardian church (Rev. 3:5) show that knowing God's plans for the future is part of becoming spiritually mature.

I have purposely used the King James Version rather than a newer translation because I have found that modern translators sometimes change the original words just to make the language flow better in today's English. Mostly, they substitute small words, such as *in* for *of* or *then* for *that*. However, many times these change the whole meaning of the sentence. Therefore, for the sake of accuracy, I hope the readers will forebear.

My personal purpose in this writing is to show the strength of the Lord "unto this generation" and His "power to every one that is to come" (Ps. 71:18). I also want to show the mighty things He has done and will do that other writers have failed to reveal because they did not address the physical judgments as "real time" events.

CONTENTS

INTRODUCTION

In his admonition to Timothy, Paul wrote: "Study to show thyself approved unto God, a workman that needeth not to be ashamed, rightly dividing the word of truth" (2 Timothy 2:15). What can we learn from this admonition? First, if we would be approved of God, we must study His Word. Second, if we would aspire to be workman, we could be ashamed before Him if we do not divide the truth correctly. Therefore, we can wrongly divide the "word of truth" (the collective inspired Word of God) due to a lack of study.

Unfortunately, this lack of study often corrupts the interpretation of the final prophecy in the Bible—the Revelation of Jesus Christ. Neglect is the main reason. Pragmatic Christians excuse their lack of study for three reasons. 1) They think it is too hard to understand; they are lazy. 2) They discredit it as a "happy hunting ground" for zealots or extremists; that disgusts them. 3) They believe it unnecessary for Christian living or evangelism; therefore unimportant. Yet, God pronounces a blessing to all who read, *hear* and keep the sayings of this book. More importantly, Jesus Christ Himself gives this book to the Church, "his servants," to show them things which "must shortly come to pass" (Rev. 1:1). These are virtually His last words spoken to His Bride.

Dare we neglect this book? How will we know these "things" if we do not study His final revelation? How can we know we have the correct interpretation if we do not rightly divide it? Failing to rightly divide the last book distorts all related prophecy because the Book of Revelation caps and organizes everything connected to the second coming of Christ. It forms the outline and the framework that integrates all other prophecies. To use a figure of speech, the prophetic word is like a picture puzzle made up of scattered pieces. The book of Revelation makes up the edge pieces. However, we must discern its divisions in order to put the pieces together.

These divisions include: 1) different time sequences, which are further divided by interruptions; 2) different groups of believers resurrected in different companies and at different times; 3) different settings for the scenes—on the earth, over the earth, middle heaven (the starry sky), and God's heaven; 4) different authorities competing with one another for supremacy; 5) even different types of interpretation in the text—literal versus figures of speech. Beyond all these, the book itself is divided into small divisions to define events. Failure to divide any of these will distort the interpretation.

The purpose of this book is to set forth these divisions, to raise questions to provoke thought, to define the related prophecies in the Old Testament and show their placement.

In short, this study will teach you how to study the Book of Revelation for yourself and connect all the dots. After all, if you understand the "what" that will happen, you will also recognize the "who" when history brings them on the world stage. You will become an able "watchman."

A brief mention of the point of view seems prudent. It is not my purpose to debate the various theological views of Revelation because I believe, as the nature of the judgments evolve, it will become clear that these events are yet to be fulfilled.

I say this because at no time since Jesus sojourned upon the earth have these particular circumstances happened. The events of 70 A.D. certainly did not fulfill them, because John received his vision some twenty years after the fall of Jerusalem. Since this was already past, what would be the point of informing the Church of its coming? Besides, that political upheaval did not change the heavens and the earth, though it tragically displaced Israel. The heavens and the earth continued in their natural courses, which is decidedly not the case in John's vision.

Jesus Himself stated that troubles at the end of the age would be so violent that nothing since the beginning of the world could compare to them (Matt. 24:21). He thus confirmed Daniel 12:1 where an angel tells Daniel about a coming time of trouble for the nation Israel that will be greater than anything that had happened after they became a nation. That means trouble greater than and more awesome than the plagues of Egypt and the crossing of the Red Sea. In Daniel's day the last great upheaval, involving the heavens and the earth had already happened (eighth century B.C.). Nothing like this has happened to the world since, certainly not since Jesus ascended. Revelation 16:18 tells about a worldwide earthquake greater than any that have happened since people were on the earth. Christ's visible return follows. Jesus has not yet come therefore, the prophesied events are still future.

Let it be clear to the reader that I speak from the point of view that when Jesus gave John the vision, He meant to convey real time and space happenings. Yes, He sometimes uses figures of speech that we will explore when we find them. Overall, however, He spoke of real events that shall soon come to pass.

Those who spiritualize portions of the vision leave us tossing on waves in a sea of uncertainty. To go beyond spiritualizing by setting aside Jesus' visible return, is to tamper with the basic tenets of Christianity—a dangerous practice. If we would not be ashamed before Him at His coming, we need to rightly divide this word of truth.

JOHN'S INTRODUCTION TO THE VISION

(REVELATION 1)

O God, thou hast taught me from my youth: and hitherto have I declared thy wondrous works. Now also when
I am old and greyheaded, O God, forsake me not; until I
have shewed thy strength unto this generation, and thy
power to every one that is to come. Thy righteousness,
also, O God, is very high, who has done great things:
God, who is like unto thee! Thou, which hast shewed
me great and sore troubles, shall quicken me again. (Ps.
71: 17–20)

Although these are the words of the psalmist, they
could have just as easily been John's words. He had
followed the Lord from his youth. Now in his old
age, he receives this awesome picture of God's righteousness and sees the judgment of the wicked earth executed
by strength and mighty power.

He introduces this picture to us by first sharing how it all came about. John has already seen the whole thing. Now he explains to the churches how it was given to him. So he tells why it was given, how it was given, where and when it was given, and who gave it to him. Afterwards, he states that he is commanded to give it in a divided manner. Therefore, even the first chapter is purposely divided in many ways.

Why the Vision Was Given

> The Revelation of Jesus Christ, which God gave unto him, to shew unto his servants things which must shortly come to pass . . . . Blessed is he that readeth, and they that hear the words of this prophecy, and keep those things which are written therein: for the time is at hand. (1:1, 3)

Unlike the title in the King James Version, the revelation is not from "St. John the Divine." He had the vision, but the revelation was from Jesus Christ. It initially came from the mind of the Father who decides everything. That is the Father's function in the Godhead. Jesus said, "I speak that which I have seen with my Father" (John 8:38). Jesus is the speaker and executor of the Father's words. Therefore, it is appropriate that God the Father gives the final revelation of the Bible through Jesus, the living Word of God. Jesus Christ's purpose as the head of the Church is to direct His body and as Bridegroom to prepare His Bride to rule, especially since these things come "shortly" (from God's perspective, not ours). He desires that the fulfillment of these days should not overtake the Church unprepared or the world left unwarned of the terrible judgments to come.

Consequently, God does not assign this task to an angel, but Jesus Himself came as "the messenger of God." He gave this vision to John to share with us, His Church, with the hope that all Christians would receive the promised blessing by reading, hearing, and keeping the things written in this book. So surely the reason for giving the vision was to share the plans of God with His friends, as he said in John 15:15, "I have called you friends; for all things I have heard of my Father I have made known unto you."

How the Vision Was Given

> And he sent and signified it by his angel unto his servant John: who bare record of the word of God, and of the testimony of Jesus Christ, and of all things that he saw. (1:1–2)

First of all, the angel of the Lord "signified" it, that is, He marked the vision with indicators that divide it. At this point, John says he bore record of three things (another set of divisions): 1) the "word of God" that he heard; (later, this is duly marked when not otherwise obvious by the words "and I heard"; 2) the "testimony of Jesus Christ" (a prophecy spoken by another[1] voicing the Lord's words), where John is part of the scene; and finally, 3) a record of "all things he saw," marked in the text by such words as "I saw" or "I looked and behold."

---

[1] The testimony of Jesus, explained in Revelation 19:10, tells us that it is a word of prophecy given by a spirit of prophecy (one of the power gifts). Some of what he heard was given indirectly in this manner.

Forty-one of these divisions appear throughout the Book of Revelation. In the last chapter of the book, John declares in the form of an oath that he saw all these things. Their purpose, aside from helping us see what he saw, is to keep the scenes separate because the events of the entire vision do not always occur consecutively. Not rightly dividing these scenes can confuse the interpretation, since they fit together in blocks.

This method of recording visions is not new because both Daniel and Ezekiel divided their visions similarly. Their visions, however, were on the whole less intricate with fewer changing scenes, and they thus employed fewer "I saw's" or "lo and behold's." Since this seems to be the method of presenting prophetic[2] visions, we need to pay close attention to them in order to understand the message.

Therefore, the method used to give the revelation was 1) spoken by the Lord, 2) spoken by a messenger voicing the Lord's words, or 3) shown to John in scenes. With some scenes, John watched as if he were viewing video clips; with others, John participated as part of the scenes.

Where and When the Vision Was Given

> I John . . . was in the isle that is called Patmos, for the word of God, and for the testimony of Jesus Christ. I was in the Spirit on the Lord's day. (1:9–10)

John states that he was exiled to the Island of Patmos, evidently because of persecution for preaching about Jesus

---

[2] Several prophets used this method to convey their visions—namely, Ezekiel, Daniel, and Zechariah.

Christ. That gives the where. He further says he was "in the Spirit on the Lord's day," a Sunday. That gives the time.

But before he gives the particulars of the vision, he composes a salutation to the churches he was earlier commanded to address.

> John to the seven churches which are in Asia: Grace be unto you, and peace, from him which is, and which was, and which is to come; and from the seven Spirits which are before his throne. (1:4)

The salutation begins, as do most epistles of the New Testament, with his name John, then names the addressees—the seven churches in Asia to which he ascribes grace and peace from God who is divided into three persons.

First, he gives a description of God's eternal nature: "from him which is, and which was, and which is to come." Then he gives reference to the Holy Spirit, described as "the seven Spirits, which are before his throne" (1:4). This reveals information John had not known until he stood before the throne himself in the vision and heard it declared (4:5). It also raises the question: Is this the same throne that belongs to the eternal one? Is this eternal one just another name for the Father? John may be declaring the grace and peace as coming from the entire Godhead.

This seems to be confirmed when he follows with a declaration of Jesus Christ the Son:

> And from Jesus Christ, who is the faithful witness, and the first begotten of the dead, and the prince of the kings of the earth. Unto him that loved us, and washed us from our sins in his own blood. (1:5)

While John describes the Father as the eternal one through the three divisions of time (present, past, and future) and describes the Spirit as seven flames of light denoting complete illumination, he describes the Son extensively by His work: 1) Jesus Christ is the faithful witness. He was the "express image" of God the Father, faithfully portraying His character to the world, and He continues to do so today through the Bible. 2) He is the firstborn of the dead—the first and only man to be resurrected from the dead to an eternal state. His very resurrection celebrates His finished work on the cross. 3) He is the Prince of the kings of the earth.

> And hath made us kings and priests unto God and his
> Father; to him be glory and dominion for ever and ever.
> Amen. (1:6)

Again we see evidence that John has been influenced by the vision in chapter 4. He refers not to secular kings now ruling the earth but to those he had seen elevated in the vision, those whom Jesus had loved and bought with His own blood and made to be kings and priests unto God and His Father. This royal Prince of the Father is to have glory and dominion forever and ever. Amen!

> Behold, he cometh with clouds; and every eye shall see
> him, and they also which pierced him: and all kindreds
> of the earth shall wail because of him. Even so, Amen.
> (1:7)

John breaks forth in a declaration of the most awesome scene that he witnessed in the whole vision—that of Christ's visible return as recorded in chapter 19. He says every eye shall see Him, specifically they who pierced Him (presumably the living Jews who still reject Him), and all shall wail because they know their judgment is at hand. Since verse 8 is not found in most manuscripts, we will ignore it.

The Giver of the Vision

> I was in the Spirit on the Lord's day, and heard behind me a great voice, as of a trumpet, saying, I am Alpha and Omega, the first and the last. (1:10–11)

John's first indication that something out of the ordinary is about to happen was a voice behind him—a great voice similar to the blast of a trumpet. Just imagine such a voice, a commanding voice resonating with great authority. The words spoken seem to confirm this, for the one speaking blatantly declares, "I am Alpha and Omega, the first and the last." This statement, though short, says it all. Jesus Christ is the beginning and the end and everything in between—complete truth, complete love, complete mercy, complete judgment, and He has complete power to carry out the judgment.

> What thou seest, write in a book, and send it to the seven churches which are in Asia; unto Ephesus, and unto Smyrna, and unto Pergamos, and unto Thyatira, and unto Sardis, and unto Philadelphia, and unto Laodicea. (1:11)

Here again we find the emphasis on seeing. This must be the reason John is careful to record each time he sees something different. The Lord commands him to write a book, not letters, so that each church receives the whole revelation. These churches are all located in Asia, a Gentile region but also populated with many scattered Jews.

> And I turned to see the voice that spake with me. And being turned, I saw seven golden candlesticks. (1:12)

John turns to face the source of the voice. He then records his first "I saw." The vision had actually begun with his hearing the voice. That is significant when we realize how much emphasis Jesus placed on "hearing" in the Gospels and continued to place emphasis on it throughout the Book of Revelation. It's a principle. The receiving of truth *always* begins with hearing.

If John knew who was speaking to him, he gives no indication. Yet John was the apostle who understood best that Jesus was the Word of God. Even if he knew it was Jesus, the awesome sight of the one now visible stretches his comprehension. First, he describes what he sees, then he describes his reaction to it. Though we have never known Christ in the flesh as John did, I am sure we would react in the same way.

John describes the setting—a series of lampstands (not "candlesticks" as rendered in the KJV). The lamp stands were unusual in that they held only one lamp instead of a menorah whose seven lamps branch from a single base and is a complete unit by itself. The number seven may suggest complete illumination, yet it requires all seven lampstands to make it so. The thought then is that no church (Jesus tells John later that these lampstands represent churches [1:20]) by itself contains all truth. Yet each church stands alone as part of a complete testimony.

> And in the midst of the seven candlesticks one like unto the Son of man, clothed with a garment down to the foot, and girt about the paps with a golden girdle. (1:13)

The glorious being standing in the midst of the lampstands suggests that He is central to their light. Furthermore, His apparel suggests the office of a priest, for he wears a floor-length robe tied about the breast with a golden girdle. The girdle itself distinguishes Him from earthly priests, particularly the high priest of Israel whose girdle was made of woven cloth in colors of blue, red, and purple. This priest wears gold representing God in His pure holiness. This leads us to believe that John sees Jesus in His role of High Priest after the order of Melchisedec.

> His head and his hairs were white like wool, as white as snow; and his eyes were as a flame of fire. (1:14)

The description of Christ's person presents a different picture, undoubtedly one of a judge. His hair is white with the texture of wool, like that of an English judge's wig. His eyes burn like flame, suggesting righteous anger. It is amazing that John is able to distinguish his eyes at all, since His whole face shines as brightly as the sun in its power. Looking directly into the sun's brightness blurs the eyes so that distinguishing the individual characteristics of the face would have been impossible. Only the flashing eyes would be discernable.

> And his feet like unto fine brass, as if they burned in a furnace; and his voice as the sound of many waters. (1:15)

His unclad feet glowed as burnished brass, giving off light like two metals fused in a furnace glow because of the extreme heat. Both His eyes and His feet remind us that our God is a consuming fire, burning away all that is less than His standard of holiness as a righteous Judge.

Then John records a change in the sound of the Judge's voice. The sound of the trumpet behind him had captured John's attention, but now face-to-face it sounds more like many waters. If you have ever stood at the top of Niagara Falls and seen the rushing water drop in a deafening roar, you heard a sound similar to what John tried to convey. Imagine such a sound relaying intelligible words!

> And he had in his right hand seven stars: and out of his mouth went a sharp twoedged sword: and his countenance was as the sun shineth in his strength. And when I saw him, I fell at his feet as dead. (1:16–17)

John completes his description by denoting seven stars in the glorious being's right hand and a sharp two-edged sword protruding from His mouth; then John collapses at the Judge's feet, utterly undone.

One cannot help but wonder how the stars in Christ's hand appeared. We naturally think of five-pointed stars as in our American flag. But what John saw had to be lights similar to what is seen in the nightly sky. Therefore, since their lights are dimmer than that shining from Christ's face, John assumes they are stars. But then Jesus refers to them as stars, removing all doubt as to what to call them.

The writer to the Hebrews explains the meaning of the two-edged sword: "For the word of God is quick, and powerful, and sharper than any two-edged sword, piercing even to the dividing asunder of soul and spirit, and of the joints and marrow, and is a discerner of the thoughts and intents of the heart. Neither is there any creature that is not manifest in his sight: but all things are naked and opened unto the eyes of him with whom we have to do" (Heb. 4:12–13). Notice this passage exactly parallels what John saw and explains the sword as a figure of speech. It is nothing less than the sharp cutting Word of God coming out of His mouth.

Here John introduces a principle concerning the interpretation of figures of speech. If we want to make any sense of this vision, we must understand that God uses more than one way to convey the message. However, the vision overall depicts a series of events that are literal time-and-space happenings. Figures of speech are marked by words such as *as a* or *liken to*, etc., showing that John is using an example of something to help us understand what he is seeing so we can see it, too.

Here we need to stop and explain something to the reader. Figures of speech abound throughout Scripture. Indeed, they constitute a veritable spiritual language all their own. John presents this picture of the glorified one in this language. Not only is it descriptive in itself, but the description also conveys deeper meanings.

New believers are subjected to more and more of these spiritual terms until they begin to speak to others in this language. For instance, take the word *light*. Among believers, *light* translates into "truth" or "knowledge." By contrast, *darkness* speaks of the absence of truth or knowledge. Jesus repeatedly spoke in this language. However, we need to distinguish between a true figure of speech and a plain-spoken word meant to be taken literally. To make everything a figure of speech goes beyond the truth and obscures the meaning.

Once we "rightly divide" a figure of speech in Scripture, it will be explained in the context unless it has already been explained elsewhere. The Bible is basically all part of one truth. Therefore, if we know what goes before, we will understand what comes after. This is a problem to people who interpret the Book of Revelation by using only its text with a few other prophecies. This book is meant to be the capstone of God's truth. It rests upon the whole Word of God, which has been built "line upon line and precept upon precept" until it brings us to the consummation of God's revelation to man. If we do our homework, we will see the picture Jesus is trying to show His Church.

Returning to the discussion of figures of speech, we have an example of both types of explanation in this first chapter. Jesus explains to John in verse 20 that a mystery surrounds the stars in His hand and the lampstands. The seven stars *are* seven angels (in this case, "messengers," as that is the original meaning of the word *angel*), and the seven lampstands *are* the seven churches. This exemplifies a figure of speech explained right in the context. The two-edged sword exemplifies a figure of speech explained outside the context. It was already explained in Hebrews, so there is no need to explain it again.

Now let's go back and reread the description of the glorious being. We will point out the figures of speech meant to make us see what John saw:

And I turned to see the voice that spake with me [of course, John didn't expect to see a voice but rather He who spoke]. And being turned, I saw [scene marker] seven golden candlesticks [which we now know represent the seven churches to whom he is writing].

And in the midst of the seven candlesticks one like unto [figure of speech] the Son of man [at this point, John did not know who this was, but he looked like a human man, at least in form], clothed with a garment down to the foot, and girt about the paps with a golden girdle. His head and his hairs were white like [figure of speech] wool [the texture of the hair qualified by a brighter white], as white as [figure of speech] snow; and his eyes were as a [figure of speech] flame of fire [flashing, licking, blazing?]; and his feet like unto [figure of speech] fine brass, as if [figure of speech] they burned in a furnace; and his voice as [figure of speech] the sound of many waters.

And he had in his right hand seven stars: and out of his mouth went a sharp two-edged sword [a figure of speech not defined as those preceding it are easily discernable. Since we know that a normal mouth contains a tongue, not a sword, the sword's meaning must be ascertained elsewhere. In this case, Hebrews 4 explained it]: and his countenance was as [figure of speech] the sun shineth in his strength. (1:12–16)

Do you see the same picture John saw as he employs all these figures of speech? Now we return to John whom we left prostrate upon the ground before the glorious one.

And he laid his right hand upon me, saying unto me, Fear not; I am the first and the last: I am he that liveth, and was dead; and, behold, I am alive for evermore, Amen; and have the keys of hell and of death. (1:17–18)

The keys, given to Christ at His resurrection, have the power to open the unseen world of spirits and resurrect them at His will.

Jesus repeats his first declaration, "I am the first and the last." Perhaps he wants to remind John of his existence in ages past, identifying Himself with the one in Isaiah 41:4 who says: "Who hath wrought and done it, calling the generations from the beginning? I the LORD [Jehovah], the first, and the last; I am he." Or Isaiah 43: 11: "I, even I, am the LORD [Jehovah]; and beside me there is no saviour." Or again in Isaiah 44:6 where He says: "Thus saith the LORD [Jehovah] the King of Israel, and his redeemer the LORD of hosts; I am the first, and I am the last; and beside me there is no God."

John probably knew these Scriptures in Isaiah, and he was sure to recognize Jesus' reference to His resurrection. Then how could he miss the three statements of "I am"? It was this name that so infuriated the Pharisees. Jesus prayed in the upper room, "And now, O Father, glorify thou me with thine own self with the glory which I had with thee before the world was" (John 17:5).

John's fear dissolves when he realizes the identity of the one before him. Having lain upon His breast at the last supper with the boldness of youth, he now recognizes in his old age the fullness of the glory of Jesus Christ his Lord, a glory far greater than what he saw on the Mount of Transfiguration. Knowing fully the one before him, John is now ready to act upon the service required of him.

> Write the things which thou hast seen, and the things
> which are, and the things which shall be hereafter. (1:19).

Once again we find reference to what John sees. Up to now, he has seen the appearance of the glorious one and heard the words spoken to him. This is the past tense of the vision, the present naturally follows, and the future after that. So a division of time is set before John into which we can separate the whole vision. The present, "the things which are," will continue until they finish their full course. Then and only then can the "things . . . hereafter" begin.

Thus, the vision divides time into three periods, but it should be noted, however, that they are not equal in duration. The things John has seen could have taken only minutes to happen. The things "hereafter" have an approximate time limit of seven years plus the thousand-year reign of Christ, a time limit found in the text of the vision and other prophecies connected with it. The "things which are" have no specific time limit. We know only that this present age already existed at the time of John and will continue until Christ's return for His Church. Therefore, we can call "the things which are" the church age.

So far, the time has extended to nearly two thousand years, making it approximately the same amount of time allotted to the development of Israel as God's people. If we add the cumulative years in the history before the flood found in the list of descendents, we have 1,661 years. The total after the flood up until the time of Abraham's promise (Abraham was fifty years old at that time, according to the Book of Jasher) was 2,003 years.

Using that as a beginning point for the development of Israel, we add fifty years until Isaac is born and 430 years to his descendents and the sojourn in Egypt. We know that the exodus occurred sometime around 1500 B.C. This gives us approximately two thousand years, give or take some overlapping years, to the end of Jesus' ministry. Surely, there must be some significance to this. We have been His people almost as long as the Israelites were His people.

If we add the thousand-year reign of Christ's earthly kingdom, we will have an approximate week of thousand-year periods until the whole universe enters eternity and death itself is destroyed. It is entirely fitting that God should complete the Bible with this final revelation, explaining to His Church His whole counsel concerning the earth. He charges His Church to illuminate this to the world until He comes. He previously charged Israel with keeping His word until His first coming. Could this be the significance of the times being so similar? Does He have two separate peoples whom He loves and to whom He has made special promises?

Whether this is true or not we will have to wait and see, but we do know that the Church will reign with Christ in the coming age. We have much to learn. We dare not neglect this book, but we must divide it correctly.

THE THINGS WHICH ARE: EPHESUS

(Revelation 2:1–7)

The mystery of the seven stars which thou sawest in my right hand, and the seven golden candlesticks. The seven stars are the angels of the seven churches: and the seven candlesticks which thou sawest are the seven churches. (1:20)

If I had divided the text of Revelation, I would have begun chapter 2 with chapter 1, verse 20. Here the Lord introduces a mystery concerning the seven churches that obviously belongs to "the things which are."

This is the first of three mysteries mentioned in this book. The second "mystery of God" (10:7) has to do with the prophetic word as found in the prophets, and the third, "Mystery Babylon" (17:5) has to do with a religious regime. Many other mysteries occur in the Gospels and Epistles as well. So the question is, What is the scriptural understanding of a mystery?

The First Mystery

Strong's *Exhaustive Concordance of the Bible* defines *mystery* from the Greek word *musterion*, which means "to shut the mouth; a secret or a mystery" (through the idea of initiation into religious rites). The word probably hails back to the Elysian mystery religions of Greece, the rites of which were so immoral and licentious that the initiated swore to secrecy to hide such debauchery from public view. Used from a Christian viewpoint, *mysteries* refer to the wonderful truths that only those in Christ can know because they must discern them by spiritual means (1 Cor. 2:14). This is why Jesus called many of the parables the "mysteries" of the kingdom of God. He gives his disciples the right to understand but not others.

Paul mentions several mysteries in the Epistles, such as the truth that the Gentiles were to be included in redemption. This was a mystery hidden since the foundation of the world (Eph. 3:5–6). Another mystery was that the nation Israel will accept Christ someday, though they reject Him now. Paul says we need to know this mystery, also (Rom. 11:25). The catching away of living saints at the time of the resurrection is a great mystery (1 Cor. 15:51). Every mention of the word *mystery* in the Bible hides something that needs to be uncovered. Hence, the same is true of the Book of Revelation.

Looking at the first mystery in 1:20, we see seven stars possessively held in the Lord's right hand, suggesting authority. They belong totally to Him; therefore, He can trust them to faithfully communicate His truth (shine their light) to each of their churches.

The first step in solving our mystery should be uncovering how God uses *stars* as a figure of speech in Scripture.

Two references make mention of stars as such. Both occur in passages having to do with the resurrection. The first is found in Daniel 12:3, "And they that be wise shall shine as the brightness of the firmament; and they that turn many to righteousness as the stars for ever and ever." Wise believers shall shine *as* (figure of speech) the "brightness of the firmament," that is, like the light of a terrestrial body with an atmosphere. And those who "turn many to righteousness" shall shine *as* (figure of speech) the "stars for ever and ever."

The second reference, found in 1 Corinthians 15:39–44, explains how a corrupt physical body is sown in death, and a glorious heavenly body is raised in the resurrection. Then Paul lists different kinds of natural bodies—beasts, fish, birds, and humans—comparing them to the natural body sown in death. Then he mentions various kinds of heavenly bodies, differentiating between the terrestrial and celestial as two kinds of glories. After that, he states that "one star differeth from another star in glory. So also is the resurrection of the dead. It is sown in corruption; it is raised in incorruption. It is sown in dishonour; it is raised in glory" (vv. 41–43). First, we bear the "image of the earthy," and then we will "bear the image of the heavenly" (v. 49). The stars are a figure of speech denoting that.

Now applying this to our mystery in Revelation 1:20, we need to say that the "stars" mentioned here are not yet resurrected since the resurrection is still future at this point in the vision. We can say that the stars held in Christ's hand are believers in each church who have already earned the glory of "turning many to righteousness." They already shine in the midst of their fellow Christians. Part of the mystery then is that believers carry these messages, not heavenly beings. That alerts us to the fact that not every mention of angels in this vision refers to heavenly beings.

Believing that we have uncovered the mystery of the stars, we now face the mystery of the lampstands. How do these relate in a figure of speech? We turn to the words of Jesus in His parable of the lampstand. He says in Luke 11:33, "No man, when he hath lighted a candle [lamp] putteth it in a secret place but on a candlestick [lampstand], that they which come in may see the light." From this we can see that He means the lampstand to be public, not private or secret. In Matthew 5:14, Jesus says, "Ye are the light of the world," speaking to believers. Then He continued with, "Let your light so shine before men, that they may see your good works, and glorify your Father which is in heaven" (v. 16). Here He confirms it as public testimony. In Mark He goes one step further.

> And He said to them, "Is a lamp brought to be put under a basket or under a bed? Is it not to be set on a lampstand? For there is nothing hidden which will not be revealed, nor has anything been kept secret but that it should come to light. If anyone has ears to hear, let him hear." Then He said to them, "Take heed what you hear. With the same measure you use, it will be measured to you; and to you who hear, more will be given. For whoever has, to him more will be given; but whoever does not have, even what he has will be taken away from him." (Mark 4:21–25 NKJV)

From this passage, we can see that all truth revealed by God will be committed to the Church as the chosen vehicle to hold up "the light." Nothing is to be hidden, including the truth of the closing chapters of God's Word. John was to share his vision with the Church.

Though the message is not hidden, our "ears" must be open to receive it. Herein we find the principle concerning spiritual growth, whether of individuals or collectively as churches. We receive truth in the measure that we are able to hear it. If we refuse a certain truth, we will not receive any more.

This is important because doctrine is laid down "precept upon precept; line upon line; here a little, and there a little" (Isa. 28:9–10). We cannot understand what comes after until we understand what goes before. We cannot learn tenth-grade math until we learn ninth-grade math, because tenth-grade math builds on the ninth. Those who have truth shall have more given them. Those who do not have truth but rather a teaching they hold as truth shall have that so-called truth taken away. Luke's version of this concept adds "that which he seemeth to have" (Luke 8:18). This emphasis upon hearing continues throughout the Book of Revelation.

Looking back to our mystery of the lampstands, we wonder why seven churches are mentioned. Why not just one lampstand to represent the Church as a whole? We must understand this mystery if we would learn anything from the letters to the seven churches. Apart from the fact that the number seven in Scripture represents completeness, God must have had a specific reason for choosing these particular seven churches. After all, the cities of Colosse, Derbe, Lystra, and Hieropolos were in the same area. We can only assume that Jesus' purpose for choosing these seven was because their conditions give instruction to the whole Church.

Turning now to the letters, first we observe that John does not see anything. Instead, these letters became a major portion of what he hears. Jesus dictates every bit of the "things which are" to him.

Second, we note that they all follow a pattern. 1) Each letter begins by addressing the "star" of the church, charging him with the message, followed by a salutation from the sender. Christ in His role as Priest and Judge describes one or more of His personal characteristics to correct the church's individual shortcomings. 2) Following that, Christ evaluates their works and their characters, either commending or condemning them. He points out a problem and suggests a solution. 3) He issues a warning of consequences if they fail to comply. 4) After the warning, Christ offers a reward to those individuals who overcome the problem outlined in the letter. 5) Finally, He leaves the choice with each individual since He admonishes in each letter, "He that hath an ear, let him hear what the Spirit saith to the churches." He continually reminds us of the importance of hearing. Obviously, each one of these seven churches has a problem, or they would not need to overcome anything.

Our third observation about these letters is that no matter what problem is defined in each church, the rewards to the overcomers graduate from church to church. They go from the right "to eat of the tree of life" in the paradise of God promised to the Ephesian overcomers (2:7) all the way to the right to sit with Christ on His throne promised to the Laodicean overcomers (3:21). This indicates a progression of spiritual development. Now we begin to see why He chose these particular churches. They are the ones with the problems He wants to highlight.

Thus, "the things which are" reveal seven problems to overcome for the Church as a whole and each individual believer in particular. The admonition addresses the individual: "He that hath an ear, let him hear . . . To him . . . that overcometh will I give." Not only is it addressed to the individual, but the individual is to hear what the Spirit says to *all* the churches, making him responsible to overcome *all* the problems if he would reign with Christ on His throne. From this we can see that although salvation is a gift, each person must earn his or her place in the rule of the coming kingdom. No wonder Jesus told James and John's mother that He could not grant her sons exalted positions in the kingdom. Those positions were not His to give (Matt. 20:23). Such positions are prepared by the Father for those chosen for their spiritual maturity. This mystery has not been taught generally and so has remained hidden from most of the Church, probably because many believers have ignored the Book of Revelation.

Expositors have noticed one facet, however: the apparent overcoming of the problems in the spiritual development of the Church through history. Looking back, we can see that the Church truly has passed through seven periods in time that remind us of the seven problems. Some individuals in each time period managed to overcome the prevailing problem, causing the Church as a whole to gradually grow toward maturity.

The Salutation

> Unto the angel of the church in Ephesus write; These things saith he that holdeth the seven stars in his right hand, who walketh in the midst of the seven golden candlesticks [lampstands]. (2:1)

Jesus reminds the church that He has the seven stars in His hand—particularly, their "star" who gives their message. He walks in the midst of all His churches observing their progress. Everything is "a go" from His perspective. What could possibly go wrong?

The Evaluation

> I know thy works, and thy labour, and thy patience, and how thou canst not bear them which are evil: and thou hast tried them which say they are apostles, and are not, and hast found them liars: And hast borne, and hast patience, and for my name's sake hast laboured, and hast not fainted. (2:2–3)

The phrase "I know thy works" occurs in the evaluation of every church. They all had works, but He was looking for more than works. Maybe we put so much emphasis on works because we think we can earn something by our works for Him. Instead, He is more interested in what we are than in what we do, probably because what we do ultimately flows from what we are. As James says, "Can the fig tree, my brethren, bear olive berries?" (James 3:12).

The great High Priest of the Church recognizes their works, their labor, their patience, and especially their zeal toward opposing false apostles. All that is well and good. They perhaps even endured some persecution in standing up for His name. He recognizes all this, but He still has a grievance against them—a grievance so grave He threatens to remove their testimony altogether.

If we were making an assessment of this church, we would see a vibrant fellowship in a metropolitan city with a large agora (marketplace), a hospital, an extensive library, two amphitheaters, and a large circus (stadium) for chariot racing. The city sprawled over several small hills and had numerous temples as well as the famous temple of Diana. We would probably look on their works and say to them, "Well done" because we know this huge city had to be full of temptations. However, the Lord does not say this. What exactly was the problem here?

The Problem

> Nevertheless I have somewhat against thee, because thou hast left thy first love. Remember therefore from whence thou art fallen, and repent, and do the first works: or else I will come unto thee quickly, and remove thy candlestick [lampstand] out of his place, except thou repent. (2:4–5)

Their works had deteriorated from what was acceptable to the Lord into something else. He states the reason: they had left their "first love." *First love* is another figure of speech. We need no explanation, for most of us knew the thrill of that experience. We wanted to spend time with our loved ones, to listen to them speak, to please them in any way we could. The bond between us was precious.

The works of the Ephesian church had changed from this sweet relationship with the Lord to a rigid standard of truth they had established. In short, they had stopped hearing His message and had developed one of their own. He knew that without a living communication between them, they would eventually grow weary in well doing. Having lost the joy of serving, they would fall back into the world. Their light would go out, and He would have no choice but to remove their lampstand.

Christ's warning was in effect, "Repent! Realize how far you have fallen from the ideal. Listen to your messenger! Hear my words to you." Jesus says, "My sheep hear my voice, and I know them, and they follow me" (John 10:27).

But this thou hast, that thou hatest the deeds of the Nicolaitanes, which I also hate. (2:6)

Christ, however, commends their love of truth and hatred of evil. Both He and they hate the deeds of the Nicolaitanes, a sect that seems to have left no trace in history. The early church father Irenaeus identified them as followers of Nicolas, one of the seven deacons in Acts 6:5. He associated them with the Gnostics, but his assessment was not founded on clear historical evidence. Clement of Alexandria defended Nicolas. So we are left with only the name for a clue. In the Greek *Nikolaites* means an "adherent of Nicolaiis." *Nikolaos* means "victorious over the people." Some believe from this clue that it was an early attempt to set up an apostolic succession, elevating so-called enlightened men (pastors, bishops, archbishops, popes) to positions of authority over the laity and taking away the priesthood of all believers. Whether this is true, we cannot tell, but this much we do know: The Ephesians did not call them false apostles. They did object to their deeds, and rightly so if the Nicolaitanes adopted the Gnostic antinomianism (as pseudo-Tertullian in the fourth century speculates). Antinomian Gnosticism held that sensuality could be overcome by indulging it to exhaustion, and they practiced the foulest debaucheries.[3]

Perhaps the Gnosticism of the first century had affected the Ephesian church more than they realized. Gnostics el-

---

[3] Editor, James Hastings, DD *The Dictionary of the Apostolic Church, Vol. II*, Charles Scribner's Sons, New York, 1918, p. 455.

evated intellectual knowledge over faith, whereas the Ephesian church elevated knowledge over love. Yet as Paul tells the Corinthians, even if we have all knowledge and understand all mysteries and have no love, it profits us nothing (1 Cor. 13:2–3). Paul expressly reminds the Ephesians in his letter to them to speak "the truth in love" (Eph. 4:15). In fact, he entreats them six times to carry out their works "in love" (1:4; 3:17; 4:2, 15, 16; 5:2). Finally, he tells them to "know the love of Christ, which passeth knowledge" (3:19).

Living and working with truth alone leads to rigidity, legalism, and rejection by the Lord. Love is the primary fruit of the Spirit, something to be cultivated in the Church and in the believer. The only works acceptable to God are deeds of faith worked *through* love (Gal. 5:6).

The Reward

> He that hath an ear, let him hear what the Spirit saith unto the churches; To him that overcometh will I give to eat of the tree of life, which is in the midst of the paradise of God. (2:7)

Notice that although Jesus writes to the whole Ephesian church, He leaves the overcoming of the problem to the individual. If we are correct in our assessment that these letters offer a progression of spiritual growth, this first church stands as a beginning. Thus, as applied to the individual, it would be a starting point also.

The first steps of new believers seem to leap with joy. Their consciences are clear. The knowledge of what the Lord has done for them is fresh and exciting. They desire to please the Lord in everything they do. Others like to be around them because of that effervescent flush of first love. However, the new believers' joy will last only as long as they hear from the Lord. If they develop a hunger and thirst for the Word of God, they will grow and overcome.

All too often, however, they depend on others to feed their new spiritual lives. Unless the Holy Spirit inspires the teaching, the words are dead. Settling for a set of truths will not keep their love alive. When adversaries come against them, they would become discouraged and lose interest in spiritual things. If they fell back into the world, their lives would not change, and they would not grow spiritually. How many times have we seen this happen?

Are they lost then, since they failed to continue? No, they genuinely believed; therefore, their sins remain covered by the blood of Christ. They fall into the category of the person spoken of in 1 Corinthians 3:15, "He himself shall be saved; yet so as by fire." Because they failed to repent of departing from their first love and walked through life devoid of hearing their Shepherd's voice, they did not produce any spiritual maturity worthy of reward. Salvation becomes their fire escape from hell, and they arrive in heaven with nothing but their eternal life. How prone we are to judge such persons as not being real Christians. Only God knows the hearts of people, and we must leave this judgment to Him.

Again, we see the importance of hearing. The persons who hear and continue to hear are the ones who overcome. They will be given access to the tree of life in the paradise of God. This same tree was denied to Adam and Eve in the Garden of Eden because they chose knowledge over life. The Ephesians were making the same mistake.

The last chapter of Revelation shows the tree of life growing in the middle of the street on either side of the river,
supplying life in its fruit and healing in its leaves. When
Jesus speaks of the heavenly dwelling place he was going
to prepare for His Church, He says, "Whither I go ye know,
and the way ye know. Thomas saith unto him, Lord, we
know not whither thou goest; and how can we know the
way? Jesus saith unto him, I am the way [the street?], the
truth [the river?], and the life [the tree?]" (John 14:4–6).

Tracing the river in Revelation back to its source, we
find that it issues from the throne—a river of life that evidently flows through the heavenly city. We assume that
wherever the river flows, by their association we would also
find the street and trees. Access to this tree and therefore
the street depicts a starting point of the journey to the throne
in a figure of speech. Failure to overcome this step is failure
to undertake the journey at all.

Chapter 3

THE THINGS WHICH ARE: SMYRNA

(REVELATION 2:8–11)

The Salutation

> And unto the angel of the church in Smyrna write; These things saith the first and the last, which was dead, and is alive. (2:8)

He who has charge of all history says basically, "I am in control. Nothing can happen to you unless I allow it. Nevertheless, I know what you are going through. I have been there before you. I know what it is like to be persecuted, hated, spit upon, and beaten for the sake of being in God's will."

The Evaluation

> I know thy works, and tribulation, and poverty, (but thou art rich) and I know the blasphemy of them which say

they are Jews, and are not, but are of the synagogue of Satan. (2:9)

The Smyrna church was suffering at the hands of Jews who enlisted Roman rulers in their attempt to stamp out Christianity. Jesus recognizes these believers' works, tribulation, and poverty, but He says, "Thou art rich"—rich in heavenly riches. He told His disciples in the Sermon on the Mount that those who are persecuted for His sake shall have great reward in heaven (Luke 6:22–23). He also recognizes their adversaries, who were acting on behalf of Satan.

Polycarp, the famous bishop of Smyrna who in his youth knew the apostle John, was the twelfth martyr in Smyrna. His trial and subsequent martyrdom show the circumstances of this church.

The times were troublesome as Satan stirred his forces against the electrifying spread of Christianity. Gnosticism, already at work before this explosion of the Christian faith, assailed the church not only from without but also from within. It tried to infuse its own doctrines into Christianity to dilute and distort the message. Heresy moved from mere divisions and differences of opinion in the Church (Titus 3:10) to "damnable heresies, even denying the Lord that bought them" (2 Pet. 2:1; see Jude 4). Valentius and Marcion led such sects in those days while Polycarp was "the principal leader of Christianity in Asia." Marcion met Polycarp on one occasion and implored him to "recognize us." Polycarp replied, "Aye, aye, I recognize the firstborn of Satan."[4] Polycarp stawartly stood for the truth. Irenaeus wrote that Polycarp taught the church in Rome on a visit to heal

---

[4] Editor, James Hastings, DD, *The Dictionary of the Apostolic Church*, vol. 2, (New York: Charles Scribner's Sons, 1918) p. 243.

a division, by saying, "There is only one truth left by the apostles and transmitted to the Church."[5]

Polycarp wrote to the Philippian church saying, "Whosoever shall not confess the testimony of the cross is of the devil; and whosoever shall pervert the oracles of the Lord to his own lusts and say there is neither resurrection nor judgment, that man is the firstborn of Satan."[6] Perhaps he alluded to Marcion. However, we know the heresy concerning the resurrection had already been accepted by Hymenaeus and Philetus, because Paul mentioned them in his letter to Timothy (2 Tim. 2:17).

It was clearly a time of controversy between the real truth and Gnoticism. Politically, the controversy that raged between the Church and Rome was intensified by the Jews who incited it; hence, the reason for Jesus' mention of so-called Jews being of the "synagogue of Satan" (Rev. 2:9).

Turning to the historical account of Polycarp's arrest, trial, and death, we quote extensively from an old dictionary printed in 1918 for those of us not scholarly enough to read from original manuscripts. The account quotes from *Martyrium Polycarpi,* a letter written by the church of Smyrna to the Church at large to give the account of their bishop's death:

> Among the minute details which the Martyrium Polycarpi gives on the arrest, trial and execution of the bishop of Smyrna, there appears a valuable date: "The martyrdom of the blessed Polycarp," we read in 21, "took place on the second day of the first part of the month Xanthicus, on the seventh day before the Kalends of

---

[5] Ibid.
[6] Ibid.

March, on the great Sabbath, at the eighth hour. He was apprehended by Herodes, when Philip of Tralles was high priest, in the proconsulship of Statius Quadrartus, but in reign of the Eternal King Jesus Christ." The martyrdom took place, therefore, on a Saturday which fell on the 23rd of February. The proconsul Stratius Quadratus is identified with the person of the same name who was consul in 142, and who, according to inscriptions, was proconsul of Asia between 151 and 157: the year 155 is the only one in which the 23rd of February falls on Saturday (Harnack, Chronologie, i. 334–356, completed by Stahlin, Christl. Griech. Litteratur, Munich, 1914, p. 977).

The proconsul, interrogating Polycarp said to him (ix. 3): "Swear the oath and I will release thee; revile the Christ," to which Polycarp replied: "Fourscore and six years have I been His servant (σγδοηκοντα και εχ ετη δουλευω αυτω), and He hath done me no wrong. How then can I blaspheme my King who saved me?" We conclude from these words that Polycarp was eighty-six years old at the time of his martyrdom, not that he had been a Christian for eighty-six years. (Harnack Chronologie, i. 323, 342 ff.).

Other Christians suffered martyrdom at Smyrna at the same time as Polycarp . . .

The Martyrium Polycarpi (1–4) mentions the tortures that were inflicted on them, and gives the name of one of them, Germanicus, whose heroism went the length in attracting the wild beast to him and inciting it to devour him, whereupon the pagan multitude shouted with fury: "Away with the atheists" (αζρε του αθου). This is the cry by which popular hatred designated the

Christians as enemies of the gods. The people demanded Polycarp (ητεγοθω Πολυκαρποχ); [this is no error but a direct quote] the people therefore knew Polycarp as the most notable of the Christians at Smyrna, as their chief (iii. 2). Polycarp remained at Smyrna in spite of the advice that his friends gave him to flee secretly . . .

Polycarp was arrested on Friday towards evening in a house (εν τινι δωματγω) in which he had found shelter: the bystanders marveled "at his age and his constancy," and wondered "why there should be so much eagerness for an old man like him" (vii. 1–2). The bishop requested one hour to pray before following them; they consented. Then Polycarp stood up and prayed, "being so full of the grace of God, that for two hours he could not hold his peace" (vii. 3), and in his prayer he mentioned "all who at any time had come his way, small and great, high and low, and all the universal Church throughout the world" (και πασηχ τηχ κατα την οικουμενη καθολικηχ εκκλησιαχ). At last he was taken to Smyrna on the Saturday morning (viii. 1). Herod the irenarch (the chief of the municipal police) pressed him to do sacrifice: "What harm is there in saying: κυριοχ καισαρ (Caesar is lord)?" He evidently wanted to suggest an equivocation to Polycarp, to save him . . . Polycarp was brought ειξ το σταδιον where the people were assembled and the proconsul was present (ix. 1). Let us remark in passing that this appearance of Polycarp before the proconsul in the open stadium is very unusual from the point of view of the forms of proconsular justice . . .

The proconsular called upon Polycarp to swear by the fortune of Caesar (ομοσον την καισαροχ τυξην) and say: "Away with the atheists" (αλρε τουχ αθεουχ).

Polycarp, casting his eyes on the multitude of pagans who filled the stadium, "sighs and raising his eyes towards heavens, says, 'Away with the atheists!'" But he refused to curse the Christ (ix. 2–3). The proconsul incited in vain. "I am a Christian," replied the bishop; "if thou wouldest learn of the doctrine of Christianity, assign a day and give me hearing." "Prevail upon the people," answered the Roman magistrate sarcastically. "As for myself," said Polycarp, "I should have held thee worthy of discourse; for we have been taught to render, as it is meet, to princes and authorities appointed by God such honour as does us no harm; but as for these, I do not hold them worthy that I should defend myself before them" (x. 2) a reminiscence of St. Paul, (Rom. 13:1–7).

The proconsul threatened to throw him to the wild beasts if he did not abjure. "Call for them," answered the bishop, "for the repentance from better to worse is a change not permitted to us; but it is a noble thing to change from untowardness to righteousness" (xi. 1). The proconsul threatened him with the stake; Polycarp replied: "Thou threatenest that fire which burneth for a season and after a little while is quenched: for thou art ignorant of the fire of the future judgment and eternal punishment, which is reserved for the ungodly. But why delayest thou? Come do what thou wilt" (xi. 2). The proconsul ordered his herald to proclaim in the middle of the stadium; "Polycarp hath confessed himself to be a Christian" (xii. 1). The whole multitude composed of pagans and Jews living in Smyrna began to shout: "This is the teacher of Asia, the father of the Christians, the puller down of our gods, who teacheth numbers not to sacrifice nor worship!" The multitude begged that

Polycarp should be burned at once (xii. 2–3). They brought fuel; the Jews were in the greatest haste. When the pile was ready, the bishop laid aside his clothes and was placed against the stake. They wanted to nail him to it; he refused: "Leave me as I am," he said, "for He that hath granted me to endure the fire will grant me also to remain at the pile unmoved, even without the security ye seek from the nails" (xiii. 3). Fixed to the stake, his hands behind his back, "he was like a noble ram out of a great flock for an offering" (xiv. 1).[7]

The account goes on to say that "the bishop then repeated in a loud voice a very remarkable prayer, for it is in the manner of a eucharistic prayer, and gives the impression of what we call a praefatio (xiv. 1–2). While dying, the bishop prayed in the ritual from which the liturgy is derived. Thus died the glorious martyr, Polycarp . . ."[8]

A painting hanging in an ancient church in Smyrna shows his actual death as being by a thrust of a sword into his side. The story is told that the fire did not kill him but rather a soldier did. This seems confirmed by the *Matyrium Polcarpi* because it mentions that Christians were refused the right to bury the body. The Jews insisted that it be burned in the manner of the heathen.

Catching a glimpse of what Christians in Smyrna faced, we can see why the Lord told them they were rich in treasures in heaven. Turning back now to the letter to Smyrna, we know what the problem was. We need only to see Jesus' solution.

---

[7] Ibid p. 244.
[8] Ibid.

The Problem

> Fear none of those things which thou shalt suffer: behold, the devil shall cast some of you into prison, that ye may be tried; and ye shall have tribulation ten days: be thou faithful unto death, and I will give thee a crown of life. (2:10)

Christ tells these believers that they will suffer, but they were not to fear. He is clear that Satan is behind the persecution. Satan, using the Romans and the Jews, seeks to stamp out Christianity through fear. It is a test of faithfulness. Jesus told His disciples not to fear what men could do, because they were limited to taking away physical life. Rather they were to fear Him who is able to destroy both soul and body in hell (Matt. 10:28).

Will these believers love their lives more than Christ and capitulate to the demands of the ungodly? Polycarp said that the brethren should "teach the faithful not to think only of their individual safety, but to think of all the brethren."[9] God did not intend that all should die. It was popular then for martyrs to receive glory. Because of this, many put themselves before the authorities instead of waiting to be arrested. If a person's faith failed, it affected the whole church. The *Martyrium Policarpi* mentions such a one.

> But one man Quintus by name, a Phrygian, newly arrived from Phrygia, when he saw the wild beasts turned coward. He it was who had forced himself and some others to come forward of their own will . . . For this cause

---

[9] Ibid.

therefore, brethren, we praise not those who deliver
themselves up, since the Gospel doth not so teach us.[10]

Such believers acted presumptuously and so did not
have the grace of God when faced with death. God chooses
His martyrs.

After telling them not to fear, Jesus offers the Smyrnians
encouragement: "I will give thee a crown of life" (2:10).
Actually, death is a shortcut to this crown. It is offered in
the Book of James as an award for living a lifetime of overcoming temptation and trials (James 1:12–17). In both cases,
the award is won by overcoming unfaithfulness.

The Reward

He that hath an ear, let him hear what the Spirit saith
unto the churches; He that overcometh shall not be hurt
of the second death. (2:11)

The overcomers will not be hurt (*adekeo*, "injured; to
unjustly suffer wrong or be offended") by the second death.
The second death separates unbelievers from God forever,
because this death follows their resurrection and judgment
(Rev. 20:14). The precious overcomers will never be in danger of that *unless* they renounce Christ.

Consider what this means. To renounce Christ as
Polycarp was asked to do would mean to give up all claims
He has on our lives, all His benefits, including the forgiveness of sins and eternal life. It would mean to publicly declare that we love our own temporary existence in this world

---

[10] Ibid.

more than we love Him. Besides that, we would cast dishonor on His name and give triumph to His enemy, Satan. We would place all that Christ suffered for our salvation in the light of "little consequence." Worst of all, we would deny the Holy Spirit any ground to inhabit our bodies and hold our souls for eternity, because in essence we would be withdrawing our faith.

This amounts to treading "under foot the Son of God" and counting "the blood of the covenant . . . an unholy thing" and doing "despite unto the Spirit of grace" (Heb. 10:29). Jesus said, "He that shall blaspheme against the Holy Ghost hath never forgiveness, but is in danger of eternal damnation" (Mark 3:29). I do not want to get into a debate concerning whether or not we can lose our salvation once it is secured, but consider the following:

Those working in a deliverance ministry, that is, delivering people from demonic invasion, have discovered that demons will not leave bodies unless: 1) the persons have forgiven all offenses of others against themselves;[11] 2) they have confessed the sins associated with the said demons and have asked the Father's forgiveness; and 3) they have renounced the evil spirits by name.

Demon spirits can enter into people when those persons have persistently cooperated with the demons in particular sins. The spirits claim the sins as their *right* to inhabit

---

[11] This frees them from the tormentor's prison inflicted on them because of their refusal to forgive (Matt. 18:34–35). This is the first step to deliverance, because if people refuse to forgive others, the heavenly Father will not forgive them (Mark 11:26). Confessing their sins (which are the grounds for the spirits' right to their bodies) and asking forgiveness is the second step to deliverance. If the persons do not perform the first step, they cannot go on to the second step, receiving the Father's forgiveness.

them, calling them their "ground." As long as the persons persist in those sins, the demons will not budge. When the individuals confess their sins to God and are forgiven, the demonic spirits lose their right to be there. By renouncing the evil spirits' names, the individuals deny the spirits and regain control over that portion of their own wills (where the invading spirits had seized control). They or some other believers can then force the demon spirits out by commanding them to leave in Jesus' name. They are able to do this because of the authority Christ delegated only to believers to speak in His name (Luke 10:17; Acts 19:13–17).

If the Holy Spirit enters the spirits of believers and dwells in their bodies because they have been obedient to the gospel and have faith in Christ's finished work (the Holy Spirit's grounds to inhabit them [Eph. 1:13]), could He not leave if they withdrew their faith and renounced Jesus' name? It seems a pointless reward for overcoming if the threat is not real. If it is impossible for believers to cast aside their salvation, why not save themselves from an unnecessary death when asked to recant?

One could argue that those who are unfaithful and cling to their physical lives by renouncing Christ might live the remainder of their days believing themselves condemned to hell. They might then fall back into sin and become useless as Christians, causing the second death to hurt them. We leave it to the reader to decide.

Some believers in every age will face persecution, and they will be called on to suffer like the Smyrna church but not all. How can Christians overcome the problem of maintaining their faith in this present age if no persecution exists?

Some persecution comes to all believers in Christ, the only difference being the degree of severity. We may not be called on to lay down our lives; however, we are all called on to be faithful to Christ's name. All new believers go through a period of rejection from friends, family, and the world if they have any testimony at all. This is especially true during their "first love" experiences if they boldly confront others with Christ's claims. To stand against this requires faithfulness.

Then, too, a lifetime of overcoming temptation and trials proves faithfulness to Christ and will earn that same crown of life promised to the suffering Smyrna saints. Whatever the circumstances, those who are faithful are *never* in danger of the second death.

Chapter 4

THE THINGS WHICH ARE: PERGAMOS

(REVELATION 2:12–17)

The Salutation

> And to the angel of the church in Pergamos write; These things saith he which hath the sharp sword with two edges. (2:12)

Jesus identifies Himself as the one who has the sword that cuts on both sides. A knight wielding such a sword would cut a swath with both the forward and the backward swing. This sword, however, does not have that purpose. Instead, as the definition shows in Hebrews 4:12, it is a piercing and separating weapon able to divide the soul from the spirit on one side and the bone from the marrow on the other. Then it goes one step beyond that and divides the soul into two parts—the mind (the thoughts) from the intents of the heart (the will). When God uses this figure of speech, we can deduce that the church in Pergamos needs to be separated from something.

The Evaluation

> I know thy works, and where thou dwellest, even where Satan's seat is: and thou holdest fast my name, and hast not denied my faith, even in those days wherein Antipas was my faithful martyr, who was slain among you, where Satan dwelleth. But I have a few things against thee, because thou hast there them that hold the doctrine of Balaam, who taught Balac to cast a stumblingblock before the children of Israel, to eat things sacrificed unto idols, and to commit fornication. So hast thou also them that hold the doctrine of the Nicolaitanes, which thing I hate. (2:13–15)

Christ says in effect, "I know your works and where you live, even where Satan's seat is." We see a parallel here. The believers' works in this church are holding fast to Christ's name and not denying the faith, both works that the Smyrna church needs to develop. Nevertheless, where they live seems to compromise their efforts because it is next to Satan's throne.

Satan's ploy with this church is not to incite fear but to invite compromise. It is easier to withstand a foe who opposes us than to withstand one who seduces us. From this we conclude that they suffer little opposition from the city's religious inclinations, at least as compared to Smyrna. The seat of Satan is more likely a political seat rather than a religious one, since a throne is associated with it. As early as 399 B.C., the city of Pergamos ruled that area of Asia Minor. Each succeeding conqueror recognized its strategic location, being on a high hill overlooking surrounding valleys. No doubt, this "throne" refers to the worldly leaders in charge.

The righteous Judge recognizes their works but fails to commend the church because their problem is grievous. He says, "I have a few things against thee." 1) They allow in their midst those holding the doctrine of Balaam. 2) They also have those holding the doctrine of the Nicolaitanes. Both these teachings dilute the Word of God to the extent that many are giving in to the world's standards. Their light is about to be overshadowed by the love of money and the world. John earlier in his letter defines the *world* as the lust of the flesh, the lust of the eyes, and the pride of life (1 John 2:15–16).

Balaam had become the biblical example of one selling himself and his message for money. Never mind that Balaam's message blessed instead of cursing Balak's enemies, the Jews. Balaam simply taught Balak how to circumvent God's commands by seduction. Invited by the Moabite women to attend a celebration to their gods (Num. 25), the men of Israel succumbed to compromise that led to sensuous activities—eating, drinking, and fornication. The Balaam doctrine led to the same thing in the Pergamos church, fulfilling the lust of the flesh.

The mention of the Nicolaitanes sect shows a spread of their influence. First seen in the letter to Ephesus where their deeds are hated by the church, here they have become a functioning part of the Pergamos church. The church's compromise and tolerance for evil is despicable and worthy of judgment.

The Warning

> Repent; or else I will come unto thee quickly, and will
> fight against them with the sword of my mouth. (2:16)

"Repent! Turn away from the world and back to the separated life!" appeals Christ, the High Priest, who intercedes to the Father. Otherwise, Jesus will come as Judge and fight against them with the sword of his mouth. Question: What will He do with the sword? Answer: Do reparative surgery by cutting out the compromising members of the church. He will remove the "rotten apples," so to speak.

Separation from the body of the faithful has always been God's practice in both the Old and New Testaments. Those sinning were cut off from the others on the basis of the Word of God. The Mosaic Law provided the following:

1. An "uncircumcised man child whose flesh of his foreskin" was not circumcised should be "cut off from his people." He had broken God's covenant (Gen. 17:14).
2. A person who ate leavened bread during the Feast of Unleavened Bread) should be "cut off from the congregation of Israel" (Exod. 12:15, 19).
3. A person who compounded oil like the holy anointing oil or put it on a stranger should be "cut off from his people" (Exod. 30:33).
4. A person who defiled the Sabbath should be "put to death," but the one who did any work on the Sabbath should be "cut off from among his people" (Exodus 31:14). We must assume from this that the Israelite in Numbers 15:32–36 who was condemned

to death was doing more than just picking up sticks on the Sabbath.

5. A person who ate blood in any form, whether an Israelite or a stranger, would be "cut off from his people" (Lev. 17:10, 12).

6. If a person was ceremonially clean, not on a journey, and did not keep the Passover, he would be "cut off from among his people." This was because he did not bring the Lord's offering at the "appointed season" (Num. 9:13).

7. A person who refused to be sprinkled with the "water of separation" after becoming unclean by touching the dead would be "cut off from among the congregation." He had "defiled the sanctuary of the LORD" (Num. 19:20).

Capitol punishment meant death, but lesser crimes meant separation to preserve the rest of the congregation. This same separation follows through into the New Testament. The immoral man in the Corinthian church was put out of the fellowship for a season (1 Cor. 5:1–5).

Does this mean that the compromising Christians in the Pergamos church are cut off from the Lord? Not if they had genuinely received Christ as Savior. They still have the option of repentance, the same as the Corinthian man. The worldly Christians are separated from the faithful to prevent further corruption of the church. We should not see every church split as a work of Satan. Sometimes it is the sword of the Lord that separates believers. Church history reeks of splits over the Word of God. All those of the Peramos church had overcome unfaithfulness, but some will never overcome worldliness.

The Reward

> He that hath an ear, let him hear what the Spirit saith
> unto the churches; To him that overcometh will I give to
> eat of the hidden manna, and will give him a white stone,
> and in the stone a new name written, which no man
> knoweth saving he that receiveth it. (2:17)

Overcomers will be given "hidden manna" to eat. Since
this figure of speech is not explained here, we must look
elsewhere for its meaning. Manna is associated with Israel's
wilderness wandering; however, we find the only mention
of hidden manna in Hebrews 9:4 where it mentions manna
in a golden pot inside the ark of the covenant. That does
not clearly explain the figure either, since that is itself another symbol. Jesus clears up the question of manna when
He says, "My Father giveth you the true bread from heaven,"
speaking of Himself (John 6:32). He says this after correcting the Jews who thought manna was from heaven.

He told them emphatically that manna was not from
heaven, meaning God's heaven. In fact, its source was merely
clouds above the earth—unusual clouds but clouds none-
theless. Psalm 74:13–14 declares that the "heads of leviathan," the mythical dragon seen in the clouds at the crossing
of the Red Sea, were broken up to become food. Psalm
78:23–25 states that God commanded the clouds to drop
down manna. So manna was only a type of Jesus, the true
bread from heaven.

The Old Testament tabernacle was known as God's
dwelling place, particularly the Holy of Holies where the
ark of the covenant stood. God commanded that manna
should be put in a golden pot and placed as a memorial

inside the ark (Exod. 16:32–34). This may be a type of the reward of "hidden manna" in heaven, of which John spoke.

The overcoming Christians in the Pergamos church grow spiritually from feeding on this manna that is hidden away from the world. They are in the world but not of the world, just as Jesus had prayed for them in the upper room. That part of the reward was ever with them in this life. The rest of the reward reaches toward the future.

Jesus also promises the overcomers a white stone with a new name written on it. This stone is not just a rock. In fact, the Greek meaning defines its purpose. The word is *psephos*. Strong's concordance defines it as "a pebble (as worn smooth by handling); by implication, of use as a counter or ballot, a verdict (of acquittal) or a ticket (of admission); a vote." In other words, this little stone is a tool either for counting or voting. Further, it is inscribed with a secret name only the owner knows. This would suggest a secret ballot. Since no one knows the true owner of the stone, its vote will be anonymous. We will have to look deeply in ancient history to find the meaning for this figure of speech. Compared to the modern electronic voting machines of today, using stones for voting was primitive.

First, we look in the Old Testament for a similar stone. Here we find only David's stone used against the giant Goliath. No help there unless we see this as a stone/vote of execution. Next, we look to history that would have been known in John's day. *Psephos* being a Greek word specifically designated for a ballot or a vote suggests we look at ancient Greek government.

When Paul was in Athens, certain philosophers took him to the Areopagus, a forum area, to hear what he had to say about his new doctrine. It is curious that he should be taken there because the name Areopagus originated five hundred years before, being a part of the evolving government of Athens when it was a major city state. A monarchy ruled Athens up until the eighth century. Then a council of nobles called the Areopagus gradually divested the king of his powers. The Areopagus ruled by oral laws passed down from generation to generation.

Representation of the people came after vigorous trade from olive orchards and vineyards transformed the economy of the city and left in its wake a disparity between those whose land was arable and those whose land was poor. Debt caused the poor to indenture themselves and gave rise to great discontent among the lower classes, threatening revolution. Solon, initially a poet, wrote that if the laws were written down, the judges of the council would be denied influence by receiving gifts. An earlier attempt to write the laws had been made by Draco, but these were unduly harsh, from which we get the expression that harsh measures are Draconian. These laws had not addressed the problem of bribery. The council gave Solon a mandate in 594 B.C. to write down the laws and to institute reforms to govern society. He installed the first council that represented the people. His political reforms included

(1) the establishment of a new council, the Council of Four Hundred, and the admission of the middle classes to membership in it; (2) the enfranchisement of the lower classes by making them eligible for service in the assembly; and (3) the organization of a supreme court, open to all citizens and elected by universal manhood

suffrage, with the power to hear appeals from the decisions of the magistrates.[12] The supreme court allowed anyone who had lost a lawsuit under any of the other courts to appeal to this jury of citizens. By the fifth century B.C. at the time of Pericles (called the father of Athenian democracy), these citizen juries had been greatly enlarged. No longer was there merely a supreme court to hear appeals from the decisions of the magistrates, but an array of popular courts with authority to try all kinds of cases. At the beginning of each year a list of 6,000 citizens was chosen by lot from the various sections of the country. From this list separate juries, varying in size from 201 to 1001, were made up for particular trials. Each of these juries constituted a court with power to decide by majority vote every question involved in the case. Although one of the magistrates presided, he had none of the prerogatives of a judge; the jury itself was the judge, and from its decision there was no appeal. It would be difficult to imagine a system more democratic.[13]

Another history book addresses the detail that may well explain the white stone in the overcomers' reward, which in the original Greek meant "a vote."

From among the members of the assembly above thirty years old, several thousand men were chosen by lot as judges or jurymen. Each jury was large—perhaps 201 or 501 men, but sometimes even over 1,000. There was

---

[12] Edward McNall Burns, Western Civilizations: Their History & Their Culture (New York: W.W. Norton, 1941), p. 159.
[13] Ibid, pp. 160–61.

no public prosecutor. Any citizen might accuse any other citizen. But the accuser and the accused would speak to the jury, the time of each being marked by a water clock. In voting each juryman deposited a white or a black stone. If the accuser didn't receive a certain number of votes, he was himself condemned.[14]

Giving a white stone as a reward to overcomers suggests they will be similarly occupied in the coming reign of Christ over the earth. As jurymen or judges governing disputes of citizens in local areas, they will vote with their stones. They probably will have black stones as well for negative votes. It is curious that a black stone retains its meaning even in our society today. Those denied membership in college Greek fraternities or sororities are said to have been "blackballed."

Looking around us today, we can see those who clearly love the world more than the Father. Only those who overcome the world will be worthy to judge it.

---

[14] Henry W. Elson, *Modern Times and the Living Past*. American Book Company, New York, 1933, p. 83. *Culture* (New York: W. W. Norton, 1941), p. 159.

Chapter 5

THE THINGS WHICH ARE: THYATIRA

(REVELATION 2:18–29)

The Salutation

> And unto the angel of the church in Thyatira write; These
> things saith the Son of God, who hath his eyes like unto
> a flame of fire, and his feet are like fine brass. (2:18)

These things saith the Son of God, the Father's heir,
emphasizing His gender. He stands against them as
the Son to whom the Father has committed all judgment (John 5:22). He confirms His judgeship by alluding
to His appearance where John sees Him as the Judge of the
Church. His eyes search in anger, showing His righteous
indignation, and His feet walk in pursuit of justice.

Brass in the Old Testament was associated with judgment by its use, that is, the brazen altar in the tabernacle

court with its fire and the brazen serpent lifted up on the stick, which Jesus compared to His death on the cross (John 3:14). Both denoted judgment for sin. By this salutation, we can see Christ expects to do more than separate in this church. Something or someone will suffer severe remonstration.

The Evaluation

> I know thy works, and charity, and service, and faith, and thy patience, and thy works; and the last to be more than the first. Notwithstanding I have a few things against thee, because thou sufferest that woman Jezebel, which calleth herself a prophetess, to teach and to seduce my servants to commit fornication, and to eat things sacrificed unto idols. And I gave her space to repent of her fornication; and she repented not. (2:19–21)

Once again Christ mentions first works and last works, deeming the last works as greater. The first works include charity (love), service, faith, and patience. Since these are all good things expected in a Christian testimony, we deduce that these good works degraded into lesser values while the latter works increased to greater abundance.

The reason for this evaluation is they have allowed a woman to take charge of the church. (Now we see why Jesus emphasizes His gender.) She claims to hear directly from God like the ancient prophets. She proclaims herself a prophetess and has usurped the male leadership of the church. This reveals a great weakness on the part of the elders of the church. They have yielded in abject disobedience to Paul's teaching concerning the qualifications for deacons and elders for church government, which surely

Timothy taught to all the churches in Asia. The first quali-
fication on that list was that they must be male (1 Tim. 3:2,
12). Only elders can rule. She did not qualify. Furthermore,
Paul did not allow any woman to usurp authority over men
because of the vulnerability of a woman to Satan's deceptions.

From the beginning, God put enmity between Satan and
the woman. As a result, Satan attacks females specifically.
Besides that, one of the perversions of sin resulting from
the fall is that women strive to rule over men. The perversion foisted on men by sin is to give up responsibility and
let the women rule. While this is natural, it is contrary to
God's appointments for the very reason of what has happened in this church.

This woman is called "Jezebel," not her real name, of
course, but another figure of speech, because her works
yield the same results as the historical Jezebel. Just as ancient Jezebel led Israel into idolatry, so this latter-day Jezebel
leads the Thyatira church into spiritual adultery, introduc-
ing doctrines originating with Satan (see v. 24).

Although the Pergamos Christians toy with the activities of the world by eating things sacrificed to idols and
succumbing to the fleshly vice of fornication, they never
deny Christ's name or their faith, holding firmly to their
doctrines. The problem arising in Thyatira is the introduction of dangerous false doctrines that deny salvation to its
adherents, if they do not already know Christ.

Being a fair Judge, Jesus gives this prophetess room to
repent and turn back to the truth, thereby overcoming the
problem of false doctrines. She refuses, ending the possibility that she can grow further spiritually. The fact that
Jesus gives her space to repent suggests that she originally

accepted the doctrines of Christ but superceded them with her own "words from God." This seems confirmed by the Judge's statement, "I will kill her children [her spiritual children, not her] with death" (v. 23).

False teaching does not lead to eternal life. Therefore, those seduced by her doctrine will follow its path to death. History abounds with examples of strong women teachers leading the unwary away from the truth to paths of death, women such as Mary Baker Eddy or Madame Blavatsky. Does this mean women cannot know the truth or teach it today? I think we need to understand the fundamental problem here is that this "Jezebel" *wants* authority over men, just as her historical counterpart. She fills herself with importance and puffs herself up in her so-called special status with the Lord. By such an attitude, she dismisses the leadership of the men. Her pride makes her open to Satan's deceptions.

In contrast, humility and submission to the Word of God and the leadership of the church characterize true spiritual women.

The Warning

> Behold, I will cast her into a bed, and them that commit adultery with her into great tribulation, except they repent of their deeds. And I will kill her children with death; and all the churches shall know that I am he which searcheth the reins and hearts: and I will give unto every one of you according to your works. But unto you I say, and unto the rest in Thyatira, as many as have not this doctrine, and which have not known the depths of Satan, as they speak; I will put upon you none other

burden. But that which ye have already hold fast till I come. (2:23–25)

The bed mentioned actually means a couch meant for sleeping, sickness, sitting, or eating. Given these choices, casting her onto such a couch for punishment can only indicate its use for sickness. The Judge inflicts this same punishment on those who eat and drink at the communion table in an unworthy manner. Paul says that if we will judge ourselves, we will not be judged. "For he that eateth and drinketh unworthily, eateth and drinketh damnation to himself, not discerning the Lord's body. For this cause many are weak and sickly among you, and many sleep [die]" (1 Cor. 11:29–30).

Taking the symbolic bread and wine in Holy Communion constitutes a joining. The bread, even as far back as the ritual sacrifices of the law, represented Christ's holy life— the unleavened bread. When we eat the communion bread, we demonstrate the joining of our lives with His. If our lives are unholy when we do this, it evidently affects our bodies, making them weak, sickly, and vulnerable to death. To avoid this action of our holy Judge, we should examine our lives, confess our sins, and be cleansed before we partake.

This "Jezebel" teaches her followers to eat things sacrificed to idols and to commit ceremonial fornication, as well as eating from the Lord's table, bringing on her the punishment of the "sickbed." Those who commit spiritual adultery with her have joined themselves to another spirit. Hear what Paul says concerning this:

Wherefore, my dearly beloved, flee from idolatry. I speak as to wise men; judge ye what I say. The cup of blessing which we bless, is it not the communion of the blood of Christ? The bread which we break, is it not the communion of the body of Christ? For we being many are one bread, and one body: for we are all partakers of that one bread. Behold Israel after the flesh: are not they which eat of the sacrifices partakers of the altar? What say I then? that the idol is any thing, or that which is offered in sacrifice to idols is any thing? But I say, that the things which the Gentiles sacrifice, they sacrifice to devils, and not to God: and I would not that ye should have fellowship with devils. Ye cannot drink the cup of the Lord, and the cup of devils: ye cannot be partakers of the Lord's table, and of the table of devils. Do we provoke the Lord to jealousy? are we stronger than he? (1 Cor. 10:14–22)

The heathen worshiped their gods by eating sacrifices and indulging in ceremonial fornication with temple priestesses. This is what "Jezebel" tries to introduce into the church. No wonder the Judge came with blazing eyes and feet.

The punishment for spiritual idolatry is tribulation. Some of the guilty ones here are real believers who have been deceived. In bringing tribulation on them, Christ attempts to correct their paths. In Romans 2:4, Paul mentions that "the goodness of God" leads to repentance. The Judge's eyes search for repentance. If believers refuse His correction, they will answer for their deeds at the final judgment seat.

By the Judge's action of searching out sin (with His eyes of flame) and walking in judgment (with His bronze feet), all the churches will see the example that He makes of this church. They will know that He searches our very reins (figure of speech denoting "will" or "direction") and hearts (the center of our beings) and will reward us individually according to the works done in our bodies (2 Cor. 5:10). The Church today has little understanding of Christ's position as Judge among us. Paul continually warns about this, especially the Corinthians who needed correction.

After warning the guilty of Thyatira, Jesus admonishes the rest—those who have not joined themselves to Satan and learned the "new revelation" from "Jezebel." These escape judgment. To them He says in essence, "Hold fast what you already have until I come." This reminds us of Jesus' words concerning hearing: "Take heed therefore how ye hear: for whosoever hath [truth], to him shall be given; and whosoever hath not [truth], from him shall be taken even that which he seemeth to have" (Luke 8:18).

When the righteous Judge comes, the Thyatira church will stand before His seat of justice. Those who fail to repent will not overcome the problem of false teaching. Therefore, the truth that they think they have will be taken away.

The Reward

> And he that overcometh, and keepeth my works unto the end, to him will I give power over the nations. And he shall rule them with a rod of iron; as the vessels of a potter shall they be broken to shivers: even as I received of my Father. And I will give him the morning star. (2:26–28)

Those who overcome the problem of false teaching by rejecting it will attain a higher position in the reign of Christ. The overcomers of the former problem of worldliness have

71

attained positions (if our assessment is correct) over civil courts, suggesting that cities are involved. Perhaps the Lord casts more light on this in the parable of the pounds, when He refers to cities as being kingdom rewards for faithful trading.

He said therefore, A certain nobleman went into a far country to receive for himself a kingdom, and to return. And he called his ten servants, and delivered them ten pounds, and said unto them, Occupy till I come. But his citizens hated him, and sent a message after him, saying, We will not have this man to reign over us.

And it came to pass, that when he was returned, having received the kingdom, then he commanded these servants to be called unto him, to whom he had given the money, that he might know how much every man had gained by trading. Then came the first, saying, Lord, thy pound hath gained ten pounds. And he said unto him, Well, thou good servant: because thou hast been faithful in a very little, have thou authority over ten cities. And the second came, saying, Lord, thy pound hath gained five pounds. And he said likewise to him, Be thou also over five cities. And another came, saying, Lord, behold, here is thy pound, which I have kept laid up in a napkin: for I feared thee, because thou art an austere man: thou takest up what thou layedst not down, and reapest that thou didst not sow.

And he saith unto him, Out of thine own mouth will I judge thee, thou wicked servant. Thou knewest that I was an austere man, taking up that I laid not down, and reaping that I did not sow: Wherefore then gavest not thou my money into the bank, that at my coming I might have required mine own with usury?

> And he said unto them that stood by, Take from him the pound, and give it to him that hath ten pounds. (And they said unto him, Lord, he hath ten pounds.) For I say unto you, That unto every one which hath shall be given; and from him that hath not, even that he hath shall be taken away from him. But those mine enemies, which would not that I should reign over them, bring hither, and slay them before me. (Luke 19:12–27)

If we understand the pound to be a figure of speech describing the truth of the gospel, the nobleman (Christ) gives each of his servants the same amount. He expects them to take this truth and "trade" it, that is, increase it. Here we need to explain that by truth we do not mean knowledge. Rather, we mean truth as it can be applied in developing faith.

One servant increases his truth tenfold, the other fivefold, not a very great increase when you consider the increase the good ground provided for the seed in the parable of the sower. That was thirty, sixty, and a hundredfold (see Matt. 13:3–8). Could it be that those who overcome the problem of worldliness receive ten or five cities as their jurisdiction? Notice the servant who hides his truth does not lose his life like the enemies but only the pound. He will not rule even one city.

By contrast, those who overcome false teaching earn positions over whole nations, ruling them with a rod of iron (Rev. 2:26–27). Their "rod" as a figure of speech connects to the "rod of iron" used by the Son in Psalm 2:9 and brought to the earth at His return (Rev. 19:15) to be used against the nations to break them. It appears that the Lord delegates the use of this rod to the overcomers in Psalm 149 where the Psalmist reveals it further.

Praise ye the LORD, Sing unto the LORD a new song, and his praise in the congregation of saints. Let Israel rejoice in him that made him: let the children of Zion be joyful in their King. Let them praise his name in the dance: let them sing praises unto him with the timbrel and harp. For the LORD taketh pleasure in his people: he will beautify the meek with salvation.

Let the saints be joyful in glory: let them sing aloud upon their beds. Let the high praises of God be in their mouth, and a twoedged sword in their hand; to execute vengeance upon the heathen, and punishments upon the people; to bind their kings with chains, and their nobles with fetters of iron; to execute upon them the judgment written: this honour have all his saints. Praise ye the LORD. (Ps. 149:1–9)

This psalm projects ahead to the time of the kingdom because we have the saints executing justice. It also shows that God still has two special peoples who are separate from each other. One group lives on earth, the other "rests" in glory. While the earthly Israel enjoys her King, she is beautified by salvation as a whole nation. Nevertheless, the saints reign from heaven. They have positions over the heathen nations and authority to execute punishments. Their weapon is the Word of God, the sharp two-edged sword. Its breaking power is the strength of iron. The "rod of iron" given to the Son by the Father and the rod promised to the overcomers are the same.

This psalm explains how this delegated power will work. The overcomers are to execute the *judgment already written*, handed down to them from the King. The "rod of iron" is nothing less than an inflexible rule of righteousness (according to the Law) that sinful people will begin to chafe under as the kingdom goes on. At this future time, not only are the Jews responsible to keep the Law of God but also the rest of the world. That includes the ceremonial laws that still apply. Those ritual laws which Jesus fulfilled in His death will probably only be taught; but the ceremonial seasons, especially the Feast of Tabernacles, are commemorative and thus still required.

To understand the nature of the overcomers' authority, we turn to Zechariah's brief description of the rule over nations during the kingdom age.

> And the LORD shall be king over all the earth: in that day shall there be one LORD, and his name one . . . And it shall come to pass, that every one that is left of all the nations which came against Jerusalem shall even go up from year to year to worship the King, the LORD of hosts, and to keep the feast of tabernacles.
>
> And it shall be, that whoso will not come up of all the families of the earth unto Jerusalem to worship the King, the LORD of hosts, even upon them shall be no rain. And if the family of Egypt go not up, and come not, that have no rain; there shall be the plague, wherewith the LORD will smite the heathen that come not up to keep the feast of tabernacles. This shall be the punishment of Egypt, and the punishment of all nations that come not up to keep the feast of tabernacles.
>
> In that day shall there be upon the bells of the horses, HOLINESS UNTO THE LORD; and the pots in the LORD's house shall be like the bowls before the altar. Yea, every pot in Jerusalem and in Judah shall be holiness unto the LORD of hosts: and all they that sacrifice shall come and take of them, and seethe therein. (Zech. 14:9, 16–21)

Worship of the LORD (Jehovah) will be mandatory. Those who fail to come will pay the consequences. Those dependent on rain for their crops will receive none. Those, like Egypt, who have no annual rainfall but depend on a river for watering their crops, will receive a plague. No one will escape who disobeys the Law.

If we look to the end of the thousand-year reign when Satan (after his release) deceives the people again, we see him causing a great rebellion. Yet God will destroy only the rebels with fire falling from heaven (Rev. 20:9). From this we see that He will administer punishment promptly, pinpointing only the guilty like the precision of our military smart bombs.

Giving the overcomers power to inflict plagues on people shows the same power Satan was able to use (with God's permission) to inflict plagues on Job. Since they overcome specifically the deception of Satan, Jesus rewards them with taking over positions that the enemy once held. Jesus seems to confirm this by adding, "And I will give him the morning star" (Rev. 2:28). Lucifer, which means "light bearer," used to be a morning star ("son of the morning" [Isa. 14:12]). At the end of the vision, Jesus claims this position for Himself saying, "I am the root and offspring of David, and the bright and morning star" (Rev. 22:16). He has delegated to these overcomers an office He now holds.

Here we need to interrupt our discussion of the overcomers to look at a change of order in the letters. Up until this church, the phrase, "He that hath an ear, let him hear what the Spirit saith unto the churches,". comes before the offer of the overcomers' reward. In this letter and the following three, the exhortation comes after the offering of the reward. We see this as another pointed division with a purpose. It means that the first three churches are different from the last four in the way they hear. Can this difference be due to immaturity, like how we might address children by saying, "Listen to me," to get their attention before we speak?

The rewards themselves give some indication, because the first three churches' rewards do not offer positions of great responsibility in the coming kingdom compared to the other four. Except for the martyrs' crowns of life, the overcomers rewards for Ephesus, Smyrna, and Pergamos are elementary. Jesus expects His followers to hear His voice, to be faithful, and to overcome the world. Being able to overcome false teaching involves a battle with the enemy.

This reminds us of a division John makes of three categories of believers. He writes in 1 John 2:12–14 to little children (whose sins are forgiven), to young men (who have overcome the enemy), and to fathers (who "have known him that is from the beginning"). We note in other scriptures that believers are often broken down into these three categories. Check out the following:

- In the parable of the vine, branches produce fruit, more fruit, and much fruit (John 15).
- In the parable of the sower, the good ground produces thirty, sixty, and a hundredfold (Matt. 13:23).
- Peter writes to believers, "The trial of your faith might be found unto praise and honour and glory at the appearing of Jesus Christ" (1 Pet. 1:7).
- Paul reminds us that Jesus has reconciled "in the body of his flesh through death, to present you holy and unblameable and unreproveable in his sight: if ye continue in the faith grounded, and settled, and

be not moved away from the hope of the gospel"
(Col. 1:22–23).

- Workers of the gospel may build the temple of God
(the Church) using three different building materi-
als: gold, silver, and precious stones. Jesus will reward them according to what they use, gold being
the most precious (1 Cor. 3:12–14).

These all show differences in degrees. We see these as
growth levels, because the more we feed on God's Word,
the more we behold His glory, and the more we are changed
into His image (2 Cor. 3:18). That, after all, is the whole
purpose of God—to have many children like His Son, Jesus,
so that He may dwell among them. The conclusion to the
reason for this division is to separate out the first three levels of Christian growth. We consider these three churches
to be in the "little children" category.

Christians who desert their faith for the pleasures of
the world will probably never face the problem of false teaching. Only those who are spiritually minded seek after more
truth. The Word of God is a hedge of protection around
believers; however, Ecclesiastics 10:8 says, "Whoso breaketh
an hedge, a serpent shall bite him." If their seeking departs
from the standard of truth revealed in the Scriptures, they
become vulnerable to deception, especially if pride in ex-
clusive knowledge motivates them. We are not talking about
holding various positions on the Word of God that arise
from different levels of understanding, but we refer to the
occult teachings of Satan that divert believers from further
spiritual growth and send unbelievers to hell.

THE THINGS WHICH ARE: SARDIS

(REVELATION 3:1–6)

The Salutation

> And unto the angel of the church in Sardis write; These things saith he that hath the seven Spirits of God, and the seven stars. (3:1)

Christ here says that He has the seven spirits of God and the seven stars. We already know the meaning of stars as a figure of speech. We have discussed the seven spirits as pictured in the golden lampstand, both in the Holy Place of the tabernacle and before the throne. This, however, does not answer the picture of their being in Christ's possession. We find reference to this in Revelation 5 where John views the throne.

> And I beheld, and, lo, in the midst of the throne and of the four beasts, and in the midst of the elders, stood a Lamb as it had been slain, having seven horns and seven eyes, which are the seven Spirits of God sent forth into all the earth. (5:6)

Here two more figures of speech portray the seven spirits of God, showing their relationship to Christ as another figure—the Lamb of God.

Looking at the Lamb, first we see His sacrifice. The Lamb was freshly slain and had seven horns and seven eyes. Hebrews 9:14 explains this: "How much more shall the blood of Christ, who through the eternal Spirit offered himself without spot to God, purge your conscience from dead works to serve the living God?" This same Christ addresses the church at Sardis. Can their problem have anything to do with dead works?

Before we seek the answer to this question, let us explore the two figures of speech. We know from its usage in the spiritual language that the word *seven* denotes completeness. For the meaning of the horns, we turn to the animal world, as it is obvious that an animal with horns has power over any without horns. Besides, horns are often found only on the male of the species, and they use their horns to establish dominion, again specifying power. The Spirit of God displayed thus would carry the same meaning—complete power to establish dominion. Seven eyes denote complete vision, supplying complete perception leading to wisdom.

Therefore, Jesus the Lamb is the one who addresses the Sardian church. This Lamb has the power and wisdom of the Holy Spirit to communicate to them through His "stars," the messengers. What could be the problem?

The Evaluation

> I know thy works, that thou hast a name that thou livest, and art dead. Be watchful, and strengthen the things which remain, that are ready to die: for I have not found thy works perfect before God. (3:1–2)

Jesus looks at their works but sees their hearts, because their works originate in their hearts. Hypocrites that they are, they say they are the church of the living God, but their dead works reveal otherwise. He says in essence, "Wake up! Recover the few things that are right but which are sliding toward death. Repent!" Spiritual life, whether of an individual believer or a church, depends on communication with the Holy Spirit. From the Lord's perspective, His Spirit was broadcasting life through their messenger, but this church was not receiving it. They had stopped listening. They were operating on truth they already had and deemed it sufficient.

It is a fact of nature that when a body stops growing, it begins to decay. We must eat every day, or without food, our bodies will eventually die. God illustrated this beautifully in the wilderness with the people of Israel. Manna came fresh every day; old manna stunk and bred worms. Likewise, spiritual growth comes from a vital infusion of new truth received daily from the Holy Spirit.

Ecclesiastical smugness accompanies the idea that we already know enough and don't need more truth. What a shock to hear the Lord imply, "You are not what you think you are."

Satan probably challenged them with false doctrine, and they overcame it. Now they feel safe because they emerged victorious. How easy it is to set up a creed of doctrine to keep others safe in the future by declaring, "This we believe," then trying to live by that creed. The Jews fell into the same trap. They established their own traditions from the Law and missed the Messiah because they refused to hear new truth from the Holy Spirit.

The Warning

> Remember therefore how thou hast received and heard, and hold fast, and repent. If therefore thou shalt not watch, I will come on thee as a thief, and thou shalt not know what hour I will come upon thee. (3:3)

Christ seemed to say, "Remember how you have heard and received truth in the past. Hold that truth fast, and repent of your current tendency to settle down in a creed." Apparently, they miss the truth of Christ's return, or they deliberately ignore it. Because of this lack, they are in danger of being caught with a loss as from a thief in the night. What can they lose? They will lose the rest of the overcomers' rewards offered to this and the two remaining churches. In other words, they will be denied the full reward earned by spiritual maturity (2 John 8).

Repeatedly, Jesus commands His disciples to watch for His coming. This requires an alertness that generates vitality. However, watchfulness requires knowledge of what is coming so they can be ready. This is what they are missing.

God has placed the fivefold ministry (apostles, prophets, evangelists, pastors, and teachers) in the churches to bring all to "a perfect man unto the measure of the stature of the fullness of Christ" (Eph. 4:11–13). Jesus wants the whole Church to come to the full understanding of who He is, what He has done for and in them, and what He will do in the future concerning the world. Why else would one-third of the Bible deal with prophecy unless He intends His Church to know about it? We will find later in the vision that the Church will have a part in the judgments He brings on the ungodly, and these responsibilities will be committed to priests. If they do not hear the current message, they will not be prepared.

In his Gospel, John had written Jesus' words concerning knowledge of "things to come."

> Nevertheless I tell you the truth; It is expedient for you that I go away: for if I go not away, the Comforter will not come unto you; but if I depart, I will send him unto you. . . . I have yet many things to say unto you, but ye cannot bear them now. Howbeit when he, the Spirit of truth, is come, he will guide you into all truth: for he shall not speak of himself; but whatsoever he shall hear, that shall he speak: and he will shew you things to come. (John 16:7, 12–13)

It was expedient for Christ to send the Holy Spirit as a revealer of truth because the Church was in its infancy. It could not absorb the whole truth all at once. Hence, His words, "I have yet many things to say unto you, but ye cannot bear them now." They had to grow in spiritual maturity to take in all the mysteries of the gospel. They had to first be grounded in the fundamentals of the faith. Besides that, He had barely introduced things concerning the future.

Later, the Holy Spirit would teach the apostles these things by guiding them to prophetic Scriptures "line upon line and precept upon precept" and by direct revelation. He worked with Paul this way. Both He and Peter have much to say concerning the future. James mentions the need for patience in waiting the Lord's coming. The Thessalonians were very concerned about it; thus, it was a popular subject in the beginning. Why would Jesus have the Holy Spirit reveal things to come if it were not important for the Church to know?

It seems strange that the Sardian Christians are indifferent to Christ's return. This is the next step in their development toward becoming useful to the Lord. Yet they are content to know only the fundamentals—what God has done for them. They are not learning about God's mighty power and majesty that the prophetic Scriptures reveal. Besides the glory revealed, His faithfulness also shows in the prophetic scriptures already fulfilled.

If we focus only on our own needs and wants, we will never get to know Christ intimately as our Bridegroom. Imagine a wife who refuses to listen to her husband's plans and desires for the future. She only wants her needs attended to, ignoring her husband's needs.

Spiritual growth which lacks full knowledge of Jesus and His plans is not worthy of a full reward. The Sardian believers need to open their ears and hear the fresh infusion of truth delivered through Spirit-filled messengers to overcome their deadness.

The Reward

Thou hast a few names even in Sardis which have not defiled their garments; and they shall walk with me in

white: for they are worthy. He that overcometh, the same
shall be clothed in white raiment; and I will not blot out
his name out of the book of life, but I will confess his
name before my Father, and before his angels. (3:4–5)

Christ acknowledges that a few in their midst have overcome the problem of deadness, and their garments are not
defiled. We have to ask ourselves how death and defiled
garments are related. Jude spoke of a defiled garment "spotted by the flesh" (Jude 23). Haggai questioned priests concerning defilement: "If one that is unclean by a dead body
touch any of these [his skirt, bread, pottage, wine, oil, or
meat], shall it be unclean? And the priests answered and
said, It shall be unclean" (Hag. 2:13). Haggai went on to
explain that Israel was unclean, and that defiled every work
of their hands or that which they offered as sacrifices. Israel was to be a priestly nation before the world. God said
they failed because they were like defiled priests.

Priests were defiled when they touched something dead.
It was a stringent requirement pressed on priests by the
Law that they touch no dead person outside of their imme-
diate family (Lev. 21:1–4). The high priest, having the
anointing oil on him, could not touch even his mother or
father after death (vv. 10–11). The Church, having the Holy
Spirit, would be similar to the high priest having the anointing oil. (Oil is the figure of speech often referring to the
Holy Spirit.) If priesthood is the overcomers' goal, then the
deadness of this church makes a glaring contrast to the living priesthood they should be. No wonder Christ expresses
revulsion when speaking of their deadness. In a picture,
the rotting flesh of their own death spots their garments.
Their priesthood is corrupted.

Christ promises that the overcomers will walk *with Him* in white. This is the first mention of a close personal contact with the Lord. They will walk with Him (go wherever He goes), communicating on the way. Their conversation will concern the plans He wants to share. Walking together suggests a certain intimacy. "Can two walk together, except they be agreed?" (Amos 3:3).

"He that overcometh, the same shall be clothed in white raiment" (Rev. 3:5). Such were the traditional garments of priests and Levites, who participated in worship (2 Chron. 5:12). Since garments often portray position (as in the case of priests), being a reward it may also apply to the same. John later confirms that the Church earns this position.

> The marriage of the Lamb is come, and his wife hath made herself ready. And to her was granted that she should be arrayed in fine linen, clean and white: for the fine linen is the righteousness [righteous acts][15] of saints. (19:7–8)

The wife has made *herself* ready; therefore, it was *granted* that she should be arrayed in fine linen. Fine linen was the fabric worn by kings and priests, which believers are called to be. The Sardian church is not prepared. Dead works can never weave her fabric. She is not expecting the Lord's coming because she is wrapped up in her own needs and creeds. The apostle John wrote in his letter about the purity developed by those looking for Christ's return, calling it their hope, because they expect to be like Him. "And every man

---

[15] Other translations indicate this righteousness is of the saints. Both the ASV and NKJV translate it thus.

that hath this hope in him purifieth himself, even as he is pure" (1 John 3:3). Only those hearing the messenger and overcoming deadness are looking for Him. Only those already acting as priests will continue to walk with the great High Priest.

The coming kingdom will have need of priests to intercede for the people. Otherwise, why will there be rejoicing in heaven over the Church's new role as "kings and priests" to rule over the earth (Rev. 5:10)?

Now we look at the negative side of the reward: "And I will not blot out his name out of the book of life, but I will confess his name before my Father, and before his angels" (3:5).

Blotting a name out of the book of life is practically impossible, unless one renounces Christ. However, many in this church hear only the dead doctrine without the convicting and quickening work of the Holy Spirit. They have taken on the name of "Christian" without the Spirit in their lives. They are not born again but are still dead in their sins. Their names will never be written in the book of life unless they repent and believe. That is the same result as having been blotted out.

How many names are written in the rolls of dead churches today? How many churches look back to former expressions of spiritual truth instead of hearing the current message of the Holy Spirit? Or worse, how many adopt popular social doctrines of the world? The bulk of the Sardian church's members are like that because the Lord said He had found a "few" who are not defiled. Therefore, this church for the most part is dead.

Christ will never blot overcomers out of the book of life. Further, He says He will confess their names before the Father and His angels. This is an act of intercession, emphasizing again "priestly" action. Therefore, we conclude that the white garments indicate positions as priests in the coming conflict and later in the religious functions of the kingdom.

Chapter 7

THE THINGS WHICH ARE: PHILADELPHIA

(REVELATION 3:7–13)

The Salutation

> And to the angel of the church in Philadelphia write;
> These things saith he that is holy, he that is true, he that
> hath the key of David, he that openeth, and no man
> shutteth; and shutteth and no man openeth. (3:7)

He that is holy, true, and has the key speaks. We know Christ is holy and that He is "the truth," but the significance of what that means to this church will have to wait until we understand the "key" and what it unlocks. Christ said He is the one who opens and no man shuts; He shuts and no man opens, stressing the fact that He and only He can control this door.

Many have studied the letter to Philadelphia and judged these believers to be without a problem. Nevertheless, this salutation indicates they not only do have a problem but also that their problem has to do with this door.

The Evaluation

> I know they works: behold, I have set before thee an open door, and no man can shut it: for thou hast a little strength, and hast kept my word, and hast not denied my name. (3:8)

Again Christ begins with their works, then adds (as He does with all the other churches) a criticism to correct them and make them better. To the first church, He says they should repent and do their first works. To the second church, He says they should not fear and be faithful. To the third church, He says they should repent or else he will bring division. To the fourth church, He says they should hold fast to what they have. To the fifth church, he says they should repent and watch. In each case, He mentions in His salutation the resources in Him to accomplish the improvement. Therefore, we expect that the open door should help their works. Finally, we come to their problem: They have little strength. They can be stronger if they take advantage of the open door He sets before them. It is so open and available to their use that He condemns them for not taking advantage of this opportunity.

The two questions are: Where does this door lead? What is behind the door that will strengthen their works? Our only clue is that it has a key called the "key of David." Looking for a connection, we find this exact term in Isaiah.

> And the key of the house of David will I lay upon his shoulder; so he shall open, and none shall shut; and he shall shut, and none shall open. And I will fasten him *as* a nail in a sure place; and he shall be for a glorious throne to his father's house. And they shall hang upon him all the glory of his father's house. (Isa. 22:22–24 emphasis added)

Eliakim was the steward or treasurer over Hezekiah's household (replacing Shebna, v. 15) and held the key of the king's storehouse from which he dispensed all resources. Isaiah used him as an example of the coming King, ascribing to Him dominion and making Him a glorious throne in His Father's house. He will be *like* a nail on which all the glory of the Father will hang.

We see the connection immediately. Jesus has the key because He is the treasurer of His Father's house. All the resources of the kingdom of God for taking dominion and bringing glory to God are behind this door. The door is open. The resources are available. Why have the believers in Philadelphia not gathered all the strength they need?

Two problems beset this church: First, they do not understand their position in Christ over the powers of darkness and therefore fail to use His mighty power to fight them. Second, they are timid because of great opposition. A controversy raged as to whether the Church still had use of the power gifts that were so evident following Pentecost. We will look at what they do not know and then why they are opposed.

First, these believers do not know their position in Christ. Yet the Christians' authority rests entirely on this knowledge. It is easy to identify with Christ in His death and resurrection, but Ephesians 2:6 tells us: "And [he] hath raised us up together, and made us to sit together in heavenly places in Christ Jesus." Speaking earlier of Jesus, Paul tells the Ephesians where Jesus sits.

> According to the working of his mighty power, which he wrought in Christ, when he raised him from the dead, and set him at his own right hand in the heavenly places, *far above all principality, and power, and might, and dominion, and every name that is named, not only in this world, but also in that which is to come:* and hath put all things under his feet, and gave him to be the head over all things to the church, which is his body, the fulness of him that filleth all in all. (Eph. 1:19–22 emphasis added)

We have a position above all these things because we are "in Christ." He remains the head; therefore, the use of this power comes directly from His command. The word *dominion* means the execution of control in a sphere of rule. Where exactly does the Church have dominion? When Jesus sent His disciples to preach the kingdom of God, He gave them authority over evil spirits and power to cure diseases. The same was true when He sent out the seventy. To them he said, "Behold, I give unto you power to tread on serpents and scorpions, and over all the power of the enemy: and nothing shall by any means hurt you" (Luke 10:19). Was this authority only given to these individuals, or did He give it to the entire Church as well? To answer this question we turn to the Great Commission, the Acts of the Apostles, and the Epistles to the Church.

First, the Great Commission in Mark:

> And he said unto them, Go ye into all the world, and preach the gospel to every creature. He that believeth and is baptized shall be saved; but he that believeth not shall be damned. And these signs shall follow them that believe; In my name shall they cast out devils; they shall speak with new tongues; they shall take up serpents; and if they drink any deadly thing, it shall not hurt them; they shall lay hands on the sick, and they shall recover. (Mark 16:15–18)[16]

These are Jesus' words. He expects the power of the Holy Spirit to follow the preaching of the gospel to demonstrate the kingdom rule of God over men. Verse 18, the reference to serpents, was never meant to be a license to handle snakes but refers to what He promised the seventy—that nothing would in any way hurt them. Paul demonstrated the truth of this when he shook off the serpent that bit him on the island of Melita (Acts 28:3–5). Jesus makes no mention of a time limit on this authority. Surely, there is just as much need to get rid of demons today as it was then, especially with the occult invasion on society. We still have sickness among us, also. Why would these gifts cease?

Looking further in the Acts of the Apostles, we find that Paul healed all that were sick on Melita after he shook off the snake. Later, he raised young Eutychus from the

---

[16] Verses 9–20 have been added to later manuscripts perhaps at a time when these experiences were being debated. They still stand in our scriptures today because they agree with the Acts and the Epistles. Who is to say that they were not dropped from scriptures where they are missing because of the same controversy.

dead when he fell from a high loft during Paul's long sermon (Acts 20:7). Paul cast a spirit of divination from a young girl in Philippi saying, "I command thee in the name of Jesus Christ to come out of her" (Acts 16:16–18). He took dominion over the spirit world. Jesus could say to demons, "Come out." Paul had to say, "Come out in the name of Jesus." The spirit yielded, not to Paul but to the name of Jesus. Was Paul able to do these things because he was an apostle or because he was baptized in the Holy Spirit? (see Acts 9:17).

When Paul traveled to Ephesus for the first time, he asked a group of believers, "Have ye received the Holy Ghost since ye believed?" Their baptism had only been in water (the baptism of repentance), but now they believed in and received Jesus and were baptized in Jesus' name. "When Paul had laid his hands upon them, the Holy Ghost came on them; and they spake with tongues, and prophesied" (Acts 19:1–7). When Philip went to Samaria and preached, many people believed and were baptized. Peter and John came from Jerusalem and prayed for these new converts, and they were filled with the Holy Spirit (Acts 8:5–17).

Thus, we can see from these scriptures that the Church in the beginning received the baptism of the Holy Spirit and exercised the power gifts. We also know that the Corinthian church exercised the power gifts because Paul rebuked them for their misuse of the gifts.

The mention of their misuse in the Corinthian church brings us to the reason the Philadelphian church is timid about entering the door. The power gifts are flashy in the hands of novices, sometimes used to show off. Besides that, the gifts attract power-greedy men such as Simon of Samaria who tried to buy the authority to baptize with the Holy Spirit (Acts 8:18–24).

Jesus predicted that many will stand before him in the judgment, calling Him Lord: "Many will say to me in that day, Lord, Lord, have we not prophesied in thy name? And in thy name have cast out devils? And in thy name done many wonderful works? And then will I profess unto them, I never knew you: depart from me, ye that work iniquity" (Matt. 7:22–23). Then whose power did they use? The power of Satan. The enemy is a great imitator of Jesus. Since he cannot defeat the power of God, he sets out to discredit it. He used unscrupulous men to confuse the early Church. The believers apparently grow tired of trying to distinguish the real from the false and "threw out the baby with the bath water."

The power of God drives back Satan's kingdom, especially in countries whose gods are evil spirits. To refuse to appropriate the gifts is to slow down the process of overcoming darkness. It is like building a house with a hammer and a handsaw instead of a nail gun and a skill saw. The house will be built but not without great physical effort. Proverbs 14:4 says: "Where no oxen are, the crib is clean: but increase is by the strength of the ox." The same could be said of the gifts. If we want to get much work done, we have to put up with the mess.

We look now at the opposition to the church at Philadelphia.

Behold, I will make them of the synagogue of Satan,
which say they are Jews, and are not, but do lie; behold,
I will make them to come and worship before thy feet,
and to know that I have loved thee. (3:9)

These people say they are Jews, but Jesus says their teaching and fellowship is of Satan. The synagogue was the gathering place for Jews in every city. The Pharisees instituted them for teaching the Law to both Jews and their Gentile proselytes. Carrying out the command that the gospel was to the Jew first and then to the Gentiles, the apostles always went to the synagogues first to preach. When the Jews who refused Christ saw the numbers won, even among their own proselytes, they were envious and turned violently against the Church, which they considered a perversion of Judaism. Their hatred disqualified them as representing God; therefore, the Lord disowned them as His people, calling them liars. Since the synagogue was the cultural center, many Christians maintained their fellowship there. The Jews came up with a way to persecute believers. They exercised what is known as hērem,[17] a sentence of excommunication, closing the door to the synagogue and the kingdom of heaven, since only Jews could enter, or so they thought. This may be another reason Jesus maintains an open door.

However, their ploy seemed to have split this church, because Jesus lumps these liars with some of the Christians. We say this because of Jesus' words: "I will make them to come and worship before your feet, and to know that I have loved thee" (3:9).

This tells of division and accusation in the church. Perhaps they are using the same accusation against the overcomers that the Pharisees used against Jesus, saying that His power came from the devil. These weak Christians side

---

[17] James Hastings, DD *The Dictionary of the Apostolic Church*, Vol. II (New York: Charles Scribner's Sons, 1918) p. 211.

with the Jews. Maybe they accuse any who will enter the door of having counterfeit spirits.

Jesus' statement seems to present both groups as worshipers of Him. He will settle the quarrel by showing His love to the obedient and elevating them to a higher position. The opposition worship "before" their feet, not "at" their feet, an important distinction. They do not worship the obedient but simply stand on a lower plane in their service to God.

Satan apparently uses these people to oppose the power of the church. He hates the power gifts because they reveal the unseen world of spirits. The Holy Spirit is like a secret agent, passing to believers bits of information to fight the powers of darkness. After using the information to uncover his deceptions, believers can take authority; Satan then is easily defeated, and his works are destroyed. Therefore, the devil has developed a whole doctrine concerning the gifts. He deceives the Church into thinking they are not for everyone. The gifts were only used to start the Church in the days of the apostles. To believe this leads one to the conclusion that any later use of the gifts comes from the devil.

Now we begin to understand Jesus' salutation of being holy and true. He has given these gifts. They are holy gifts coming from the Holy Spirit. They are true gifts, not false, because they come from the one who baptizes with the Holy Spirit. Jesus had addressed the fear of receiving demonic gifts earlier when He taught on prayer.

And I say unto you, Ask, and it shall be given you; seek, and ye shall find; knock, and it shall be opened unto you. For every one that asketh receiveth; and he that seeketh findeth; and to him that knocketh it shall be opened. If a son shall ask bread of any of you that is a father, will he give him a stone? or if he ask a fish, will he for a fish give him a serpent? Or if he shall ask an egg, will he offer him a scorpion? If ye then, being evil, know how to give good gifts unto your children: how much more shall your heavenly Father give the Holy Spirit to them that ask him. (Luke 11:9–13)

Ask for what you need, seek for things or people that are lost, and knock on closed doors that you may enter, is how we normally understand this scripture. That, however, is not the meaning Jesus seems to have in mind. He once said to His disciples, "From the days of John the Baptist until now the kingdom of heaven suffereth violence, and the violent take it by force" (Matt. 11:12). From the time that John appeared until Jesus came, the Jewish religious world was electrified by John's preaching, which forced change on people. Energetic listeners passionately grabbed hold of John's teaching, then of Jesus' teaching. In other words, they pressed themselves into the kingdom.

Jesus encourages the same thing here when He says to ask, seek, and knock. However, when we look at the passage carefully, we find He is talking about asking, seeking, and knocking for *more* of the Holy Spirit. Why should we ask for more of the Holy Spirit when we received Him at our salvation? *Because we are weak.* Jesus breathed the Holy Spirit into His disciples behind closed doors after His resurrection (John 20:21). Yet He commanded them to wait in Jerusalem for power from on high—the baptism of the Holy Spirit—before attempting to do His work.

Looking at the parable, we see a contrast in the gifts: bread versus stone, a fish versus a serpent, and an egg versus a scorpion. "If a son shall ask bread of any one of you that is a father" shows Jesus is talking to believers. He further confirms this when He says, "How much more shall *your* heavenly Father give?" (Luke 11:13 emphasis added). The real question is: Who is asking, and who is their father? If God is our Father, we will get true gifts. If Satan is our father, we will get counterfeits. Satan offered a stone to Jesus for bread. "Serpents" and "scorpions" are figures of speech representing Satan's ministering spirits and the power of the enemy (Luke 10:19). No child of God should fear to ask his or her Father for more of the Holy Spirit.

The Warning

> Because thou hast kept the word of my patience, I also will keep thee from the hour of temptation, which shall come upon all the world, to try them that dwell upon the earth. Behold, I come quickly: hold that fast which thou hast, that no man take thy crown. (3:10–11)

First, Christ gives a promise: "Because thou hast . . . I also will . . ." and after that a warning. Understanding the promise hinges on the meaning of the terms the "word of my patience" and the "hour of temptation." We note that the first words are specific and possessive: "of my patience." Looking back in the Scriptures to find a reference to Jesus' patience, we see that Paul spoke of it to the Romans.

> We then that are strong ought to bear the infirmities of the weak, and not to please ourselves. Let every one of us please his neighbor for his good to edification. For even Christ pleased not himself; but, as it is written, The reproaches of them that reproached thee fell on me. For whatsoever things were written aforetime were written for our learning, that we through patience and comfort of

99

the scriptures might have hope. Now the God of patience and consolation grant you to be likeminded one toward another according to Christ Jesus. (Rom. 15:1–5)

John also refers to the patience of Jesus Christ in Revelation 1.

I John, who also am your brother, and companion in tribulation, and in the kingdom and patience of Jesus Christ, was in the isle that is called Patmos, for the word of God, and for the testimony of Jesus Christ. (1:9)

"Patience" meant to not think of themselves by fighting back but to endure as Christ endured reproaches. Now we begin to get the idea of what Jesus meant by keeping the word of His patience. They cheerfully endure the opposition of their weaker brothers and let their reproaches fall on them. Jesus finds that worthy of a promise. Now we are left with trying to understand the promise.

Christ explained that the "hour of temptation" is a time coming upon the whole world to try them in God's court of judgment. Looking at the Greek meaning of the word *keep*, we get more understanding. *Teros* means "to guard from loss or injury by keeping an eye upon." Jesus promises to guard the Philadelphian overcomers from injury or loss during the hour of what we call the great tribulation: that seven-year period described as Daniel's last week (Dan. 9:27) when God deals with both the Jews and the world for their rejection of Christ.

The reference to the hour is significant. Jesus says no man can know the day or the hour of His coming. Nevertheless, when He does come, it will happen simultaneously throughout the whole world. That means it will be a different hour of the day in all twenty-four time zones and on two different days for those next to the international dateline. In that hour, the age of grace will end, and the time of judgment will begin. Within one hour, sudden changes will grip the whole earth.

How can Jesus keep the saints from loss at this hour? Jesus says in Revelation 22:12: "And, behold I come quickly [suddenly]; and *my reward is with me*, to give to every man according as his work shall be" (emphasis added).

We conclude from this that the hour of the judgment seat of Christ is right after His appearing following the resurrection. Therefore, keeping the overcomers from loss during this time is to preserve their reward. This fits right in with His warning when He said in effect, "Behold, I come quickly. Do not waver; keep hold of what you have. Let *no man* take your crown! *No man* can open the storehouse door; *no man* can shut the storehouse door. So let *no man* take away your crown with his teaching, his reproachful opposition, or anything else that people can do." By this warning, Christ confirms that the "hour of temptation" refers to His coming.

The Reward

> Him that overcometh will I make a pillar in the temple of my God, and he shall go no more out: and I will write upon him the name of my God, and the name of the city of my God, which is new Jerusalem, which cometh down out of heaven from my God: and I will write upon him my new name. (3:12)

To become a "pillar" employs a figure of speech. Speaking plainly, what do pillars do? They hold up structures. Since the temple or dwelling place of God in the New Testament sense is the Church, pillars are the strength of it. In Galatians 2:9, Paul speaks of "James, Cephas [Peter], and John, who seemed to be pillars" of the church in Jerusalem. By this he ascribes to them leadership and feels they are able to perceive the truth of his calling. Later, in his letter to Timothy, Paul calls the Church itself "the pillar and ground of the truth" (1 Tim. 3:15). Pillars uphold. A pillar in the temple of God holds up the beauty and majesty of God's truth. "He shall go no more out" confirms one's "pillarship." Pillars do not move; they stand.

However, this statement speaks also of relationships. Since the pillars are "in the temple," they do more than just walk with Christ. Unlike the Sardian overcomers, these are constantly in His presence. He will write the name of the glorious new Jerusalem on them. Names written on them implies titles of positions of importance. This honor, however, is based on whether they have overcome all the previous problems presented before this. In other words, they as individuals continue to hear what the Spirit says to all the churches and respond by overcoming the problems, thereby growing more spiritually mature.

In his description of the new Jerusalem in Revelation 21:22, John says, "And I saw no temple therein: for the Lord God Almighty and the Lamb are the temple of it." Thus, these pillars stand in the almighty power of God and the Lamb. Earlier, John was told that the city was "prepared as a bride adorned for her husband" (21:2). The city is also a figure of speech describing the Church where God lives. A temple is a place to meet with God. Since the believers live with God, it is no longer necessary to meet with Him.

To be a pillar of the temple is to be a pillar of the city, also. No wonder, then, that they are marked as the strength of God. It is entirely appropriate that their reward for attaining strength is to become the strength of the city.

One more reward Christ will bestow on these believers. He will write on them His new name (3:12). He has been called Servant, Mighty Angel, Captain of the Lord's hosts, Son of Man, Savior, Prophet, Priest, King, Lamb, and Bridegroom. To have a new name probably applies to His upcoming status as Judge of the earth. If so, it may be the same name mentioned in Revelation 19:11 where Christ was "called Faithful and True, and in righteousness he doth judge and make war." To have this same name conferred on believers may mean they will have a part in this judgment.

Chapter 8

THE THINGS WHICH ARE: LAODICEA

(REVELATION 3:14–22)

The Salutation

> And unto the angel of the church of the Laodiceans write;
> These things saith the Amen, the faithful and true wit-
> ness, the beginning of the creation of God. (3:14)

We find a division in this salutation. When Christ
salutes the first church, He addresses the angel
of the church of Ephesus. In all the rest, He addresses the angel of the church in Smyrna, in Pergamos, in
Thyatira, etc. Now He addresses the angel of the church
not in Laodicea or even of Laodicea but the church of the
Laodiceans. It is as if He is not involved because they have
taken it over without Him. It has become their church, not
His church. While the Ephesian church has set up their

own truth, it appears that the Laodiceans have set up their own church.

No wonder Jesus says to them in effect, "I am the Amen, the finisher of the church, not you. I am the faithful and true witness; I am the beginning of the creation of God." His title in this letter compares to the title He uses in His letter to Smyrna. He tells them He is the first and the last. Here He says much the same thing except that He reverses it. He is the Amen, the final say, the author and finisher of their faith. He is also the beginning of all things. "All things were made by him: and without him was not any thing made that was made," says John when he begins his Gospel (John 1:3). In between being last and first, He is the faithful and true witness, perhaps inferring that they are not. He is the all-powerful ruler over both the creation and His Church. He will charge on His white horse to judgment, wearing the title "Faithful and True," the one who judges righteously and makes war. The entire story told by His title spells out power and majesty. With such splendor as a resource, what can possibly be their problem?

The Evaluation

> I know thy works, that thou art neither cold nor hot: I would thou were cold or hot. So then because thou art lukewarm, and neither cold nor hot, I will spue thee out of my mouth. Because thou sayest, I am rich, and increased with goods, and have need of nothing; and knowest not that thou art wretched, and miserable, and poor, and blind, and naked: I counsel thee to buy of me gold tried in the fire, that thou mayest be rich; and white raiment, that thou mayest be clothed, and that the shame of thy naked-

ness do not appear; and anoint thine eyes with eyesalve, that thou mayest see. (3:15–18).

Their works reveal their condition. They are halfhearted. They are not cold, so they are alive. Neither are they hot, that is, they have no enthusiasm for the Lord. A strange condition indeed, considering how He addresses them. He says in effect, "You make me sick to my stomach. You say, 'I am rich and increased with goods. I don't need anything.'"

The Laodiceans have settled into a comfort zone. They have supplies beyond what they need for life, for that is the meaning of being rich. Being poor means not having enough to meet one's needs. Actually, they are more than rich; they are privileged to possess many luxuries, things that make life pleasant. They do not even need God, because they have the resources to do work for Him.

Notice that Christ does not mention anything wrong with their hearing. Being the last church addressed with the final problem to overcome, they have probably heard all the messages sent to the other churches. They have overcome it all.

They know all about the Lord's coming. No doubt, they even speak in tongues occasionally. Nevertheless, they have settled down to wait for His return in comfort. The excitement of overcoming former problems has passed. They are bored. They know it all. There is nothing more for them to learn. Yet they are so much like the world, it hardly notices them.

Their works are without enthusiasm, and they do not accomplish all they can. Their problem: They have lost their zeal for the Lord. His evaluation of their condition is opposite to theirs. He says in effect: "You are ignorant. You do not even know you are wretched and miserable. You are poor, you are blind, and you are naked." Their wretchedness and misery stems from the other three conditions. They may know all about supernatural healing, but they are not experiencing it. They are poor because they measure themselves against the world. They may say to themselves, "If God is our provider, then we must be spiritually privileged. God is so pleased with us that He made us rich. After all, we're the sons and daughters of the King." Maybe they had prosperity teachers in those days, too. As a church, they appear to be without influence in the world.

Jesus told the Laodiceans that if they want to reverse their poverty, they need to buy gold from Him. As we mentioned before, *gold* is a figure of speech denoting the purity and holiness of God. With this gold, the believers can make an impact on the world that a mature church *should make*. This is the last church needing to overcome the last problem. By doing so, it would reveal to the world not only that Jesus is Savior but also a splendid King who will come to judge them. Such a testimony would leave the world guilty and ripe for judgment at Jesus' return.

To understand what Jesus says about gold, we need to find a meaning for this figure of speech. What does He mean by His command, "Buy of me?" Salvation is a gift. The only way people can buy of God is to fulfill the conditions of a promise causing God to keep His Word. Where do we find a promise concerning gold tried in the fire? Peter tells us, "The trial of your faith, being much more precious than of gold that perisheth, though it be tried with fire . . . (1 Pet. 1:7a). Such gold has had all impurities melted out by fire. By explanation, he means pure gold. God uses gold, one of the most valuable metals on earth, to describe the preciousness of faith in His eyes. It is *more* valuable than gold, just as wisdom is *more* valuable than rubies. When Christ says to buy gold from Him, He means that they should develop faith so they can do great things for His glory. He glorifies Himself by showing His power. What good are the power gifts if they are not used with faith?

The Lord tries to motivate the Laodiceans to accept their status *in Christ*, to take the tools He has given so that this last church, this mature church would leave the world without doubt concerning the majesty and might of the Lord Jesus Christ. Let this last church glean from the earth all who will believe its testimony before Jesus comes to judge. I say "last church," speaking of the development of the Church as a whole. Just as individuals develop maturity by overcoming all the problems spoken of in these letters, so also will the collective Church through the ages. Therefore, overcoming the last problem brings maturity to the Church just before Jesus' coming.

Now let us look at how the church can use "gold" to improve their works. In 1 Corinthians 3:12, Paul shows gold as being the most precious material used in building the Church. Thinking of gold as a building material, we look to the tabernacle and the temple, which were also houses of God and spiritual pictures of Christ and His Church. In both, after the boards were overlaid with gold and set up God appeared with His glory and power. The same will be true of the Church if her "boards" are overlaid with proven faith. His glory will descend on her, and the world will see it.

Jude exhorts the Church to "earnestly contend for the faith" (v. 3) against wickedness both in the world and the Church in the "last time." He writes, "But ye, beloved, building up yourselves on your most holy faith, praying in the Holy Ghost, keep yourselves in the love of God" (vv. 20–21). Praying in the Holy Spirit is one of the power gifts—praying in an unknown tongue. Jude says this builds up one's faith. To understand this, we turn to Paul's explanation to the Corinthians: "He that speaketh in an unknown tongue edifieth himself; but he that prophesieth edifieth the church" (1 Cor. 14:4).

Paul is correcting a misuse of the gift. Speaking in an unknown tongue comes as an evidence of power following the baptism in the Holy Spirit. Clearly, Paul means them to use the gift in the prayer closet, not everyone speaking in tongues all at once in a church meeting. Paul maintains that anyone seeing this would think they are crazy. The correct use of the gift in the church is one person conveying a message from God in an unknown language, another person interpreting the message in a known language, thereby prophesying to the whole church. But more specifically, someone in their midst can see this as a sign that God is truly speaking *to him* because he knows the language that is unknown to both the speaker and the interpreter. This is a double witness to him that God is in their midst. That is the correct way to use the gift publicly.

Otherwise, speaking in tongues is a gift to build up the individual with more of the Holy Spirit. One must yield to the Spirit his "rudder" or "helm," as James calls the tongue (James 3:4). By yielding his tongue to the Holy Spirit, he yields his whole person, enabling the Spirit to pray through him about specific needs of which the person's mind has no knowledge. He speaks the mysteries (hidden things) of God (1 Cor. 4:2). The constancy of yielding to the Holy Spirit builds up a fullness of the Spirit inside himself so when called on to exercise power in a situation, the voice of the Spirit's instruction is clear. Paul said, "I thank my God, I speak with tongues more than ye all" (1 Cor. 14:18). Look at the success of his works! Imagine a church filled with such believers acting in faith with power. It would know no bounds. God would be glorified. "Buy of me gold!" He says.

Christ added, "Buy of me . . . white raiment, that thou mayest be clothed, and that the shame of thy nakedness do not appear" (Rev. 3:18). As before, we seek the meaning of the figure of speech. What does "white raiment" mean? We found that it refers to the priesthood in Sardis. Here, however, "nakedness" seems to qualify its meaning. Nakededness implies an openness to sin. Adam's nakedness posed no problem until he had knowledge of sin; then he was ashamed. Therefore, from the beginning, nakedness is associated with shame. Isaiah walked naked before the nation Israel to proclaim the coming shame of the nation.

The lack of raiment for this church proclaims the same. These believers are in danger of exposing themselves before the world as frauds. They proclaim that they are representatives of the kingdom of God, but they deny the power thereof by acting no different from the world. Without zeal, they are ineffective. What a shame! Jesus says in effect, "Cloth yourselves in my glory, be the priests you claim to be, represent to this world the King of righteousness, and serve Him unequivocally!"

Christ also tells the Laodiceans, "Anoint thine eyes with eyesalve, that thou mayest see" (3:18). He urges them to medicate their blindness. Jesus uses blindness as a figure of speech to describe the spiritual condition of the Pharisees and Sadducees, but earlier God promises blindness to those who chose to disobey His laws (Deut. 28:28). The apostle Peter writes that the person who lacks virtue, knowledge, temperance, patience, godliness, brotherly kindness, and love "is blind, and cannot see afar off, and hath forgotten that he was purged from his old sins" (2 Pet. 1:9). Most likely, this is the cause of the blindness in this church. They have forgotten and cannot see afar off. They are nearsighted. If they remembered, they would be thankful, grateful, and enthusiastic.

Here I wish to break into this discussion to point out that each letter also can refer to the Church in various historical periods. It has already passed through these problems. The Church of the Reformation broke free of certain false teaching in the Catholic church. Then came the great studies of the nineteenth century concerning prophecy where everything concerning end times was duly debated and fought over. During the twentieth century in the Pentecostal and charismatic revivals, part of the Church once again acknowledged and practiced the power gifts. Though not all participated in the changes wrought through the Spirit, the Church at large was aware of them. It is always by individual choice whether to hear or not. Therefore, the Church has arrived at the final problem in its overall development.

Naturally, each of these periods has had overcomers as well as underachievers. Nevertheless, the voice of the Spirit to each of these periods moved the Church further along to maturity. That means that though today's Church may stand at the end of the problems, only a potential few are ready to overcome the last problem. They have participated in all the other problems and overcome them. Therefore, today's Church is a conglomeration—believers left over from all seven churches.

Believers in today's Church offer excuses for their shortsightedness; yet no excuse is valid. Here are the seeming problems:

- They cannot *see* because their emphasis is in the wrong place. "You cannot love others unless you *love yourself*," they say. "Therefore, 'know thyself' and 'to thine own self be true.'" Self-esteem has replaced God-esteem; psychology has replaced soteriology.[18] Esteeming oneself rather than esteeming others (Phil. 2:3) resonates the Church's new philosophy. The Laodiceans' words reflect this: "I am rich, and increased with goods, and have need of nothing" (Rev. 3:17). "Increased with goods" shows that they are rich in substance; however, that seems to be in addition to their personality riches. Can that refer to their self-esteem?

- Some believers today cannot *see* the need of the world for Christ's gospel of salvation because they cocoon themselves in their "riches"; therefore, they concentrate on raising the poverty level of the world through a social gospel.

- They have lost their *vision* of the power of the gospel message. They say that the old gospel is not enough, is not relevant to the world today; thus, we need to relate to the world to win them. We need music like the world's music and entertainment like the world's entertainment. We need to put on a show and gather in the crowds. Blind!

- They cannot *see* that conditions are ripe for Christ's imminent appearing. Perhaps they expected Him to come earlier. When He did not meet their expectations, they lost their zeal for His coming. Worse, perhaps they changed their doctrinal position on

---

[18] Soteriology =theology of salvation through Christ's blood.

His return. Some even expect to bring in the king-dom without His coming. No zeal!

Blindness seems to plague an era in decline. Samson, the last recorded judge in the Book of Judges, finished his life blind—as did also Zedekiah, Israel's last king. Now the last church is blind.

Concerning the three faults that Christians in the Laodicean church need to overcome, Paul writes of his own challenge with them.

> That I may know him [*gain wisdom concerning God's ways in order to overcome blindness*], and the power of his res-urrection [*gain proven faith for use in His service to over-come poverty*], and the fellowship of his sufferings [*grow in righteous character to overcome nakedness*], being made conformable unto his death; if by any means I might *attain* unto the resurrection of the dead. (Phil. 3:10–11 additions in italics added)

Paul was striving for the full reward. Like some in the Philadelphian church, he had overcome weakness, and he knew all about Christ's second coming. However, it takes an ongoing zeal to overcome complacency. Paul aimed to be victorious!

Paul certainly had much to discourage him near the end of his life. Friends had turned their backs on him. Some of his young helpers had deserted the kingdom and gone back to the world.[19] In addition, he faced a gruesome death at the hands of the Romans.[20] Yet he triumphed when he

---

[19] 2 Tim. 4:10
[20] 2 Tim. 4:6.

said, "I have fought a good fight, I have finished my course, I have kept the faith: henceforth there is laid up for me a crown of righteousness" (2 Tim. 4:7–8).

Mature Christians who walk in much truth may become weary in their spiritual battles. They are tempted to no longer "fight the good fight of faith" to the end (1 Tim. 6:12). Because they pose the greatest threat to Satan, he opposes them vigorously. It would be easier for them to sit back, smug in their knowledge of the truth, and wait for the Lord to come rather than to fight with zeal to the end.

Looking back on the three things complacent Christians lack, we can sum them up as follows: They are hindered by a lack of doing works of faith (God's ministry); a lack of being what they ought to be (conformed to Christ's image); and a lack of seeing (from God's point of view). No wonder they are wretched and miserable. In their complacency, they have lost the means to use God's power.

The Warning

Jesus tells the Laodiceans, "As many as I love, I rebuke and chasten" (3:19). In John's Gospel, He also says, "He that hath my commandments, and keepeth them, he it is that loveth me: and he that loveth me shall be loved of my Father, and I will love him, and will manifest myself to him" (John 14:21). He will rebuke and prod to keep us moving because He loves us.

Returning to the idea that this church belongs to the Laodiceans, not to Christ, we find Him outside the church knocking to get in.

> Be zealous therefore, and repent. Behold, I stand at the door, and knock: if any man hear my voice, and open

the door, I *will* come in to him, and will *sup* with him, and he with me. (3:19–20 emphasis added)

The Reward

To him that overcometh will I grant to sit with me in my throne, even as I also overcame, and am set down with my Father in his throne. (3:21)

To "sup" or eat with Christ shows total understanding not only of His ways but also of His plans—a communed fellowship. To do His works means to use the same power the apostles used as adult sons. It means to accomplish His will and display His glory to the world, to do the works of the Father. Jesus tells His disciples, "Verily, verily, I say unto you, He that believeth on me, the works that I do shall he do also; and greater works than these shall he do; because I go unto my Father" (John 14:12). He was able to do this by sending the Holy Spirit. He does not say, "You shall do" as He said to the apostles, but "he that believeth," he who has faith, shall do works that glorify the Father through the Son. Doing greater works than Jesus did would set the world up to see God just as the Church did in its beginning. It would force a choice on them, but it would also feed Christ. Jesus says, "My meat [food] is to do the will of him that sent me, and to finish his work" (John 4:34). It is also His "meat" to do the Father's will through us. We shall dine together! We feed on Him, and He feeds on our work through Him. Oh, Christian, do you not long to set a feast before our Lord?

To overcome as Christ overcame is to reign over all the circumstances of life. This requires true faith, a fully developed Christ-like character, and an understanding of the purposes of God. No wonder He counsels us to obtain these qualities. Christ is knocking to get into a church that has shut Him out. It is up to us to hear His voice, open the door, and let him in. "He that hath an ear, let him hear what the Spirit saith unto the churches" (3:22). Again, He emphasizes the importance of hearing.

The reward for overcoming complacency is the ultimate limit, higher still than pillars. Christ will actually share His throne with overcoming believers. Surely, these are the hundredfold reproducers of seed mentioned in the parable of the sower (see Luke 8:5–15).

Conclusion to the Letters

The first three problems of the churches directly relate to the parable of the sower. Showing the relationship of rewards to the production of good seed, we can compare the lack of production from seed that fell on stony ground to the problem of unfaithfulness; persecution defeated them (Luke 8:6, 13). We can look at the reduced growth of the good seed in thorny ground in relation to worldliness; the cares of this world defeated them (vv. 7, 14). If we go back to Revelation 1, we can compare the Ephesian church's lack of hearing to birds consuming the sower's seed, which removes the possibility of reproduction (vv. 5, 12).

Reserving the thirty–, sixty–, and one hundredfold reproduction for the four remaining problems, we have a two-to twenty-ninefold reproduction of seed to apply to those that overcome the first problems. While this low production of seed does little to glorify the Lord, great numbers of Christians will progress no further. Jesus explains that "the seed is the word of God" (Luke 8:11). In Matthew's account of this parable, Jesus tells His disciples,

"It is given unto you to know the mysteries of the kingdom of heaven" (Matt. 13:11). He wants them to understand His Word about His kingdom and the preparation of the Bride to reign. Overcomers of the first three problems in Revelation 2 will reign over less responsibility.

Looking back at the reward scale from the top, this is how it appears to work: First, those who are born again by the Spirit but fail to hear God and obey will live inside the heavenly city but receive no reward. Their capacity to know and enjoy God has yet to be developed.

Second, those who begin well hear God but do not continue walking in His way. Instead, they fall back into the life of their old natures or are unfaithful in other ways. These will eat from the tree of life, but they will be denied a crown of life.

Third, those believers who mix the world into their Christianity choke their growth so they cannot be trusted as judges over the world. However, their souls will never be in danger of the second death.

Fourth, those Christians who begin well but are trapped by Satan in a false doctrine may have overcome worldliness and earned positions as judges, but they will be denied higher positions over nations.

Fifth, those who overcome false doctrine (the young-men category of believers) but settle into dead doctrines of tradition will rule the nations but will not walk with Christ in white as kingdom priests.

Sixth, those who learn about Jesus' plans for the future but fail to gain His mighty power by acquiring the power gifts will become kingdom priests.

Seventh, those who overcome weakness will earn the position of pillars that always stand in God's presence *at* the throne. Nevertheless, they fail to continue in zeal and develop "faith tried in the fire"; therefore, they will be denied a position *on* the throne with Christ. That is reserved for those who earn the full reward.

We see that God reserves positions of honor and glory for those who can overcome most or all the problems. Those who overcome will glorify the Lord. Yet the ability to overcome depends on our ability to hear. It is no wonder Christ repeatedly says in these letters, "He that hath an ear, let him hear."

Looking back on the rewards, we see a progression reaching from the outskirts of paradise to the very throne itself. Thus, the position of each person's kingdom service depends on his or her spiritual maturity.

Finally, we come to the end of "the things which are." Whether we view these letters as a historical sequence or a maturity scale, they exhort us to growth. The very word *overcome* demands a struggle. Victory brings maturity, and maturity brings rewards, responsibilities, and fitness to reign. May we all hear what the Spirit is saying to the churches.

Chapter 9

THE RAPTURE: A DOCTRINAL INTERLUDE

> After this I looked, and, behold, a door was opened in heaven: and the first voice which I heard was as it were of a trumpet talking with me; which said, Come up hither, and I will shew thee things which must be hereafter. And immediately I was in the spirit: and, behold, a throne was set in heaven, and one sat on the throne. (4:1–2)

Finished with the last sentence of the dictation, John looks up from writing the "things which are" to find himself alone again. He looks around to see what will happen next.

Suddenly, a door opens in heaven. As he marks the beginning of a new scene, the reverberating trumpet-like voice invites and commands him to come up through the door. It appears then that he will view "things which shall be hereafter" from a heavenly vantage point, from the other side of the open door.

Before we continue with John, it seems appropriate to discuss what happens (if anything) to the Church in this change of scenes. Is God finished with the Church on earth at this time? Do believers view the nations under judgment with John from heaven, or are they left behind to suffer with the nations?

The question of whether Christians are involved in the tribulation of the "things . . . hereafter" has been vigorously debated for years. Obviously, where we place the rapture of the Church in the scheme of things will color the whole picture of prophetic events. Placing it at the wrong time in the sequence will change the interpretation. The pretribulation rapture position seems to fit best with the Scriptures overall. The following arguments provide reasons.

Separation of Peoples

First, we will consider God's separate dealings with His peoples: Israel and the Church. Many have discounted Israel, saying the Church has replaced her. However, one of the mysteries we mentioned before has to do with Israel's future salvation. Then, too, we call to mind the combined roles of Jesus in His appearance to John.

In the introduction, we said that "His angel" would divide (signify) the entire vision. At the end of Revelation, the Lord states this again in the form of an oath saying, "I Jesus have sent mine angel to testify unto you these things in the churches" (22:16). We see Him there in His Mighty Angel role. Though Israel has rejected Jesus as Messiah, they know the one who rescued them from Egypt with "a mighty hand, and with an outstretched arm" (Deut. 26:8). They know Him as God's Mighty Angel.

The Book of Revelation is not the only place where we find references to a personal messenger of God. For instance:

> Behold, I send an angel before you, to guard you on the way and to bring you to the place which I have prepared. Give heed to him and hearken to his voice, do not rebel against him, for he will not pardon your transgression; for my name is in him. But if you hearken attentively to his voice and do all that I say, then I will be an enemy to your enemies and an adversary to your adversaries. When my angel goes before you, and brings you in to the Amorites, and the Hittites, and the Perizzites . . . and I blot them out . . . and I will make all your enemies turn their backs to you. (Exod. 23:20–23, 27 RSV)

This special angel had God's name and spoke His words. He was specifically commissioned to lead Israel and fight her battles as she journeyed through the wilderness to the Promised Land.

The Israelites failed to obey God's command because of unbelief. As a result, they could not enter the land during Moses' lifetime. Therefore, the angel was sent again in Joshua's day. God did not tell Joshua of His coming; instead, he met Him face to face. The angel had the form of a man and had a sword in His hand. He said He was the Captain of the Lord's hosts. When Joshua fell at His feet to worship Him, the Captain told him to take off his shoes because he was standing on holy ground.

An angel would not receive worship; and since the words He spoke were the same as those spoken to Moses by the "I am that I am," the eternal, self-existing God (Exod. 3:14), we can conclude that this person was God. Because He had the form of a man, we believe, as other commentators, that this was the preincarnate appearance of the Lord Jesus. Furthermore, since the Captain of Joshua 6 came to accomplish what was promised to the personal angel of Exodus 23, we conclude they were the same.

Isaiah confirmed this with his description of an avenger in the wine press treading out the grapes of wrath against Israel's enemies. First, he asks: "Who is this that cometh from Edom, with dyed garments from Bozrah? this that is glorious in his apparel, traveling in the greatness of his strength?" (Isa. 63:1). Then the Lord answered:

> I that speak in righteousness, mighty to save . . .For he said, surely they [Israel] are my people, children that will not lie; so he was their Saviour. In all their affliction he was afflicted, and *the angel of his presence* saved them: in his love and in his pity he redeemed them; and he bare them, and carried them all the days of old. (Isa. 63:1, 8–9 emphasis added)

This is no ordinary presence. Would an angel speak of Israel as his children, or could he be their Savior? Because He is coming to be their Savior, expositors agree that the avenger is Christ judging the nations. Though the treading of the wine is a type of future judgment, Isaiah saw the avenger and recognized Him as Israel's special redeeming angel from the days of Moses and Joshua. Therefore, the "angel of his presence" who "carried them all the days of old" refers to the same person who identified Himself to Joshua as the Captain of the Lord's hosts. He is the same invincible angel who redeemed Israel from Egypt and led them to the Promised Land. By picking up this role again, it is strong evidence that He is ready to work with Israel once more.

It is not surprising then that Christ separated His operations with His two peoples into two distinct periods. Although the glorious one seen by John in Revelation 1 has a combined role of Priest and a person of power, the letters He dictates speak solely to the Church. On the other hand, the "things which shall be hereafter" have to do with the Jews, Jerusalem, the temple, Gentile rulers, and nations. There is no reference whatever to the Church. Is God telling us that although the role of Jesus as Priest/Mighty Angel is to both peoples, He works with them separately and at different times?

Not only are the times divided into two separate viewings for John, but he also sees them from two separate locations. The Priest/Mighty Angel dictates the letters to the churches to John on earth. The Priest/Mighty Angel comes to John. However, John sees from heaven the "things . . . hereafter" dealing with Israel and the nations. He goes to the Priest/Mighty Angel. God could show the whole vision to John on earth. Why doesn't He? Can this change in John's location, who represents a servant of Christ, signify that the whole Church will view the "things . . . hereafter" from the same vantage point as John? I think this can be the significance of separate views in separate locations.

Besides the separation in dictating letters and showing scenes, we have the fact that after Revelation 3, there is no indication in the text that the Church is still on earth. Scripture does not mention her again until chapter 19, verse 14 where the King prepares His army. Nor does Scripture place her on earth in a symbolic way.

On the other hand, the text names Israel tribe by tribe and shows her in a figure of speech as well. The sealing of the twelve tribes of Israel in chapter 7 puts a severe strain on making this refer to anything other than literal Israel, since the tribes are specifically named. Even to the point that the tribe of Dan is omitted in favor of the half tribe of Manasses. Besides, by naming the tribes individually, the woman of Revelation 12 shows Israel as Jesus' mother. The Church could never give birth to Christ; rather, it is the other way around. Thus, both the tribes' names and the figure of speech point to Israel rather than to the Church.

Because God separates the vision concerning the churches and Israel and because He fails to mention the Church again during the events taking place on earth, this seems to be strong evidence that the Church simply is not there.

The Firstfruits of Resurrection

In Paul's first letter to the Corinthians, he gives a long dissertation on the resurrection in which he includes the order of its occurrence. He says, "As in Adam all die, even so in Christ shall all be made alive. But every man *in his own order*: Christ the firstfruits; afterward they that are Christ's at his coming" (1 Cor. 15:22–23 emphasis added). (The word *order* is a military term denoting a division or a company, in this case of believers.) We know Revelation 20 mentions the resurrection of martyred tribulation saints. Jesus raises these up after He returns to set up His kingdom. They are the last "order" to be included in what is termed the first resurrection or the resurrection of the redeemed. However, other resurrections take place earlier, for instance, the two witnesses and later the saints of Revelation 11. Obviously, the Lord's coming in the air for the

Church, the firstfruits of all the redeemed must occur some-time before this also.

James says that the Church is begotten as "a kind of firstfruits of his creatures" (James 1:18), indicating a general harvest of born-again ones to follow. As the firstfruits, the Church is the beginning, the first in the line of companies. The martyred tribulation saints are the last. Since *firstfruits* is a figure of speech for the resurrection, does this not indicate a separate and following resurrection for the martyred Israelites?

Add to this the description Paul gives of the rapture. He says that the end of the Church age will be heralded "with the voice of the archangel, and with the trump of God."[21] Paul also says that the catching away of the Church to heaven occurs at "the last trump" (1 Cor. 15:52).

The "last trump," according to W. E. Vine, is a military allusion and does not refer to the trumpet judgments later in the vision.[22] When Jesus returns to the earth to set up His kingdom, He leads *several armies* back to earth. Thus, Scripture pictures the rapture as a military trumpet calling up a military company.

Can this possibly refer to the reverberating trumpet-sounding voice of the Mighty Angel? Is He sounding the final roundup of the Church from earth so He can deal with Israel? Is "the last trump" the same talking trumpet that calls John to heaven? We believe Paul describes the rapture this way because Jesus showed it to him in this manner, probably in vision form. Paul states the truth of it prophetically, saying: "For this we say unto you by the word of the

---

[21] 1 Thess. 4:16.
[22] W. E. Vine, *An Expository Dictionary of New Testament Words*, vol. 4 (London: Oliphants, 1953), p. 160. God uses trumpets in the Word for different purposes: calling His people together is but one.

Lord" (1 Thess. 4:15). Would not the Holy Spirit use the same symbols with John as He did with Paul?

Therefore, I believe the rapture of the Church is the "firstfruits," the first company in the order of resurrections. Further, its time in the sequence belongs just prior to John's arrival before God's throne,[23] John's call to heaven may be a picture of the Church's call to heaven.

Hints That the Church Is in Heaven

While no evidence exists in the Book of Revelation from chapter 3 to chapter 19 that the Church is on earth, the text gives several indications that she is in heaven. One of these has to do with crowns. The other has to do with the return of the armies to earth. Both these indications hint strongly that Jesus calls up the Church between Revelation 3 and 4.

CROWNS

The group of elders John sees in this scene of "things . . . hereafter" wear crowns of gold (4:4). Paul speaks of several crowns believers can earn. He says the Olympiads run races to obtain corruptible crowns, but we run the Christian race to obtain incorruptible ones (1 Cor. 9:25). "So run," he exhorted, "that ye may obtain" (v. 24). Paul tells the Thessalonians, "For what is our hope, or joy, or crown of rejoicing? Are not even ye in the presence of our Lord Jesus Christ at his coming"? (1 Thess. 2:19). Shortly before his death, Paul tells Timothy, "I have fought a good fight, I

---

[23] John saw the promise to the Laodicean overcomers fulfilled. The elders were wearing crowns and sat encircling Christ's throne. Obviously, they were rewarded earlier before John arrived.

have finished my course, I have kept the faith: henceforth there is laid up for me a crown of righteousness" (2 Tim. 4:8). The twenty-four elders wearing crowns of gold in John's vision may typify believers—those receiving a full reward.

NOT ISRAEL

We can eliminate Israelites as part of this group of elders, because God does not promise heavenly crowns to them. Israel's future blessings and rewards all relate to earth. He promises them a priesthood (Isa. 66:21) and a ministry to the Gentiles (v. 19). The Gentiles will recognize them as the chosen seed of God (vv. 22–23). As priests, they will receive the riches of the Gentiles for this ministry.

Scripture makes only one mention of crowns in reference to Israel. The city of Jerusalem will become a crown of glory and a royal diadem in the Lord's hand, for He will cause Israel's sons to "marry" the land, and it will flourish bountifully (Isa. 62:3–5). Thus, in the restored and bejeweled Jerusalem, the Lord will establish His royal capitol, and it will be a "crown of glory" to Him.

God will install "David," a literal human descendent of King David, as ruler over Israel during the millennium (Jer. 30:9; Hos. 3:5). He will be a living type of the Lord Jesus Christ, because he will take the place of the high priest and offer sacrifices for Israel, while the King-Priest officiates over the world from the heavenly New Jerusalem. Thus Israel's rewards are tied to the land and do not include crowns and seats in[24] Christ's heavenly throne.

---

[24] This denotes more than just a location. It shows position: in His authority, in His presence, in His circle, since the thrones "are round about" His Father's throne.

Furthermore, God promises earthly rewards to restored Israel, whom the Mighty Angel is just getting ready to redeem. Therefore, it is too soon in the vision for the crowned elders to represent restored Israel. Nor can they be Old Testament saints, for, as we will prove later, they are not yet resurrected.

On the other hand, Scripture speaks of believers as a "royal priesthood" (1 Pet. 2:9), and they are promised specific crowns for overcoming: "Be thou faithful unto death, and I will give thee a crown of life" (Rev. 2:10). Christ promised the Laodicean overcomers a place in His throne (Rev. 3:21). Therefore, it seems likely that the crowned elders represent the Church, not Israel.

NOT ANGELS

The crowns also eliminate the possibility that the elders refer to angels. The writer of Hebrews says, "For unto the angels hath he not put in subjection the world to come" (Heb. 2.5). We shall see later that the Church, not heavenly beings, shall administrate the judgments on the earth.

Besides, the Greek word used for crowns is *stephanos*, a trophy of honor gained for victory in the games. Angels do not compete and overcome to gain honor. According to Jude 9, their honor and positions are already established.

Further, these elders intercede for those whom God has made kings and priests. "The four and twenty elders fell down before the Lamb, having every one of them harps, and golden vials full of odours, which are the prayers of saints . . . .and hast made us unto our God kings and priests: and we shall reign on the earth" (Rev. 5:8, 10). A kingdom of priests—a royal priesthood—from every nation surely refers to the Church, because elders commonly intercede for the Church. Would angels perform such priestly duties? I think not, since even Christ had to become a man before He could be an effective priest (Heb. 2:14–17).

John calls the ruling body "elders," that is men with apparent age and wisdom. To John, *elder* was a familiar term applied to the ruling bodies of men both in Israel and the Church. Surely, John saw the elders as men. Therefore, the elders show that the Church is in heaven from the beginning of the "things hereafter."

MORE PROOF

In Revelation 17:14 and 19:11–16, an army is being prepared to return to earth. At His coming, the Lamb (Christ) will fight against God's enemies.

> These shall make war with the Lamb, and the Lamb shall overcome them: for he is Lord of lords, and King of kings: and they that are with him are called, and chosen, and faithful. (17:14)

Those who will fight with Christ are called, chosen, and faithful. The Holy Spirit calls them to sanctification. They are chosen by the foreknowledge of God the Father and are faithful to trust the finished work of Christ (2 Thess. 2:13; 1 Pet. 1:2; Jude 1:1). The Scripture applies these attributes specifically to the Church.

Speaking about the Bride of the Lamb, Revelation 19:8 says, "To her was granted that she should be arrayed in fine linen, clean and white: for the fine linen is the righteousness of saints." Later in the chapter, the armies (mentioned also in the chapter 17) accompanying the King of kings and Lord of lords to the final battle on earth, "followed him upon white horses, clothed in linen, white and clean" (Rev. 19:14). Since we recognize the Lamb and the Lord as the same, we may surmise that both these companies clothed in fine linen represent the same group. Therefore, if the Bride is included in the armies, when did she arrive in heaven? To come with Him, it seems reasonable that she has previously ascended.

Jude 14–15 confirms this: "And Enoch . . . prophesied of these, saying, Behold, the Lord cometh with ten thousands of his saints, to execute judgment upon all." According to this, the army will be made up of saints, and Revelation 19:14 tells us they will come from heaven with the Lord. Therefore, the crowned elders, representing a company of priestly rulers, and the Bride in fine linen riding on white war steeds present strong evidence of the Church being in heaven during the "the things which shall be hereafter."

THE WRATH OF GOD

Paul, writing to the Thessalonians about the return of the Lord, says: "For God hath not appointed us to wrath, but to obtain salvation [from wrath] by our Lord Jesus Christ" (1 Thess. 5:9). He mentions the same truth earlier in his letter when he describes how the Thessalonian believers "turned to God from idols to serve the living and true God; and to wait for his Son from heaven, whom he raised from the dead, even Jesus, which delivered [past tense] us from the wrath to come" [future tense] (1 Thess. 1:9–10). These scriptures seem to agree that the Church will not be subject to God's wrath. Paul equates the "wrath" of God (1 Thess. 5:9) with the "day of the Lord" (1 Thess. 5:2), a time spoken about regarding Israel but not the Church.

In Luke 21:36, Jesus says to His apostles: "Watch ye therefore, and pray always, that ye may be accounted worthy to escape all these things that shall come to pass, and to stand before the Son of man." Jesus knew He would be in heaven at that time. To escape future wrath meant being in heaven with Him.

Other scriptures shed additional light on how the wrath of God will affect the Church. Peter says the "day of the Lord will come as a thief in the night" and will bring great destruction to the world (2 Pet. 3:10). But "nevertheless we, [the Church] according to his promise, look for new heavens and a new earth, wherein dwelleth righteousness. Wherefore, beloved, seeing that ye look for such things, be diligent that ye may be found of him in peace, without spot, and blameless" (2 Pet. 3:13–14). "That ye may be found of him" sounds like a reference to the second coming of Christ. How can believers be found of Him in peace if they will experience His wrath? Why should Peter encourage us to look for new heavens and a new earth if we will be present when He remakes them? No, Peter is not preparing us to endure wrath but to know about future things so we will not be "led away with the error of the wicked" (v. 17). Furthermore, Peter never told us how to stand in the terrible judgments but rather to look for the Lord's coming in the midst of the world's increasing wickedness (2 Pet. 3:1–4).

Conclusion

In conclusion, we believe the Priest/Mighty Angel separates the "things which are" from the "things which shall be hereafter" into two different times to illustrate His separate works with each body of believers. He further separates the presentation of the periods by allowing John to view one on earth and the other in heaven. The text confirms the separate working by dealing only with the Church in the first period and only with Israel and its relations with Gentiles in the second period.

After separating the two peoples, we see Israel represented on earth as a sealed company mentioned tribe by tribe and by a woman who gives birth to a ruling son. However, the twenty-four elders represent the Church in heaven. Apart from the elders and certain messengers to be revealed later, John makes no mention of the Church from chapter 3 to chapters 17 and 19, where she prepares herself to reign and returns with the Lord. From this, we conclude that Jesus will call up His Church, reward them, and retire them from active service on earth while He deals with Israel.

The Church is also spoken of as the "firstfruits of his creatures" (James 1:18), the company that will be resurrected first after Christ. Add to this how the Mighty Angel's voice corresponds to the "shout" and the "trump" at the rapture (1 Thess. 4:16). The trumpet will herald the close of one time and the beginning of another. The trumpet may alert believers to their final move from earth to heaven. John himself may illustrate the Church's rapture when he responds to the Captain's voice.

We have further proof that God works consistently in separate dealings with the Church and Israel. We have the crowned elders. The elders of chapter four have proved to be the Church by the process of elimination. They cannot be Israel (Old or New Testaments) because the time of their appearing is too soon in the vision. The elders are not angels but men because John can differentiate between them by their appearance. Furthermore, they cannot be angels, because they act as priests. That leaves the elders to signify the Church, placing believers in heaven at the start of the "things which shall be hereafter."

Moreover, Christ's salvation exempts the Church from the wrath to come in "the day of the Lord." She has every right to look forward to His coming, her "blessed hope." He gives her knowledge of future things so she will remain faithful and stand in the last evil days before His coming.

Therefore, we conclude that the break in the time after John finished "the things which are" designates the secret catching away and rewarding of the Church before the "things which shall be hereafter" begin.

In response to the trumpet's command, "Come up hither" (Rev. 4:1), John wanted to obey. But the door, after all, was in heaven. Then he made an exciting discovery: "And immediately I was in the spirit" (v. 2). Leaving his body behind on Patmos, John traveled upward in the spirit through the open door.

Chapter 10

THE HEAVENLY SETTING

(Revelation 4)

And immediately I was in the spirit: and, behold, a throne was set [*lay outstretched*] in heaven, and one sat on the throne. And he that sat was to look upon like a jasper and a sardine stone: and there was a rainbow about the throne, in sight like unto an emerald. (4:2–3 addition in italics)

Excitedly, John marks the change in scene by saying, "And, behold," inviting his readers to see with him the wonders now filling his spiritual eyes.

Light emanates from the throne in all directions. From the center, sparkling like finely set gemstones, God sat resplendent in all His glory. John in his Gospel wrote about the Lord being the "light of life" (John 8:12). John also wrote in his first Epistle: "God is light, and in him is no darkness at all" (1 John 1:5). Is it not fitting that his first glimpse of heaven should be this same light?

The light reflected looks *like* jasper and sardine or carnelian gemstones. This figure of speech may signify that the Father and the Son sit as one, while at the same time distinguishing between their separate works. The jasper light would indicate one, and the sardine or carnelian light would indicate the other. Later on in the vision, John tells us that the walls of the heavenly city are also jasper. Walls speak of limitations that are totally in the Father's hands, since all obey His will, even the Son. Therefore, the jasper stone typifies the Father, while the reddish sardine, speaking of sacrifice, typifies the Son. John's first glimpse of the throne reveals the "Father of lights" and the "Light of life" shining together as one.

We pause in the light description to note another spiritual significance indicated by these particular stones. The jasper was the last stone in the breastplate of the high priest, while the sardius (same stone as the sardine) was the first stone. Can this be a confirmation of Jesus' salutation to the Laodiceans that He was the first and the last? On the other hand, can it mean that the one on the throne now represents His ancient people Israel? Is He displaying the last and the first stones of the breastplate over His heart, just as the earthly high priest wore the name-engraved stones over his heart? Can God be showing His desire and concern for Israel now that it is time to begin the "things . . . hereafter" and Israel's redemption? Whatever the answers to these questions, the colors of light tell a story of their own.

The Portrait of Light

Like sparkling reflections from crystalline stones, the royal atmosphere is alive with color. Although jasper is a variety of quartz found in many colors, the most desirable as a gemstone is a translucent bright yellow-green. George Frederick Kunz, once America's foremost gemologist, also assigns a green hue to precious jasper.[25] The sardine or carnelian stone (depending on the type) reflects a red light. It is associated with two different varieties of quartz: carnelian is a flesh-colored stone, and sard is a bright orange-red to brownish-red stone. We cannot know exactly which color John saw, but we suspect it was the bright orange-red to brown-red. That would make the light radiating from the seat of the throne as bright yellow-green and a burnt orange-red.

It is an interesting fact that certain values of red and green complement each other, making a whole. All the color needed to make up visible light not found in one color is found in the other. These, called complements, together create the full light spectrum. It would be great if we could say this is true of the colors on the throne. However, there is not enough of the primary blue color to make it complete. Another color, however, is involved. The emerald green associated with the rainbow can supply an ample amount of blue (emerald green is a blue-green) to complete the spectrum. This would make the light at the throne complete and confirm John's words: "God is light, and in him is *no darkness* at all" (1 John 1:5, emphasis added).

The rainbow arching over the throne introduces the third member of the trinity. The Holy Spirit presents Himself before the throne in a series of sevens. In the beginning of Revelation, John salutes the churches from the seven spirits of God before the throne (1:4). Seven lamps burning

---

[25] George Frederick Kunz, *The Curious Lore of Precious Stones* (New York: Dover Publications, 1971), p. 90.

before the throne are these seven spirits of God (4:5). The Lamb has seven horns and seven eyes which are also the seven spirits (5:6). The light pattern arches above God's throne in the seven colors of the rainbow (4:3).

The statement of John concerning the rainbow resembling an emerald stone is puzzling. A rainbow is a refraction of light broken into seven colors by rain or a mist. So how can John say it is emerald-green? Marvin Ford, who was clinically dead for thirty-five minutes, clears up the mystery with his description of the throne.

> The throne of God filled my consciousness with the reddish-brown and yellow glow of chalcedony, a precious quartz, surrounded by the glistening aura of emerald-green light. A majestic rainbow arched over the throne like a massive crowning dome, and the throne seemed to extend for miles along a transparent sea of golden glass, stretching into the far distance to accommodate millions of worshiping angels and departed spirits.[26]

Evidently, the green aura seen by both Ford and John shines from the throne toward the rainbow and perhaps fades into it.

The rainbow shimmering across the long, outstretched throne suggests that the light has been broken in the presence of a great cloud. Rainbows require prisms to break the light. In a figure of speech, water often represents the Holy Spirit in Scripture. In the last chapter of Revelation, John sees a "pure river of water of life, clear as crystal, proceeding out of the throne of God and of the Lamb" (22:1). A

---

[26] Marvin Ford, *On the Other Side* (Plainfield, N. J.: Logos, 1978), p. 174.

cloud also is a figure of the Holy Spirit in Scripture, as well as the "latter rain" (Joel 2:23) and "rivers of living water" (John 7:38). Thus, the rainbow is the light pattern of the Holy Spirit showing that a cloud is present and is the source of the river flowing forth. This completes the portrait of the Godhead. The rainbow and the emerald aura show that the Holy Spirit is in the picture. The emerald-green radiating from the throne completes the spectrum of light: Father, Son, and Holy Spirit all occupy the throne. Set before John, then, is nothing less than a picture of the Godhead painted in strokes of light.

The Sound-and-Light Show Surrounding the Throne

> And out of the throne proceeded lightnings and thunderings and voices: and there were seven lamps of fire burning before the throne, which are the seven Spirits of God. And before the throne there was a sea of glass like unto crystal. (4:5–6)

Though the throne is the source of light and glory, all around are reflections of that glory. Starting with the floor in front and extending beneath, we see the color of the foundation of the throne. John tells us that "before the throne there was a sea of glass like unto crystal" (4:6). Ford saw it as a vast sea of transparent golden glass. This slick pavement, seen from below by the seventy elders of Israel when they received the covenant with Moses in the wilderness, was a different color. Exodus 24:10 says: "And they saw the God of Israel: and there was under his feet as it were a paved work of a sapphire stone, and as it were the body of heaven in his clearness."

Ezekiel saw the throne itself as the color of a sapphire stone resting on a "terrible" or awesome crystal that looked like the firmament or sky.[27] The elders also saw a blue crystal under the throne. The sapphire stone of the ancients is believed today to be the lapis lazuli, an ultramarine blue.[28] Why it was golden when Ford saw it we cannot tell. Perhaps it changes colors. However, we rather think it was also blue when John viewed it because he called it a sea. Ford would have called it a sea regardless of the color because of his knowledge of Revelation. John, on the other hand, described it as he saw it, and it is probably blue like the sea.

Picturing the sea as a solid crystal like ice, yet with the color and clarity of a gemstone, emphasizes its long-lasting beauty and rigidity. One can stand and walk on this sea. Since the figure of speech for the Word of God is water (Eph. 5:26) and the greatest body of water is a sea, a blue sea pictures the throne of God founded on His unchanging, everlasting, and all-encompassing Word.

Other lights contribute to the wondrous scene. Flickering upon the bright blue sea, soft yellow-orange flames burn on the seven lampstands. All this light is merely the visible manifestation of God, the source of almighty power.

Paul writes: "The King of kings, and Lord of lords; who only hath immortality, dwelling in the light which no man can approach unto; whom no man hath seen, nor can see: to whom be honour and power everlasting. Amen."[29] Evi-

---

[27] Ezek. 1:22, 26.
[28] Kunz, George Frederick *Curious Lore of Precious Stones*, (New York: Dover Publications, 1971) p. 293.
[29] 1 Tim. 6:15–16.

dently, he saw this same display when caught up to heaven himself.

The Father's Voice

We cannot move on with the description of the throne without listening to the sounds issuing from it. Bursts of white lightning shoot forth from the throne accompanied by peals of thunder (4:5). In the center of this picture, the "Father of lights" sits on His throne and sounds forth His authority with "lightnings and thunderings and voices" (4:5).

It is the Lord of the thunderstorm psalm: "The voice of the LORD is upon the waters: the God of glory thundereth. . . . In his temple doth everyone speak of his glory. The LORD sitteth upon the flood [the sea?]; yea, the LORD sitteth king for ever."[30]

Job's friend, Elihu, described this awesome sound:

Hear attentively the noise of his voice, and the sound that goeth out of his mouth. He directeth it under the whole heaven, and his lightning unto the ends of the earth. After it a voice roareth: he thundereth with the voice of his excellency. . . . God thundereth marvelously with his voice. (Job 37:2–5)

Psalm 29:3 says: "The voice of the LORD is upon the waters: the God of glory thundereth." John himself had witnessed the sound of it previously and recorded it in his Gospel. The voice came in response to Jesus' request for the Father to glorify His own name. A voice came from

---

[30] Psalm 29:3, 9–10.

heaven saying, "I have both glorified it, and will glorify it again" (John 12:28). To others standing by, the voice sounded like thunder.

The Father's voice sounds different from those of the Son and the Holy Spirit. Jesus, as High Priest of the Church, speaks to John in a voice sounding like many waters (Rev. 1:15). As Israel's Mighty Angel, He speaks with a voice like a trumpet (Rev. 1:10). The Holy Spirit demonstrated how He speaks in a still, small voice within each believer as He did to Elijah in the cave (1 Kings 19:12). The Father's voice, however, sounds like thunder. It is important to distinguish the voices because it helps with the interpretation of the vision.

Those Present at the Throne

> And round about the throne were four and twenty elders sitting, clothed in white raiment; and they had on their heads crowns of gold. (4:4)

John, completely awed by the glory of the one on the throne, gradually becomes aware of the presence of twenty-four men seated around the throne (4:4). The men wear white garments and have golden crowns on their heads. He recognizes them at once as elders, those who have developed maturity in the faith. Perhaps he can still hear the ringing words of the earlier scene, "To him that overcometh." Are not these the overcomers who purchased gold from Christ and are clothed in white garments (3:18)? They had applied salve to their eyes (3:18), conferring wisdom, so they can be trusted with great authority. They have obviously overcome as Christ overcame; thus, He seats them around the throne as He promised (3:21).

The number twenty-four may refer to the priests, the descendants of Aaron. David divided Eleazar and Ithamar's sons into twenty-four groups to handle the twenty-four courses of temple service (1 Chron. 24:1–18). These were accounted governors of the sanctuary and governors of God. We shall see later that the twenty-four crowned elders of Revelation function as priests also. If the elders represent the Church, as we believe, then this is only a representative number, just as David's appointed priestly service was representative. Only so many from each course served at the same time, and then they rotated.

Likely, the priesthood of the Church will have the same sort of rotation. Therefore, not all those who have overcome every problem will be before Him at one time. Nevertheless, they are the representation of the whole Church—the royal priesthood, the chosen generation in general—even though they themselves are the top overcomers of the Church

The Seven Spirits

> And there were seven lamps of fire burning before the throne, which are the seven Spirits of God. (4:5)

Notice that John states without explanation that the "seven lamps of fire . . . are the seven Spirits of God." He had seen the tongues of fire burning over the believers on Pentecost. No one has to tell him the meaning of these lamps. He suddenly understands that he is standing in the real temple in heaven, looking at the real lampstand, of which the lampstands in the tabernacle and the temple were only shadows.

God's ultimate purpose in the earth is to dwell among His people. Sin spoiled His fellowship with Adam and Eve in the garden. When He established His tabernacle in the wilderness, He set forth the way into His presence by various furnishings with accompanying services. The heavenly counterparts show the true functions of each.

Entrance into the earthly tabernacle was through the gate in the fence, through the five pillars with the hangings, through the four pillars holding up the veil, and finally into the presence of God who dwelt in the cloud over the mercy seat. When John responds to the invitation, "Come up hither," he passes through the door into heaven and is immediately in the presence of the throne, unhindered by intermediate steps.

The Heavenly Tabernacle

Heaven holds the same furniture as the earthly tabernacle and temple but without the shadows. In heaven, the lampstand is the Holy Spirit—the testimony of truth. The throne is the mercy seat resting on a foundation of holiness and law, like the ark filled with electric resurrection power, as witnessed by the thunder and lightning. (Aaron's rod that budded pictured the resurrection.) The Church, seated on the throne of grace, is the showbread of God's presence (known formerly as the "bread of faces"), His people with whom He has become one. The golden altar of incense does not appear in this chapter but shows up later in chapter 8 where Israel's Mighty Angel intercedes for the earthly saints.

The brazen altar burns somewhere before the throne beyond the sea of glass. Later, John sees martyrs' blood collected there (Rev. 6:9).

In his temple, Solomon turned the laver of the tabernacle into a large basin called the brazen sea, which was held up by twelve bronze oxen. It represented cleansing by the Word of God (see Eph. 5:26). Here we see it expanded even more and called a "sea of glass," where the redeemed stand on the Word to praise and serve, since cleansing is no longer necessary. Later, we will see these same furnishings present in the final tabernacle when Christ dwells with us in the heavenly Jerusalem.

The Seraphim

And round about the throne, were four beasts full of eyes before and behind. And the first beast was like a lion, and the second beast like a calf, and the third beast had a face as a man, and the fourth beast was like a flying eagle. And the four beasts had each of them six wings about him; and they were full of eyes within: and they rest not day and night, saying, Holy, holy, holy, Lord God Almighty, which was, and is, and is to come. And when those beasts give glory and honour and thanks to him that sat on the throne, who liveth for ever and ever, the four and twenty elders fall down before him that liveth for ever and ever, and cast their crowns before the throne, saying, Thou art worthy, O Lord, to receive glory and honour, and power: for thou hast created all things, and for thy pleasure they are and were created. (4:6–11)

John's sweeping gaze turns back to the throne once more. As his eyes grow accustomed to the light, he makes out four glorious living creatures hovering in and around the central throne. Like gentle giants in some fantasy tale, they blinked with eyes all over their bodies. Steve Lightle encountered them in an intense dealing with God. He described one of them this way:

> He was very, very large. The room had a high ceiling— perhaps a good twenty feet—and the belt buckle of this creature was about twenty-five feet high. He was a creature of God and stood higher than the roof of the house. I don't even know how to put this into words, but he was not limited by the physical dimensions of the house or this world. They each had three pairs of wings. They stood absolutely motionless and yet they knew everything and could see everything that was going on all around in every direction—up, down, around, everywhere—just like it says in the Bible.[31]

The earthly creature that each seraph resembles symbolizes a facet of Christ's ministry. The head of the first creature looks *like* a lion. This depicts Christ as the Lion of Judah, the rightful King of Israel, the Messiah. The second creature looks *like* a calf. He depicts Christ as the servant who was a sacrifice on God's altar. The third, with the head of a man, depicts Jesus as the Son of Man, the one tempted in all points as we, yet without sin, that He might become an effective High Priest. The fourth creature is *like* a soar-

---

[31] Lightle, Steve *Exodus II*, (Kingwood, TX: Hunter Books, 1983) p. 62

ing eagle that lives in the heights of heaven. The eagle represents the Mighty Angel, the very Son of God.

Although they resembled earthly creatures, they each had six wings, indicating they belonged to the heavenly realm. The cherubim have four wings, showing their assignment to earth, since the number four represents creation and the natural realm. The seraphim engage in the ceaseless activity of exalting the one on the throne. Being full of eyes, they see His glory from every angle. They constantly find more for which to praise Him and so lead the rest in worship. In fact, when they give glory, honor, and thanks to Him "who liveth for ever and ever," the twenty-four elders fall down before Him, too (4:9–10).

The living creatures, represented by the ark and the veil in the Mosaic tabernacle, complete the picture of the real throne in heaven. In the earthly tabernacle, two golden cherubim overlooked the mercy seat on the ark of the covenant in the Holy of Holies. Two more were embroidered on the inner veil, making four surrounding the ark. We are told in Hebrews 10:20 that the veil was a type of Christ's flesh, torn so we can have access to God's throne of grace. Therefore, the two cherubim on the veil may represent Christ's earthly ministry in His first coming. The other two may represent Christ's ministry in His second coming when He will reign as King.

Isaiah saw the same six-winged creatures at the throne. However, at that time they hid their faces under their wings (Isa. 6:2). Perhaps this was true of the cherubim in the tabernacle. May we speculate and suppose that the calf-like and man-like creatures were featured on the veil, since Christ's ministry on earth now is complete and the veil rent? That would leave the lion-like and the eagle-like creatures attached to the ark (which depicts the throne) to represent the other two. Christ has come and fulfilled the first two offices and shortly will fulfill the other two. Is He not fulfilling His role as Mighty Angel at this time? The creatures are constant reminders of His work.

Eyes completely covered their wings (their means of travel), portraying their all-seeing perception. The eyes portray Christ as one able to see in all directions, thus full of wisdom. Therefore, they go forth in the complete wisdom of God.

These creatures have one task wherever they go and from which they take no rest. They cry, "Holy, holy, holy, Lord God Almighty, which was, and is, and is to come" (4:8). They always glorify the Father, just as Christ did on earth. They apparently lead the worship in heaven, for when they burst forth in praise, they prompt the elders to do the same.

Can this be the exalted place from which Satan fell? He was once full of wisdom and beauty. His ability to create music would have been a great asset in leading worship. Ezekiel called him a covering cherub (Ezek. 28:14), a position similar to the Old Testament cherubim. Isaiah said, "How art thou fallen from heaven, O Lucifer, son of the morning!" (Isa. 14:12), for truly this was a lofty position.

Now, after the living creatures cry, "Holy, holy, holy," the elders cast their crowns at the Lord's feet and bow low, saying, "Thou art worthy, O Lord, to receive glory and honour, and power" (4:10–11).

Concluding the description of the heavenly setting where the "things which shall be hereafter" begin, we see the throne along with John, set as a magnificent jewel in the midst of light and splendorous color. We hear the power of it as the Father sends forth His thunderous commands. We join in the adoration of His creatures as we identity with the elders around the throne. We worship the one revealed in the tabernacles of God (both the exodus tabernacle and the one in heaven). Now we wait expectantly with John to see what the future holds for the earth.

Chapter 11

THE WORTHY ONE

(REVELATION 5)

And I saw in the right hand of him that sat on the throne
a book written within and on the backside, sealed with
seven seals. (5:1)

Following the worship, John's attention returns to the
one seated on the throne. Nothing fascinates him
more than the splendor of the Almighty. The elders
and angels performing their worship cannot compare.
Growing more accustomed to the effulgence, he makes out
the form in the midst.

A curious sealed scroll in the right hand of the one seated
on the throne catches his eye. It is curious because it is
written not only on the inside as is customary but also on
the back as well. Here we interrupt John's observation to
point out an important division. Since the scroll was written on both sides, it would have to be turned over to read

the back. Writers consistently overlook this detail. In God's eyes, however, this detail is so important that He devotes a whole scene to it.

Two other details are worth mentioning. First, the one on the throne holds the book in His right hand, indicating it is an official ordinance. Second, it has seven stamped seals that have to be individually opened before it can unroll. One seal stamped with an earthly king's signature was enough for men to recognize it as the king's command. God's seven seals declare it complete, unalterable, and most likely judicial. Therefore, it requires a proper person to authorize its opening, because whoever opens it must be prepared to prosecute according to its contents. It is a legal document drawn up to cleanse the earth by decreeing the destruction of God's enemies.

Zechariah included a description of it in his visions concerning this future time.

> Then I turned, and lifted up mine eyes, and looked, and behold a flying roll. And he said unto me, What seest thou? And I answered, I see a flying roll; the length thereof is twenty cubits, and the breadth thereof ten cubits. Then he said unto me, This is the curse that goeth forth over the face of the whole earth: for every one that stealeth shall be cut off as on this side according to it; and every one that sweareth shall be cut off as on that side according to it. And I will bring it forth, saith the LORD of hosts, and it shall enter into the house of the thief, and into the house of him that sweareth falsely by my name: and it shall remain in the midst of his house, and shall consume it with the timber thereof and the stones thereof. (Zech. 5:1–4)

The size of this scroll is significant. It is the same size as the porch of Solomon's temple. Clearly, it is not a book suitable for men to read. But by making it this size, God may well be saying to us: "People of earth, you cannot come into My presence and worship Me in the millennial age unless you first pass through this 'porch' of cleansing judgment."

This scroll, written on both sides like the seven-sealed scroll, groups curses on one side for offenses of man against his fellowmen and on the other side for offenses against God. Inside are written the judgments for breaking the last five commandments. Outside are written those that judge for breaking the first five commandments,[32] the offenses against God personally.

Is this truly a copy of the same scroll that John sees in the Father's hand after it has been opened and completely unrolled? It would certainly explain why the seven-sealed book is written on both sides. God will judge offenses against Himself according to the one side and offenses against mankind's fellowmen according to the other side. Understanding this helps with the interpretation of the sequence. It tells us when to turn the scroll over and read the back side.

The Search for a Man

And I saw a strong angel proclaiming with a loud voice, Who is worthy to open the book, and to loose the seals thereof? And no man in heaven, nor in earth, neither

[32] Some do not include "honour thy father and thy mother" in God's half of the Law, but we must remember that to rebel against parents is to rebel against the authority set by God and is therefore against God.

under the earth, was able to open the book, neither to look thereon. And I wept much, because no man was found worthy to open and to read the book, neither to look thereon. (5:2–4)

A scene change claims John's attention. A strong angel exclaims with a loud voice, "Who is worthy to open the book, and to loose the seals thereof?" (5:2). What man indeed can initiate the wrath of God and unleash it on the earth? They make a thorough search. Is there any one among all the saints in heaven or among those still alive on earth who can open this book? Finally, the searchers go so far as to look over the trapped souls in hell, but they find no one who can cast the "first stone." Therefore, the answer to the angel's question is: No one is worthy to enforce the law, to commence the cursing. All are guilty and therefore themselves under its curse.

Tenderhearted John, the pastor, weeps. He grieves not because no one can open the book so he can see what is in it but because of sin's devastation and what it has worked in all people. Every person who lives or who has ever lived is disqualified. No one is worthy. None even dare look on the book.

Overwhelmed by this realization, John almost misses the next scene.

The Lion of Judah from the Root of David

And one of the elders saith unto me, Weep not: behold, the Lion of the tribe of Juda, the Root of David, hath prevailed to open the book, and to loose the seven seals thereof. And I beheld, and, lo, in the midst of the throne and of the four beasts, and in the midst of the elders, stood a Lamb as it had been slain, having seven horns and seven eyes, which are the seven Spirits of God sent forth into all the earth. (Rev. 5:5–6)

An elder[33] brings John back to the present by saying: "Weep not: behold, the Lion of the tribe of Juda, . . . hath prevailed to open the book." Wiping away his tears, John regains his composure.

The scene changes again. Suddenly, in the middle of the living creatures and the elders, a Lamb appears, looking as if it has just been killed, yet it is alive. Seven horns (perfect power) rise menacingly from its head. Seven eyes (perfect wisdom) look confidently about. The fatally bleeding yet living Lamb clearly typifies Christ as the innocent victim offered in sacrifice. He alone is worthy. He bore the curse on the cross that all people might be free from it. Now He, the Lamb who will yet become the Lion of Judah, steps forward with deliberation to receive the book. He has every right to open it.

For centuries, God warned of the fate of those who rejected His way of salvation. Untold numbers of prophecies had been proclaimed concerning the evil days that will come on the earth to the unsuspecting. The hundreds of years of grace end at the unrolling of the scroll. That long-awaited day of God's wrath has finally come. The Lamb will start the proceedings.

---

[33] It is curious that the elders appear to know what is happening even before it happens. Later, an elder explained to John about the great multitude (Rev. 7:13). Daniel, the prophet, saw a pair of saints (not the same pair) on two separate occasions who seemed to know what was going to happen to Israel in the future (Dan. 8:13–14; 12:5). This seems to be the privilege of the Church (John 14:26; 2 Pet. 1:19; Rev. 1:1).

The Lamb takes the scroll from the Father's right hand. We assume the bright lights shining from the throne have diminished now that the center of attention is on the book. John clearly sees only one on the throne. From this we understand that each scene displays a different truth. Here the Father and the Son are separated, where before they were shown together. The Father's right-hand Son receives the book from the Father's right hand. In John 5:22, John recorded Jesus' declaration that "the Father judgeth no man, but hath committed all judgment unto the Son." That is why He receives the book.

> And he came and took the book out of the right hand of him that sat upon the throne. And when he had taken the book, the four beasts and four and twenty elders fell down before the Lamb, having every one of them harps, and golden vials full of odours, which are the prayers of saints. (5:7–8)

When the Lamb takes the book, the four creatures and the twenty-four elders fall prostrate before Him in worship. Earlier, they cast their crowns before the Father; perhaps it was not fitting to wear crowns in the presence of the Almighty. We are not told if they have put them back on. They do have, however, two other items for worshiping the Lamb. Each possesses a harp for offering musical praise and a golden vial full of odors, which are the prayers of saints. They appear to be worshiping in a priestly administration representing all the Church. The sweet odor ascends to the Father. The twenty-four elders fall down before the throne, pouring out praise with their golden vials.

> And they sung a new song, saying, Thou art worthy to take the book, and to open the seals thereof: for thou wast slain, and hast redeemed us to God by thy blood out of every kindred, and tongue, and people, and nation; and hast made us unto our God kings and priests: and we shall reign on the earth. (5:9–10)

Out of this sweet praise, voices break forth into spontaneous harmony—the resonant harmony of a "new song." New songs spring melodiously from the heart of each individual worshiper. Therefore, the words are not in unison as in a known song, but they may have the same theme. The tune is not the same, either, but each person composes his or her own melody from the heights and depths of joy and praise within. Given at the same time, the overall effect is a beautiful sonorous harmony.[34]

The appearance of the Lamb with the marks of His suffering fresh on his body prompts this fresh outbreak of worship. The worshipers can plainly see the passion pressed on their Lord. The contrast between this man and all others cannot be denied. The exalted plane to which He has lifted them, the unworthy, inspires the "new song." Its overall theme is: "Thou art worthy to take the book . . . for thou hast redeemed us to God by thy blood." Not only has the Lamb redeemed them, but He also has made them kings and priests to reign over the earth. This song swells around the Lamb, who alone is worthy to judge those who have spurned this blessing.

---

[34] The Holy Spirit is teaching the Church to sing a "new song" in worship these last days. Israel sang it in the Old Testament times (see Ps. 33:3; 96:1; 98:1).

The Sevenfold Angelic Worship

> And I beheld, and I heard the voice of many angels round
> about the throne and the beasts and the elders: and the
> number of them was ten thousand times ten thousand,
> and thousands of thousands; saying with a loud voice,
> Worthy is the Lamb that was slain to receive power, and
> riches, and wisdom, and strength, and honour, and glory,
> and blessing. (5:11–12)

So caught up with the events centered around the
throne, John is almost startled to hear praise go up from
numberless angels surrounding this central scene. There
are so many that his attempt to number then ends up a
large indeterminate estimate. The praise of the believers
prompts this angelic outburst; yet they praise the Lamb from
a different point of view entirely. They have not benefited
from His sacrifice personally. These angels have never fallen
into sin. Still His sacrifice has been a demonstration to them
of the grace and mercy of God. They have watched with
great interest the godly character that Christ was able to
build into a rebellious people. They praise His work in ac-
complishing the salvation of the Church.

Angels declare His worthiness because of what they have
seen, not for what they have received. Their praise is sev-
enfold. The believers, mindful of the great grace that enables them to be there, focus on the right of Christ to judge
the earth that has rejected Him. The angels, however, focus
on what Christ is worthy to receive because of His sacrifice.

(1) He is worthy to receive mighty power. This is the word for force, not authority. He received mighty power at the resurrection. It was necessary for His administration of the Church. Paul says, "The exceeding greatness of his [God's] power to us-ward who believe, according to the working of his mighty power" (Eph. 1:19). Paul expresses a desire to know this "power of his resurrection" because it is the secret to victory in all things (Phil. 3:10). Thus, the death of Christ earns for him this mighty power for all time. The angels declare he deserves honor for this.

(2) He is worthy to receive riches. Paul tells us that there are "riches of the glory of his [God's] inheritance in the saints" (Eph. 1:18). God makes investments in people, not things. To have believers resemble the image of Christ fulfills God's purpose for us: to have many sons like His Son Jesus. To explain this further, Jesus said, "Herein is my Father glorified, that ye bear much fruit" (John 15:8). To produce the fruit of the Spirit is to produce the likeness of Christ. Thus, the riches for which the angels praise Him are the excellence of saints made possible through His mighty working power. No wonder the angels praise Him. They have seen the obstacles He overcame in making people like Himself. Let Him be honored with these riches.

(3) He is worthy to receive wisdom because He has demonstrated to all principalities and powers another side of God's character. This is His ability to act righteously toward a fallen race and at the same time to be merciful. His display of grace shown to mankind reveals wisdom angels could never have imagined, since they are a pure unfallen race. Even redeemed Paul marvels at the wisdom in this. He says, "O the depth of the riches both of the wisdom and knowledge of God! how unsearchable are his judgments,

and his ways past finding out!" (Rom. 11:33). Let the Lamb receive honor for His wisdom.

(4) He is worthy to receive strength, the ability to work effectively, because He became God's "arm of salvation." The descriptive phrase, "With a strong hand, and with a stretched out arm" (Ps. 136:12) shows God's effectual power to work. In this word picture, the hand and arm always work together. Jesus implies that the "finger of God" is the Holy Spirit (see Luke 11:20). We understand the phrase "under the hand of God" to mean "under the power of the Spirit." If the hand is the Spirit, then the arm is the Son, God's means to extend His Spirit to men. This is further explained in its use in the Old Testament. Isaiah calls Jesus the "arm of the Lord." He begins: "Who hath believed our report? and to whom is the arm of the LORD revealed?" (Isa. 53:1). Again, Isaiah says: "Behold, the Lord God will come with strong hand, and his arm shall rule for him" (Isa. 40:10). "And on mine arm shall they trust" (Isa. 51:5). Repeatedly, in the Old Testament we are told He saved His people by his "mighty hand, and the stretched out arm" (Deut. 7:19). From all this we conclude that the angels speak of Christ's dependence on the Holy Spirit for working power. He is worthy to receive strength, because He never works independently of the Father or the Holy Spirit. The strength of unity deserves praise! Give Him honor for this strength.

(5) Worthy is the Lamb that was slain to receive honor because He "humbled himself, and became obedient unto death, even the death of the cross" (Phil. 2:8). Proverbs tells us, "Before honour is humility" (Prov. 15:33). Peter also confirms this: "Be clothed with humility: for God resisteth the proud, and giveth grace to the humble. Humble yourselves therefore under the mighty hand of God, that

he may exalt you in due time" (1 Pet. 5:5–6). Honor has to do with recognition and an exalted position. We are commanded to give honor to whom honor is due (see Rom. 13:7). We are to honor our parents and give double honor to elders who rule and teach well (see 1 Tim. 5:17). Therefore, to receive honor is to receive an exalted position. For His humility, Jesus receives the position to which "every knee should bow . . . and that every tongue should confess that Jesus Christ is Lord" (Phil. 2:11). Render to Him, therefore, the honor due His name, say the angels.

(6) Worthy is He to receive glory (an increase in fame with a good report) because of His suffering. "But we see Jesus, who was made a little lower than the angels for the suffering of death, crowned with glory and honour; that he by the grace of God should taste death for every man" (Heb. 2:9). Not only does He receive glory for His own suffering but from all those who suffer for His name's sake. Peter says: "If ye be reproached for the name of Christ, happy are ye; for the spirit of glory and of God resteth upon you: on their part he is evil spoken of, but on your part he is glorified" (1 Pet. 4:14). The ability to endure abuse from the world all comes from Christ's sustaining grace. He is worthy to receive glory!

(7) Worthy is He to receive blessing, happiness, or joy, because He endured the cross in order to obtain our fellowship. "Looking unto Jesus the author and finisher of our faith; who for the joy that was set before him endured the cross, despising the shame" (Heb. 12:2). Yes, He is worthy of blessing because the evidence of this fulfilled joy, the Church, is in His presence. Let Him be honored with blessing. Let it be full.

He has accomplished all He set out to do. The seven-fold praise is both appropriate and complete. The angels are witnesses that this is so. They cannot help but praise Him. He is worthy "to receive power, and riches, and wisdom, and strength, and honour, and glory, and blessing" (Rev. 5:12).

Universal Praise

> And every creature which is in heaven, and on the earth, and under the earth, and such as are in the sea, and all that are in them, heard I saying, Blessing, and honour, and glory, and power, be unto him that sitteth upon the throne, and unto the Lamb for ever and ever. And the four beasts said, Amen. And the four and twenty elders fell down and worshipped him that liveth for ever and ever. (5:13–14)

When the angels finish their chorus, John hears all creation sound forth its approval of Christ. This implies more that just animals with audible voices but also inanimate creation, such as plants, stones, and even stars. The time for creation's groaning under the curse is about to end. Paul tells us: "For the earnest expectation of the creature waiteth for the manifestation of the sons of God. For the creature was made subject to vanity, not willingly, but by reason of him who hath subjected the same in hope, because the creature itself also shall be delivered from the bondage of corruption into the glorious liberty of the children of God" (Rom. 8:19–24).

Creation is willing for Christ to take the book and open the judgments because this will remove the death and decaying processes under the cursed law of sin and death.

Then a cancerous earth and a solar system filled with spiritual wickedness will be cleansed and remade to conform to the rest of a perfectly ordered universe.

At the end of the tribulation (so named because of the terrible judgments) when the contents of this book have been served and the judgments duly processed, then the sons of God, the redeemed, will be manifested. Their reign in the kingdom will begin. At that time, creation will enter a new phase. They will be liberated from the curse to live in "new heavens and a new earth, wherein dwelleth righteousness" (1 Pet. 3:13).

Creation's groans turn to praise: "Blessing, and honour, and glory, and power, be unto him that sitteth upon the throne, and unto the Lamb for ever and ever" (Rev. 5:13). Truly, they are willing for the Lamb to open the book. The four living creatures simply say, "Amen." For the third time, the elders are on their faces in worship. He is worthy!

OPENING THE SEALS

(REVELATION 6)

And I saw when the Lamb opened one of the seals, and I heard, as it were the noise of thunder, one of the four beasts saying, Come and see. (6:1)

As worship ends, a hush of expectancy falls over the scene. It is time to open the book. The Lamb breaks open the first seal. John records, "I saw," and a new scene appears before him. The scene seems to be spotlighted in front of the throne, where all heaven watches with intense interest as the plans of God unfold, being announced by the Father's voice[35] through the living creatures.

---

[35] This is curious because up until now they say only "Holy, holy, holy." Either this is their normal sound or they speak *as* the Father. Appropriately, they condemn those who have rejected Christ's work, which they represent as a figure (king/lion; ox/servant; man/priest; flying eagle/Son of the Highest)

Since the book contains judgments to be administered after its opening, breaking the seals can only be preliminary action leading up to the final judgments. Thus, the seals portray a sequence of literal happenings, sometimes set in spiritual language and other times in actual description of the events. Some scenes take place on earth and some in heaven, both types clearly shown by their settings. In this chapter, dividing the scenes as marked will show how important this is to interpreting the events correctly.

The first four seals are a unit, describing steps engaged in a devastating war. One of the living creatures or beasts introduces each stage of this war. Together they show the final fulfillment of the "beginning of sorrows" described by Jesus in His Olivet discourse (Matt. 24:8). The fifth seal switches the action back to heaven. The sixth seal gives John a startling view of earth from space, delaying the opening of the seventh seal to another chapter.

The White Horse and the Red Horse

The first of the living creatures, possibly the one which resembles a lion, thunders, "Come!"

> And I saw, and behold a white horse: and he that sat on him had a bow; and a crown was given unto him: and he went forth conquering, and to conquer. (6:2)

A white horse prances into view. The rider carries an archer's bow. John watches while an unnamed entity places the victor's crown on the rider's head. Then the conqueror riding the white horse continues his victorious campaigns to the extent that he becomes obsessed with the drive to conquer more.

For identification of the rider, we have three clues: the color of his horse, the bow in his hand, and his intentions. First, the color: White stands for victory and/or righteousness. Overcomers of chapter 2 wore white, symbolizing their victory over their old natures by their attainment of Christlike characters. David wrote in his repentant psalm, "Wash me, and I shall be whiter than snow" (Ps. 51:7), the symbol for victory in God's cleansing power to make righteous. Later in the vision, Jesus rides a white horse to a righteous victory in judgment at Armageddon.

Horses, on the other hand, are associated with warfare all through the Scriptures. Proverbs 21:31 says: "The horse is prepared against the day of battle." Only kings could afford to keep horses, which they used for warfare. The people used donkeys for travel and oxen for plowing. A white horse, then, symbolizes victory in war for a perceived righteous cause.

Missiles shot from a bow can pierce the enemy without any close contact. The bowman needs a strong arm and a good aim to be successful. Having such a reputation, he could conceivably conquer by threats. The situation developing in this symbolism suggests a power that gains control over others without actually taking peace from the world. It keeps the rest of the world at bay by intimidating threats of attack. Heaven crowns the conqueror's efforts with success or perhaps even a real crown. Therefore, he deceives himself into thinking he can gain his complete objective, and he goes out with that intent.

It is not easy to put a name to this power in the world today. Years ago, one might have assigned this role to Communism. When the seal is opened, the bow is already in the hand of the rider, indicating that the conqueror is not new at this game. The only thing new is the success that authority in heaven has now granted. This will, in turn, prepare the setting for the next seal, which is unique because it is opened *in this same scene.*

> And when he had opened the second seal, I heard the second beast say, Come and see. (6:3)

John does not repeat the little scene-marking phrase, "And I saw." When Jesus opens the second seal, John hears one of the creatures (the calf-like creature?) say, "Come and see." Then "there went out another horse," which we presume goes to overcome the former rider—still spotlighted from the first seal—who will continue to conquer until stopped.

> And there went out another horse that was red: and power was given to him that sat thereon to take peace from the earth, and that they should kill one another: and there was given unto him a great sword. (6:4)

Action in the scene changes abruptly as the red horseman overtakes the white horseman. Whereas the war pictured before was scattered, perhaps a war of terror in a relatively peaceful world, it now becomes an open, bloody confrontation symbolized by the red horse. Another major power bent on preventing the "conqueror's" takeover makes a last desperate effort to save the world.

The red horseman receives "a great sword." This sword is so great, we are told in the description of a later seal, that the war fought with this weapon wipes out one-fourth of the world's population. This sword becomes the means to destroy peace on the earth, plunging civilization into a world-devastating war. We may dub this "great sword" nuclear, at least until a greater weapon is developed. What else can wreak such havoc, killing over 600 million people in one war?

The statement that the red horseman has power to take peace from the earth suggests that he represents a nation. Many commentators identify the white horseman as the antichrist, but the second seal makes it plain that the horsemen kill one another. Thus, the white horseman does not survive to participate in later events. If the red horseman is the head of a nation, then the white horseman is also the head of a nation, or at least he has a large following that threatens the world.

The red horseman has been given a weapon ("a great sword") that is mighty to kill. The word for *kill* used in this passage is a little-used Greek word[36] that means "to slaughter, as in a sacrifice." Its usage here suggests something is being offered up. Can it be that the nation of the red horseman has finally offered the supreme sacrifice to save the world from the conqueror?

Contributing to this thought is the fact that the calf-like creature, which represents Christ's sacrifice, is the most likely one to call this seal into action. Men have rejected God's sacrifice of mercy, and now He offers them the alternative: judgment. This is all preliminary, however. Men against men bring death and destruction, with only two seals open.

---

[36] The most used Greek word in the New Testament for *kill* means "to put to death." The Greek word used here, *spazo*, means "to butcher or slaughter as an animal for sacrifice" and is used only four or five times (according to Strong's Concordance).

The Black Horse

> And when he had opened the third seal, I head the third
> beast say, Come and see. And I beheld, and lo a black
> horse; and he that sat on him had a pair of balances in
> his hand. And I heard a voice in the midst of the four
> beasts say, A measure of wheat for a penny, and three
> measures of barley for a penny; and see thou hurt not
> the oil and the wine. (6:5–6)

After Jesus opens the third seal, the man-like creature
directs, "Come and see." Then John says, "And I beheld,
and lo," the words for a changed scene. Gone are the former
two horsemen. In their places stands a black horse with a
rider. Instead of instruments of war, this rider holds a balance scales in his hand. Then comes the command from
among the four living creatures (the throne), "A measure
of wheat for a penny, and three measures of barley for a
penny; and see thou hurt not the oil and the wine" (6:6). It
is a clear command of limitation: Hurt only the barley and
the wheat.

The war situation remains, since the horse is still in the
picture. Of the color, Jeremiah says, "Our skin was black
like an oven because of the terrible famine" (Lam. 5:10).
Thus, both the horse's color and the rider's balance scales
suggest an extreme famine due to the devastation. To understand what the voice said, however, we need to know
the relationship of wheat and barley to oil and wine.

In the Old Testament, God set seven feasts for Israel to
keep each year (Lev. 23). These festivals fell at the time of
various harvests. The first three, the Passover, the Feast of
Firstfruits, and the Feast of Unleavened Bread, came in the
spring of the year (March/April) and were associated with

the barley harvest. The fourth, Pentecost, came fifty days after Firstfruits in June and was associated with the wheat harvest. The last three, the Feast of Trumpets, the Day of Atonement, and the Feast of Tabernacles, came in the fall (September/October) and were associated with the oil and the wine harvest. These festivals all have prophetic significance, and the first four (those associated with wheat and the barley) have already been fulfilled.

Christ fulfilled the first feast, Passover, when He died on the same day and hour that the official national Passover lamb was sacrificed in the Temple. Thus, Christ became our Passover Lamb (1 Cor. 5:7). Then begins the festival week of unleavened bread. The unleavened bread speaks of Christ as the sinless sustenance He gives to all those who take advantage of the salvation He accomplished, the pure Bread of Life, also symbolized in the Communion bread. The Feast of Firstfruits falls on the day after the special Sabbath of that same week. Christ arose from the dead on this very day when Israel waved the firstfruits of the barley harvest before the Lord. Therefore, He became the "firstfruits" of the resurrection (1 Cor. 15:20). The Holy Spirit fulfilled Pentecost when He anointed believers on the fiftieth day after the Feast of Firstfruits during the wheat harvest. This marks the beginning of the Christian Church.

Therefore, the barley and wheat embodied in the first four festivals speak of the scope of Christianity. Consequently, the judgment of war and famine seems to be directed toward those who have heard the gospel preached and rejected it.

Now we deal with a point of speculation. The nations affected in this passage may be those where Christianity has had its greatest influence, such as the United States and

Canada, where the gospel can be heard at any time on radio or television. Christianity may also be strong in Russia, especially after the raising of the Iron Curtain. However, missionaries report that France, Germany, and other European countries are nearly pagan. Furthermore, they seem to be associated with Italy in the vision; therefore, we surmise they are not affected, since both theirs and Israel's turn for judgment comes later. The fulfillment of the first four festivals, then, seems to pertain to countries where Christianity has had the greatest influence today.

They do not involve Israel because of her unbelief: "Even unto this day, when Moses is read, a veil is upon their heart" (2 Cor. 3:15). The people of Israel do not yet believe, and the remaining Feast of Trumpets, Day of Atonement, and Feast of Tabernacles have to do spiritually with Israel's repentance, redemption, and refinement. Since these festivals are yet unfulfilled, those they pertain to, especially Israel, may be exempt. What is important to note is the command, "Hurt not the oil and the wine," refer to the three latter feasts. Add to this argument the fact that the word translated *hurt* in the command means literally "to be unjust." Since a "veil covers their heart," it would be unjust to include Israel in this judgment of war and famine. Therefore, the Middle East escapes judgment—for now.

The Pale Horse

> And when he had opened the fourth seal, I heard the voice of the fourth beast say, Come and see. And I looked, and behold a pale horse: and his name that sat on him was Death, and Hell followed with him. And power was given unto them over the fourth part of the earth, to kill

with sword, and with hunger, and with death, and with the beasts of the earth. (6:7–8)

Jesus opens the fourth seal. The black horse fades from view. The eagle-like creature invites the next rider to center stage. Immediately, a pale horse appears. (In the Greek, *pale* as a color stood for a putrid light green.) This color suggests an absence of life-giving blood. The symbolic men associated with this horse also echo the fearful finality of death by their names. On the horse sits a rider called Death, followed by a footman called Hades.

Heaven grants them power, in the sense of the right to act, over one-fourth of the earth. With heaven's permission, "Death" and "Hades" may kill up to 1,756,664,000 people, (a theoretic number based on one-fourth of the projected population of the world by 2010). Their methods include the sword, suggested earlier as a nuclear "sword," and its effects are deadly and capable of killing this staggering number of people. The deadly duo connected with this horse will decimate by hunger as the famine spreads, perhaps radiation sickness brought on by contaminated food supplies. Biological warfare may also be a factor. Suspended smoke and dust could block the sunlight over the affected countries, destroying agriculture and contributing to famine. The spirits of death and suicide[37] have opportunity to enter people through depressed emotions and disease. Finally, the beasts of the earth run wild. Without their natural food, starving animals prey upon mankind.

---

[37] Death and suicide demons are often encountered in the deliverance ministry. Their work is to bring about people's death prematurely in any way they can.

The death angel, dispensed from Satan's ranks, directs the war, while demons ("Hades" means the unseen world) take every advantage against people. Hell reigns. Despair is everywhere. People kill for morsels of bread. Survival of the fiercest replaces the law of the land as anarchy takes over.

The victims of the pale horse are those who have rejected the light of the gospel. Since both "light" and "salt" (the Church) have been removed from the earth, the life-repressing forces of the unseen world are left without restraint.[38] The powers of darkness control their victims in the midst of these depressing circumstances.

It is interesting that the living creatures, in turn, direct the action of the first four seals. We suggest that the nature of each beast fits the action of the seal. The lion-like creature, which represents Christ as King, calls forth and crowns the conqueror on the white horse. Then the sacrificial calf-like creature calls forth the sacrificial slaughter, the red horse. Next, the man-like creature introduces regulation into the marketplace because of famine, the black horse. The eagle-like creature, which represents Christ who has the power of life and death, gives the death angel free reign in the scene of the pale horse.

All this suggests righteous judgment against those who have known about Christ and rejected Him. God repays Russia for the martyrs' blood it shed. God judges the United States and other Christian nations for spurning the gospel light. I particularly mention Russia and the United States

---

[38] Jesus said that the Church was to be light and salt. With the light of the Church gone, the darkness (the demonic world) will reign without hindrance. Salt, a preserving agent, also being removed, causes the world to spoil in its own wickedness.

because these two nations have enough nuclear weapons to destroy in this magnitude.

It seems apparent that the light of the Church has been removed for three reasons: 1) the severity of these judgments; 2) the lack of restraint on the powers of darkness; and 3) those who "turned to God from idols to serve the living and true God" will be rescued from "the wrath to come" (1 Thess. 1:9–10). We have not yet come to the time of God's wrath. This preliminary judgment displays only the wrath of men. Still, it is directed toward "them that know not God, and that obey not the gospel of our Lord Jesus Christ" (2 Thess. 1:8).

The Martyrs

> And when he had opened the fifth seal, I saw under the altar the souls of them that were slain for the word of God, and for the testimony which they held: and they cried with a loud voice, saying, How long, O Lord, holy and true, dost thou not judge and avenge our blood on them that dwell on the earth? And white robes were given unto every one of them; and it was said unto them, that they should rest yet for a little season, until their fellow servants also and their brethren, that should be killed as they were, should be fulfilled. (6:9–11)

Jesus opens the fifth seal, but no living creature summons the actors to this scene. So John just says that he sees martyrs under the altar. John probably sees their blood, since that is what one would expect to find. They cry out like Abel's blood. He may see bodies. Whatever he sees, we know they are dead. He is shocked to find people under the altar of sacrifice. Yet it is not hard for John to understand why they are there. He himself is in exile for the same reason—"for the word of God, and for the testimony of Jesus Christ" (Rev. 1:9).

Saints' blood under the altar raises the question, which saints? If the Church is no longer on earth but has been resurrected and rewarded and since the text does not tell us of any new believers at this point, we have to surmise what else may be happening. The sequence thus far mentions only the rearranging of the world's political power structure. It says nothing about God's people. Before one-quarter of the world destroys itself, Jesus evidently calls a new set of witnesses. They have believed the Word and tested it because they have a testimony of what God can do. These believers have been sacrificed on God's altar, so to speak. Opposition to their testimonies has caused their martyrdom sometime before their appearance here.

When John sees their blood, he remembers the blood under the altar at Jerusalem. He had seen the priests pour out the blood of lambs and goats at the base of the temple altar many times. Like that blood, these souls have been collecting. Their righteous blood cries out for justice in the same way that Abel's blood cried from the ground. They cry for justice against their butchers: "How long, O Lord, dost thou not judge and avenge our blood?" God tells them they must wait until the iniquity of their murderers reaches its fullness. More of their brethren will be killed.

In the meantime, they receive white robes. It appears another company of saints is being resurrected, because the robes being given here are stately robes of honor, their reward for martyrdom. The Greek word used for robe is *stole*, according to W. E. Vine.[39] Luke uses the same word for the

---

[39] Vine, *Expository Dictionary*, p. 199.

robe put on the prodigal son to honor him. A full robe with a train, it was also the kind worn by the Pharisees to honor themselves. After they receive their robes, God invites these martyrs to rest while the judgment continues.

How, you might ask, can we see this as a resurrection? First, it is obvious that blood cannot speak. What we have is a figure of speech representing life after death. These souls, though alive, are without immortal bodies. They appeal for justice; thus, they remember their murderers, proving they have souls. They are alive with eternal life (furnished by the Holy Spirit), but they have been collecting in a "holding tank" under the altar. They are unclothed spirits. They have not yet made an appearance before the throne. Now they are invited to do so in an attitude of rest. The idea of giving robes to voices would be ridiculous; therefore, a change in their status has occurred. To be given robes at this time shows that they are now living spiritual souls with bodies.

The reason for picturing them here may be to set the time and place in the sequence for this resurrection and to connect it to other important events. We shall see in the next chapter who these believers are and what God calls them to do.

The Overturning

> And I beheld when he had opened the sixth seal, and. lo, there was a great earthquake; and the sun became black as sackcloth of hair, and the moon became as blood; and the stars of heaven fell unto the earth, even as a fig tree casteth her untimely figs, when she is shaken of a mighty wind. And the heaven departed as a scroll when

it is rolled together; and every mountain and island were moved out of their places. (6:12–14)

The Lamb breaks open the sixth seal. It becomes obvious as the scene progresses that John has been transported back to the vicinity of the earth where he watches a world age end right before his eyes.

A world age is a period of time between worldwide physical destructions. For instance, the Genesis flood ended the antediluvian world age. Herodotus, the Greek historian, mentions ancient Egyptian accounts of four worldwide destructions since they were a nation.[40] Afterwards, the surface of the earth is different, and civilizations begin anew.

As John looks on, the surface of the earth shudders with a great earthquake. The stricken sun becomes black as a "sackcloth of hair"; the moon turns bloody red. Stars plummet to earth like green figs torn from a tree in a fierce gale. The heavens depart and roll out of sight like a rolled-up scroll. Every mountain and island moves out of its place.

Commentators have stumbled over this and similar passages for years, spiritualizing the meanings, calling it apocalyptic language. Perhaps it was difficult for them to conceive of anything this violent happening to the earth. Maybe they could not visualize a cause great enough to produce these effects.

Geologists, on the other hand, are keen on understanding the violence of nature written in the rocks. Folded rock strata, massive molten rock intrusions, even shifting continents—these all tell of great catastrophic events which hap-

---

[40] Immanuel Velikovsky, *Worlds in Collision* (New York: Doubleday, 1950), p. 105.

pened to the earth in the past. Men have partially recorded many of these events. Because of the nature of these events, they are at best sketchy reports. People were more interested in survival than recording history. Therefore, the accounts, especially those recorded in Scripture, are more like the outcrops geologists use to determine the under burden. The detailed truth remains hidden for the most part.

Looking at these outcrops, we can piece together much of the past that civilization has forgotten. The following scriptures show one prominent factor. God *always* involves the heavenly bodies when He judges the whole earth. This is why the heavens declare the righteousness of God (Ps. 50:6). He uses them to cleanse the world.

First, we look a general statement.

> Of old hast thou laid the foundation of the earth: and the heavens are the work of thy hands. They shall perish, but thou shalt endure: yea, all of them shall wax old like a garment; as a vesture shalt thou change them, and they shall be changed. (Ps. 102:25–26)

God controls the workings of the heavens and the earth. In this psalm, He declares His right to change them like garments when they grow old. The Hebrew word for *perish* used in the Old Testament literally means "to wander away," "to lose one's self"; by implication "to perish, break, be undone." Seeing this meaning makes us realize the reason *for* its meaning. The breaking apart or the wandering away of the heavens and earth means great destruction. It does not mean, however, the total annihilation of the heavens and earth but a mere changing of their former outward designs, their "clothes," if you will.

Speaking of the exodus of Israel from Egypt, the psalmist says, "The earth shook, the heavens also dropped at the presence of God" (Ps. 68:8). On another occasion, he says, "Then the earth shook and trembled. . . . He bowed the heavens also, and came down" (Ps. 18:7, 9). "The LORD also thundered in the heavens, and the Highest gave his voice; hailstones and coals of fire. Yea, he sent out his arrows, and scattered them; he shot out lightnings, and discomfited them" (Ps 18:13–14).

Then fifty years after the exodus, God aided Joshua when He "cast down great stones from heaven upon them unto Azekah, and they died: they were more which died of hailstones than they whom the children of Israel slew with the sword" (Josh. 10:11). During that battle, the sun did not go down for more than a day.

Still later, God helped Deborah and Barak in battle when the "heavens dropped" and "the stars in their courses fought against Sisera" (Judg. 5:4, 20).

God also says, "I will shake the heavens and the earth" (Hag. 2:21; see Heb. 12:26). Ezekiel prophesies, "All the men that are upon the face of the earth, shall shake at my presence, and the mountains shall be thrown down. . . . And I will rain upon him, and upon his bands [an enemy army], . . . an overflowing rain, and great hailstones, fire, and brimstone" (Ezek. 38:20, 22).

The raining of hailstones (meteorites) involves the heavens. Peter mentions that the heavens were involved in the great flood: "The heavens were of old, and the earth . . . whereby the world that then was, being overflowed with water, perished: but the heavens and the earth, which are now . . . reserved unto fire against the day of judgment" (2 Pet. 3:5–7). *Both* the heavens and the earth were changed at the time of the flood.

God seems to use the heavenly bodies in two ways when the earth undergoes His judgment: He either pummels the earth with space debris, dropping stones out of the sky—meteorites (hailstones in the Hebrew denote stones from heaven, either rock or ice, but mostly associated with fire [see Josh. 10:11; Ps. 78:48]). Other times He sends a large body into the earth's gravitational field, affecting its motion, like the day the sun stood still. Isaiah tells about a time when the earth will actually leave its orbit: "Therefore I will shake the heavens, and the earth shall remove out of her place, in the wrath of the LORD of hosts" (Isa. 13:13). The ancients associated these catastrophic times with judgment because this was when God displayed His great power and glory. They would call on God to bow the heavens and come down to judge the wicked. Isaiah 64:1–3 is such an example:

> Oh that thou wouldest rend the heavens, that thou wouldest come down, that the mountains might flow down at thy presence, as when the melting fire burneth, the fire causeth the waters to boil, to make thy name known to thine adversaries, that the nations may tremble at thy presence! When thou didst terrible things which we looked not for, thou camest down, the mountains flowed down at thy presence.

This is not poetic language. These are real-time events! If we do not understand these actions of God as literal happenings, much valuable background for seeing the awesomeness of the judgments is lost. Using the conditions that Revelation 6:12–14 sets forth, let us explore what a literal explanation would entail.

First, the catastrophe is widespread. It includes the whole earth and at least part of the solar system. The sun, moon, and stars act abnormally.

Second, the black sun indicates a prolonged total eclipse seen over the whole earth. The sun hides behind another body, turning "black as sackcloth of hair." The midday sky darkens to night. Only the bright ring of the sun's corona marks its place in space. Enveloped in shadow, the earth detects a body, close in, whose earthshaking effects can already be felt. Yet the body that blocks the sun cannot be the moon, because it is clearly visible a distance away.

Third, something has happened to turn the moon's silvery reflective surface to a bloody red hue. Consequently, this bright red orb glows in the darkened sky. We say "bright" because the body coming in between the earth and the sun does not block the light reflecting off the moon.

Fourth, the earth's path through space changes. Multitudes of meteorites fall, pockmarking the earth's surface. The number and driving force of their impact on earth, suggested in the figure of the fig tree, indicates that either the earth leaves its regular orbit to encounter a large meteor belt or that great amounts of unexpected space debris crosses the earth's normal course. Either explanation reveals a drastic change in the earth's corner of the solar system.

Fifth, in the midst of this shower of stars, the horizon shifts, moving against the starlit sky. The light from bright shooting stars streaming downward is suddenly crossed by more blurred streaks. The stationary starlight of hundreds of stars moves horizontally. The overall effect suggests white starlit characters written in reversed-out print on a dark scroll. Then these characters are further blurred into lines by rapidly rolling up the scroll. The whole awesome backdrop of heaven appears like a full sheet of written lines streaking across the sky.

Apparently, the earth turns over. That explains why the sky looks like lines on a scroll. The sky remains stationary; only the earth moves. Points of light become lines because of the movement. This shifting horizon, depicted in the rolling of the scroll, is what an observer standing on the earth would see if the earth's geographic poles suddenly reversed.

Finally, the sixth condition required to give a literal interpretation is a force great enough to cause "every mountain and island" to move out of their places in a *worldwide* earthquake. Any force great enough to shift the axis of the earth or turn it upside down would also affect its rotational velocity. Sudden braking of the rotational spin would cause a speed differential between the lighter outer crust of the earth and its heavy viscous center. (Please note that the overall average of the earth's crust is only 28 miles in depth.) Such friction of the continental plates sliding over the semi-fluid interior and clashing one against the other could rearrange the surface geography. The earthquake, then, could result from a slowed and overturned earth.

The foreign body invading the earth's corner of the solar system is reacting with the earth according to the laws of physics. Both bodies carry electrical charges because of their mass and motion. Both have gravitational pulls. Because of attraction between such bodies, their courses and speeds can be changed when they come in close enough range to interact one with the other. If they come only close enough for the electromagnetic attraction to be involved, a spark of electricity might pass between them in the form of a giant thunderbolt. In this case, the magnetic poles would reverse, and the magnetic fields would break up and reform. Magnetic north would become magnetic south and vice versa.

Apparently, this has happened many times in the past. Geophysicists have counted 171 reversals of the earth's magnetic field in lava flows in the mid-ocean ridges between the continental plates.[41] They know this is true because of the inclination of magnetic particles in the flows.

> When rock is liquefied it is nonmagnetic, but cooling to 580 Centigrade (Curie point), it acquires a magnetic state and [the particles of metal in the flow line themselves up with the nearest magnetic field.] After solidifying, lava rock retains its magnetic property, and would retain it even though it became displaced or the magnetic orientation of the earth changed [again].[42]

Some of these reversals have taken place in historical times. Clay pots reveal the same evidence. Particles in the clay line up with and point to a particular magnetic inclination before firing, but after firing they were set, leaving behind a record of the magnetic inclination of that period. Most interesting is the discovery that the last time the reversal of the magnetic field took place was in the eighth century before the present era, or twenty-seven centuries ago. The observation was made on clay fired in kilns by the Etruscans and the Greeks.[43]

---

[41] Continental plates are large blocks of the earth's crust floating on a semifluid interior. They fit together rather like pieces of a puzzle. A whole continent may comprise one piece.

[42] Immanuel Velikovsky, *Earth in Upheaval* (New York: Doubleday, 1955), p. 143.

[43] Ibid, p. 146.

Isaiah lived at this time and saw the earth turn over. He could say with certainty, "Behold, the LORD maketh the earth empty, and maketh it waste, and turneth it upside down" (Isa. 24:1). Yet his prophecy which begins with these words refers to a future time because he also says, "The earth . . . shall fall, and not rise again" (Isa. 24:20). Since we see it falling again in Revelation, the prophet surely refers to the time of John's vision.

We cannot say that every time the magnetic poles reverse, the earth turns over or shifts its geographical poles since it only takes a supercharge to reverse the polarity. However, there does have to be a source for the supercharge. Evidence of changes in the geographical poles abound in the earth's geologic records but not to the extent of magnetic changes. It seems reasonable to expect that any time a foreign body tangles with the earth, much electrical activity exists, just as many flashes of lightning occur in a single summer storm.

But the mechanism for reversing the geographical poles, the north pole becoming the south pole and vice versa, requires a unique situation. The electrical charge of the nearest pole would encounter a large electrically charged dust cloud (or even direct influence from the head of such a body) having the same polarity. Magnetic repulsion would flip the earth over just like a little white magnetic dog flips around when the black one is moved too close to its rear. While such a condition might develop when the earth tangles with a comet whose tail has the same charge as the closest pole, the opportunities for electrical exchange between the earth and the comet's head would be more numerous. So though the conditions may exist for a magnetic pole reversal, they may not always exist for a geographic pole reversal.

Now we move into an area of controversy. There is no question but that the earth has turned over in historical times. Geological and historical evidence confirms this. The debate centers on the cause. Geologists demand an extra-terrestrial cause to explain the reversals and the widespread destruction recorded in rock strata. Astrophysicists are not prepared to admit such a cause. Immanuel Velikovsky, drawing from ancient literature and histories, formulated a theory that the planet Venus (acting originally as a comet) tangled with the earth at the time of the exodus of Israel from Egypt and later with Mars in Isaiah's day.[44] He describes these encounters as the cause of the destruction. Since Venus now conforms to their understanding of the laws, astrophysicists can find no indications that this encounter happened.

Though leading scientists would like to be sympathetic to Velikovsky's theory, they see too many evidences that seem to contradict it. In addition, they are turned off by the religious leanings of those who follow Velikovsky and by his apparent lack of understanding of certain portions of celestial mechanics. J. Derral Mulholland, dealing with the problems of Velikovsky's comet changing the orbits of Venus and Mars, says:

> One could hypothesize two additional planet-sized objects entering the solar system, one encountering Venus, the other Mars, in just such a way as to produce near-circular orbits, then exiting the system without another trace. Or one could appeal to a *host of angels*

---

[44] Ibid, p. 146. The theory is presented in *Worlds in Collision* by Immanuel Velikovsky, who attempts to show that "the perfectly ordered solar system" occasionally runs amuck with dire results on the earth.

pushing in just the right direction. *Neither is believable.*[45] (Emphasis added)

Thus scientists have a tendency to stick rigidly to God's natural laws without making allowance for His exceptions or interferences, angelic or otherwise. George W. Gamow (one of the foremost advocates of the Big Bang theory) summarizes the scientific thinking in this matter:

> I am not religious, and when asked how God created the universe, usually answer that He invented the basic laws of Physics and Chemistry, and ordered the universe to follow these laws. Thus from the very beginning the Universe was developing according to strictly scientific laws, and the God never tried to interfere with that development. [46]

Gamow obviously believes in a Creator God but does not allow Him any latitude in His own creation. We laymen tend to side with evidence supplied by scientists because of their great minds, except for one thing. Velikovsky's research into the traditions of ancient cultures to support what he hypothesizes about the past perfectly explains the conditions of the future found in John's vision of Revelation. How can scientific facts account for that? What if Velikovsky and the scientists are both right?

---

[45] Donald Goldsmith, Norman W. Storer, Peter J. Huber, Carl Sagan, J. Darrel Mulholland, and David Mossison, *Scientists Confront Velikovsky* (New York: W. W. Norton, 1977) p. 113

[46] Letter received from Prof. George W. Gamow, University of Colorado, 4 March 1961.

What if God did interrupt the normal scheme of things to perform His word to Israel, leaving behind only debatable evidence for the geologists and astrophysicists to assess? If true, later generations would have to accept these accounts by faith. Hebrews 11:13 confirms this idea. Translated literally from the Greek as it reads in *The Interlinear Greek-English New Testament*:

> By faith—we apprehend to have been framed—the worlds [ages]—by [the] word of God—so that not from appearing—the things seen—having being.

The word for *worlds* refers to the ages, equating it with what Herodotus called "world ages." The different world ages existed because God periodically made changes in His creation. These changes apparently involved new bodies not formerly seen.

The controversy between geologists and astrophysicists is not resolved. Yet Velikovsky's theory satisfies both the geologic record and the historical record. It allows an occasional body to interfere with the course of the earth in space. Moreover, his theory seems to agree with the Bible. Therefore, we feel free to use Velikovsky's research to explain otherwise obscure portions of the prophetic scriptures.

By comparing the information Velikovsky collected to present his theory with the conditions laid down in Scripture, we surmise that a large extraterrestrial body, perhaps a comet with a long dusty tail full of debris, tangles with the earth. After eclipsing the sun, it moves close enough to the earth to react with it electromagnetically, striking the earth with a giant thunderbolt. (An electric charge, when striking a magnet, will reverse its polarity.) An electrical charge from a heavenly body or a charged dust cloud might conceivably do the same to the earth, since it in itself is a huge magnet. If the body were large enough, if it approached the earth so that its tail crossed the earth's path, and if the magnetic pole nearest the approach were the same polarity, it would flip the earth over by magnetic repulsion. The gravitational attraction of the comet at the same time would cause a veering in the earth's orbit and a braking of rotation that would bring about a worldwide earthquake.

Summing up now what the literal interpretation of Revelation 6:12–14 shows, this is what we understand: First, a foreign body invades earth's place in space, coming near enough to attract its magnetic field but not close enough to collide. The gravitational attraction causes the earth to slow its rotation, which results in the first earthquake. The body comes directly in between the earth and the sun as shown by the eclipse, closer even than the orbit of the moon around the earth. Its tail covers the moon with a reddish dust, scattering space debris which peppers the earth like falling figs from a wind-shaken tree. Before veering away from the earth, it sends forth a charge of electricity in the form of a gigantic thunderbolt, neutralizing the charges of the two bodies. This charge strikes the earth, reversing the electromagnetic polarity. The polarity of the head of the comet now being the same as the nearest magnetic pole, they would repel one another. This would cause the body of lesser mass (apparently, the earth) to turn entirely over, reversing the geographic poles, thus moving the mountains and islands out of their places.

This sums up the overview John sees from space. But imagine the perspective of people on earth. They see the sky roll away like a rolled-up scroll. Then the earthquake shatters much of civilization as we know it. Since it is worldwide, the earthquake leaves no safe haven. Most of the world's cities lie in a mangled rubble of twisted steel and concrete, reminiscent of the falling of the trade towers in New York City. Some of the population may have sought safety away from the cities, since they have seen the catastrophe coming. God moves His people to safe ground, as revealed in later chapters. Although the eclipse of the sun, the red moon, the shower of stars, and the overturning occur in the sixth seal, the body responsible for the catastrophe has already been sighted. Christ gives people's reactions:

> And there shall be signs in the sun, and in the moon, and in the stars; and upon the earth distress of nations, with perplexity; the sea and the waves roaring; men's hearts failing them for fear, and for looking after those things which are coming on the earth: for the powers of heaven shall be shaken. (Luke 21:25–26)

These words of Christ recorded in Luke give the same specifics found in Revelation 6 regarding the sun, moon, and stars, plus one new detail—the roaring sea, which we will discuss in the next chapter.

> And the kings of the earth, and the great men, and the rich men, and the chief captains, and the mighty men, and every bondman, and every free man, hid themselves in the dens and in the rocks of the mountains; and said to the mountains and rocks, Fall on us, and hide us from the face of him that sitteth on the throne, and from the wrath of the Lamb: for the great day of his wrath is come; and who shall be able to stand? (6:15–17)

The nations are perplexed. Heart attacks strike down the fearful. Men cannot fight these forces with weapons. The cities empty as people scurry for shelter, kings and common people alike. They crawl into caves and dens to hide from falling meteorites and to escape collapsing structures. Tumultuous noise, from the grating and grinding of the earth's crust as it seeks to make adjustments in the different blocks along fault lines, ruin people's hearing. Chasms open and close, trapping those trying to escape. Men cry out to the rocks to hide them from the wrath of the Lamb.

They acknowledge that it is time for God's judgment. They confess their own guilt. Because the martyrs of the former scene have given an effective witness, victims of the sixth seal know the source of their judgment, and they expect wrath from the Lamb they have rejected. These words of the fugitives indicate that things have been happening in the religious and social world that we are not aware of from our text so far.

With John, we have been watching the political, economic, and natural events. We have followed the edge of a puzzle, if you will. Now we need to go back and fill in the middle of the picture, a picture that presents a choice: on the one hand, life and safety; on the other hand, death and destruction.

WEATHER CURRENTS

TIER UPON TIER

At the equator, where the big painting cuts the globe to reveal the ocean currents there, the deepest layer (1) is cold water on the sea floor. Then comes a slow-moving current (2). On top of it is the swift Cromwell current (3), 100 to 1,000 feet below sea level. Above it are surface currents (4), quickened by easterly trade winds (5). Over them the stratosphere is swept by the erratic Berson Westerlies (6) at 60,000 feet and the powerful Krakatoa Easterlies (7) at 80,000 feet. North of the equator, surface winds (8) help produce tropical clouds and whirl into low pressure storms. High above, the Jet Stream (9) spurts at 35,000 feet and the Polar Vortex (10) towers between 40,000 and 200,000 feet. The Jet Stream, formed where warm southern air meets with cold northern air, lashes around the mid-latitudes at up to 300 mph. Its undulations affect the surface winds, which in turn affect surface currents at sea.

So, in patterns wrought by earth's heating, wind and water surge and spin, layer on layer...* in the normal course of events. But if the motion of the earth should change or the heat absorbed increase, drastic weather would ensue. Needless to say, if the earth suddenly turned upside down, the winds and waves would wreak havoc everywhere.

INCOMING SOLAR RADIATION

DUST

REFLECTED
SUNLIGHT

CLOUDS

PACIFIC OCEAN CRUST

EQUATOR

(7)

(6)

(5)

(4)

(3)

(2)

(1)

(8)

ABSORBED
SUNLIGHT

OUTGOING INFRARED RADIATION

(10)

(9)

(8)

Chapter 13

THE SEALED COMPANY

(REVELATION 7)

The seventh seal remains unbroken, but the scene changes anyway. A parenthetical pause interrupts the sequence. John sees the earth before the destruction of the sixth seal. Four angels hold four winds in check.

> And after these things I saw four angels standing on the four corners of the earth, holding the four winds of the earth, that the wind should not blow on the earth, nor on the sea, nor on any tree. And I saw another angel ascending from the east, having the seal of the living God: and he cried with a loud voice to the four angels, to whom it was given to hurt the earth and the sea, saying, Hurt not the earth, neither the sea, nor the trees, till we have sealed the servants of our God in their foreheads. (7:1–3)

Two scenes loom before us. First, we see four angels maintaining the status quo of the winds until they receive the order to change to judgment mode. They remain poised and ready to act. The second scene introduces the reason for the delay. Apparently, what we see here is a flashback to the beginning before the Lamb opens any of the seals, perhaps to immediately after the catching away of the Church.

Because of the command given to the angels, "Hurt not the earth, neither the sea, nor the trees" (v. 3) and because we know the earth cannot overturn without affecting the sea or the trees, we surmise that the four winds contribute to the destruction in the sixth seal. Therefore, this scene will help us catch up to the rest of the story by filling in the missing details.

The Winds

Not too much was known about the affects of winds on weather until 1957. That year the scientists of sixty-six nations worked together to unlock some mysteries of the earth. *Life Magazine* reported, "In that historic year, the International Geophysical Year (IGY), man placed the world under his multi-instrumented eye and wrung from it facts hitherto unknown." Out of this research, we learn how winds and ocean currents create the earth's weather. The article in *Life* went on to say:

> The ocean movements, the clouds, the polar gales all add up to the weather. The painting [see color plates] shows the mechanism that drives the weather, with the currents of the sea and air that are created by a great global exchange of heat. The process begins when the sun's radiation streams to earth. About 65% of it is ab-

sorbed by the planet, then it is gradually given off as heat. It is this warmth heating the atmosphere from below rather than—as most people believe—from above, that helps power the weather. Warm, light water and air begin to rise at the equator. As they move poleward, they are replaced by colder, heavier water and air coming in underneath from the north. Because the earth rotates, these north-south movements are shifted toward east and west. The swirling, heat-exchanging masses become layered into tiers of globe-circling currents.[47]

Contrary to what most people think in reference to the four winds, the scientists uncovered a complicated weather system. This does not, however, negate what this passage (Rev. 7:1–3) tells us. The number four in Scripture stands for the natural creation. The *four* angels in charge of the *four* winds simply emphasize the involvement of the natural realm.[48] Rather than being the straight north, south, east, and west surface winds, the easterly, westerly, and polar vortexes, etc. occur in different layers of the atmosphere. (The writers of biblical times simply spoke of the surface winds that blew over their local habitations.) Scientists found that the normal, natural winds arise from a combination of heat absorption and the rotation of the earth. In the event that more heat is absorbed into the air or the rotation is disturbed (turning over would certainly cause an interruption of the normal flow of air), the winds would

[47] "The New Portrait of Our Planet," *Life Magazine,* 7 Nov. 1960 New York: Time Inc., Also printed in Life's Pictorial Atlas p. 24

[48] Vallowe, Ed F. *Keys to Scriptural Numerics,* (Forest Park, GA: Ed. F. Vallowe Evangelistic Association, 1974) p. 60

become fierce. Both these conditions would exist should the earth suddenly flip upside down.

Besides causing earthquakes, the scraping together of tectonic plates would generate tremendous heat from friction. Lava flows, especially in the trenches where crust is destroyed as one plate slides under another, would release heat to the ocean currents and consequently to the air. With such heating, the oceans would actually boil[49] in places, causing the air to rise like hot-air balloons making winds.

Add to this heat released from the oceans the heat from the lava furnaces created in the cracking crust on the surface. Beyond additional heat increasing the winds, the drag on the normal air currents caused by the sudden veering of the earth creates another problem. Whole temperature zones suddenly displaced in an overturning of the globe—cold air from polar vortexes rushing into tropical areas and vice versa—would create violent tornadoes and hurricanes all over the earth's surface from the mixing temperatures.

This, too, has happened in the past. Men have discovered frozen mammoths with vegetation still in their mouths encased in ice, testifying to a sudden displacement of location and temperature. The meat was so fresh, they feasted on the thawed carcasses.

Besides being heated, the sea would be displaced. The fluid waters keep their bounds now because of gravity and stable motion, much like water in a bucket that is being swung at a steady speed. Nevertheless, disturb the motion of the bucket or change the speed of the swing, and the water will leave its bounds and come over the sides. The same thing would happen to the ocean. Sweeping tidal

---

[49] Isaiah mentions the waters boiling (Isa. 64:2).

waves would splash against the inland mountains, washing away great forests of trees ripped up by the violent winds.

According to historical traditions, this did happen in the past when the earth tangled with a comet that disturbed its rotation. Immanuel Velikovsky, writing from accounts in ancient manuscripts, reconstructs this as follows:

> The shifting of the atmosphere under the impact of the gaseous parts of the comet, the drift of air attracted by the body of the comet, and the rush of the atmosphere resulting from the inertia when the earth stopped rotating or shifted its poles, all contributed to produce hurricanes of enormous velocity and force and of world dimensions. Manuscript Troano and other documents of the Mayas describe a cosmic catastrophe during which the ocean fell on the continent and a terrible hurricane broke up and carried away all towns and forests.[50]

Velikovsky shows how disturbances of the earth's rotation would affect the winds and cause the oceans to sweep up on the land, washing away forests. No wonder then that angels are holding back the winds lest they hurt the earth, the *sea,* and the *trees.*

Velikovsky, formulating a working hypothesis to explain what would happen if such a pole shift took place, writes:

> At that moment, an earthquake would make the globe shudder. Air and water would continue to move through inertia; hurricanes would sweep the earth, and the seas would rush over the continents, carrying gravel and sand

---

[50] Immanuel Velikovsky, *Worlds in Collision* (New York: Doubleday, 1950), p. 67.

and marine animals, casting them on the land. Heat would develop, rocks would melt, volcanoes would erupt, lava, flowing from fissures in the ruptured ground would cover vast areas. Mountains would spring up from the plains and travel on the shoulders of other mountains, causing faults and rifts. Lakes would be tilted and emptied, rivers would change their beds; large land areas with all their inhabitants would slip under the sea. Forests would burn, and hurricanes and wild seas would wrest them from the ground on which they grew and pile them, branch and root, in huge heaps.[51]

Since the destructive force of wind and water acting together in a pole exchange would destroy vast populations of people, it becomes clear why the Lord commands the angels to hold back the winds. God wants a chance to offer His mercy. He has a specially called people to warn the world of impending disaster. They will preach the gospel of the kingdom to all nations, offering them an alternative to the coming judgment.

Still occupying his position close to the earth, John observes an angel ascending over the globe from the east. He comes on special assignment, carrying the seal of God. Crying out a command to the other angels, he says, "Hurt not the earth, neither the sea, nor the trees, till we have sealed the servants of our God in their foreheads" (7:3). We are not told how long before the catastrophe this sealing takes place, but it seems likely that God would not leave the world without a witness after the Church is gone. Therefore, we suspect they will be called before the war begins, perhaps

---

[51] Immanuel Velikovsky, *Earth in Upheaval* (New York: Doubleday, 1955), p. 136.

during the relatively peaceful period. This allows time for the witnesses to preach the gospel, to warn the people of coming disaster, and for persecution against them to develop.

Curious about the end times, His disciples ask Jesus, "Tell us, when shall these things be? and what shall be the sign of thy coming and of the end of the world?" (Matt. 24:2).[52] Jesus' answer seems to confirm our reasoning. First, He warns that the world will seek after religious leaders: "Many shall come in my name, saying, I am Christ; and shall deceive many. And ye shall hear of wars and rumours of wars: see that ye be not troubled: for all these things must come to pass, but the end is not yet. For nation ["ethnos"] shall rise against nation ["ethnos"], and kingdom against kingdom" (Matt. 24:5–7).

For years translators have made this passage say "nation . . . against nation," and rightly so except in this case a more literal translation may be called for. The word *nation* literally means a "race," a "tribe," specifically a "foreign (non-Jewish)" one; by implication, a "pagan" one. Since Jesus follows his "ethnos" against "ethnos" with "kingdom against kingdom" which also implies "nations," He would be repeating Himself if the word "nation" were meant. However, as always, we understand the words after they happen. Ethnic battles fill nearly every corner of the globe today. We mention a few: Palestinians versus Israelis; Hindus versus Islamics in western India; Tamils versus Sinhalese of Sri Lanka; Irish Catholics versus Protestants in Ireland;

---

[52] Curiously, Jesus answered their questions in reverse order, first giving the signs of the end of the age (vv. 4–26), then the signs of His coming (vv. 27–31), and finally the time (vv. 32–36).

Kurds versus Turks and Iraqi on their borders; Hindus versus Pakistani people in Kashmir; Serbs versus Albanians; tribal wars in Africa; French Canadians versus English-speaking Canadians. This list is only partial; however, it is enough to prove my point. Ethnic hatreds have given rise to terrorism across the globe.

After civil struggles come physical disasters. Jesus says that great earthquakes, famines, pestilence, fearful sights, and great signs will appear in the heavens.[53] The narrative background of Matthew and Luke repeats the conditions in the first six seals: "But *before all these,* they shall lay their hands on you, and persecute you, delivering you up to the synagogues, and into prisons, being brought before kings and rulers for my name's sake . . . .And some of you shall they cause to be put to death" (Luke 21:12, 16, emphasis added).

The implication of being brought before synagogues denotes a Jewish witness to Jews. Preaching the name of Christ to Orthodox Jews is heresy. We might deduce from this obvious civil power in religious hands that a revival of Judaism has taken place. Since Jesus says that people will seek after religious leaders, Judaism will enjoy increased sway over its adherents even as Islamic leaders enjoy an increase of power today. Indeed, the whole world seems to be more religious. The Jews are no exception; therefore, we should expect to find them defending their faith.

The opportunity to witness to kings and rulers seems to come after imprisonment. This reminds us of Paul's witness—first to his brethren, then to the Gentiles, and after that to kings and rulers—during his imprisonment. These witnesses apparently are scattered all over the world in or-

---

[53] Matt. 24:29.

206

der for the gospel to be preached to all nations as Jesus says. After delivering the message, the whole world stands warned: "For then there will be great tribulation, such as has not been from the beginning of the world until now, no, and never will be" (Matt. 24:21 RSV Taken from The Layman's Parallel Bible). The overturning of the earth is apparently the beginning of "the end" spoken of by Jesus, while everything else up to this point is merely the "beginning of sorrows" (Matt. 24: 6, 8).

The Sealed Company

> And I heard the number of them which were sealed: and there were sealed an hundred and forty and four thousand of all the tribes of the children of Israel. (7:4)

Getting back to the vision, John hears the number of witnesses called forth: 144,000 of all the tribes of Israel—twelve thousand from each tribe. The angel carrying the seal is most likely Israel's Mighty Angel with the earnest of the Holy Spirit to give to these especially called Jews, just like the seal put on Christians from the Church age. Who else but Israel's Mighty Angel can grant them the stamp of God's ownership? Placing the seal in their foreheads contrasts to the name written on the forehead of Babylon—the false witness, the false church—and later copied by the antichrist for his followers (see Rev. 13 and 17).

The sequence of the tribes' sealing differs from the usual order of their birth. Reuben, the firstborn, is sealed second, while Judah, the fourthborn, comes first. The tribe of Dan is omitted, and Manasseh, a son of Joseph, is substituted and appears in sixth position instead of fifth. The reason for this order can be discerned when we look at the meanings of their names as given at the times of their births.[54]

Looking at them in the order given, the ministry, persecution, and ultimate victory of these saints emerge. The first, Judah, means, "Now will I praise the LORD" (Gen. 30:35) and can be interpreted as their recognition of Jesus as their Lord. Perhaps they will be called in the same sudden manner as Paul. One minute they are devoted Jews, but when confronted with the glorious Mighty Angel, they become completed Jews as they lay hold of Jesus, *the* seed of Abraham.

The second, Reuben, means, "The LORD hath looked upon my affliction" (Gen. 30:32). The witnesses begin a personal walk with Christ and run into opposition. The third, Gad, means, "A troop cometh" (Gen. 30:11). Their witness is received by others. The fourth, Asher, means, "Happy am I . . . and blessed" (Gen. 30:13). They experience joy at the results of their ministry. The fifth, Naphtali, means, "With great wrestlings have I wrestled . . . and I have prevailed" (Gen. 30:8). Persecution persists.

The sixth, Manasseh, means, "God . . . hath made me forget all my toil, and all my father's house" (Gen. 41:51). The witnesses will be imprisoned for heresy against the Jews, some even betrayed by their own family and friends.[55] The seventh, Simeon, means, "I was hated" (Gen. 29:33). The world will hate the witnesses because of their stand for Christ's name. The eighth, Levi, means, "Now this time will my husband be joined unto me" (Gen. 29:34). The witnesses will be caught up to join Christ and the Church in heaven. The ninth, Issachar, means, "God hath given me

---

[54] Gen. 29:30–35; 30:6–13, 18–24.
[55] Luke 21:16.

my hire" (Gen. 30:18). The raptured witnesses will be rewarded, as was the Church. The tenth, Zebulun, means, "God hath endued me with a good dowry" (Gen. 30:20). They bring to Christ the righteousness He has developed in them and are clothed in white raiment. The eleventh, Joseph, means, "God hath taken away my reproach" (Gen. 30:23). Their tears are wiped away, and they are lifted up in honor. The twelfth, Benjamin, means, "The son of my right hand" (Gen. 35:18). The witnesses will be awarded positions of authority in the kingdom of God. Dan, the tribe left out, means, "God hath judged me" (Gen. 30:6), a meaning that is out of character with the ministry of these witnesses.

By choosing and sealing these specific tribes in this order, God lets their names signify exactly what they will do. We marvel at the preciseness of the details in God's revelation to us.

The Great Multitude

> After this I beheld, and, lo, a great multitude, which no man could number, of all nations, and kindreds, and people, and tongues, stood before the throne, and before the Lamb, clothed with white robes, and palms in their hands; and cried with a loud voice, saying, Salvation to our God which sitteth upon the throne, and unto the Lamb. (7:9–10)

After the sealing of the witnesses, the scene flashes ahead to show the outcome of their ministry as the setting moves back to heaven. John looks on with amazement at the great multitude from every kindred, nation, people, and language. These are obviously resurrected saints because, clothed in white robes, they wave palm branches triumphantly before the throne. Meanwhile, the gospel has reached all parts of the globe, as their origins declare. The whole world stands guilty and ripe for judgment.

The praise of this multitude differs from any offered so far: "Salvation to our God which sitteth upon the throne, and unto the Lamb" (7:10). As we will see later, the people in this multitude have not had lifetimes to mature as believers. Perhaps the vast majority can be classified as "babes in Christ." They simply thank God for saving them, and they are especially aware of having escaped the great judgment predicted by the witnesses.

> And all the angels stood round about the throne, and about the elders and the four beasts, and fell before the throne on their faces, and worshipped God, saying, Amen: Blessing, and glory, and wisdom, and thanksgiving, and honour, and power, and might, be unto our God for ever and ever. Amen. (7:11–12)

After the great multitude's praise, the angels fall down on their faces to worship God. Breaking forth into praise, they chant it in a seven-fold form of prayer, saying: "Amen [let it be]: Blessing [happiness], and glory [good report], and wisdom [good action], and thanksgiving [gratitude], and honour [elevated position], and power [right to rule], and might [strength], be unto our God for ever and ever. Amen" (7:12). They pray in effect, "Let these things come to God as a result of the great multitude saved through the testimony of the sealed company."

Although this multitude is the result of the Jewish witnesses' ministry, the witnesses themselves are not featured before the throne in this passage. We would naturally expect the sealed company to be resurrected and/or caught up at the same time as their converts because they will have warned the world and gathered this harvest of souls. However, God is making preparations to call a new set of witnesses to testify for Him in the Middle East during the most severe judgments. These sealed Jews have a part in this calling not yet mentioned in our text. Therefore, we will have to wait until Revelation 14 to find out more about this. In that chapter, the vision spotlights *them* before the throne, even though the *time* of the event may be simultaneous with the review of this multitude.

> And one of the elders answered, saying unto me, What are these which are arrayed in white robes? And whence came they? And I said unto him, Sir, thou knowest. And he said to me, These are they which came out of great tribulation, and have washed their robes, and made them white in the blood of the Lamb. Therefore are they before the throne of God, and serve him day and night in his temple: and he that sitteth on the throne shall dwell among them. They shall hunger no more, neither thirst any more; neither shall the sun light on them, nor any heat. For the Lamb which is in the midst of the throne shall feed them, and shall lead them unto living fountains of waters: and God shall wipe away all tears from their eyes. (7:13–17)

When an elder asks John to identify this group, he replies, "Sir, you know." The elder then explains that these people have come out of great tribulation,[56] have washed

---

[56] This is not what is commonly known as the "Great Tribulation," taken from Matthew 24. See chapter 17.

their robes, and "made them white in the blood of the Lamb" (7:14). It appears then that most of their righteousness is appropriated, not earned as with the Church. Therefore, they will learn to worship in the temple in heaven, where they will be led and fed by Christ and will grow further in understanding.[57]

With the parenthetical part of our picture puzzle filled in, we are ready to watch Jesus remove the last seal. Then the document will unroll and expose the front side of the scroll. Up until this time, only the outside of the scroll has been visible. It is time to look inside.

[57] Rev. 7:17.

Chapter 14

THE OPEN SCROLL

(Revelation 8)

> And when he had opened the seventh seal, there was silence in heaven about the apace of half an hour. (8:1)

Finally, the Lamb opens the seventh seal. Instead of coming events being previewed as before, a dead silence falls over the scene. John estimates the silence to last for half an hour. The book has been fully unrolled, and the judgments are laid out in order; yet the prosecution rests.

Why? Perhaps some will repent after the awful destruction of the overturning. More likely, Jesus will visit the earth to proclaim his title to it, now that the official seals have been broken. Revelation 10 shows this. If the latter is the case, it explains why the courtroom is silent. The prosecutor is absent.

During this break in the action at the throne, let us look at other prophetic scriptures that pertain to what has happened so far. Peter, preaching to the crowd of Jews in the temple when he healed the lame man, says that Christ will remain in heaven until the restitution of all things, "which God hath spoken by the mouth of *all his holy prophets* since the world began" (Acts 3:21, emphasis added). This means that besides speaking to Israel's problems current to their own time, the prophets also tell about things concerning Jesus' return.

We mentioned earlier that the prophetic picture is like a puzzle. John's vision provides a sequence of events and structure. Like the edge of a puzzle, it defines the picture. Many other pieces interlock with the edges and fill in the middle. When we place one piece of a puzzle to its matching piece, they complement each other in the whole picture. However, they are exactly alike at their matching edges. The same is true of a prophetic puzzle. Pieces join when they touch the same incident in the sequence of events. For instance, take the "overturning." Isaiah speaks about it with almost the same wording as John, yet he gives different details. By this we can place Isaiah's whole prophecy into the sequence in Revelation. Look at the following verse:

And all the host of heaven shall be dissolved, and the heavens shall be rolled together as a scroll: and all their hosts shall fall down, as the leaf falleth off from the vine, and as a falling fig from the fig tree. (Isa. 34:4)

According to this verse, the heavens break up, then roll together like a scroll, and their hosts (space debris) fall to the earth like figs. This sounds like the same situation described in Revelation. This verse, however, belongs in the middle of a battle, revealing more of the political history of this time. Isaiah 34 describes a time when the indignation of the Lord is against *all* nations and their armies. At the end of the prophecy, Isaiah gives what I believe is the key to linking the scattered pieces of the end-time puzzle together. He says:

> Seek ye out of the book of the LORD, and *read*: no one of these shall fail, none shall want her mate: for *my mouth* it hath commanded, and *his spirit* it hath gathered them. (Isa. 34:16, emphasis added)

This verse almost seems out of context because it falls in the midst of a description of birds of prey being given an inheritance where they can live with their mates. It would make no sense at all to search the "book of the Lord" to find a mate for a bird! However, it does make sense to see the fourth verse quoted above as a mated verse that links to the one in Revelation. Here we must search the Word to find the mate. Actually, there are two more mated verses in this same prophecy that link to other prophecys. Therefore, by searching the Scriptures for these "mated" verses, we can piece the whole puzzle together through the guidance of the Holy Spirit. By studying the relationship of these prophetic links, we find what may be the center of the picture. By this, we mean an event that divides the "things which shall be hereafter" into two-part sections:

The first half lines up with the "beginning of sorrows," spoken of by Jesus in the Olivet Discourse, and ends with the overturning. The second half begins with the opened scroll and ends at the return of Christ to the earth with His saints. Since the passage in Isaiah ends the first section of the prophetic time and makes way for the second, we see it as central. Being central, this piece joins many other pieces. As one might imagine, an event as important and divisive as this would be shown in its different aspects in several major prophecies. Besides John's vision and Isaiah, both Joel and Ezekiel give prominence to this central event. The event: the Russian invasion of Israel.

Pieces Central to the Puzzle: The Russian Invasion

The Russian invasion of Israel, being a major event in the prophetic picture, must be placed in its proper sequence. Various opinions have been put forth. Naturally, placing it incorrectly would change the interpretation. That is why the prophecy in Isaiah 34 is so crucial. It shows a direct link with Revelation 6, placing it in the order of events.

This passage also links with Ezekiel 38 and 39, which many Bible students recognize as being the Russian invasion of the Middle East. The prophet Joel, who prophesied about two invasions—that of the Russians and later of many nations at the Battle of Armageddon—rounds out the prophecies in Ezekiel and Isaiah. Thus, by mating verses, the event is placed without a strain to the interpretation.

We will attempt to outline these links for the reader. Understand, however, that other books have established the interpretations of Ezekiel 38 and 39. Most Bible scholars accept them. Because of this, we put forth the emphasis on the natural catastrophe connected with it rather than the political.

First, we look at the verse in Isaiah 34 that mates with the verse concerning the overturning in Revelation 6:14 where the heavens appear to roll up like a scroll.

Come near, ye nations, to hear; and hearken, ye people:
let the earth hear, and all that is therein; the world, and
all things that come forth of it. For the indignation of
the LORD is upon all nations, and his fury upon all their
armies: he hath utterly destroyed them, he hath delivered them to the slaughter. Their slain also shall be cast
out, and their stink shall come up out of their carcases,
and the mountains shall be melted with their blood. *And
all the host of heaven shall be dissolved, and the heavens
shall be rolled together as a scroll: and all their host shall
fall down, as the leaf falleth off from the vine, and as a fig
falling from the fig tree.* For my sword shall be bathed in
heaven: behold, it shall come down upon Idumea, and
upon the people of my curse, to judgment. The sword
of the LORD is filled with blood, it is made fat with fatness, and with the blood of lambs and goats, with the fat
of the kidneys of rams: for the LORD has a sacrifice in
Bozrah, and a great slaughter in the land of Idumea. (Isa.
34:1–6, emphasis added)

Reading it in context, we see the events of Revelation 6
with added detail. We learn that when the earth overturns
and the sky rolls out of sight in a blur, the destruction that
accompanies it falls on a great battle. Most likely, this is the
last battle of the war which was started between the red
horseman and the white horseman in the second seal. It
seems that now all nations are involved (see v. 2).

The final phase of this war appears to be in the Middle
East, because verse 6 in our prophecy tells us that the
"sword of the Lord" will effect a great slaughter in
Idumea. This was a section of land in the southern plateau of Israel that the Edomites annexed when Babylon

carried Israel into captivity.[58] This great slaughter on the mountains southeast of Jerusalem, described more fully in the ensuing verses of this prophecy (Isa. 34:8–17), turns into a sacrifice benefiting unclean birds gathered with their mates. The Lord makes such a complete devastation of the area during the overturning that it becomes a living picture of hell.

> And the streams thereof shall be turned into pitch, and the dust thereof into brimstone, and the land thereof shall become burning pitch. It shall not be quenched night nor day; the smoke thereof shall go up for ever: from generation to generation it shall lie waste; none shall pass through it for ever and ever. But the cormorant and the bittern shall possess it; the owl also and the raven shall dwell in it. (Isa. 34:9–11)

Rivers of pitch feed everlasting flames. The atmosphere reeks with the searing stench of brimstone (burning sulfur). In the smoke-filled darkness, unclean birds fly, making a parallel to the unclean spirits of hell. These extract pleasures from the remains of men, as do the literal birds who gather to consume the fallen army.

Not only does verse 4 interlock with Revelation 6, but also verse 8 confirms this as the time of the sixth seal, the great day of God's wrath: "For it is the day of the LORD's vengeance, and the year of recompenses for the controversy of Zion" (Isa. 34:8).

So at the opening of the sixth seal, apparently the dissolving of the heavens rains destruction on the armies invading Israel. The squabbling of the nations over Zion is

---

[58] Ezek. 36:5.

the reason for God's direct intervention in the final battle of the war. He overturns the earth at this time, creating a surface hell in the area of the battlefield. Princes and common men alike fall side by side as the invading army is reduced. Ezekiel describes the invaders:

> And I will turn thee back, and [leave but the sixth part of thee],[59] and will cause thee to come up from the north parts, and will bring thee upon the mountains of Israel: and I will smite thy bow out of thy left hand, and will cause thine arrows to fall out of thy right hand. Thou shalt fall upon the mountains of Israel, thou, and all thy bands, and the people that is with thee: I will give thee unto the ravenous birds of every sort, and to the beasts of the field to be devoured. (Ezek. 39:2–4)

Are the weapons of this army reduced to those of the past because the havoc already caused by using modern weaponry made them too dangerous to the world? Or is God merely speaking metaphorically, using the common weapons of their day? Then again, it could be possible that the armies have simply run out of gasoline and can no longer use engine-powered might. Later, we learn that this is an army of horsemen (Ezek. 38:4).

If our assessment is correct about this piece of the puzzle, other verses will mate back to Isaiah as well. Let us trace the outline of sections of Isaiah and Ezekiel to see how they match. To confirm the identification of the invading army, look again at Isaiah 34:

---

[59] Other translations differ. The Holy Scriptures, Translated from the Original Languages, by J. N. Darby, indicates it is an uncertain word. He translates it "lead thee" NAS translates it "drive you."

And all the host of heaven shall be dissolved, and the heavens shall be rolled together as a scroll: and all their host shall fall down, as the leaf falleth off from the vine, and as a falling fig from the fig tree. For *my sword* shall be bathed in heaven: behold, it shall come down upon Idumea, and upon the people of my curse, to judgment. (Isa. 34:4–5, emphasis added)

And now in Ezekiel:

And I will call for a *sword* against him throughout all my mountains, saith the Lord God: every man's sword shall be against his brother. And I will plead against him with pestilence and with blood; and I will rain upon him, and upon his bands, and upon the many people that are with him, an overflowing rain, and great hailstones, fire, and brimstone. (Ezek. 38:21–22, emphasis added)

Both these scriptures describe the falling of meteors. Both describe a heavenly sword, which provokes men to use swords against their fellow soldiers. In these scriptures, the sword comes to kill the sacrifice of the Lord (Isa. 34:6). The expression "bathed in heaven" (Isa. 34:5) may refer to the appearance of a heavenly body that becomes the "sword" involved in this great slaughter. According to tradition, such an attack from heaven occurred in Isaiah's day. Velikovsky says the planet Mars took on the appearance of a sword when God destroyed Sennacherib's army during the siege of Jerusalem.[60] Isaiah had predicted it earlier:

---

[60] Immanuel Velikovsky, *Worlds in Collision* (New York: Doubleday, 1950), p. 261.

Then shall the Assyrian fall by the sword, not of a mighty man; and the sword, not of a mean man, shall devour him: but he shall flee from the sword, and his young men shall be discomfited. And he shall pass over his strong hold for fear, and his princes shall be afraid of the *ensign* [the sword in the heavens], saith the LORD, whose fire is in Zion, and his furnace in Jerusalem. (Isa. 31:8–9, emphasis added)

Sennacherib's army would not be afraid of an ordinary sword. They were soldiers after all. It was the supernatural "sword" that caused their panic. In addition, the Babylonians of the eighth century prayed to Mars, who was the great sword god.[61] Therefore, it seems that the "sword of the Lord" could be a shape seen in the heavens. It comes to make a sacrifice.

The sword of the LORD is filled with blood, it is made fat with fatness, and with the blood of *lambs* and *goats*, with the fat of the kidneys of *rams*: for the LORD hath a sacrifice in Bozrah, and a great slaughter in the land of Idumea. And the unicorns shall come down with them, and the *bullocks* with the bulls; and their land shall be soaked with blood, and their dust made fat with fatness. (Isa. 34:6–7, emphasis added)

Now back to corresponding verses in Ezekiel:

And, thou son of man, thus saith the Lord God; Speak unto every feathered fowl, and to every beast of the field,

---

[61] Ibid, p. 262.

Assemble yourselves, and come; gather yourselves on every side to my sacrifice that I do sacrifice for you, even a great sacrifice upon the mountains of Israel, that ye may eat flesh, and drink blood. Ye shall eat the flesh of the mighty, and drink the blood of the princes of the earth, of *rams*, of *lambs*, and of *goats*, of *bullocks*, all of them fatlings of Bashan. (Ezek. 39:17–18, emphasis added)

Here we see the same rams, lambs, goats, and bullocks, the same blood, and the same sword, even the same location—the mountains of Israel. The sacrifice in both Ezekiel and Isaiah appear to be the same. During the sacrifice, "every man's sword shall be against his brother" (Ezek. 38:21) where, in the confusion of the heavens raining hailstones, fire, and brimstone, the army will finish itself off.

Scripture identifies this northern army earlier in Ezekiel's prophecy as the army of Gog from the land of Meshech and Tubal (Ezek. 38:2). The mainline teachers of prophecy have traced these ancient races to their present-day descendants in Russia.[62]

The next thing we want to examine is the reason God allows this invasion of the Middle East.

So will I make my name *known* in the midst of my people Israel; and I will not let them pollute my holy name any more: and the heathen shall know that I am the LORD, the Holy One in Israel. Behold, it is come, and it is done, saith the Lord God; this is the day whereof I have spoken . . . .And I will set my glory among the heathen, and

---

[62] One of the best descriptions of this prophecy is found in J. Dwight Pentecost, *Things to Come* (Findlay, Ohio: Dunham, 1958), p. 326.

all the heathen shall see my judgment which I have executed, and my hand that I have laid upon them. So the house of Israel shall *know* that I am the LORD their God from *that day and forward* . . . .Neither will I hide my face any more from them: for *I have poured out my spirit upon the house of Israel*, saith the Lord God. (Ezek. 39:7–8, 21–22, 29, emphasis added)

The time has come for God to call His own nation back to Himself—to call national Israel, not just a few selected Jews. As Isaiah put it: "For it is the day of the LORD's vengeance, and the year of recompenses for the controversy of Zion" (Isa. 34:8). Ezekiel speaks of Gog provoking God's wrath against the nations.

And it shall come to pass at the same time when Gog shall come against the land of Israel, saith the Lord God, that my fury shall come up in my face. For in my jealousy and in the fire of my wrath have I spoken, Surely in that day there shall be a great shaking [earthquake] in the land of Israel. (Ezek. 38:18–19)

Because of God's great jealousy, there is a "great shaking" in Israel. In fact, the prophet Joel describes the reason for the jealousy.

Then will the LORD be jealous for his land, and pity his people. Yea, the LORD will answer and say unto his people, Behold, I send you corn, and wine, and oil [and the festivals that go with them], and ye shall be satisfied therewith: and I will no more make you a reproach among the heathen: But I will remove far off from you the northern army, and will drive him into a land barren and desolate, with his face toward the east sea, and his hinder part toward the utmost sea [the area of Idumea], and his stink shall come up, and his ill savour shall come up, because he hath done great things. (Joel 2:18–20)

In His great jealousy, God drives off the "northern army." It is the same Russian army whose stink comes up to "stop the noses" in Ezekiel's prophecy (39:11). Joel mentions the outpouring as well:

And ye shall know that I am in the midst of Israel, and that I am the LORD your God, and none else: and my people shall never be ashamed. And it shall come to pass afterward,[63] that I will pour out my spirit upon all flesh; and your sons and your daughters shall prophesy, your old men shall dream dreams, and your young men shall see visions: And also upon the servants and upon the handmaids in those days will I pour out my spirit. And I will shew wonders in the heavens and in the earth, blood, and fire, and pillars of smoke [volcanoes]. The sun shall be turned into darkness, and the moon into blood, *before* the great and terrible day of the LORD come. And it shall come to pass, that whosoever shall call on the name of the LORD shall be delivered: . . . as the LORD hath said, and in the remnant whom the LORD shall call. (Joel 2:27–32, emphasis added)

This outpouring of God's Spirit evidently will happen before the army overtakes the land, prior also to the physical destruction of the overturning. It may happen even as

---

[63] After they know that God is in their midst.

far back as the fifth seal, since the signs in the sun and moon appear in the sixth seal. Ezekiel speaks of it in the past tense after the destruction is over.

One more prophecy belongs to this section of the puzzle. Looking now at Jesus' Olivet Discourse, we find that, although Israel has received an outpouring of the Holy Spirit, her troubles are only beginning.

> And when ye shall see Jerusalem compassed with armies, then know that desolation thereof is nigh. Then let them which are in Judea flee to the mountains; and let them which are in the midst of it depart out; and let not them that are in the countries enter thereinto. For these be the days of vengeance, that all things which are written may be fulfilled. And they shall fall by the edge of the sword, and shall be led away captive into all nations: and Jerusalem shall be trodden down of the Gentiles, until the times of the Gentiles be fulfilled. (Luke 21:20–22, 24)

Jerusalem will not be a safe place when the great earthquake hits. The Lord warns His people to flee. When they see the armies gather for battle, it is a sign to flee from the city and from the surrounding countryside.

Political problems will multiply for the nation of Israel at this time also. Although God will defeat the Russian army, later other political figures will step in to claim the victory. Farther on in the vision, we will learn that the Palestinians, perhaps along with the armies of Jordan, Syria, Lebanon, Egypt, and United Europe, had been allied with Israel in this war. The Arabs have been waiting for an excuse to re-take Israel. The Israeli–Arab coalition remains in control of Jerusalem after the war. We will see when we take up the power structure of this coalition that Israel eventually loses control and therefore comes under Gentile rule once more.

We have looked at pieces of our picture puzzle that form the center from the prophets. Later, these will join to the fuller description of the religious and political drama appearing in Revelation 11, 12, and 13. For now, with the background of the central pieces filled in, we see a more complete picture of the devastation, both of the battlefield and of the earth as a whole. Heaven waits in hushed silence to see what the seventh seal will bring.

The Mighty Angel Begins Prosecution

And I saw the seven *angels which stood before God*; and to them were given seven trumpets. And another angel came and stood at the altar, having a golden censer; and there was given unto him much incense, that he should offer it with the prayers of all saints upon the golden altar which was before the throne. And the smoke of the incense, which came with the prayers of the saints, ascended up before God out of the angel's hand. (Rev. 8:2–4 emphasis added)

Thirty minutes of silence ends as action at the throne resumes. John watches as the seven angels who stand before the throne receive seven trumpets.

Another Angel stands at the altar of incense with a golden censor in His hands. Since this is a priestly act, we suspect that He is the Mighty Angel acting as the High Priest of redeemed Israel. Out of His censor ascends smoke to which the Angel adds the prayers of saints.

Before we go on with the narrative, let us pause to look more closely at the angels who receive the trumpets. Since the Angel offering the incense must almost certainly be the Lord Jesus in His role as Priest after the order of Melchisedec, perhaps the term *angels* here may refer to messengers rather than beings of heavenly origin. In this passage, even Jesus is called a messenger. Later, we will see that the Mighty Angel has just returned from taking possession of the earth (the reason for the thirty-minute silence at the throne). Now He resumes the action. The seven angels are each to deliver a message. That makes them messengers. They are to sound out the instructions written in the book. Besides giving their role, John tells us that these are the seven angels ("messengers") *that stood before God* (see Rev. 8:2 above). We remember that the reward for the Philadelphian overcomers was to become pillars who stand as truth in the temple of God (see 3:12). The messengers above sound forth the truth of the judgments. Can it be that the Church is already assuming some responsibility with Christ over the earth? We will raise this question again later in the vision, but for now we return to the narrative.

Filled with worship and thanksgiving, the prayers of the earth's saints ascend out of the Angel's hand. They glorify the Lord, first, for their redemption and second, for the destruction of the Russian army, which reveals that the God of Moses is with Israel once again. Recall Ezekiel's prophecy: "So the house of Israel shall know that I am the LORD their God from that day and forward" (Ezek. 39:22). Israel's petitioning for justice against her enemies will be heard since she now has the Mighty Angel to avenge her.

> And the angel took the censer, and filled it with fire of
> the altar, and cast it into the earth: and there were voices,
> and thunderings, and lightnings, and an earthquake. And

the seven angels which had the seven trumpets prepared themselves to sound. (8:5–6)

In response, the Angel casts fire off the altar toward the earth. Voices, thunderings and lightnings proceed from the throne. God the Father responds to the prayers for vengeance. This results in another earthquake. In heaven, the messengers under the Lord's command prepare to announce the forthcoming action by sounding their trumpets.

In this section on the trumpets, we will see only the actions described on the front of the scroll just opened. They announce the details. The actions will be carried out later. On the scroll are written the judgments of God led by His priestly Angel, known also as Captain of the Lord's hosts or the Lion of Judah. These judgments are inscribed on the front of the scroll, which are for the offences of men against men. They compliment the greater judgments written on the back of the scroll, which are for the offenses against God the Father, which we will see later in the vision. The interface of the two will be mentioned only briefly in the next section on the trumpets. As we said before, the trumpet blasts are only the announcements of the plagues. Nevertheless, God takes this opportunity to explain what will be involved.

The First Trumpet

The first angel sounded, and there followed hail and fire mingled with blood, and they were cast upon the earth: and the third part of trees was burnt up, and all green grass was burnt up. (8:7)

The first angel sounds his trumpet to describe the first plague. The hail mentioned here is from the Greek word *chalaza*[64] that means to "let loose" or "let fall," used always in the New Testament as "an instrument of divine judgment." The corresponding word for hail in the Hebrew is *barad*, used by the prophets and Moses. According to Jewish sources, *barad* means "meteorite" more often than "ice." I read in *Discover* magazine that meteors (even as small as grapes) slam into the earth's atmosphere at the speed of 37 miles per second. Imagine the force of a meteorite making it all the way to the earth's surface!

Immanuel Velikovsky, referring to the Midrashic and Talmudic writings, says that the hail that fell on Egypt was hot.[65] This explains how hail can be mingled with fire. The plagues of Egypt were very similar to this time. In fact, the prophet Micah says it will be like the coming out from Egypt:

> According to the days of thy coming out of the land of Egypt will I shew unto him marvellous things. The nations shall see and be confounded at all their might: they shall lay their hand upon their mouth, their ears shall be deaf. They shall lick the dust like a serpent, they shall move out of their holes like worms of the earth: they shall be afraid of the LORD our God, and shall fear because of thee [Israel]. (Mic. 7:15–17)

These marvelous things God will show have more might than what the nations have. All their nuclear weaponry will appear puny by comparison. Nuclear attacks aim at certain

[64] W. E. Vine, *An Expository Dictionary of New Testament Words* (London: Oliphants, 1953), p. 188.

[65] Velikovsky, *Worlds in Collision*, (New York: Doubleday, 1950) p. 51.

locations, whereas meteorites rain universally. People will crawl into caves and dens like worms, seeking protection.

The dust they will lick is the "blood" that will fall along with the hail and fire ordered by the trumpet. Velikovsky, writing about the catastrophe that accompanied the exodus from Egypt, describes this dust.

> A celestial body that only shortly before had become a member of the solar system—a new comet—came very close to the earth. The account of this catastrophe can be reconstructed from evidence supplied by a large number of documents. The comet was on its way from its perihelion and touched the earth first with its gaseous tail . . . .It was about this comet that Servius wrote: "Non igneo sed sanquineo rubore fuisse" (It was not of flaming but bloody redness). One of the first visible signs of this encounter was the reddening of the earth's surface by a fine dust of rusty pigment. In sea, lake and river, this pigment gave a bloody coloring to the water. Because of these particles of ferruginous or other soluble pigment, the world turned red.[66]

Reconstructing the events of the sixth seal in light of this information, we now understand how the moon can be turned to blood. Evidently, a comet, similar to what appeared during the exodus, will be turned loose some time before the sixth seal. The moon will enter the tail of the comet first as it approaches the earth. Its approach will eclipse the sun.

---

[66] Ibid, p. 48.

Then there must be an electrical[67] exchange between the earth and the approaching body that reverses the magnetic and geographic poles,[68] causing the earth to turn upside down. The earthquake of the seventh seal indicates that the earth will still be in the grip of this body. Even at the time of the battle, the earth will pass through part of the tail. Ezekiel says the invading army will be rained on "with blood and . . . an overflowing rain, and great hailstones, fire, and brimstone" (Ezek. 38:22).

The earth will move at a closer range during the first trumpet, receiving larger chunks of the comet's tail. Great meteorites will fall and destroy one-third of the earth's trees, i.e., those that remain from the overturning.

Velikovsky tells about the time of the exodus when hail or meteorites fell. He says they exploded with deafening noise, and fire ran along the ground, but the people were more frightened of the noise than the hail.[69] The terrible noise will affect the victims of this trumpet judgment, also. Micah tells us "their ears shall be deaf" (Mic. 7:16). Ezekiel mentions the fire rain that will fall with the exploding meteorites on the army of the north.

Velikovsky maintains that crude petroleum formed in the atmosphere when hydrogen and carbon gases of the comet's tail mingled with oxygen of the earth's atmosphere,

---

[67] Zeus/Jupiter was known to the ancients for his ability to hurl thunderbolts of lightning. Velikovsky ascribes the same power to comets at close range. *Worlds in Collision*, pp. 172–73.

[68] Then there must be an electrical exchange between the earth and the approaching body that reverses the magnetic and geographic pole. Immanuel Velikovsky, *Earth in Upheaval* (New York: Doubleday, 1955), p. 146.

[69] Velikovsky, *Worlds in Collision*, (New York: Doubleday, 1950) pp. 53–54.

and it became a rain of fire. He says, "If carbon and hydrogen gases, or a vapor of a composition of these two, enter the atmosphere in huge masses, a part of them will burn, binding all the oxygen available at the moment; the rest will escape combustion, but in swift transition will become liquid" and fall like rain. He tells of accounts around the world that speak of whole populations being destroyed in this sticky rain that burned with a black smoke. Even green grass will burn with such fuel upon it.[70]

Therefore the destruction of the first trumpet causes a rain of "blood," (red dust), hail and fire upon the earth. We wonder how people can survive such destruction. Yet we know they do from the scriptures that deal with political and religious events. Even so, the population will shrink with each advancing judgment.

The Second Trumpet

> And the second angel sounded, and as it were a great mountain burning with fire was cast into the sea: and the third part of the sea became blood; and the third part of the creatures which were in the sea, and had life, died; and the third part of the ships were destroyed. (8:8–9)

A second trumpet sounds. But this time, instead of exploding hailstones falling, a chunk of the comet's tail, its size like "a great mountain burning with fire," is cast into the sea. We presume this sea is the Mediterranean, since this was the larger sea of the geography known to John. As

---

[70] The "fatness" of the sword of the Lord is probably this same crude oil. Just as animal fat fueled the fires of animal sacrifices, so crude oil may very well fuel the burning of the invading army.

a result, "a third part of the sea [becomes] blood." The water will turn bloody red. Dusty pigment from the mountainous chunk not only colors the water red but it also poisons it.

Therefore, John records, "the third part of the creatures that were in the sea, and had life, died." The tidal wave created from such a large displacement of water destroys a third of all ships, probably dumping them on the shorelines. Damage along the coast adds to the destruction.

Scientists discussing the tremendous explosion that leveled several dozen square miles of Siberian forest in 1908 guessed the width of the falling object to be 1,500 feet, much smaller than a mountain. Yet falling at 25,000 mph could convert its energy into widespread destruction. One of these scientists, an astronomer at Fernbank Science Center in Atlanta, Georgia, Dr. Richard Williamon, commented that if such an object plunged into the ocean, it would cause a tidal wave that would inundate some coastal cities. Imagine what an object the size of a mountain could do!

The Third Trumpet

> And the third angel sounded, and there fell a great star from heaven, burning as it were a lamp, and it fell upon a third part of the rivers, and upon the fountains of water; and the name of the star is called Wormwood: and the third part of the waters became wormwood; and many men died of the waters, because they were made bitter. (8:10–11)

As the third angel sounds, the earth begins to cross the center of the comet's tail, where a piece breaking off the main head is larger than a mountain. This piece, called a star, we would more likely call a small asteroid. The falling star glows like a burning lamp whose blue-white incandescence increases as friction from falling through the earth's atmosphere heats it hotter and hotter. The friction builds until it reaches its peak, whereupon the whole body explodes, spraying an elliptical pattern of debris. Apparently, this is what astronomers call a detonating meteor.

> On November 15, 1859, a meteor of this class passed over New Jersey; it was visible in the full sunlight and was followed by a series of terrific explosions, which were compared to the discharge of a thousand cannons. Other meteors are so large that they reach the earth before complete evaporation takes place, and we get what is called a fall of meteoric irons or meteoric stones, often accompanied by loud explosions.[71]

The author of this quote, the then director of a solar physics observatory, goes on to say that, in the largest of these falls, the elliptical ground pattern was eighteen miles long by five miles wide. This should give us some idea of the "greatness" of the falling star John sees. A meteor that is capable of spraying meteoric iron over one-third of the earth's rivers might be several miles in diameter.

The star is named "wormwood" because it turns the waters bitter. Many men died after drinking the contaminated waters. Not even spring water would be safe. Surface water, dissolving the soluble mineral dust and carrying it down from above, would emerge in the springs. Later in the vision, we

---

[71] Sir Norman Lockyer, KCB, *Elementary Lessons in Astronomy*, (London: Macmillan and Co., Limited, 1909) p. 180

will learn which third of the earth receives this galling spray. We remember that though these announcements tell of judgments written in the order in which they will occur, they will not follow one another immediately. Therefore an indeterminate amount of time passes between their actual happenings. The messengers proclaim before the throne exactly what the scroll decrees. The Two Witnesses relay them to the beast's kingdom. This will become more clear when we see the political figures who play against this background of physical events on the earth. I say this at this point because the "wormwood" factor in the star is a strict response to idolatry as spoken of by Jeremiah (9:13–15).

The Fourth Trumpet

> And the fourth angel sounded, and the third part of the sun was smitten, and the third part of the moon, and the third part of the stars; so as the third part of them was darkened, and the day shone not for a third part of it, and the night likewise. And I beheld, and heard an angel flying through the midst of heaven, saying with a loud voice, Woe, woe, woe, to the inhabiters of the earth by reason of the other voices of the trumpet of the three angels, which are yet to sound! (8:12–13)

The fourth angel sounds his trumpet and a strange thing happens. The light received from the sun, moon, and stars shining on the earth diminishes by one-third. It is not that the bodies will give any less light, but the earth will receive less because time will change. Both day and night will be shortened by one-third. This means that the earth will turn on its axis in sixteen hours instead of twenty-four.

Recently, astronomer Darren Williams and his colleges at Pennsylvania State University in studying the various orbits of the earth and their corresponding temperate bands, explored the problems the earth should have if it changed to an elliptical orbit. (The present orbit is near circular.) Following Kepler's physical laws they determined that when the earth approached nearest to the sun it would greatly accelerate. During that time it would also be subjected to great heat, but life would be able to endure it because of the oceans ability to absorb the heat. That in turn would allow life to survive when farthest from the sun for then the oceans would release their heat.[72]

The exploding star of the preceding trumpet has hit one-third of the earth's surface broadside, and the impact may increase the earth's speed of rotation or even push it into an elliptical orbit. But whatever the cause of the shortening of the day, it protects the elect of God. Jesus says: "And except those days should be shortened, there should no flesh be saved: but for the elect's sake those days shall be shortened"[73] (Matt. 24:22). When taken literally, these words attest to some sort of tremendous change in the natural pattern of time.

Velikovsky says this has happened before. In relating folklore of primitive people, he states:

The traditions of many primitive races speak of a "lower sky" in the past, "a larger sun," a swifter movement of

---

[72] Weed, William Speed "Circles of Life" Discovery Magazine, November 2002, p. 44

[73] The number of days cannot be changed because they are specifically numbered—the last half of the week = 1290 days.

the sun across the firmament, a shorter day that became longer after the sun was arrested on its path.[74]

The ancient peoples kept records of the heavenly bodies because they affected their daily lives. The lower sky may be a description of a closer (larger) sun. The swifter movement could indicate a faster rotation, making the sun appear to travel its course swiftly. The ancient people were concerned with the winter and summer solstices because by this means, they determined if the solar system (especially the sun) were running on schedule. If not it sometimes meant catastrophic events could be expected or, at the least, bizarre weather patterns. These affected their daily lives and crops and often became the basis for religious activity.

Apparently, after the fourth trumpet, the normal laws of physics that govern the earth's rotation will be superceded by the unusual circumstances of the judgments. The earth will also receive great heat from the sun (see Rev. 16:8–9). Nevertheless, because the earth turns faster, it provides less exposure to the heat before nightfall, thus protecting life. This accompanying disaster of burning heat will be discussed when we examine the back side of the scroll and the vials of wrath. The trumpet judgments, as we mentioned at the beginning of this section, are not the fullness of God's wrath but only the initiating forces. The vial judgments on the back of the scroll develop to the fullest the destruction begun on the front.

Next, an angel flies through the middle heaven (where the stars are), announcing a division in the judgments. The last three trumpet disasters will be so much greater in terror

---

[74] Velikovsky, Immanuel *Worlds in Collision*, (New York:: Doubleday, 1950) p. 187.

compared to the former four that the angel calls them "woes." The worst is yet to come!

Chapter 15

WOE UPON WOE

(REVELATION 9)

The Fifth Trumpet

The fifth angel sounds. John shudders as he tries to imagine what new tragedy could be worse than what he has already seen. But the angel had promised woes, and the first woe is on its way. John records with horror:

> And the fifth angel sounded, and I saw a star fall from heaven unto the earth: and to him was given the key of the bottomless pit. And he opened the bottomless pit; and there arose a smoke out of the pit, as the smoke of a great furnace; and the sun *and the air were darkened* by reason of the smoke of the pit. And there came out of the smoke locusts upon the earth: and unto them was

given power, as the scorpions of the earth have power. And it was commanded them that they should not hurt the grass of the earth, neither any green thing, neither any tree; but only those men which have not the seal of God in their foreheads. And to them it was given that they should not kill them, but that they should be tormented five months: and their torment was as the torment of a scorpion, when he striketh a man. And in those days shall men seek death, and shall not find it; and shall desire to die, and death shall flee from them. (9:1–6, emphasis added)

This judgment seems to have a spiritual fulfillment. Even literal expositors differ on the interpretation because the star is personalized: "to *him* was given the key," and "*he* opened the bottomless pit" (9:1). Some believe the star signifies an angel or perhaps Satan himself rather than a literal heavenly body.

The bottomless pit (like quicksand) or abyss, as some translators put it, is traditionally believed to be the prison of the most wicked spirits (Jude 6). Then, too, a spiritual interpretation seems confirmed at the end of the passage where the king over the locusts is said to be an evil angel called Abaddon or Apollyon (v. 11). The star, opening the way for hoards of extremely perverse spirits to rise into the upper world, would plunge civilization into great spiritual darkness. We tend to agree. All this does indeed show spiritual circumstances.

We also believe, however, that the judgment is literal as well. We think both the literal and spiritual interpretations go hand in hand. In fact, we believe a law of double meaning can be applied to many descriptive passages in Revelation. The spiritual meaning has been applied in the past, but the literal meaning has often been ignored. Understanding the literal circumstances seems to be the *missed message* of Revelation. So looking at this judgment in the literal sense, let us consider what happens to the earth.

The falling star—a meteor or perhaps an asteroid—collides with the earth. Asteroids are irregular chunks of rock believed to be remnants of an ancient exploded planet that orbits the sun between Mars and Jupiter. In this case, it more likely is a component of the body tangling with the earth. In the disruption of the heavenly order, an astral chunk several miles in diameter could be sent on a collision course with the earth.

Whatever it is, the body that invades the earth's space does not detonate in the air, as the former "star." Instead, this star receives a "key" to the bottomless pit, giving it the ability to penetrate the crust by creating an opening. Therefore, it plunges through the rigid crust of the earth into the soft (bottomless) interior.

Any body colliding with the earth with enough force to push its way through twenty-eight or more miles of crust would also cause dire side effects. The worldwide earthquake that resulted from the overturning of the earth in the sixth seal has probably weakened the fault system of the earth, especially the divisions between the tectonic plates.[75] The fallen star now adds more stress. Of course, the amount of energy expended depends upon the mass and speed of the star. The addition of the star's mass to the earth sends forth shock waves of energy from the point of entry. The displacement would cause waves similar to those sent out

---

[75] Tectonic plates are large sections of the earth's crust that float upon the semifluid interior and fit together somewhat like pieces of a jigsaw puzzle.

when a stone is thrown into a pool of water. This energy would express itself ultimately by cracking and forcing open divisions between continental plates, forcing lava to pour through the openings to the earth's surface. The surface of the earth would darken in the smoke. New volcanoes would erupt to relieve inner pressure along the fissures. Sending up plumes of ash and black smoke, pouring out hot molten rock, they would set forests aflame and boil the ocean water.

In this scenario the whole earth appears to be on fire. What is visible takes on a primordial look not unlike Genesis 1:2: "And the earth was without form, and void; and darkness was upon the face of the deep." Jeremiah saw it, too.

> I beheld the earth, and, lo, it was without form, and void; and the heavens, and they had no light. I beheld the mountains, and, lo, they trembled, and all the hills moved lightly. I beheld, and, lo, there was no man, and all the birds of the heavens were fled. (Jer. 4:23–25)

A stupendous volcano forms over the star's point of entry. Thick, black smoke and basaltic ash, combined with the dust of the collision, boil miles high up into space like a gigantic smelting furnace. Other volcanoes around the globe contribute their share of gloom to the atmosphere and plunge the world into a "shadow of death" so thick it can be felt and tasted. People near the 1980 eruption of Mount St. Helens in Washington State choked on gray ash in the air. But that eruption was miniscule in comparison to the global eruption foretold in Revelation 9.

A discovery made in Gubbio, Italy, indicates a similar incident occurred in the geologic past. Geologist Walter Alvarez, who was looking for evidence of magnetic reversals in the limestone deposits in the Apennine Mountains, found a one-centimeter layer of ash and clay. It was entirely void of fossils and sandwiched in between limestone layers. When the sample was analyzed, geologists found a high concentration of iridium, a metal extremely rare in the earth's crust. On further investigation, the same deposit was found in Denmark, Spain, and New Zealand.

Since the deposit was so widespread and contained a metal common to meteorites but rare on earth, geologists concluded that its source was extraterrestrial. Besides, the deposit was laid down at the same time in geologic history in which the dinosaurs became extinct. From this evidence, Alvarez and his father, Nobel prize physicist Luis W. Alvarez, along with Frank Asara and Helen V. Michel, both nuclear chemists at Lawrence Berkeley Laboratory, proposed the following theory:

At the end of the Cretaceous geologic epoch, an asteroid, some six miles or more in diameter, crashed into the earth's crust.[76] In an instant, it excavated a crater one hundred miles or so in diameter, throwing up dust and debris along with volcanic ash. The smoke and dust surrounded the earth and so darkened it that all plant foliage died or became dormant, breaking down food chains. Before enough light was restored, the enormous dinosaurs with their voracious appetites died.[77]

---

[76] A giant ring, the remnant of such a collision, was later found near the Yucatan Peninsula.

[77] Robin Bates, "The Asteroid and the Dinosaurs," *Science Magazine*, May 1981, p. 67.

However, the destruction of this woe may at least match if not exceed that occasion. This star will probably be larger than the asteroid in that ancient episode or else will travel at a greater speed. The darkness will no doubt be thicker, the disturbance of the earth's crust greater, and the surface change more widespread. We expect vegetation and animal life will be almost totally destroyed, leaving the remaining population without food and desperate to survive.

If that were not bad enough, people's distress becomes unbearable because many insect-like vermin will ascend out of the pit along with the smoke. Although they are called locusts, they do not feed on vegetation. Instead, they seek out people who do not have the seal of God on their foreheads. They sting with the fierceness of scorpions, inflicting great pain. Death, however, is not within their power. Yet people will wish to die rather than endure the torment of these creatures, and this situation lasts for five months.

It is clear from the description of the locusts that they are not native to the earth. Rather, they are especially prepared instruments of judgment like those God used against Egypt. Recall the plagues of lice, locusts, and flies. About the flies in particular, Velikovsky says that conditions of that area were probably conducive to some insect plagues, but the noxious dog-fly associated with the planet-god Baal Zevuv was a new species. He contends that the comet brought this new breed to the earth in *its tail*.

That may well be the case in this woe. A new species of insects inflicted on earth from outer space is within the realm of possibility. The Voyager III flyby of the planets Jupiter and Saturn in 1981 revealed that some of their satellites have conditions where life-producing proteins can be formed. Who is to say that these strange-acting locusts have not ridden to earth on a star?

Who knows what God has prepared in outer space with which to scourge the earth? He said to Job, "Hast thou seen the treasures of the hail, which I have reserved against the time of trouble, against the day of battle and war?" (Job 38:22–23). God has weapons prepared for trouble. The "star" may simply be the vehicle that brings them.

The locusts are real enough, but they signify a far greater menace spiritually. The vilest, most depraved spirits from the lowest level of hell have been turned loose on earth to prey on humans. The depraved spirits may attach themselves to the bodies of these locusts as they ascend out of the abyss, using them as vehicles to accomplish their destruction. (Spirit creatures cannot work extensively in the earthly realm without physical bodies.)[78] We suspect that they inhabit the locusts' bodies because of their description, which God evidently planned for in their creation. Together they will bring great distress. This is how they looked:

> And the shapes of the locusts were *like* unto horses prepared unto battle; and on their heads were *as it were* crowns like gold, and their faces were *as* the faces of men. And they had hair as the hair of women, and their teeth were *as* the teeth of lions. And they had breastplates, *as it were* breastplates of iron; and the sound of their wings was *as* the sound of chariots of many horses running to battle. And they had tails *like* unto scorpions, and there were stings in their tails: and their power was to hurt men five months. And they had a king over

---

[78] Demonic spirits can influence and entice human minds as spirits, but they need physical bodies to do physical damage.

them, which is the angel of the bottomless pit, whose name in the Hebrew tongue is Abbadon, but in the Greek tongue hath his name Apollyon. (9:7–11, emphasis added)

John uses figures of speech in the description of the locusts to depict their demonic characters. Their overall shapes look *like* horses, armor-plated for battle. This signifies their warlike nature. They have come to stir up strife and keep men at war with one another. They wear crowns on their heads, not of gold but *like* gold (an imitation), which shows their determination to rule, even though their authority is not from heaven, but from the king of the pit. (They do rule their victims, however, when they transfer themselves from the body of the locust to the body of the men they sting.) Their faces being *like* men, show they have intelligence, therefore they can communicate and cooperate with each other against their victims. Also, they can conceal their demonic activity under the guise of human effort in the people they control. Their long, flowing hair, like the hair of women, reveals their seductive natures in drawing people into sin. Their teeth, *like* lions' teeth, shows their fierceness, their power to induce fear, and their ability to grasp and tear their victims.

The breastplate of armor *like* iron shows they are not vulnerable to attack and are practically invincible. Anyone determined to have their own way in sin is vulnerable. Sin attracts them. Although they present no threat to the elect, the wicked have no defense against them. The sound of their coming strikes fear in their victims, for their wings sound like thundering chariots on the move. Coming out of darkness, the locusts/demons will intimidate their victims with sound effects long before they attack. The sound of their wings fill the wicked with terror, not knowing when or where they will strike. The fear they induce give great power to the forces of darkness. Even under natural circumstances, a flying band of locusts is frighteningly loud. Imagine being pursued in the dark by these supernatural locusts, knowing you are their "foliage!" Their king, the dark angel from the pit who directs their activities, is named "Destroyer"; therefore, they accomplish his work–they destroy. True to their nature, locusts travel in bands. (Demons also organize into gangs or bands.) Together they will destroy the lives of everyone they touch.

People will be in varying degrees of darkness, both spiritual and literal. Creatures lurking in that darkness create terror far beyond any monster movie Hollywood could ever produce. They prey on humans rather than plants because, in the darkness and ash, foliage plants are dying. Besides, they were commanded to feed on the wicked. Men love darkness rather than light, so God gives them darkness! The first woe has been revealed.

The Sixth Trumpet

And the sixth angel sounded, and I heard a voice from the four horns of the golden altar which is before God, saying to the sixth angel which had the trumpet, Loose the four angels which are bound in the great river Euphrates. And the four angels were loosed, which were prepared for an hour, and a day, and a month, and a year, for to slay the third part of men. And the number of the army of the horsemen were two hundred thousand thousand: and I heard the number of them. And thus I saw the horses in the vision, and them that sat on them, having breastplates of fire, and of jacinth, and brimstone: and the heads of the horses were as the heads of lions; and out of their mouths issued fire and smoke and brimstone. By these three was the third part of men killed, by the fire, and by the smoke, and by the brimstone, which issued out of their mouths. For their power is in their mouth, and in their tails: for their tails were like unto serpents, and had heads, and with them they do hurt. And the rest of the men which were not killed by these plagues yet repented not of the works of their hands, that they should not worship devils, and idols of gold, and silver, and brass, and stone, and of wood: which neither can see, nor hear, nor walk: neither repented they of their murders, nor of their sorceries, nor of their fornication, nor of their thefts. (9:13–21)

The sixth angel blows his trumpet, but instead of action beginning when it sounds as in the other trumpets, a command issues forth from the horns of the altar of incense. This is the piece of furniture in the temple that stands for prayer and intercession. Evidently, the command, "Loose the four angels which are bound in [at][79] the great river Euphrates,"[80] comes in answer to a specific prayer.

Then we are told these angels have been reserved for a specific hour and day to slay a third of mankind. An important event will take place at this time, which we will be shown later in the vision (Rev. 11:7–14). Two of God's special witnesses will be slain. This judgment falls in answer to the believing prayers of Jewish saints. Therefore, the command comes forth from the horns of the altar of incense.

---

[79] George Ricker Berry, *The Interlinear Greek-English New Testament* (Grand Rapids: Zondervan, 1958, 1973), p. 640.

[80] Rev. 9:14.

These four angels have apparently been assigned to this task for some time and stand in readiness for the precise moment to arrive. Thus, time alone binds them. Their position connects to a specific place on earth, the Euphrates River, because their work prepares the way for the events of the last trumpet, as we shall shortly see.

Each angel commands a vast army. Their number, four, stands for creation—the natural world. And four is associated with the four directions. So these four armies come against the whole earth. They have dominion over it all. It is by God's grace, then, that only one-third of the world's population dies.

John hears the number of this vast army announced—twice ten thousand times ten thousand. Then he sees the armies in a vision. They are cavalries of invincible warriors, wearing breastplates of jacinth and brimstone. The bright red-orange color of jacinth (a variety of zircon) combines with the pale yellow of the brimstone (sulfur), giving the warriors' breastplates a fiery appearance. In fact, that is all John sees of the warriors, since the fierceness of their steeds is overwhelming.

The horses are actually more destructive than the warriors. The heads look like lions' heads with manes full-blown and probably fiery. Moreover, their mouths spew fire, smoke, and burning sulfur. The horses' tails look like serpents' heads, which also hurl missiles at their victims below.

Although these armies are under spiritual leadership, they come against the earth as a literal plague. Clearly, this army cannot be made up of men. Rather, it appears to be an astronomical army capable of spraying burning crude oil and sulfur down to earth. This has happened before. Concerning a near collision between Mars and Venus during the commotion of Uzziah's time (mentioned by Isaiah), Velikovsky says this:

> When Mars clashed with Venus, asteroids, meteorites and gases were torn from this trailing part [of Venus] and began a semi-independent existence, some following the orbit of Mars, some other paths. These swarms of meteorites with their gaseous appendages, heads and tails, were newborn comets; flying in bands and taking on various shapes, they made an uncanny impression. . . . They also ran along different orbits, grew quickly from small to giant size, and terrorized the peoples of the earth. [Isaiah calls them "the terrible ones" (Isa. 25:51)] They bring pestilence and cause earthquakes.[81]

The second woe results in more destruction than the first. Two hundred million of these horsemen attacking from the sky, hurl hot stones, boiling oil, and flaming sulphur. They also dump stifling sulfurous gases on the population. Once more the number of people diminishes in the terrible judgment of the sixth trumpet.

Nevertheless, those left alive after the horrendous plague do not repent of the "works of their hands." Remember, a good deal of time elapses between judgments. Idolatry, under the influence of the demonic hoard unleashed in the first woe, has by now reached epidemic proportions. Like the darkness of India where people worship many gods of gold and silver, wood and stone, these rebels will worship gods that promise protection from the harsh elements at work in judgment. The work of the demons behind these

---

[81] Immanuel Velikovsky, *Worlds in Collision* (New York: Doubleday, 1950), p. 281.

gods is evident from the list of sins people refuse to repent of—murder, witchcraft (practiced by use of drugs), fornication, and theft. The demons do a thorough job. They have successfully deceived people to the point that this severe judgment does not affect a change of their hearts. That is, all except a remnant in Jerusalem. Revelation 11 includes the conclusion to the second woe:

> And that same hour was there a great earthquake, and the tenth part of the city fell, and in the earthquake were slain of men seven thousand: and the remnant were affrighted, and gave glory to the God of heaven. (11:13)

Events in Revelation 11 show that this judgment is directed against people for the specific act of killing God's witnesses, which we will take up later, hence, the mention of the second woe in Revelation 11 as well as in chapter 9. Chapter 11 also includes the detail that the astronomical army in that woe will cause a great earthquake (11:13). This seems to confirm that we are dealing with the same phenomenon described by Velikovsky, i.e., that small, independent comets can produce earthquakes.

In this case, however, the earth itself attracts the mass from the invading comets instead of another planet. The writhing movement of the small comets, casting debris from the whip-lashing tails, indicate that they will struggle between two forces. This effects earth by causing movement of the surface, perhaps like tidal waves resulting in minor earthquakes all around the earth. Of course, the comets, being smaller, come crashing down, causing great destruction wherever they land. The earthquake mentioned in Revelation 11 will probably be only one of many, the one connected to the Middle East.

With the earthquake, woe two has been announced.

Chapter 16

THE LITTLE BOOK

(REVELATION 10)

The third and final woe waits. John holds his breath, expecting the ultimate wrath to break forth. However, as before, the mighty "prosecutor" interrupts the sequence between the sixth and seventh judgments to add new pieces to the puzzle already outlined. These pieces add religious, social, and political actions played against the colorful background of the trumpet judgments.

So we will backtrack again. In fact, we will piece together a large center piece of the puzzle with those we have already put together in chapter 14 from the prophets. This

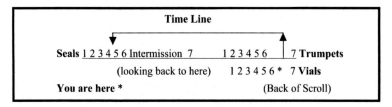

Time Line

Seals 1 2 3 4 5 6 Intermission 7   1 2 3 4 5 6 | 7 **Trumpets**

(looking back to here)   1 2 3 4 5 6 *   7 **Vials**

You are here *   (Back of Scroll)

large piece begins with verse 1 of Revelation 10 and continues until verse 1 of Revelation 12. It wraps around the sixth seal, locking onto both sides. Yet it belongs in the time sequence after the Lamb breaks the seventh seal before the trumpet judgments begin. Surprisingly, the portions of this piece found in Revelation 11 and 12 link to events as far back as the fifth seal. No wonder, then, that the "prosecutor" stops the action. Many details must be added to make the picture plain. From this point on, the puzzle, the mystery of John's vision will be constantly embellished by colorful overlays which add more and more details to the picture. Some will overlap like this present piece. Nevertheless, in the end, we will form a complete picture. The important thing to remember is that we are still gathering a few isolated pieces that relate to things already discussed, yet we will introduce new facts as well. From this point on, we will furnish the reader with a time line showing where the chapter begins in the sequence.

Returning now to the puzzle piece under examination, we begin with the judicial procedure emanating from the throne.

> And I saw another mighty angel come down from heaven, clothed with a cloud: and a rainbow was upon his head, and his face was as it were the sun, and his feet as pillars of fire: and he had in his hand a little book open: and he set his right foot upon the sea, and his left foot upon the earth. (10:1–2)

John calls this personage a "mighty angel," but the further description and work of this being causes us to think

He is Israel's Mighty Angel. Maybe the Mighty Angel is so obscured by the cloud and rainbow that John does not recognize Him as the glorious one he has already met. Or perhaps the size of the angel confuses John. A being that stands on the shore, one foot in the water and the other on the sand, is surely not what John sees. Likely, he sees a towering being with one foot in the middle of Africa and the other in the middle of the Atlantic Ocean. Regardless of his size, the Angel has the same sun-blazing face and fiery feet as the Alpha and Omega John met at the beginning of the vision.

The appearance and mission of this Mighty Angel is the same as the one seen by Ezekiel when he was called to service.

> And above the firmament that was over their heads[82] was the likeness of a throne, as the appearance of sapphire stone: and upon the likeness of the throne was the likeness as the appearance of a man above upon it. And I saw the colour of amber, as the appearance of fire round about within it, from the appearance of his loins even upward, and from the appearance of his loins even downward, I saw as it were the appearance of fire, and it had brightness round about it. As the appearance of the bow that is in the cloud in the day of rain, so was the appearance of the brightness round about. This was the appearance of the likeness of the glory of the LORD. And when I saw it, I fell upon my face, and I heard a voice of one that spake. (Ezek. 1:26–28)

---

[82] See Exod. 24:10.

Ezekiel receives a message from this glorious one. He falls down under the power of His displayed glory. Ezekiel knew he was in God's presence; yet the one on the throne had the form of a man. Is not this the Captain of the Lord's hosts, the mighty personal Angel sent to save Israel in Exodus? He sits on a throne resting on a chariot powered by four living creatures (Ezek. 1:19). The "Man" has come to deliver a warning of judgment from God into the hands of Ezekiel.

The righteousness and mercy of God demand that people be warned. The scroll that Ezekiel receives was written on both sides with judgments, lamentations, and woes against Israel. Even though God knew that stiff-necked Israel would not respond, His sense of legal righteousness must be satisfied. It is the same situation in Revelation. The seven-sealed book, written on the front and the back, spells out judgment, lamentation, and woes. People must be warned!

> And [the angel] cried with a loud voice, as when a lion roareth: and when he had cried, seven thunders uttered their voices. And when the seven thunders had uttered their voices, I was about to write: and I heard a voice from heaven saying unto me, Seal up those things which the seven thunders uttered, and write them not. (10:3–4)

Since the Mighty Angel has a similar description and mission to the personage in Ezekiel, we believe He is the same glorious one: Jesus, the Captain, the Lord of hosts, the Mighty One of Israel. Worthy of His office, the Lamb descends with the might of the Lion of Judah. During the thirty-minute intermission after the last seal was broken on the scroll in the Father's hand (Rev. 8:1), He comes to declare openly His right to execute justice. The words will be spoken prophetically and then given through the mouths of His witnesses. Just as He did with Ezekiel, the Captain of the Lord's hosts decrees the judgments ahead of the trumpet plagues so that the earth may be warned of what is to come.

> And the angel which I saw stand upon the sea and upon the earth lifted up his hand to heaven, and sware by him that liveth for ever and ever, who created heaven, and the things that therein are, and the earth, and the things that therein are, and the sea, and the things which are therein, that there should be time no longer: but in the days of the voice of the seventh angel, when he shall begin to sound, the mystery of God should be finished, as he hath declared to his servants the prophets. And the voice which I heard from heaven spake unto me again, and said, Go and take the little book which is open in the hand of the angel which standeth upon the sea and upon the earth. And I went unto the angel, and said unto him, Give me the little book. And he said unto me, Take it, and eat it up; and it shall make thy belly bitter, but it shall be in thy mouth sweet as honey. And I took the little book out of the angel's hand, and ate it up; and it was in my mouth sweet as honey: and as soon as I had eaten it, my belly was bitter. And he said unto me, Thou must prophesy again before many peoples, and nations, and tongues, and kings. (10: 5–11).

In His hand, again in like manner to Ezekiel (see Ezek. 2:9), the Mighty Angel carries a little open book. This scroll has not been sealed with wax and imprinted. This open book refers to a custom[83] of the Jews at the purchase of property. When such a transaction took place, it was customary to write down the conditions agreed upon, along with evidence of purchase in the presence of witnesses. Then this document was sealed with wax and imprinted. Another document of the same evidence was made but remained open. If for any reason the open copy was contested, the sealed copy, a second witness, could be opened and confirm the evidence.

The little book in the hand of the angel represents the public document. The world belongs to the Lamb of God. He has purchased it with His own blood. However, before He can rule over it as the Prince of Peace, He will judge the earth's wickedness as the Captain of the Lord's hosts because He is the one in command of the heavenly bodies. This little book in the Angel's hand may be just a smaller copy ("little book" is diminutive) of the seven-sealed book (the scroll) in heaven. This copy is open to the public and is small enough so people can read it.

The Angel roars with a voice *like* a lion, the symbol for a king. Proverbs 19:12 tells us, "The king's wrath is as the roaring of a lion." With a roar, He makes the public announcement with authority: Let all the world hear the evidence and terms of the purchase spoken in the rage of the insulted, righteous Ruler. Both the Father and Son unite in the declaration. The "lion" roars the terms of the front side of the scroll. Seven thunders rumble—a confirmation by the Father follows. Most likely, He proclaims the back side of the scroll; therefore, John is told not to write what the seven thunders say. These terms will be recorded later in

---

[83] Jer. 32:11, 14.

the vision under the vial judgments. The lion's roar and the seven thunders signify what God is about to accomplish.

Special prophets receive the declaration. The Angel lifts His hand and swears by the Creator who lives forever and ever that "there should be time no longer [no more delay]" (v. 6). The trumpets have announced that the King has taken up his rule. When the seventh angel "begins to sound, the mystery of God will be finished as he declared to his servants the prophets" (v. 7).[84] These were not just Old Testament prophets but those evidently called before the seventh trumpet begins to sound. They remove the mystery of what God is doing in the earth.

Let us pause here to point out another division in the text. If the complete mystery of God's judgment is unveiled by the seventh trumpet, then six of the seven vials of wrath which are yet to be announced have already been poured out before this trumpet sounds. This supports the idea that the judgments written on the back side of the scroll will not be fulfilled after the trumpet judgments cease, as most believe. Rather they are executed successively—the first trumpet judgment followed by the vial of wrath poured on top, the second trumpet followed by the second vial of wrath, etc. Otherwise, how could it be said that when the seventh trumpet sounds the mystery will be finished?

By the time of the seventh trumpet, the meaning of the dark prophecies are all too clear to a reeling world. Knowledge of God's judgment is not lacking; therefore, ignorance is not an excuse. All will hear what God is doing. All will be responsible for what they hear because God will send forth the voice of prophecy wherever people remain.

---

[84] My paraphrase.

John becomes the example of the special prophets, a stand-in, if you will. In the next chapter, we will see the actual prophets called to ministry. Now a voice calls to John saying, "Go and take the little book which is open in the hand of the angel which standeth upon the sea and upon the earth" (v. 8). John obeys. Again the angel says, "Take it, and eat it up; and it shall make thy belly bitter, but it shall be in thy mouth sweet as honey" (v. 9). John eats it and confirms the angel's words. (To eat it signifies making the message part of him.) It is sweet to know the will of God, but such a message turns to bitterness when the world reacts to it. The little book contains a message of woe. Ezekiel experienced the same thing when he received his prophetic calling. No doubt, the future prophets whom John represents in the vision will experience it also.

Next, John receives the scope of the prophetic message. The angel says, "Thou must prophesy again before many peoples, and nations, and tongues, and kings" (v. 11). This command is curious since we have seen John prophesy all the way to the seventh trumpet. When it sounds, all the terms of the scroll will be fulfilled. The angel said, "Thou must prophesy *again.*" John must repeat it. This time he must proclaim the back of the scroll to people in all walks of life, even to kings.

The prophetic word will reach the remaining world. God will hold people responsible for their reaction to the warning!

Chapter 17

THE TWO LAMPSTANDS

(REVELATION 11)

We begin this chapter with John still in the presence of the Mighty Angel. We know the scene has not changed because of the absence of the scene dividers—"and I saw," "I looked and lo," etc. The angel continues John's preparation to prophesy to "many peoples, and nations, and tongues, and kings" (10:11).

Giving John a reed, the mighty angel says: "Rise, and measure the temple of God, and the altar, and them that worship therein" (11:1)

Time Line

(Front)

Seals <u>1 2 3 4</u> ▼ <u>5 6 7</u> **Intermission *** ▲   <u>1 2 3 4 5 6</u>   7   **Trumpets**

Looking back to here   1 2 3 4 5 6 7   **Vials**

You are Here *   (Back)

Evidently, the prophets for whom John has been standing in are among these worshipers. In his measuring, John sets them apart for God's special use. But before we discuss what John measures, let us look at what he was commanded not to measure.

> But the court that is without the temple leave out, and measure it not; for it is given unto the Gentiles: and the holy city *shall they tread under foot* forty and two months. (11:2, emphasis added)

Matching this verse with another in Jesus' Olivet Discourse, we get a fuller picture of the situation in Jerusalem at this moment. Luke's version says:

> And they shall fall by the edge of the sword, and shall be led away captive into all nations: and Jerusalem shall *be trodden down of the Gentiles,* until the times of the Gentiles be fulfilled. (Luke 21:24, emphasis added)

Earlier in the discourse, Jesus explained how this would be.

> And when ye shall see Jerusalem compassed with armies, then know that the desolation thereof is nigh. Then let them which are in Judea flee to the mountains; and let them which are in the midst of it depart out; and let not them that are in the countries enter thereinto. (Luke 21:20–21)

These scriptures were partially fulfilled when the Roman emperor Titus destroyed Jerusalem in A.D. 70 and scattered the Jews. However, physical disasters from heavenly bodies did not occur at that time. Therefore, we may have here a double interpretation which is totally fulfilled at this latter invasion. By connecting the above verses to what John was told in Revelation 11:2 concerning the Gentiles occupying the city, we learn that the measuring occurred at the same time as the gathering of armies to Jerusalem for battle. At this time, the fifty plus years of Israel's present occupation of Jerusalem will come to an end once more. Believers are told to flee because of the desolation that will result from this battle.

The "desolation [that] is nigh" probably speaks of the overturning of the earth in the sixth seal (which in this sequence has not happened yet). Matthew and Mark both mention another desolation in their accounts. Matthew says:

> When ye therefore shall see the abomination of desolation, spoken of by Daniel the prophet, stand in the holy place, (whoso readeth, let him understand:) then let them which be in Judea flee into the mountains. (Matt. 24:15–16; see also Mark 13:14)

The "abomination" that brings desolation mentioned in this account and those following, refers to an idol that is set up in the temple's Holy Place. (The Tanakh, the Jewish version of the Old Testament in English, translates Daniel 9:27 saying the idol will be set up at the corner [of the altar].) The last verse of the scripture above (Matt. 24:16) ties back to Luke's account, because after Luke mentions Jerusalem being surrounded by armies, the next verse says: "Then let them which are in Judea flee to the mountains" (Luke 21:21).

Matthew and Mark tell the "elect," the name for believers in the Olivet Discourse, to flee when they see the idol set up, while Luke tells them to flee when they see armies gather. From this, we conclude that these two events happen at the same time. Consequently, the piece of the puzzle from Revelation 11:2 interlocks with both the imminent invasion of Jerusalem and the setting up of the abomination of desolation.

We know the invading army is Russian because we have already put together other pieces of this section of the puzzle. We know the destruction forthcoming is because of God's jealousy for His people. Now we learn that an abominable idol that has been set up on holy ground provokes His wrath. The armies surrounding Jerusalem would most likely be allies gathered to defend the city against Russia. Their defense, however, fails to save the city because Russia advances farther south into Idumea before she falls. Besides taking the city, the invading army ravishes the whole countryside of Judea; hence, the warning to believers to flee to the mountains.

Since Jesus referred to the "desolation of abomination" in Daniel's prophecy as something we need to understand, we will now fit together pieces from this prophet and see how they relate to this time. The abomination mentioned belongs in the middle of a prophecy concerning a political leader.

> And arms shall stand on his part [the political figure], and they shall pollute the sanctuary of strength, and shall take away the daily sacrifice, and they shall place the abomination that maketh desolate. (Dan. 11:31)

Gathered to this political leader, the allied "arms," that is, the gathered armies, will agree to stop the Jewish sacrifices and erect an idol. So it is through the leadership of this person that the "abomination" will be set up. Later, Daniel gives the time in connection with the setting up of the idol.

> And from the time that the daily sacrifice shall be taken away, and the abomination that maketh desolate set up, shall be a thousand two hundred and ninety days. (Dan. 12:11)

This verse presents the time in days, spelling it out precisely. It is the same time given to the Gentiles to tread down the city of Jerusalem. At this time, we note that the earth's orbit has change. If we divide 42 months into 1,290 days, we have a 30.7-day month or a 368.4-day year.[85]

This adds weight to our interpretation that the overturning and especially the change in rotation in the fourth trumpet judgment had caused the earth to change its solar revolution. This seems confirmed in another scripture in Daniel concerning the same political leader. Here we find more reference to time with the need to change the calendar.

> And he shall speak great words against the most High, and shall wear out the saints of the most High, and *think to change times* and laws: and they shall be given into his hand until a time and times and the dividing of time. (Dan. 7:25, emphasis added)

---

[85] Some expositors have confused this detail by dividing the 42 months into the 1,260 days of Israel's protection in chapter 12. But we cannot divide apples into oranges. Gentile months must be divided into Gentile days.

The Gentiles, under this political leader, have been ordained by God to rule for this specific stretch of time. Though the calendar will change during this period, their days of power will remain the same. "Times" in this passage refer to years. Forty-two months divided by twelve months equals three and one half years—a time (one year) and times (two years) and the dividing of time (one-half year). By giving the time in years, months, and days, God emphasizes the limitation of Gentile power.

The final mention of the "abomination" that makes "desolate" occurs in the seventy-week prophecy of Daniel 9. After prophesying about the sixty-nine weeks until the Messiah would be cut off, Daniel says concerning the seventieth week:

> And he shall confirm the covenant with many for one week: and in the midst of the week he shall cause the sacrifice and the oblation to cease, and for the overspreading of abominations he shall make it desolate, even unto the consummation, and that determined shall be poured upon the desolate. (Dan. 9:27)

The setting up of the "abomination" will happen in the middle of a "week" of years (seven). We know this because the period following its placement is absolutely defined as three and a half years. If three and a half years is half the time, then the "week" (seven) refers to years. This prophecy provides the framework of time for "the things which shall be hereafter." The Church age, a secret hid in God[86] from ages past, comes as a parenthesis between the sixty-ninth and seventieth week of the prophecy. Since we know

---

[86] Eph. 3:2–5.

the sixty-nine weeks of years had already been fulfilled when Jesus died (the Messiah cut off Dan. 9:26), we can expect God to begin to fulfill the rest of this prophecy after the Church is taken up to heaven.

But getting back to the verse at hand, besides learning about the time, we find the political leader makes a covenant with "many." Evidently, the covenant has been in force for some time, because the political leader merely confirms it when he comes to power. He rises to power about the same time the seven-sealed book is brought forth for opening. The "many" involved in the covenant may be a united Europe and a united Middle East, including Israel. These may draw up a treaty of mutual protection against the aggression that began even before the opening of the second seal.

The covenant provides mutual benefits. European nations may excuse themselves from a worsening relationship between two major nuclear powers (the United States and Russia or possibly China). Then a united Europe may draw the Middle Eastern Arabs to their side because of dependence on their energy resources. Israel, apparently now at peace with her Arab neighbors, receives a part in the covenant having religious overtones, such as guaranteed rights to the temple mount, sacrifices, oblations, etc. The Arabs probably receive military aid and manufactured goods in exchange for their oil. The covenant satisfies everyone.

After three and a half years, the political leader breaks the covenant with Israel (because of the war), stops the sacrificing, and erects an idol. Actually, he will institute a religion that we will examine when we learn more about this man. When he does, he will initiate God's jealous wrath and bring destruction to the land. During the last forty-two months of Gentile rule, this evil leader will take over Jerusalem. For this reason, the angel tells John not to measure the court or the city.

John Measures the Faithful

> And there was given me a reed like unto a rod: and the angel stood, saying, Rise, and measure the temple of God, and the altar, and them that worship therein. (11:l)

As we said in the beginning, John is still in the same scene as he was in Revelation 10. In the time sequence, it is somewhere in the middle of the prophetic week, probably during the thirty-minute break after the Lamb opens the last seal. There a voice instructed John to receive the little book from the angel's hand. Now the angel (the same angel that spoke to him before? Or the Mighty Angel?) says, "Rise, and measure" and, presumably, go to Jerusalem to do the measuring. To understand the significance of this, we need to know why these people gather to this particular place. To do this, we will back up in our narrative again.

An important event has already taken place at the temple prior to the Mighty Angel's descent to claim the earth, an event that has not yet come to light in our text. What John views when he goes to measure the temple is really a flashback. The Lion of Judah had already come to earth to claim His kingdom with the final seal broken, revealing the document. However, during the calling up and resurrection of the saints in the fifth seal, others had been commissioned to take their places. These are the ones He wants John to measure. Therefore, we will go back to the fifth seal and catch up on what is happening to these people.

In an earlier chapter, we pieced together scriptures from the prophet Joel that described the destruction of the Russian army. These connected to the sixth seal. The verses before those describing the sun darkening and the moon turning to blood tell of Israel corporately pleading with God because of the advancing army. Marauding bands had stripped the land to the north of food like a great hoard of locusts. The devout in Israel pour into the temple in Jerusalem to implore the Lord in earnest prayer: "Blow the trumpet in Zion, sanctify a fast, call a solemn assembly" (Joel 2:15).

We note that their coming into the temple coincides with their feast days, because these terms refer respectively to the Feast of Trumpets, the Day of Atonement,[87] and the Feast of Tabernacles. This sets the time of the invasion at the fall harvest, the harvest of oil and wine. At this time, the restrictive command to "hurt not the oil and the wine" of the third seal lifts. The time has come to fulfill the last three festivals of the Jews.

> Gather the people, sanctify the congregation, assemble the elders, gather the children, and those that suck the breasts: let the bridegroom go forth of his chamber, and the bride out of her closet. (Joel 2:16)

This, however, is be no ordinary feast day where one has a choice of attending or not attending. The decree compels all to be present, from babes in arms to newlyweds. With the Russians hoards approaching, Israel will face her greatest peril since it became a nation in 1948. They need everyone's pleas to God.

---

[87] The fast on the Day of Atonement is spoken of in the phrase "afflict your souls" (see Lev. 16:31; 23:26–32).

> Let the priests, the ministers of the LORD, weep *between the porch and the altar*, and let them say, Spare thy people, O LORD, and give not thine heritage to reproach, that the heathen should rule over them: wherefore should they say among the people, Where is their God? (Joel 2:17, emphasis added)

Crowds press into the temple courtyards in response to the cry. The priests and ministers lead the travailing prayers. We know the idol has not yet been set up at this time because the priests and ministers still have access to the altar. Also, the huge crowd of faithful Jews who respond to the desperate cry fill the courtyard. This would be impossible if the idol is there because of the people's devotion to God.

Ten days earlier, the first day of the gathering (the Feast of Trumpets), the blowing of the rams' horns had called faithful Israel to real repentance. It will come in response to a prophetic word from the Lord.

> Therefore also now, saith the LORD, turn ye even to me with all your heart, and with fasting, and with weeping, and with mourning: and rend your heart, and not your garments, and turn unto the LORD your God: for he is gracious and merciful, slow to anger, and of great kindness, and repenteth him of the evil. (Joel 2:12–13)

Led by their priests, repentant Israel receives an unexpected blessing: *spiritual rebirth*. The weeping crowd had continued to grow from the blowing of the trumpets until the Day of Atonement when Christ appears and redeems them. We will take up Israel's redemption in detail in the next chapter. Here we wish only to establish that weeping priests and ministers, between the temple porch and the altar, stand on the ground that John measures off for the Lord.

Now returning to the vision, John hears the Mighty Angel say:

> And I will give power unto my two witnesses, and they shall prophesy a thousand two hundred and threescore days, clothed in sackcloth. These are the two olive trees, and the two candlesticks standing before the God of the earth. And if any man will hurt them, fire proceedeth out of their mouth, and devoureth their enemies: and if any man will hurt them, he must in this manner be killed. These have power to shut heaven, that it rain not in the days of their prophecy: and have power over waters to turn them to blood, and to smite the earth with all plagues, as often as they will. (11:3–6)

Of "them that worship therein" (v. 1), two will have a special ministry that consists entirely of prophecy. During the period of 1,260 days (out of the 1,290 days given to the Gentiles), these two witnesses are untouchable, publicly announcing the contents of the little open book. They will have no other priestly duties after the idol is set up, since it is forbidden to offer daily sacrifices because of the broken covenant. Therefore, they stand like two golden lampstands, shedding light on God's plans for the earth.

The two witnesses minister the prophecies in much the same way Elijah and Moses did, who confronted the political leaders of their countries. Rain is withheld because of the idolatry, just as in the days of Elijah. Since many Jews will be sold as slaves, especially children,[88] the bondage calls forth plagues similar to the days of Moses. Also like Elijah,[89] the witnesses will speak words of fire, and God will send fire on their enemies. They prophesy concerning the absolute sovereignty of God.

Puzzle Pieces from Zechariah's Visions

Zechariah, writing at the time of Israel's restoration from Babylonian captivity, also includes pieces to our picture puzzle. He mentions two olive trees connected to a lampstand. These pieces are found in the midst of a series of visions. The verse in Revelation 11:4 describing the two witnesses, "These are the two olive trees, and the two candlesticks[90] standing before the God of the earth," mates with this verse in Zechariah: "Then said he, These are the two anointed ones, that stand by the *Lord of the whole earth*" (Zech. 4:14, emphasis added).

The phrase "stand by the Lord of the whole earth" would hardly be adequate to consider as a mated interlock except that Zechariah describes the two olive trees previous to the phrase. The trees stood on either side of a golden lampstand. They connected to the lampstand by golden pipes, and through them golden oil flowed directly from the trees to the lampstand. Zechariah describes the whole symbol, whereas they are simply labeled for John.

All this emphasis on gold confirms what God had told Zechariah earlier: "Not by might, nor by power, but by my spirit, saith the LORD of hosts" (Zech. 4:6). Gold indicates the glory is God's; He does it all. He pipes the oil, the Holy Spirit, from the source to the lampstand without the aid of

---

[88] Joel 3:6.
[89] 2 Kings 1:10.
[90] Lampstands

human hands. This indicates much more than an anointing, rather, a constant flow.

Although this series of visions in Zechariah was given to encourage Israel after they came back to the land following the Babylonian captivity, it becomes clear as the visions progress that they deal mainly with Israel's return at the end of this age. There are ten visions in the series. They offer the same overall sequence as John's vision, especially the last six. They begin with the gathering of Israel back to the land and continue until the Messiah builds the millennial temple. Because of this parallel, we will fit them into our puzzle as the pieces touch those in John's vision.

Now concerning the pieces in view—the lampstands, we find that both occurrences refer to testimony, but the emphasis is different. In Zechariah's vision, it is on the source of the testimony (golden lampstand, golden pipes, golden oil), while in John's vision, we see the emphasis on the recipients—the witnesses and the content of their message. Together, they show the absolute authority of the two witnesses who represent God on earth.

Being heard by the rebel world, the witnesses themselves seem to have unlimited power. Even though they merely obey God, just as Moses and Elijah obeyed God by announcing His plans, they appear to cause plagues. They announce drought, it comes. They announce that the sea will be turned to blood, it does. Bitter waters, falling stars, blackened atmosphere—all from the little open book. Through the witnesses, God speaks to the authorities in Jerusalem. The rest of the world will hear as the Egyptians heard in the days of Pharaoh. News filters down to the populace from official notices. The government will blame the witnesses for the plagues. The message will divide the people. Some will fear

God and act accordingly; others will actively oppose and try to kill His servants.

The False Victory

> And when they shall have finished their testimony, the beast that ascendeth out of the bottomless pit shall make war against them, and shall overcome them, and kill them. (11:7)

At the end of their 1,260 allotted days, thirty days before the Gentile authority runs out, the enemy regroups. "The beast that ascendeth out of the bottomless pit" may refer to Apollyon, the Destroyer, king over the demons of the first woe. On the other hand, it could refer to Satan himself, who is absolute king over them, and who, as we will find out in the next chapter, will be cast out of heaven to earth. Whoever he is, he will provide temporary strength as the opposition grows fierce.

Tension mounts. Zealots on both sides regroup for the final showdown. A supernatural war breaks out: the saints of God on one side, testifying of their God, the wicked on the other, seduced by Satan and his demons. To the advocates of the occult, the power plays will appear like the "black magic" wars of primitive witch doctors, i.e., where spirits do battle for their masters, using spiritual laws and raw force. False miracles abound. Satan's servants counterfeit the fire of God. With the death of the two witnesses, the forces of darkness win a major victory.

> And their dead bodies shall lie in the street of the great city, which spiritually is called Sodom and Egypt, where also our Lord was crucified. And they of the people and

kindreds and tongues and nations shall see their dead bodies three days and an half, and shall not suffer their dead bodies to be put in graves. And they that dwell upon the earth shall rejoice over them, and make merry, and shall send gifts one to another; because these two prophets tormented them that dwelt on the earth. And after three days and an half the Spirit of life from God entered into them, and they stood upon their feet; and great fear fell upon them which saw them. And they heard a great voice from heaven saying unto them, Come up hither. And they ascended up to heaven in a cloud; and their enemies beheld them. (11:8–12)

The victory celebration is short, only three and a half days. God turns the defeat into a victory for the forces of light. Life, the greatest miracle of all, cannot be duplicated or counterfeited by Satan. Dismayed and in great fear because their resurrection verifies the teaching of the saints, the celebrants receive just retribution—the second woe!

And the *same hour* was there a great earthquake, and the tenth part of the city fell, and in the earthquake were slain of men seven thousand: and the remnant were affrighted, and gave glory to the God of heaven. And the second woe is past; and, behold, the third woe cometh quickly. (11:13–14, emphasis added)

Those left alive must acknowledge, just like Israel of old standing before Elijah, that the God in heaven is the God of the Scriptures, not just a neutral force to be manipulated by the beast. He is Lord indeed!

The mention of the second woe connects these incidents with those surrounding the sixth trumpet judgment.

We know this because we were told that the fifth trumpet judgment ended the first woe (Rev. 9:12). We remember that the second woe was ordered from the golden altar of incense in answer to prayer for judgment.

Now we understand why. The gross wickedness of the people in killing the prophets and celebrating their deaths bring judgment in the "same hour." It is greatly deserved!

> And the seventh angel sounded; and there were great voices in heaven, saying, The kingdoms of this world are become the kingdoms of our Lord, and of his Christ; and he shall reign for ever and ever. And the four and twenty elders, which sat before God on their seats, fell upon their faces, and worshipped God, saying, We give thee thanks, O Lord God Almighty, which art, and wast, and art to come; because thou hast taken to thee thy great power, and hast reigned. (11:15–17)

The seventh and last trumpet sounds. Triumphant shouts ring out in heaven, and the twenty-four elders fall on their faces, worshiping and praising God. The consummation of the age is in sight. The saints rejoice! Soon they are to descend with Christ to the earth.

The Indignation

But on earth, the nations are angry. They gather for a showdown—a fight to establish supremacy over the world. This recalls a prophecy concerning Old Testament saints. Isaiah speaks about his own and others' resurrections from the grave:

> We have been with child, we have been in pain, we have as it were brought forth wind; we have not wrought any

deliverance in the earth; *neither have the inhabitants of the world fallen.* Thy dead men shall live, together with my dead body shall they arise. Awake and sing, ye that dwell in dust: for thy dew is as the dew of herbs, and the earth shall cast out the dead. Come, my people, enter thou into thy chambers, and shut thy doors about thee: hide thyself as it were for a little moment, until the indignation be overpast. For, behold, the LORD cometh out of his *place to punish the inhabitants of the earth for their iniquity:* the earth also shall disclose her blood, and shall no more cover her slain. (Isa. 26:18–21, emphasis added)

Isaiah talks about the pregnancy of Israel. For a long time, the seed of the Messiah had been developing, but the pain Israel felt was like false labor. Though her pain was great like that of birth, all that came from it was the passing of gas (wind). God had shown Isaiah that the time of his own resurrection connected to the time when He would return to earth and personally see to the judgment. It is only "a little moment" that they wait in their chambers until time to return with Him to see the guilty damned. Time enough for them to receive their rewards. Compare this passage with the next in Revelation 11.

And the nations were angry, and thy wrath is come, and the time of the dead, that they should be judged, and that thou shouldest give reward unto thy servants the prophets, and to the saints, and them that fear thy name, small and great; and *shouldest destroy them which destroy the earth.* (11:18, emphasis added)

Another segment of the redeemed rise from the dead and receive their rewards—Old Testament believers consisting of the prophets of God (God's anointed servants), the saints (Israel, set apart under the covenants), and finally, all those who feared God's name. These latter ones include those who feared God before the setting apart of a nation for Himself. Some of the greats might be Abimelech, the king of Gerar in Abraham's day, or the queen of Sheba. Examples of the "small" might be Job's friends. Job, as a prophet–priest, belongs to the category of servant. These rise together just as Isaiah said, "Thy dead men shall live, together with my dead body" (Isa. 26:19).

Paul spoke of the resurrection occurring in segments: "But every man in his own *order:* Christ the firstfruits; afterward they that are Christ's at his coming. Then cometh the end" (1 Cor. 15:23–24, emphasis added). The Lord comes for each order separately. The word for "order" in the Greek, *tagma,* denotes a military term such as company,[91] regiment, platoon, etc. Since the leader of this military division is our Captain,[92] we view these various orders as companies.

As we mentioned before, seven orders of resurrections occur in John's vision. We have witnessed four thus far, if we count the Alpha and Omega who told John He was dead but now is alive, as representing the resurrection of our Lord. Besides Christ, we have the Church, the Jewish mar-

---

[91] W. E. Vine, *An Expository Dictionary of New Testament Words* (London: Oliphants, 1953), vol. 3, p. 145.

[92] There are many titles for the Lord's relationship with Israel. Joshua saw Him as Captain of the Lord's hosts. He is called the Mighty Angel, the Holy One, the Mighty One of Israel, but Captain suits as a title here because of His military stance.

tyrs with their Gentile multitude (most of which are raptured from among the living), and the two witnesses. Now,
the Old Testament saints make the fifth resurrection. There
will be two more before we finish the vision, making seven
in all.

It is interesting to note that the large companies of Christians resurrected thus far have participated in two mysteri-
ies hidden in ages past—Christ living in believers and the
salvation of Gentiles as well as Jews. The two witnesses,
however, are prophets of the newly redeemed Israel. It is
their death that provokes God's "indignation," a term used
over and over in regard to the gathering of nations for the
final outpouring of His wrath.[93]

The two witnesses are more related to Old Testament
saints than to the others. They know the Mighty Angel better than the indwelling Christ of Christians. On the other
hand, the sealed company (the 144,000) and their Gentile
converts are sealed with the Holy Spirit just like members
of the Church, herself a combination of Jews and Gentiles.
So the resurrections appear to be grouped according to like-
nesses.

Old Testament saints knew nothing about the "hidden
mystery." Their only interest was to see the wicked pun-
ished. They are resurrected just in time to witness that event.

The Third Woe

John does not witness the resurrection of Old Testament saints. In fact, this entire chapter, with the exception
of his measuring and this last activity at the throne, has
been told to John by the angel. It was among the things

---

[93] Isaiah 13:5; 26:20; 66:14; Jer. 10:10; Dan. 8:19; Zeph. 3:8.

that he "heard." But now the active scene divider "saw" becomes the passive "was seen" as John views the ark along with everyone else.

> And the temple of God was opened in heaven, and there was seen in his temple the ark of his testament; and there were lightnings, and voices, and thunderings, and an earthquake, and great hail. (11:19)

After the announcement of the resurrection, John sees the temple in heaven open. He can look right in and see the ark of the covenant. Lightnings, voices, and thunderings—the activities of the throne issue out of the ark. Later, we will see that the temple had been closed to view until now.

The seventh trumpet sounds. The final and most devastating woe of all falls. Yet John only mentions thunderings, lightnings, an earthquake, and great hail.

Therefore, it is obvious that we will have to learn more before we can understand the nature of this last stroke of judgment. The fullness will come when we put together the other pieces written on the back of the scroll.

Chapter 18

THE SUNLIT WOMAN

(REVELATION 12)

With the fall of the second woe (the end of Revelation 11), we have almost reached the end of the writings on the front side of the scroll. Revelation 12 crosses this same stretch of time again but with a different set of details.

This chapter is one of the overlays we mentioned. The Mighty Angel told John the rest of the contents of Revelation 11 after he had measured the faithful. That chapter was part of the things that John heard. Now we will look at the measuring from another perspective and see it through the eyes of people on earth.

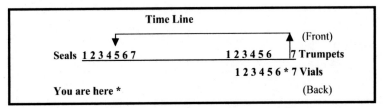

The Sign

> And a great *sign*[94] was seen in the heaven (12:1, Inter-
> linear Greek–English New Testament, emphasis added)

John introduces this new scene with a voice change in the verb. Since the beginning, the scene dividers of John's report have introduced each new scene with verbs in the active voice: "I saw," "I looked," "I beheld," etc. But at the mention of the temple in heaven being open and the ark being visible at the second woe (11:19), John switches to the passive voice and says, "There was seen." At the beginning of this scene, he also uses a passive verb.[95]

At the close of the sixth seal, the vision halted to introduce God's witnesses for that period. Here we see the same thing. The trumpet judgments stop after the sixth trumpet/vial to introduce the players in the last half of the week. In the last chapter, we saw God's elect measured and two prophets, like Moses and Elijah, called to speak for God.

Now the vision spotlights a woman who clearly gives birth to Christ. She is first seen in the form of a sign in the sky, but later in the chapter, it shows her living on earth. Her adversary is the devil, and her testimony identifies her as the people of God. Therefore, the woman, first shown as a symbol birthing Christ, goes on to represent certain believers in the second half of the week.

---

[94] The KJV translates this "wonder," but it is the same Greek word "semelon" translated "sign" in Revelation 15:1.

[95] *Optomai*–passive when used objectively as a person or thing being seen. Vine, *Expository Dictionary*, p. 65.

The voice change may simply indicate that John views these scenes in the company of others. Much of what he saw before was clothed in spiritual figures of speech or representation of events. Declaring something to be seen in the heavens as a sign would mean that God intended people on earth to see it, not just John. How else could it be a sign? Therefore, we assume from this that the heaven meant here is the starry heaven. The dragon of verse 3 confirms this by casting down a third part of the stars of heaven to earth. This means that although the sign foretells certain spiritual events, they are also actual happenings in themselves and can be seen by others besides John. If this is the case, then the sign appears in the sky where the inhabitants of earth can see it, too.

> And there appeared a great wonder in heaven; a woman clothed with the sun, and the moon under her feet, and upon her head a crown of twelve stars: and she being with child cried, travailing in birth, and pained to be delivered. (12:1–2)

All eyes gaze heavenward as a spectacle of wondrous nature develops—a woman appears in the sky, so distinct in shape that one need not use his imagination to trace her outline. Her long flowing robes glisten, reflecting the orange glow of a hazy sunrise or a dusky sunset. Lifting her up as a lovely space sculpture, the rising moon provides a pedestal under her feet. A crown forms around her head, made up of twelve stars. A closer look at this queen of heaven reveals a bulging belly, great with child. The woman, located in outer space, can be seen by the whole world.

Suddenly, the newly formed space sculpture comes to life. She bends over, hands on her loins—her time has come.

Her body language confirms that birth pangs are upon her. Thrashing about, she mimics pain. Every eye on earth watches in fascination.

> And there appeared another wonder in heaven; and behold a great red dragon, having seven heads and ten horns, and seven crowns upon his heads. And his tail drew the third part of the stars of heaven, and did cast them to the earth: and the dragon stood before the woman which was ready to be delivered, for to devour her child as soon as it was born. (12:3–4)

Fascination, however, turns to terror when a dreadful figure appears. A great red dragon advances toward the woman. His appearance resembles a fiery Chinese dragon, except he has seven heads instead of one, with ten horns distributed among them. His mighty tail sweeps a third of the stars of heaven and flings them to earth. Switching his tail impatiently, he waits to devour the male child about to be delivered.

For centuries, theologians used this scripture passage to describe Satan's fall from heaven, taking one-third of God's angels in his rebellion. It truly is a picture of his hatred for the woman through the ages and his fervent desire to kill her seed. Nevertheless, it is also a real-time and space event in this sequence. Mankind has reason to fear! They see the trajectory of the bodies involved. In fact, Luke 21:26 says, "Men's hearts failing them for fear, and for looking after those things which *are coming* on the earth" (emphasis added).

> And she brought forth a man child, who was to rule all nations with a rod of iron: and her child was caught up

unto God, and to his throne. And the woman fled into the wilderness, where she hath a place prepared of God, that they should feed her there a thousand two hundred and threescore days. (12:5–6)

The woman brings forth a royal Son who will ascend his Father's throne and receive a scepter of inflexible rule. The woman, however, must remain on earth, and God will honor her with special protection. Her special relationship with the Father is because of the birth.

Deprived of his prey, the dragon, later identified as the devil or Satan, finds himself under attack. The time has come for the archangel Michael and his army to clear the heavens of the devil's influence. Satan tries to defend his territory, but he and his fellows are no match for the forces of God acting with authority from the throne.

And there was war in heaven: Michael and his angels fought against the dragon; and the dragon fought and his angels, and prevailed not; neither was their place found any more in heaven. And the great dragon was cast out, that old serpent, called the Devil, and Satan, which deceiveth the whole world: he was cast out into the earth, and his angels were cast out with him. (12:7–9)

Angry because he is cast down, Satan goes after the woman to vent his wrath on her, but she escapes him. Given wings like those of a great eagle, she flies to a place of safety.

How much of John's report that actually can be seen by earth dwellers is not clear. In fact, we wonder how John knew the time allotted for the woman's protection, since nothing in the action reveals this. Nor does the fact that she has a protected hideout show up in the sign. Perhaps this came to him as a word of knowledge that he pronounces prophetically.

The time mentioned, 1,260 days (the same time allotted to the two witnesses), informs us that we are looking at the second half of the week again. That is all but the last thirty days. (See the time line at the beginning of the chapter.) The 1,260 days end at the sixth trumpet or second woe. Beyond that, the Gentile ruler has only thirty days left before the Lord takes over the kingdom.

The woman in the sky signifies the woman hidden by God during this time. She can be identified by the symbols and her man child Christ, who is foretold as He who will rule with a "rod of iron" (Ps. 2:9). The figure of speech, the "sun-moon-twelve-star combination" occurs in Joseph's dream in Genesis 37. Jacob interpreted these to mean himself, his wife, and his twelve sons. These descendents of Jacob literally became Israel. Christ, the Messiah, was born to their descendents. However, Israel did not recognize Him as their Messiah. He is about to be born to them again, this time spiritually. Now they will recognize Him. Therefore, the woman in the sky, travailing in birth, signifies Israel.

The Woman in Travail

Although the woman is an actual physical sign in the sky, she also proclaims this very important event on earth. Like the Bethlehem star at Christ's physical birth, the man child announces the spiritual birth of the Messiah to Israel. Since both birth announcements are written in the sky, they pronounce their heavenly origin.

Isaiah, speaking of Christ's physical birth, says:

Before she travailed, she brought forth; before her pain came, she was delivered of a man child. Who hath heard

such a thing? who has seen such things? Shall the earth
be made to bring forth in one day? or shall a nation be
born at once? for as soon as Zion travailed, she brought
forth her children. (Isa. 66:7–8)

Out of *her* travail, Israel brings forth children. When
Jesus was born to her in Bethlehem, she felt no pain at all.
But when the nation travails, she brings forth born-again
children. After her travail, her children become witnesses
for God during the last half of the prophetic week.

Having looked briefly at the birth announcement in the
sky, let us now turn to the birth itself. Here we look at the
circumstances on earth to see how they correlate with the
birth announcement. We began the last chapter with John
setting aside the temple (and those who worshiped there)
for God's purposes. This dealt mainly with the two witnesses, the "two lampstands" who belong to the priesthood.
We must remember, however, that the faithful remnant of
Israel had gathered at the same time to travail with God in
prayer because of the advancing army. Therefore, they are
included in the measuring, because they were present when
the two witnesses were anointed for service.

We have already established that Israel received the Holy
Spirit sometime prior to the "overturning" and the destruction of the Russian army. Now we need to establish that the
travailing woman brings forth Christ to her nation. Since
the lampstand and olive tree symbols mate with the same
symbols in Revelation for the two witnesses, let us turn
back to the visions of Zechariah and see how other visions
relate to Israel's spiritual rebirth.

Of Zechariah's ten visions, the puzzle piece that we
matched up earlier (the two olive trees) is found in the

seventh vision. The piece we wish to put in place now is found in the fifth vision. The first four are preliminary and are not directly connected to this part of the picture. But for the sake of background, we will state them briefly:

Zechariah's first vision deals with the jealousy of the Lord for His people because of how the nations are treating them (Zech. 1:7–17). The second and third visions concern how He comes against the powers that have scattered them and prevented their return to the land (1:18–21). The fourth vision deals with the measuring of Jerusalem so that the glory of God and the scattered sons of Israel may return (2:1–13). These things have been partially fulfilled and are being fulfilled today. The scattering began with the destruction of Jerusalem by Rome in A.D. 70 and has continued as each nation has rejected Israel and cast them out, gassed, or pogrommed them. The land was measured for their return at the close of World War I.

God has come against every nation since that tried to prevent Israel's return to their land. They are not, however, all back yet. The war depicted in the first four seals will send Jews scurrying to their homeland and the apparent safety of the Middle East. The next step would be to establish the new covenant with the nation. That brings us to the events that connect with the woman giving birth. The fifth vision of Zechariah says:

> And he showed me Joshua the high priest standing before the angel of the LORD, and Satan standing at his right hand to resist him. And the LORD said unto Satan, The LORD rebuke thee, O Satan; even the LORD that hath chosen Jerusalem rebuke thee: is not this a brand plucked out of the fire? Now Joshua was clothed with filthy garments, and stood before the angel [the Mighty

Angel?]. And he answered and spake unto those that
stood before him, saying, Take away the filthy garments
from him. And unto him he said, Behold, *I have caused
thine iniquity to pass from thee, and I will clothe thee with
a change of raiment.* And I said, Let them set a fair mitre
upon his head. So they set a fair mitre upon his head,
and clothed him with garments. And the angel of the
LORD stood by. And the angel of the LORD protested
unto Joshua, saying, Thus saith the LORD of hosts; If
thou wilt walk in my ways, and if thou wilt keep my
charge, then thou shalt also judge my house, and shalt
also keep my courts, and I will give thee places to walk
among these that stand by. (Zech. 3:1–7)

In the vision, the high priest Joshua symbolically represented the people before God; therefore, the whole nation
of Israel, clothed in filthy garments, stands before the
Messenger of Jehovah (the Mighty Angel). Isaiah 64:6 says
that "all our righteousnesses are as filthy rags." This reveals the figure of speech for human righteousnesses (good
works) without Christ. The fact that Joshua (the high priest
of Zechariah's day represents Israel in this latter-day happening) stands before God in filthy garments indicates symbolically that the nation is back in the land in this second
fulfillment worshipping as they did of old. They are still
trying to establish their own righteousness through the ceremonial law. The offering that their high priest brings before God is an offering of works. We established in chapter
17 that the call to repentance and prayer to God to save
them from the Russian takes place during the fall festivals.
On the Day of Atonement, the high priest enters the Holy
of Holies to represent Israel before God.

So Zechariah's portrayal of the high priest standing before God fits in exactly with what should be taking place at this time. The picture of Satan standing at the right hand of the angel also fits into this time slot. He resists the removal of the self-righteous "rags," which he has promoted. Israel cannot approach God clothed in her own righteousness. Like the dragon in the sky, Satan tries to hinder this vital spiritual change in Israel.

Nevertheless, Israel receives a clean set of garments and a charge to walk in God's ways. This appears to depict a cleansing from self-righteousness to being clothed in God's "garments of salvation" (Isa. 61:10). The fair mitre is part of the uniform of the priesthood. The angel charges the cleansed priests to earn positions as permanent priests in the eternal kingdom.

So, then, this vision depicts Israel after she has return to the land and to her ceremonial worship. However, her return to worship is marred by the same mistake made at the first return to the land in Zechariah's day—the setting up of the Talmudic additions and traditions. This was the condition despised by Christ when He walked among them. Paul spoke of it also:

> For I bear them record that they have a zeal of God, but not according to knowledge. For they being ignorant of God's righteousness, and going about to establish their own righteousness, have not submitted themselves unto the righteousness of God. (Rom. 10:2–3)

"Joshua," being confronted by the angel, submits to and is clothed with God's righteousness. Since Joshua represents the Israelites symbolically, it means the gospel message penetrates the hearts of the crowd gathered to celebrate the Day of Atonement. God redeems them instantly! Then He fills them with power as a collective body, just as He did the Church on the Day of Pentecost.

Besides receiving changes of raiment, another tremendous event takes place before the two witnesses are commissioned. Vision six precedes immediately before the one that portrays the two olive trees and lampstands.

> Hear now, O Joshua the high priest, thou, and thy *fellows* that sit before thee: for they are men wondered at: for, behold, I will bring forth my servant the BRANCH.[96] For behold the stone that I have laid before Joshua; upon one stone shall be seven eyes [the Holy Spirit, Rev. 5:6]: behold, I will engrave the graving thereof, saith the LORD of hosts, and *I will remove the iniquity of that land in one day.*[97] (Zech. 8:8–9, emphasis added)

God promises to unveil His Branch to two groups of men: to the "fellows that sit before thee" and to Israel represented by Joshua. The "fellows" that sit before Joshua are

---

[96] Jer. 23:5–7.

[97] In chapter 2, Zechariah prophesies that "the Lord shall inherit Judah his portion in the holy land, and shall choose Jerusalem again" (Zech. 2:12). This cleansing and reclaiming of the land shows that His favor and blessings are now toward Israel. The land occupies an important place in the covenants of the Jews. He warned repeatedly that a sinful people defile the land (Lev. 18:25, 27). Therefore, this cleansing provides for Israel's new relationship with God. Although God redeems the people and the land, it will still be three and a half years before they can enjoy this blessing. The Gentile usurpers and the Jewish collaborators still have rights to the land during the remainder of the judgment period.

special because the power of God is already evident in their lives. They are "men wondered at." They tell Israel about God's servant, the Branch. Jeremiah defines the Branch as the King whose name is "the Lord our Righteousness," He who regathered Israel (Jer. 23:6). Therefore, the Branch is none other than Israel's Messiah.

Jesus Christ, the Branch, suddenly stands in their midst as their King, but He is a king who bears wounds in His body. With the message of God's righteousness confirmed, they can plainly see that it is not by works of righteousness that they have done, but by His grace alone are they redeemed.

After Israel recognizes the Branch, God forces her to recognize the engraved cornerstone once rejected by them. Jesus stated plainly when He was on the earth that He was the stone which the builders rejected (Matt. 21:42). Peter says, "But unto them which be disobedient, the stone which the builders disallowed, the same is made head of the corner" (1 Pet. 2:7). Zechariah tells us:

> And it shall come to pass in that day, I will seek to destroy all the nations that come against Jerusalem. And I will pour upon the house of David, and upon the inhabitants of Jerusalem, the spirit of grace and of supplications: and *they shall look upon me* whom they have pierced, and they shall mourn for him, as one mourneth for his only son, as one that is in bitterness[98] for his firstborn. (Zech. 12:9–10, emphasis added)

---

[98] In order to understand this bitterness, one needs to know the blind hatred and prejudice orthodox Jews feel for anything connected with Christianity. To learn that their precious Messiah is the Jesus of the Christians and had been available to them all along will be a traumatic, emotional event, This will be especially true if, like Paul, they will be

At last, they understand! At last, the full truth dawns upon them. Isaiah prophesied their exact words:

> Surely he hath borne our griefs, and carried our sorrows: *yet we* did esteem him stricken, smitten of God, and afflicted. But he was wounded for our transgressions, and he was bruised for our iniquities: the chastisement of our peace was upon him; and with his stripes we are healed. (Isa. 53:4–5, emphasis added)

Jesus of the Christian faith *is* the Messiah after all! What is more, this personal appearance of Christ fulfills the rituals of the Day of Atonement. So leaving the prophets for a moment, we will look into the Law and see this precious "appointment with the Messiah" portrayed by ritual.

In Leviticus 16:7–10, we read that two goats were required for the atonement of Israel's sin for one year. One goat died as a sin offering; the other became a scapegoat to remove their sins. Jesus had to *appear alive* to fulfill the type of the scapegoat.

Before the high priest offered the goats, he offered a bullock for himself and his house, the priesthood. The first sacrifice signifies the redemption Christ secured for the Church, His royal priesthood, "whose house are we" (Heb. 3:6). The blood of the bullock was then sprinkled on the mercy seat that pictured its application at the throne. After that, the first goat was slain and its blood was also sprinkled

---

filled with hatred toward Him because of the witness of redeemed Jews, which in this case will be the 144,000. Their days of mourning will include great regret as they ponder the sufferings their ancestors endured because of their stiff-necked and deliberate blindness as a people

by the high priest, who entered behind the veil with blood *a second time for Israel's sake.* Returning from the Holy of Holies, the high priest then sprinkled blood on the Holy Place, on the curtains that covered the tabernacle, and on the altar outside. He thus cleansed and dedicated a place for Israel to worship and serve Him in righteousness for another year. Finally, he sprinkled the blood of both the bullock and the goat on the horns of the altar (Lev. 16:18).

> And when he hath made an end of reconciling the holy place, and the tabernacle of the congregation, and the altar, he shall bring the live goat: and Aaron shall lay both his hands upon the head of the live goat, and confess over him all the iniquities of the children of Israel, and all their transgressions in all their sins, putting them upon the head of the goat, and shall send him away by the hand of a fit man into the wilderness. (Lev. 16:20–21)

After all the holy ground (the same portion measured by John) had been sprinkled with blood, the high priest laid his hands on the live goat. At this appearing, Jesus will become Israel's scapegoat. He died as the bullock and the first goat over nineteen hundred years ago. One death suffices for both the Church and Israel. The sprinkling of the two bloods together on the horns of the altar and the burning of the two carcasses together (Lev. 16:27) without the camp show this. The Church received its benefit, but it was not efficacious then for Israel because she refused to believe. When she believes, the blood can be sprinkled on the mercy seat in heaven at a separate entrance behind the veil (when the man child is caught up to the Father's throne).

But first, Christ must appear before the Israelites—alive. He does not have to die again to redeem them. He simply shows them His wounds. When He leaves, He will carry away all their sins.

It takes two goats, then, to typify Christ's redemption of Israel. Isaiah describes the effect of the first goat:

> And the Redeemer shall come to Zion, and unto them that turn from transgression in Jacob, saith the LORD. As for me, this is my covenant with them, saith the LORD; My spirit that is upon thee, and my words which I have put in thy mouth, shall not depart out of thy mouth . . . for ever. (Isa. 59:20–21)

The first goat redeems by blood and brings access to the Spirit. Paul describes the function of the second, the scapegoat:

> For I would not, brethren, that ye should be ignorant of this mystery, lest ye should be wise in your own conceits; that blindness in part is happened to Israel, until the fulness of the Gentiles be come in. And so all Israel shall be saved: as it is written, There shall come *out of* Sion the Deliverer, and shall turn away ungodliness from Jacob: for this is my covenant unto them, *when I shall take away their sins.* (Rom. 11:25–27, emphasis added)

The Deliverer removes their sins. The former scripture says He comes *to* Zion, the latter says He comes *out of* Zion. Connecting these verses in Isaiah and Romans in this manner shows the fuller detail seen by combining mated verses. In His coming and going, the Deliverer takes away their sins.

With the sin question solved, God gives Israel a charge: "Thus saith the LORD of hosts; If thou wilt walk in my ways, and if thou wilt keep my charge, then thou shalt judge my house, and shalt also keep my courts, and I will give thee places to walk among these that stand by" (Zech. 3:7). The charge tests Israel's faithfulness so they can earn rewards in the coming kingdom just like the Church.

Again it is Zechariah who says:

> In that day there shall be a fountain opened to the house of David and to the inhabitants of Jerusalem for sin and for uncleanness . . . .And it shall come to pass, that in all the land, saith the LORD, two parts therein shall be cut off and die; but the third shall be left therein. And I will bring the third part through the fire, and will refine them as silver is refined, and will try them as gold is tried: they shall call on my name, and I will hear them: I will say, It is my people: and they shall say, The LORD is my God. (Zech. 13:1, 8–9)

Jehovah lights the refiner's fire because Israel must be tried as silver and gold in a furnace to test their faithfulness to see if it is greater than that their forefathers. Satan makes the fire very hot as he seeks to destroy God's people.

The Preachers

We have looked at the nation's redemption in Zechariah's visions as depicted by Joshua, the high priest, and his change of garments. Now let us identify those who sit before Joshua, the "men wondered at." Paul, by a verse that mates with Isaiah's account of Israel's redemption, speaks of the time when Israel will believe:

How then shall they call on him in whom they have not
believed? and how shall they believe in him of whom
they have not heard? and how shall they hear without a
preacher? And how shall they preach, except they be
sent? as it written, How beautiful are the feet of them
that preach the gospel of peace, and bring glad tidings
of good things! (Rom. 10:14–15)

Paul asks who will preach to Israel about salvation? Who
indeed can preach to Israel at a time when they will listen?
Answer: only those who are divinely sent. Can it be these
men of power who have inspired great wonder?

Paul says blindness that happened to Israel will remain
"until the fullness of the Gentiles be come in" (Rom. 11:25).
After this, Israel will hear and receive spiritual truths. The
144,000 Jewish witnesses have already brought in the last
great harvest of Gentile souls, the multitude of believers
during the first half of the week. Therefore, we might assume these "men of power" to be the Jewish witnesses who
have completed their mission to the world and return to
Jerusalem to preach to those in Israel who fear God. The
time certainly fits.

For a clue to the identity of the preachers, let us look at
the prophecy in Isaiah that Paul quotes (Isaiah 52). But
first, let us establish its setting. Isaiah chapter 50 tells about
the humiliation of Christ: "I gave my back to the smiters,
and my cheeks to them that plucked off the hair: I hid not
my face from shame and spitting" (Isa. 50:6).

The next chapter shows the call of the preachers. Isaiah
talks of them as "ye that know righteousness, the people in
whose heart is my law" (Isa. 51:7). This means that they
have already benefited from the New Covenant promise by
Jeremiah, which states:

> Behold, the days come, saith the LORD, that I will make
> a new covenant with the house of Israel, and with the
> house of Judah: . . . After those days, saith the LORD, I
> will put my law in their inward parts, and write it in
> their hearts. (Jer 31:31, 33)

It seems that the preachers are believers already. We have
seen that the members of Sealed Company (144,000) are
severely persecuted for their testimony during the first half
of the week. If these are the same preachers, then, there
should be some mention of it here in Isaiah. Finishing the
verse started earlier, Isaiah says:

> Fear ye not the reproach of men, *neither be ye afraid of
> their revilings.* For the moth shall eat them up like a gar-
> ment, and the worm shall eat them like wool: but my
> righteousness shall be for ever, and my salvation from
> generation to generation. (Isa. 51:7–8, emphasis added)

The witnesses cower in the face of revilings and persecution to the point that the Spirit has to exhort them to get
moving. He reminds them of His mighty works in the past
by saying:

> Awake, awake, put on strength, O arm of the LORD
> [Christ as Mighty Angel?]; awake, as in the ancient days,
> in the generations of old. Art thou not it that hath cut
> Rahab, and wounded the dragon? Art thou not it which
> hath dried the sea, the waters of the great deep; that
> made the depths of the sea a way for the ransomed to
> pass over? (Isa. 51:9–10)

Wake up, says the prophet, to the "arm" of the Lord,
the arm to be revealed to Israel (Isa. 53:1). Isaiah calls on

that same mighty angel who wounded Egypt (Rahab) and cut up the dragon (Leviathan) [99] in the wilderness to feed the people, to come back into action for Israel.

> Therefore the redeemed of the LORD shall return, and come with singing unto Zion; and everlasting joy shall be upon their head: they shall obtain gladness and joy; and sorrow and mourning shall flee away. I, even I, am he that comforteth you: who art thou, that thou shouldest be afraid of a man that shall die, and of the son of man which shall be made as grass; and forgettest the LORD thy maker, that hath stretched forth the heavens, and laid the foundations of the earth; and hast feared continually every day because of the fury of the oppressor, as if he were ready to destroy? and where is the fury of the oppressor? The captive exile hasteneth that he may be loosed, and that he should not die in the pit, nor that his bread should fail. But I am the LORD thy God, that divided the sea, whose waves roared: The LORD of hosts is his name. And *I have put my words in thy mouth*, and I have covered thee in the shadow of mine hand [the power of the Holy Spirit], *that I my plant the heavens, and lay the foundations of the earth, and say unto Zion, Thou art my people.* (Isa. 51:11–16, emphasis added)

Why, indeed, would these witnesses be afraid of men? God has spoken to them: He who has almighty power. "I, even I," He says, "am he that comforteth you" (Isa. 51:12). Those exiled captives emprisoned for proclaiming the gospel take hope and are soon be released. They

---

[99] Ps. 74:13–14.

come from all over the world. Therefore, the redeemed shall (emphatically) return with a special message to preach to "Zion," those gathered in Jerusalem to celebrate the feasts. They will come with joyful anticipation. They will meet the Lord!

The preachers proclaim a mixed message. Yes, God will plant new bodies in the heavens. Yes, He will relay the foundations of the earth. But take heart, O Zion, they say, He wants you to know that you are His people! In spite of the mighty judgments, you will be preserved and refined in the fire.

> Awake, awake, stand up, O Jerusalem, which hast drunk at the hand of the LORD the cup of his fury; thou hast drunken the dregs of the cup of trembling, and wrung them out. . . . Thus saith thy Lord the LORD, and thy God that pleadeth the cause of his people, Behold, I have taken out of thine hand the cup of trembling, even the dregs of the cup of my fury; thou shalt no more drink it again: but I will put it into the hand of them that afflict thee; which have said to thy soul, Bow down, that we may go over: and thou hast laid thy body as the ground, and as the street, to them that went over. (Isa. 51:17, 22–23)

God removes the cup of judgment from Israel. No more will Gentile armies run over her without dire consequences. The Lord's jealousy for His people rises in wrathful indignation.

The Sealed Company will preach this whole message, delivered with great authority from the Spirit, to those gathered at the temple to celebrate the Feast of Trumpets. Remember, the faithful of Israel had gathered in the first place to implore God to save them from the invading Russian Army. God answers them in power via the 144,000 witnesses or at least a representative of this group, those who survived the persecution.

These Jewish witnesses are there to "sound the trumpet" of God's message of repentance to them. That would be the first day of the seventh month, the Feast of Trumpets. By the tenth day or the Day of Atonement, many will have crowded into the temple courtyard to hear the Word preached with power. By this time, the crowds will continue to increase until the witnesses move outside on the mountain to preach. All Jerusalem will wonder at the men and their message.

And Israel begins to wake up! Repentance and travail overcomes the worshipers as they recognize that Christ, whom they rejected, is indeed their Messiah. The Sealed Company preaches the same message John the Baptist preached at Christ's first coming: Repent, for the kingdom of God is at hand! "Therefore my people shall know my name: therefore they shall know in that day that I am he that doth speak: behold, it is I" (Isa. 52:6). They recognize the authority of God in the Sealed Company's words.

> How beautiful upon the mountains are the feet of him
> that bringeth good tidings, that publisheth peace; that
> bringeth good tidings of good, that publisheth salvation;
> that saith unto Zion, Thy God reigneth! (Isa. 52:7)

Paul refers to this verse as "the feet of *them*," but here it reads "the feet of *him*." Could this be a reference to Jesus, the Branch, the Lord our Righteousness, appearing in their midst, spoken of by Zechariah?

Thy watchman shall lift up the voice; with the voice together shall they sing: for they shall see eye to eye, when the LORD shall bring again Zion. Break forth into joy, sing together, ye waste places of Jerusalem: for the LORD hath comforted his people, he hath redeemed Jerusalem. The LORD hath made bare his holy arm [Christ] in the eyes of all the nations; and all the ends of the earth shall see the salvation of our God.[100] (Isa. 52:8–10)

After Israel realizes that God's Spirit is truly in their midst, the "arm" of the Lord is made bare. We found this expression to mean Jesus, the Savior, when we discussed the word picture of "his mighty hand and outstretched arm" (Rev. 5). Therefore, the "arm" being made bare means Christ unveiled to Israel in person. Verse 14 of this same chapter further confirms this: "As many were astonied at thee; his visage was so marred more than any man, and his form more than the sons of men" (Isa. 52:14).

When they see His wounds, they are astonished. "Surely he hath borne our griefs" (Isa. 53:4). It is the same scene, depicted by Zechariah, of the builders' Cornerstone once rejected but now laid bare before Israel. The scapegoat of Leviticus 16 presents Himself alive to carry away Israel's sins. So besides redeeming the nation, He confirms His messiahship in person, just like He confirmed His resurrection in person before many witnesses.

---

[100] Every eye will see Him when He comes in the clouds.

The Birth Announcement

Before the praise offered for salvation and probably as a confirming sign during the preaching, the spectacular pageant of the woman begins to form in the sky. A heavenly body suddenly erupts, scattering dust and debris through thousands of miles in space. The clouds of dust take on the shape of a woman. She stands out as she reflects the sun's rays from her glistening, dusty dress. She is close by—in our own solar system. Appearing above the moon, she may even be bright enough to be seen in the daytime.

Her head, the main mass of the body affected, reveals a circle of twelve points of light, which when seen from the earth look like a crown. In our solar system, only one body is near enough to fulfill this requirement: the planet Jupiter with its many moons. Although Saturn is thought to have anywhere from twelve to eighteen satellites, its greater distance and the moons' smaller sizes are not as likely to be seen.

On the other hand, the physical conditions on Jupiter are conducive to producing the results ascribed to this new body in space. Jupiter's family of satellites and rings contains the ice, rocky debris, dust, and sulfur dumped on the earth during the trumpet judgments. Also, the planet abounds with organic substances, such as methane gas and perhaps other hydrocarbons which could produce crude petroleum (fuel of the fire rain) under the right conditions.

But the most interesting and perhaps the most likely physical condition on Jupiter that could bring about this sign in the heaven is the giant red spot. This large feature (large enough to contain two earths) is thought to be a great high-pressure storm of swirling dust and gasses whose color is possibly due to traces of phosphorous and organic molecules being transported from below.[101] The red spot has been seen through telescopes since 1665 and became especially brilliant in 1878. Located just south of the red spot is a newly formed white spot (only sixty or so years old), also a high-pressure cell but with different trace elements. Should some disturbance occur in Jupiter's charged atmosphere (Voyager found the Jovian atmosphere to be continually crackling with lightning)[102] to expel these storms, we might see a new comet or comets enter the solar system. This depends, of course, on whether these storms have substance at the center of their swirls.

Such a hypothesis was suggested in *Pensee*, a magazine published by the Student Academic Freedom Forum. An article by H. Ragnar Forshufvud concerning the red spot says:

> I propose the reconsideration of the solid-body hypothesis. How could a solid body be floating in the atmosphere of Jupiter? My answer is: by electrostatic repulsion. It should be noted that during the Exodus disaster, electrostatic attraction between Venus and the Earth was comparable to and probably stronger than gravitational forces. The proof is that the waters fell back immediately after the discharge. [Both

---

[101] Rick Gore, "What Voyager Saw: Jupiter's Dazzling Realm," *National Geographic*, Jan. 1980 Vol. 157, #1, p. 8.
[102] Ibid, p. 11.

Josephus and King David mention this lightning at the crossing of the Red Sea.[103]] Now if Venus was electrically charged, the force that allowed Venus to leave Jupiter may have been, quite simply, electrostatic repulsion. If you calculate the voltage Jupiter must have had to make this possible, you arrive at something on the order of 10 [to the power of 19] volts. If Jupiter had this high voltage, it probably has about the same today. This could explain how a solid body is able to float around in the atmosphere. No one has yet been able to explain the red color of the spot. I suggest that the solid body is surrounded by a red ferrous dust, which is kept there by magnetic forces. The Greek used to say that Athena sprang out of the head of Zeus, which is to be interpreted as a description of the fact that Venus was expelled from Jupiter. Could it be that Zeus is pregnant again?[104]

Jupiter had a reputation in mythology for giving birth to children. Besides Venus, the great goddess Diana of the Ephesians was said to have fallen from Jupiter (Acts 19:35).

Velikovsky, reporting in *Yale Scientific* on the feasibility of comets originating in our solar system through colliding bodies in space, says: "In such near collisions, eruptive forces could exceed escape velocities, and the

---

[103] Whiston,William (translator) Josephus, *Antiquities of the Jews*, Book II, chapter 16, sec 3 p. 64 (Grand Rapids: Kregal Publications, 1867,1963,1964,1966,1967,1969) See also Ps. 77:16–18.

[104] H. Rugnar Forshufvud, "The Red Spot," *Pensee*, (Portland, OR: Student Academic Student Forum, Fall 1972) p. 46.

red spot on Jupiter could conceivably be the locus of a major eruption."[105]

Therefore, we propose that because of the physical conditions of Jupiter and the possibility of the red spot housing a body large enough to greatly affect the earth in an encounter, this may be the source of the new comet. The giant red spot, along with the white spot below, may be, in fact, the expelled bodies seen in the sign—bodies, which at some time in the expulsion, take on the appearance of living figures. The eruption itself, along with Jupiter, would form the woman, while the red spot would form the red dragon. That would leave the white spot or some other feature in Jupiter's atmosphere to form the man child.

We believe the red dragon fits the figure or body that will tangle with earth. As mentioned before, Velikovsky's sources describe comets of bloody rather than fiery redness. This fits our dragon. The so-called mythical dragons (ancient comets) Hydra and Typhon had a hundred heads that spit fire.[106] They, too, resemble our dragon, having multiple heads. Leviathan, the dragon of the exodus, also had more than one head (Ps. 74:13–14). Therefore, it is most likely that, of the three figures, the dragon becomes the comet that terrorizes the earth. This body, then, causes the physical judgments, eclipsing the sun, dusting the moon, turning over the earth, and causing the trumpet judgments, directly or indirectly.

---

[105] I. Velikovsky, "Venus: A Youthful Planet," *Yale Scientific*, April 1967, p. 9.

[106] *Little and Ives Webster's Dictionary*, "Classical Mythology," sec. 12, pp. 1805, 1823.

The man child ascends immediately to the throne in heaven. The body that represents this figure apparently shoots off on a new trajectory and disappears. The woman at some point develops wings and appears to fly away as the dust and gases rearrange, and dissipate. Somewhere in this succession of displays, the comet appears as a bloody sword. Revelation 12:7–12 mentions another. Michael, the archangel, along with his army, replace the other figures.

> And there was war in heaven: Michael and his angels fought against the dragon; and the dragon fought and his angels, and prevailed not; neither was their place found any more in heaven. And the great dragon was cast out, that old serpent, called the Devil, and Satan, which deceiveth the whole world: he was cast out into the earth, and his angels were cast out with him. And I heard a loud voice saying in heaven, Now is come salvation, and strength, and the kingdom of our God, and the power of his Christ: for the accuser of our brethren is cast down, which accused them before our God day and night. And they overcame him by the blood of the Lamb, and by the word of their testimony; and they loved not their lives unto the death. Therefore rejoice, ye heavens, and ye that dwell in them. Woe to the inhabiters of the earth and of the sea! for the devil is come down unto you, having great wrath, because he knoweth that he hath but a short time. (12:7–12)

Now, it is obvious from this passage that we are dealing with a spiritual situation. Yet it is equally true that the dragon's descent poses a literal threat to the inhabitants of both the earth and sea. What we have here is a unique instance where God uses pageantry in the sky to picture spiritual happenings. Fully written in the sky for all the world to read, it presents a warning, an omen, if you will. But before we take up the spiritual message written there, let us continue with the physical description.

As the dragon separates from the woman, other bodies become involved. The sky fills with two separate armies. Missiles and thunderbolts pass back and forth between them. Eventually, the body representing Michael in the pageant overcomes the dragon and thrusts him out of Jupiter's orbit on a collision course with the earth.

The portrayal of war games in the sky may seem too far out for belief; but it has happened before. Josephus records a similar happening when Titus destroyed Jerusalem in A.D. 70. In his book, *Wars of the Jews*, Josephus says:

> Thus there was a star resembling a sword, which stood over the city, and a comet, that continued a whole year . . . . Besides these, a few days after . . . on the one and twentieth day of the month Artemisius, a certain prodigious and incredible phenomenon appeared; I suppose the account of it would seem to be a fable, were it not related by those that saw it, and were not the events that followed it of so considerable a nature as to deserve such signals; for, before sun-setting, chariots and troops of soldiers, were seen running about among the clouds. [107]

Evidently, God used the sword as a spiritual omen against Jerusalem. The sword was a sign written in the sky.

---

[107] Josephus, *Complete Works, Wars of the Jews*, ed. William Wiston, p. 582.

The pageantry of the army showed that the city would be destroyed in the war. And it was. Likewise, the comet of this latter-day sign takes on the appearance of a sword coming to perform the sacrifice of the invading army on its way to Jerusalem. Isaiah's prophecy (Isa. 34:5) mentioned a sword "bathed in blood in heaven." Apparently, the comet continues to change its shape. Isaiah viewed it after the dragon shape and the armies had both disappeared. The sign, then, is a continuing expression of what God is doing spiritually. Therefore, the spiritual nature of the sign is just what the action implies.

Putting the events pictured together with what we already know, we will place them in our puzzle. We know from Old Testament prophecies that Israel is reborn by an outpouring of the Spirit sometime before the Russian invasion. We know the 144,000 witnesses return to Jerusalem to preach the gospel to the Jews. This is confirmed later in the vision when they stand on Mount Zion with the Lamb (Rev. 14). We know some witnesses are martyred because the opening of the fifth seal spoke of their blood under the altar. We interpreted the "giving out of robes" to the martyrs as the time of their resurrection. The opening of the fifth seal sets the time in that sequence. Since we know that Jesus appears to declare His messiahship to Israel and stands with the 144,000 (all of them, which presupposes that some are resurrected), that connects their resurrection with His appearing. Therefore, by this connection, we know that Israel gives birth spiritually sometime after the opening of the fifth seal but before the destruction of the overturning in the sixth seal, which destroys the Russian army.

And when the dragon saw that he was cast unto the earth,
he persecuted the woman which brought forth the man

child. And to the woman were given two wings of a great eagle, that she might fly into the wilderness, into her place, where she is nourished for a time, and times, and half a time, from the face of the serpent. (12:13–14)

When the sign appears, it starts the action—the birth and everything connected with it. But the rest of the events pictured in the sky continue in sequence throughout the last half of the prophetic week. These events include war in heaven, the hiding of the woman, and the persecution.

The catching away of the man child at the end of the birth, however, signifies another important event. Besides the Messiah becoming Israel's scapegoat to carry away their sins, He enters heaven (goes behind the veil a second time) on the behalf of Israel, fulfilling the ritual of the Day of Atonement. After the sprinkling of the blood, He becomes their High Priest before God the Father. However, when He returns to heaven, He takes the 144,000 witnesses with Him, leaving behind a new body of redeemed ones—the woman, Israel. (The converts of the 144,000, the great multitude of chapter 7, will be raptured from among men all over the world at the same time. We say this not from scriptural proof but conjecture. If God removed the Church from His wrath, would He not also remove these believers from the severest judgments, leaving behind a truly guilty world to suffer them?) We look at the rapture of the 144,000 in detail in chapter 20. Suffice it here to say that the whole process of Israel's spiritual rebirth takes place under the pageantry of fearsome signs in the heavens.

Finishing the story presaged in the sky, the spiritual picture of the war in heaven is rather obvious. Satan, no longer tolerated in the heavens, must base his operations on the earth itself. The war in the heavens prevents his interference with the man child's spiritual birth to Israel. With the man child safely caught up to the throne, he goes after the real woman—Israel.

The Woman on Earth

The woman, however, receives earnest instructions concerning the hardships ahead. God had prepared a place for her to hide. The two witnesses and part of Israel's priesthood, who are God's testimony to the Gentile conquerors, remain behind. On signal, the rest of the faithful are exhorted to flee. The setting up of the idol, perhaps an image made to look like the dragon in the sky, signals the time.

Evidently, a time lapse occurs between the appearing of the sign and the eclipse of the sun at the sixth seal—time enough for Israel to be redeemed and the idol to be constructed and set up. Time enough also for the woman to flee. But once the idol is set up, the die is cast. Then begins the last half of the week: the great tribulation, spoken of by Jesus.

> When ye therefore shall see the abomination of desolation, spoken of by Daniel the prophet, stand in the holy place, (whoso readeth, let him understand:) then let them which be in Judea flee into the mountains: Let him which is on the housetop not come down to take any thing out of his house: neither let him which is in the field return back to take his clothes. (Matt. 24:15–17)

The armies have gathered. The abomination has been set. Time has run out. Next, a great thunderbolt strikes the earth. Jesus says:

> For as the lightning cometh out of the east, and shineth even unto the west; so shall also the coming of the Son

of man be. For wheresoever the carcase is, there will the eagles be gathered together. (Matt. 24:27–28)

Several events take place one after the other—the electrical discharge from the approaching comet, the horizon shifts, the great earthquake, and finally, birds of prey gathered around the slaughtered army to eat the sacrifice.

And the serpent cast out of his mouth water as a flood after the woman, that he might cause her to be carried away of the flood. And the earth helped the woman, and the earth opened her mouth, and swallowed up the flood which the dragon cast out of his mouth. And the dragon was wroth with the woman, and went to make war with the remnant of her seed, which keep the commandments of God, and have the testimony of Jesus Christ. (12:14–17)

The encounter of the earth with the dragon produces a flood of water that threatens to destroy the fleeing woman. The great earthquake opens a crevice, swallowing the menacing flood, and the woman escapes to higher ground.

Many Bible scholars believe her secret hideout, the place prepared by God, is the ancient Nabatean city of Petra. W. E. Blackstone, author of *Jesus Is Coming*, invested his life savings in Bibles and tracts and sent them to Petra where they were supposedly buried, awaiting the arrival of the Jewish remnant. However, guides told me on my trip to Petra in 1998, that although Christian groups keep bringing literature, the Jordanian government keeps destroying it. It has become a nagging problem for the government.

Petra, once the glory of the Nabateans and later the Romans, lies south of the Dead Sea on Mount Seir about sixty miles from Jerusalem. Located on high table land whose edges drop off sharply into the Arabah, Petra has limited entrances. One is a mile-long gorge 300 feet high and 30 feet wide at the widest point, the other has four-wheel access across extremely rough terrain. Tombs and houses carved out of solid rock stretch for about three miles. All in all, it is a fairly safe place of refuge during the ravages of nature and persecutions of men.

The woman, who hides safely during the bulk of the judgments, does not represent the whole nation of Israel. We know this because of other references to persecution and martyrdom. Luke mentions those taken captive when the city falls (Luke 21:24). Joel tells of Jewish children sold as slaves (Joel 3:6), and John speaks of the remnant of the woman's seed whom Satan persecutes (Rev. 12:17). At the end, John sees believers resurrected who were beheaded for refusing to worship the image at the temple (Rev. 20:4). Therefore, we have to understand that the woman only represents those in the place of refuge. Away from their hideout, they are vulnerable.

Nevertheless, Israel's faith becomes unshakeable as each judgment progresses. She does not whine and complain as she did at the first exodus. Instead, she might well repeat the words of the psalmist:

God is our refuge and strength, a very present help in trouble. Therefore will not we fear, though the earth be removed, and though the mountains be carried into the midst of the sea; though the waters thereof roar and be troubled, though the mountains shake with the swelling thereof. Selah. There is a river, the streams whereof shall make glad the city of God, the holy place of the tabernacles of the most High. God is in the midst of her; she shall not be moved: God shall help her, and that right early. The heathen raged, the kingdoms were moved: he uttered his voice, the earth melted. The LORD of hosts is with us; the God of Jacob is our refuge. Selah. Come, behold the works of the LORD, what desolations he hath made in the earth. He maketh wars to cease unto the end of the earth [the overturned earth?]; he breaketh the bow, and cutteth the spear in sunder; he burneth the chariot in the fire. Be still, and know that I am God: I will be exalted among the heathen, I will be exalted in the earth. The LORD of hosts is with us; the God of Jacob is our refuge. Selah. (Psalm 46)

The woman grows strong in faith as she witnesses the exploits of her God. She truly reflects the glory of the Sun of Righteousness.

Here we pause to answer the question raised in the first chapter: Does God have two separate peoples He loves and to whom He has made special promises? The answer must be yes. Actually, He indicated this to Abraham when He made the promise that he (Abram) would father many nations. In Genesis 13:16, God promised that Abram's seed would be a numerous as the dust of the earth. In Genesis 15:5, He promised that Abram's seed would be as numerous as the stars that cannot be numbered.

To Abraham's son Isaac, God repeated only the promise concerning the stars (Gen. 26:4). To Jacob, Abraham's grandson, God repeated only the promise concerning the dust of the earth. Why? I believe He meant to set apart two peoples to be His witnesses, an earthly people and a heavenly people. Both Israel and the Church are descendents of Abraham: the Jews by circumcision, the Church by faith (Rom. 4:16). The Church superceded Israel in receiving the blessing first, because of Israel's disbelief.

Now during this week of judgment, God remembers His promises to Israel and gives her another chance. Therefore, God always intended to have two peoples to represent Him in two different ages. Although Israel's promises were delayed, they have not been lost. God fulfills His every word.

Chapter 19

THE ADVERSARIES

(Revelation 13)

The controversy comes to a climax. Will Satan rule the world or will God? John has already met those on God's side. Now the Lord shows him Satan's chosen leaders whom the devil inspires to war against God and His people. John watches the evil kingdom's leaders as they emerge in visionary pageantry. Describing the scene, he says:

> And I stood upon the sand of the sea, and saw a beast rise up out of the sea, having seven heads and ten horns, and upon his horns ten crowns, and upon his heads the name of blasphemy. And the beast which I saw was *like unto* a leopard, and his feet were *as* the feet of a bear, and his mouth *as* the mouth of a lion: and the dragon gave him his power, and his seat, and great authority. (13:1–2)

John's location remains the earth, this time on its surface, specifically at the seashore. As John looks at the dreadful beast, he notices the resemblance to the fierce dragon he had seen in the previous episode. He counted the beast's heads and horns as it emerged out of the water. Yes, it had the same seven heads and ten horns as the dragon but with one difference. Instead of the crowns resting on the heads as they did on the dragon, they encircled the horns themselves. Nevertheless, with the same blasphemous name stamped on all the heads, the beast reflects the dragon's antichrist nature. A definite similarity exists between the dragon's heads and the beast's heads.

Speaking in spiritual language, seven—the number designating completeness—combined with heads signifying leadership, translates into complete or absolute leadership in both the dragon and the beast. The number ten speaks of law and responsibility (rule) while the horn presents power in the sense of strength. Both add up to power. Crowns speak of authority to rule. The sea represents the Gentile nations (see Dan. 7:2–3).

Giving meaning to the figures of speech, what John sees rising from the nations (the sea) is a Gentile empire with the leadership (heads) completely dedicated to antichrist activity (blasphemous) and with the authority (crowns) and the strength (horns) to govern what remains of the world. Therefore, the spiritual message reads as follows: The empire, with backing from the dragon's heads, leads people to rebel against God.

John notes a closer view as he indicates another scene change. Rising higher in the water, the rest of the beast comes into view. Here the similarity to the dragon ends. Instead of a reptile, the body of the beast is *like* a leopard but with certain exceptions. His feet, for instance, are *like* bear feet. His mouth is different as well, broader and with larger teeth, *like* a lion's mouth.

Although John describes seven heads on the beast, we presume that one head actually leads. Perhaps the other heads form a collar about its neck. These other heads may have led in the past but now the beast is under the leadership of the one who has suffered a death blow. Yet this mortally wounded head has somehow revived, causing the whole world to wonder (Rev. 13:14). We will learn more about this aspect of the empire when we look at Revelation 17.

The dragon or devil gives the beast supernatural power. He backs the empire's authority with a display of spiritual power, probably using occult practices and sorcery. This deceives people to believe in the government's divine right to rule.

The Territory

The unseemly beast before John describes in figures of speech the last world empire, but the beasts themselves describe earlier empires. The animals used—leopard, bear, lion, and the ten-horned creature—depict the same four kingdoms that the prophet Daniel predicted would rule the world until the time of the saints' reign. The leopard stood for the Grecian Empire; the bear, the Media-Persian; the lion, the Babylonian; while the ten-horned creature stood for the Roman Empire (Dan. 7:2–7).[108] Though yet future in Daniel's day (except for Babylon), these four empires became history before Christ's first coming. Since

---

[108] The number ten stands for law, which was Rome's main cultural contribution to civilization.

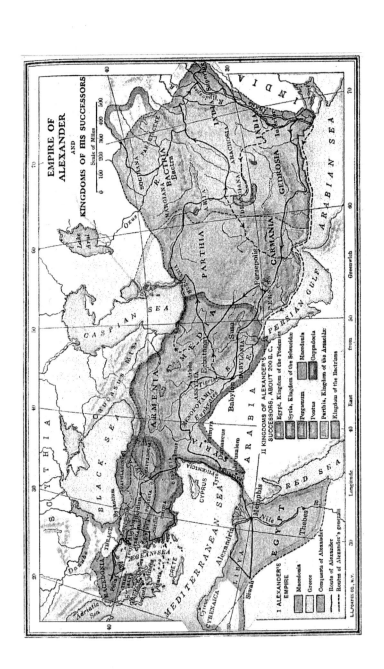

EMPIRE OF
ALEXANDER
AND
KINGDOMS OF HIS SUCCESSORS

Scale of Miles
0   100   200   300   400   500

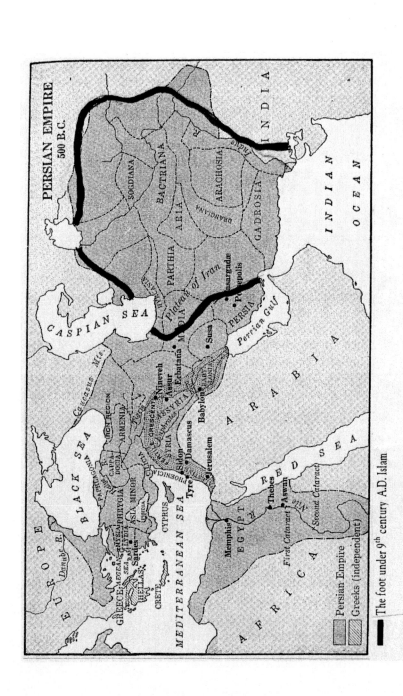

PERSIAN EMPIRE
500 B.C.

INDIA

INDUS R.

SOGDIANA

BACTRIANA

ARIA

ARACHOSIA

DRANGIANA

GADROSIA

PARTHIA

Plateau of Iran

Pasargadae
Persepolis

MEDIA

PERSIA

Persian Gulf

Susa

INDIAN OCEAN

Oxus R.

Jaxartes R.

CASPIAN SEA

Ecbatana

Caucasus Mts.

HILL REGION

Nineveh

Asur

ASSYRIA

Tigris R.

Euphrates R.

Babylon

BABYLONIA

ARMENIA

CAPPA-DOCIA

PAPHLAGONIA

Fertile Crescent

SYRIA

Damascus

PHRYGIA

ASIA MINOR

PAMPHYLIA

LYDIA

MYSIA

CILICIA

PHOENICIA

Sidon

Tyre

Jerusalem

ARABIA

BLACK SEA

EUROPE

Danube R.

GREECE

AEGEAN SEA

HELLAS

Sardis

ATTICA

CRETE

CYPRUS

MEDITERRANEAN SEA

Memphis

EGYPT

Nile R.

Thebes

Aswan

First Cataract

Second Cataract

RED SEA

AFRICA

Persian Empire

Greeks (independent)

The foot under 9th century A.D. Islam

the Roman Empire preceded the saints' rule, it is the only one necessary to revive. But the figure of speech employed here may not refer to history at all but rather to geography.

Since God suspended His timetable concerning Israel after Jesus' death, these empires passed on to others until the end time. Now the symbols that characterize them come back into the picture, this time not in succession but in combination. The image shown to Nebuchadnezzer revealed all the nations that would rule over this land. This combination may well describe the geographic locations of those in power since the previously mentioned four empires covered more or less the same territory, the Middle East. (God does not concern Himself with the rest of the Greek or Roman empires.) So then, it is reasonable to assume that the bulk of the territory that comprises the beast's body will remain the Middle East, with the symbols defining the limits. Also, we note that it is only the heads that particularly relate to Rome, not the territory.

The overall shape of the beast is like a leopard with certain modifications. Most of the territory of the ten crowns of Revelation compares to the Grecian Empire's holdings. One difference, however, is the feet. They are like the bear.

The Media-Persian boundaries were more extensive than the Grecian boundaries. Both reached beyond the Indus River but the Media-Persian Empire extended farther to the northeast. (See maps) Today that territory includes Armenia, Azerbaijan, Uzbekistan, Turkmenistan, Afghanistan, Pakistan and a southeastern portion of Kazakhstan, but not India. All of these states are predominantly Muslim. Egypt, Israel, Syria, Lebanon, and as far east as Romania were the extent of the Roman Empire eastward. Thus, Iraq and Iran were never part of Rome's territory. However, they were principle countries in the Persian Empire. Therefore, we could say that the foot of Media-Persia extended from Iraq to Kazakhstan.

After the advent of Muhammad and the rise of Islam the Arabs began to expand their territory. As they moved farther and farther east and north they moved their capitol to Iraq. Though the people converted to Islam were varied, the Arabs kept the ascendancy of ruling power. The Abbasids rulers, at the height of their Islamic Empire in the ninth century, reconsititured the whole Pre-Islamic Empire territory besides Arabia. Actually, the part we would call the foot is almost identical to the Persian boundaries. That explains why the whole region today is predominantly Islamic.

Besides the feet, the other exception to the Grecian Empire is the mouth, the member that ingests food for the kingdom. This "mouth of a lion" refers to Babylon or present-day Iraq. Located on the Persian Gulf, we shall see later that Iraq is destined to become an economic portal for importing food when the judgments become severe. This may become the empire's feeding mouth. The speaking mouth has a connection to spiritual Babylon, although he too comes from the Middle East. The ten heads and horns of the beast show a historic connection with the Roman Empire in Europe, the last great empire prophesied in Daniel that ruled this territory in the past. Seeing the territory in this light makes us realize that today this same area (with the exception of Israel) is held by Islamic powers, perhaps by the descendents of the same nations the psalmist decries:

Keep not thou silence, O God: hold not thy peace, and be not still, O God. For, lo, thine enemies make a tumult: and they that hate thee have lifted up the head. They have taken crafty counsel against thy people, and consulted against thy hidden ones. *They have said, Come, and let us cut them off from being a nation: that the name of Israel may be no more in remembrance.* For they have consulted together with one consent: they are confederate against thee: the tabernacles of Edom, and the Ishmaelites; of Moab, and the Hagarenes; Gebal, and Ammon, and Amalek; the Philistines with the inhabitants of Tyre; Assur is also joined with them: they have holpen the children of Lot. Selah . . . .Let us take to ourselves the houses of God in possession . . . .As the fire burneth a wood, and as the flame setteth the mountains on fire; so persecute them with thy tempest, and make them afraid *with thy storm.* (Ps. 83:1–8, 12, 14–15, emphasis added)

Count the peoples. There are ten.

The Ruler

And I saw one of his heads as it were wounded to death; and his deadly wound was healed: and all the world wondered after the beast. And they worshipped the dragon which gave power unto the beast: and they worshipped the beast, saying, Who is like unto the beast? who is able to make war with him? And there was given unto him a mouth speaking great things and blasphemies; and power was given unto him to continue forty and two months. And he opened his mouth in blasphemy against God, to blaspheme his name, and his tabernacle, and them that dwell in heaven. (12:3–6)

The beast signifies the kingdom or empire in power; the heads speak of the government, while the horns, especially the horn with the mouth, speak of those who will rule this empire. Daniel says concerning these horns:

I considered the horns, and, behold, there came up among them another little horn, before whom there were three of the first horns plucked up by the roots: and, behold, in this horn were eyes like the eyes of a man, and a mouth speaking great things. (Dan. 7:8)

Daniel says to the angel showing him the vision:

I would know the truth of . . . the ten horns that were in his head, and of the other which came up, and before whom three fell; even of that horn that had eyes, and a mouth that spake very great things, whose was more stout than his fellows. I beheld, and the same horn made war with the saints, and prevailed against them. (Dan. 7: 19–21)

[The angel replied to Daniel:]

And the ten horns out of this kingdom are ten kings that shall arise: and another shall rise after them; and he shall be diverse from the first, and he shall subdue three kings. (Dan. 7:24)

Daniel refers to the ruler of the kingdom in power when the Lord returns to set up His kingdom. This same mouth in Revelation speaks for the whole beast. Daniel further declares in his next vision (Daniel 8) that this "little horn" is a descendent of one of Alexander the Great's four generals who divided his kingdom after his death.[109]

> And *out of one of them came forth a little horn*, which waxed exceeding great, toward the south [Egypt], and toward the east [Babylon], and toward the pleasant land [Israel]. And it waxed great, even to the host of heaven; and *it cast down some of the host and of the stars to the ground, and stamped upon them*. Yea, he magnified himself even to the prince of the host, and by him the daily sacrifice was taken away, and the place of his sanctuary was cast down. And an host was given him against the daily sacrifice by reason of transgression, and it cast down the truth to the ground; and it practised, and prospered. Then I heard one saint speaking, and another saint said unto that certain saint which spake, How long shall be the vision concerning the daily sacrifice, and the transgression of desolation, to give both the sanctuary and the host to be trodden under foot? And he said unto me, Unto two thousand and three hundred days; then shall the sanctuary be cleansed. (Dan. 8:9–14, emphasis added)

Mentioned are the three kings this man will subdue—Egypt, Babylon, and Israel. Isaiah says a day comes when these nations will be strong allies (see Isa. 19:23–25). Naturally, this strong alliance would have to be diminished before any other leadership could control the Middle East.

---

[109] Dan. 8:8, 21–23.

The "little horn" of Daniel 8 is often interpreted as being fulfilled by Antiochus Epiphanes IV because he entered the temple, desecrated it, and took away the daily sacrifice. He also persecuted the Jews with great cruelty.

While he certainly does indicate the type of man this end-time tyrant will be, he could never fulfill the passage fully because the end-time tyrant cast down "stars to the ground, and stamped upon them" (Dan. 8:10). This causes the world to marvel and say, Who can make war like him? Is not this "little horn" claiming to use stars as weapons for his battles? Is he not taking personal credit for the destruction of the Russian army? He magnifies himself even against Michael, the prince of the host. He identifies himself with the dragon in the sky. He takes away the daily sacrifice and sets up the "abomination that brings desolation" (the idol that provokes God's jealousy)—the warring "god of forces."

From his appearance on the political scene until Jesus cleanses the sanctuary at His coming, this little horn has 2,300 days of power. That would mean he rises to power early in the prophetic week, 1,010 days before the last 42 months (1,290 days = 42 months; 1,290 + 1,010 = 2,300). This is why it is said that "power was given unto him *to continue* forty and two months" (Rev. 13:5). He has already come to power, probably during the great war of the four horseman. We know he makes a holy covenant with Israel, but in the midst of the week, he breaks it (Dan. 9:27).

Perhaps this is when the Arab–Israeli coalition forms. Let us say that by the "little horn's" efforts, he conforms to an alliance between the Middle East coalition and the European economic community against other powers that threaten or are already at war. The covenant includes a political agreement between Judaism, Islam, and the United Protestant/Roman Catholic church in Rome—hence, its title, the "holy covenant." The alliance promises peace in Europe and its vital Middle-East connections as well as the preservation of religious sites. The miraculous destruction of the Russian army, which had entered the alliance's territory, convinces the remaining world of the "little horn's" divine right to rule. Therefore, at the beginning of the forty-two months, he takes on more power.

> And it was given unto him to make war with the saints, and to overcome them: and power was given him over all kindreds, and tongues, and nations. (13:7)

The widespread power over kindreds, tongues, and nations comes from the religious prominence he enjoys. His solution to the problem of peace in a world recently ravaged with nuclear war finds acceptance with all people, except those who know God and His plans. The saints alone oppose his religious claims and so invoke the wrath of the "little horn."

Daniel tells more about this king:

> And in the latter time of their kingdom [Alexander's four generals], when the *transgressors are come to the full,* a king of fierce countenance, and understanding dark sentences, shall stand up. And his power shall be mighty, but not by his own power: and he shall destroy wonderfully, and shall prosper, and practice, and shall destroy the mighty and the holy people. And through his policy also he shall cause craft [deceit] to prosper in his hand; and he shall magnify himself in his heart, and by peace shall destroy many: he shall also stand up against the Prince of princes [Jesus, Rev. 1:5]; but he shall be broken without hand. (Dan. 8:23–26, emphasis added)

This king of "fierce" or, literally, robust countenance hypnotizes his audiences in the same manner as Hitler. His influence has spiritual help.

> And then shall that Wicked be revealed, whom the Lord shall consume with the spirit of his mouth, and shall destroy with the brightness of his coming: even him, whose coming is after the working of Satan with all *power and signs and lying wonders,* and with all deceivableness of unrighteousness in them that perish; because they received not the love of the truth, that they might be saved. And for this cause *God shall send them strong delusion, that they should believe a lie:* That they all might be damned who believed not the truth, but had pleasure in unrighteousness. (2 Thess. 2:8–12, emphasis added)

Under the dragon's influence, the leader's occult powers flourish. Ultimately, he will destroy the two witnesses, suggested by the "mighty and holy people" (Dan. 8:24). The ability of this leader to "destroy wonderfully" could refer to his apparent use of stars in battle. His sudden rise to power, along with his popularity with the people, will go to his head. In the end, he proclaims himself god and stands blasphemously against the Lord Jesus Christ. Daniel describes his audacity:

> And the king shall do according to his will; and he shall exalt himself, and magnify himself above every god, and shall speak marvelous things against the God of gods, and shall prosper till the indignation be accomplished: for that that is determined shall be done. Neither shall he regard the God of his fathers, nor the desire of women, nor regard any god: for he shall magnify himself above

all. But in his estate shall he honour the God of forces: and a god whom his father knew not shall he honour with gold, and silver, and with precious stones, and pleasant things. Thus shall he do in the most strong holds with a strange god, whom he shall acknowledge and increase with glory: and he shall cause them to rule over many, and shall divide the land for gain. (Dan. 11:36–39, emphasis added)

The blasphemous king honors the dragon, the comet in the sky, the manifestation of the "god of forces" because of the assistance it appears to give his military campaigns. In fact, this may be the image he erects at the temple site. Whatever the image may be, it is definitely the dragon's power that men worship.

The people deceived by the "divine" nature of this power lose all freedom. This leader even takes their land away from them (for their own good, of course), but they still worship him:

And all that dwell upon the earth shall worship him, whose names are not written in the book of life of the Lamb slain from the foundation of the world. (Rev. 13:8)

Although the world falls at his feet, those whose names are written in the Lamb's book of life do not. It seems that this attitude of worship does not come about until the beast appears to have performed the feat of raining stars on the Russian army. Remember, the accompanying destruction (the overturned earth) has left most of civilization in shambles. The 144,000 witnesses had warned the world; therefore, those who refuse their message were left behind at the rapture of the great multitude (their Gentile converts). Only scattered peoples have survived the judgment of the overturning. Europe and the Middle East, where God is working out His program, represent civilization's last stand. Eastern hoards invade at the end, but we have no indication as to who they are.

Therefore, the organized "world," all that is left, consists of a relatively small population compared to the world as we know it now. Therefore, the conflict between gods divides the entire population. Who is the true Savior: God, who destroyed Russia as prophesied many hundreds of years ago, or the "little horn" with his preposterous claims.

A Warning

John pauses now in the description of the beast to prophesy to those alive during this period. He warns that those who cooperate with this wily leader will suffer the consequences.

> If any man have an ear, let him hear! He that leadeth into captivity shall go into captivity: he that killeth with the sword must be killed with the sword. Here is the patience and faith of the saints. (13:9–10)

It is a great temptation to simply go the way the world is going—join in the hostilities and take the path of least resistance under this leadership. Nevertheless, God calls forth a people to stand for righteousness and resist evil. He puts them through a refining fire to purify them as silver (Zech. 13:9). Therefore, He warns with great detail about this antichrist to come so believers can resist him.

The False Prophet

After warning the saints, John sees another beast rise:

> And I beheld another beast coming up out of the earth; and he had two horns like a lamb, and he spake as a dragon. And he exerciseth all the power of the first beast before him, and causeth the earth and them which dwell therein to worship the first beast, whose deadly wound was healed. And he doeth great wonders, so that he maketh fire come down from heaven on the earth in the sight of men, and deceiveth them that dwell on the earth, by the means of those miracles which he had power to do in the sight of the beast; saying to them that dwell on the earth, that they should make an image to the beast, which had the wound by a sword and did live. (13:11–14)

This beast emerges out of the earth. By contrast to the sea, which signifies the Gentiles, this beast comes from the solid earth, the Jews. The sea in Scripture represents the nature of the faithless, wave driven and tossed by every wind of doctrine. The solid ground, on the other hand, represents stability. Nations come and go, but the Jews stubbornly remain an unassimilated nation clinging to their traditions based on a God-given faith. The solid earth, then, refers to the fundamental faiths that originated in Jehovah. The beast, at first, arises from and appears to fulfill the goals of these three fundamental faiths: Judaism, Christianity, and Islam.

Therefore, the beast out of the earth represents a religious kingdom, whereas the beast out of the sea represents a political kingdom. One is superimposed upon the other. The fact that the beast from the earth resembles a lamb shows that the religious system claims to save mankind (by their peace?). The two horns represent the two men who exert authority. One is the Antichrist spoken of later in Revelation as simply the beast; the other one described in this passage is later called the false prophet.[110] Although ten horns (ten men) are the power behind the political beast, only two men represent the power in the religious system: the false god and the prophet who promotes his worship.

The beast-like lamb purports to bring in the long-expected Jewish kingdom and presents the ruler, the political beast, as Israel's long awaited Messiah. But the redeemed Jews recognize him as an imposter because his mouth gives him away. He speaks like the dragon. Of those Jesus said would come, this lamb is the ultimate in false prophets—*the* false prophet—foretold to show great signs and wonders. Jesus told the Jews: "I am come in my Father's name, and ye receive me not: if another shall come in his own name, him ye will receive" (John 5:43). Therefore, this important Jewish religious figure gives the name and claim of the beast credence to the point that unredeemed Jews accept him. The false prophet claims to fulfill a passage which speaks of a prophet like Moses:

> I will raise them up a Prophet from among their brethren, like unto thee, and will put my words in his mouth; and he shall speak unto them all that I shall command him. And it shall come to pass, that whosoever will not hearken unto my words which he shall speak in my name, I will require it of him. (Deut. 18:18–19)

---

[110] Rev. 19:20.

The false prophet arises from among them, of their brethren. He appears to perform wonders like Moses. He speaks words to which they must listen. He leads the coalition of Jews, so-called Christians, and Moslems to worship a new god—not Jehovah of the Jews or Jesus of the Christians[111] nor Allah of Islam but the self-exalted "little horn" who unites and supercedes all religions.

This poses no problem for those who follow Islam, because they believe in a succession of prophets. No longer is Mohammed considered to be the last prophet. Another has come and has manifested himself as god. The passionate followers of Islam see no conflict in a god that wars. They can wholeheartedly accept him. Have they not fought the battles of Allah for centuries? Now under the influence of the false prophet, the beast will look like Messiah to the Jews and like Christ to the "Christians" and like the Mahdi[112] to the Moslems.

Paul speaks of the two leaders of this religious system. He calls the beast the "man of sin" and the false prophet that "Wicked" one "whose coming is after the working of Satan with all power and signs and lying wonders" (2 Thess. 2:3, 8–9). The implication is that the religion of these leaders, besides being idolatrous, is morally depraved. In the

---

[111] Remember, these are not real Christians but members of the false church left behind at the rapture. They are Christian in name only.

[112] *Mahdi* (Arabic for "the guided one). The future leader of Mohammedans expected to appear as a messiah to establish the better age to come. Vergilious Ferm, ed., *An Encyclopedia of Religion* (New York: The Philosophical Library, 1945), p. 463. He is the divinely inspired leader awaited by the Muslim masses who is to bring perfect Islam and social justice before the end of the world. *Encyclopedia Britanical, Fifteenth Edition.* (Philip W. Goetz, Editor-in-Chief (Aukland, Geneva, London, Manila, Paris, Rome, Seoul, Sydney, Tokyo. Toronto; University of Chicago, 1985), p. 121.

past, idol worship was accompanied by ceremonial prostitution, but the most depraved moral sin recorded in the Bible is sodomy or homosexuality. Speaking of the death of the two witnesses, Jerusalem is called spiritual Sodom (Rev. 11:8). Could this refer to her two leaders' relationship? We were told in Daniel regarding the beast: "Neither shall he regard the God of his fathers, nor the desire of women" (Dan. 11:37). This points to such sins as those mentioned in Romans 1, the sins of reprobate minds. Thus, the leaders of this new religion condone and celebrate their reprobate lifestyle.

Looking back at John's description of the false prophet, we watch as he continues:

> And he had power to give life unto the image of the beast, that the image of the beast should both speak, and cause that as many as would not worship the image of the beast should be killed. (13:15)

Giving life to the image of the beast makes one wonder if the image has been computerized. We see that the image reveals those who refuse to worship it. Computer technology today makes it possible to catalog every person alive with a unique number. Assigned by the government just like social security numbers, it would be no problem for computers to check the population against mailing addresses, employment records, or census registrations, etc., to see if all had received their stamped numbers. We believe that computers may very well be involved in this life-and-death struggle perhaps through cameras located in the idol.

The dragon, Satan, through his control of the beast and the false prophet, seeks to destroy the remnant of the woman's seed. Later in the vision, John sees that their victims are beheaded for their witness for Jesus and because they refuse to worship the beast. Nevertheless, "They overcame him by the blood of the Lamb, and by the word of their testimony; and they loved not their lives unto the death" (Rev. 12:11).

The Economic Rule

Besides having complete control over the religious activities of people, the government of the two horns dominates the economy as well. Thus, they maintain a tight control over the population. Remember the heads of the beast stand for the type of government in control, while the body represents the territory. Later, we will learn that the governments are connected to Rome.

> And he causeth all, both small and great, rich and poor, free and bond, to receive a mark in their right hand, or in their foreheads: and that no man might buy or sell, save he that had that mark, or the name of the beast, or the number of his name. Here is wisdom. Let him that hath understanding count the number of the beast: for it is the number of a man, and his number is Six hundred threescore and six. (13:16–18)

This government controls every facet of the commercial world. The last government in power when the barbarians destroyed ancient Rome was the bureaucracy. It was similar to this last-day government. This wounded head has revived. Remember, the heads stand for the type of government in control. We believe the beast's rule shows this same type of government, a bureaucracy. Therefore, by examining the history concerning the wounded head, we can learn more about the present rule under its revived head.

At the time of Diocletian and subsequently Constantine, the economic situation in the Roman Empire had all but collapsed. Earlier emperors had given large estates to a favored few, and this had forced small farmers out of business. They, in turn, became *coloni* who accepted small portions of large estates in exchange for labor. Others fled to the cities, causing unemployment and unrest. Eventually, to cope with the problems

> Constantine decreed that henceforth no colonus could leave the soil and that his children had to accept the same status as that of their father. His economic absolution went further. Everyone was 'chained to his post.' In the cities the same caste system was applied to members of the corporations or guilds. All guilds whose activities were essential to the state, such as supplying grain, baking, transportation, and entertaining the city mobs, were made hereditary organizations, a member of which was bound to his occupation and even had to marry the daughter of a member of his guild. . . . The same hereditary principle was applied to the city's middle class, from whose ranks came the decuriones, who were members of the municipal curia or council. The decuriones were made responsible for the collection of the taxes and had to make good any deficit in the revenue. Many of the decuriones tried desperately to evade the crushing burden. Some joined the army, others the church and some even became coloni. The desperate measures instituted by Diocletian and Constantine were to no avail. In the long run the remedy was as bad as the disease from which the empire suffered. The principate had given way to

the dominate, a vast bureaucracy had been created, and the economic regimentation chained men to the soil and to their guilds.[113]

The great republic of Rome had degenerated into Oriental despotism. The once powerful beast with teeth of iron described by Daniel was now weak and had to be divided into eastern and western sections in order to regulate the massive government.

Other historians describe this period:

Thus, under this Oriental despotism, liberty disappeared, and the once free Roman citizen lost his independence. Even the citizen's wages and the prices of goods he bought or sold were, as far as possible, fixed for him by the state. The emperor's countless officials, who were little better than spies, kept an eye upon even the humblest citizen. They watched the grain dealers, butchers, and bakers and saw to it that they properly supplied the public and never deserted their occupation. In a word, the Roman government now attempted to regulate almost every interest in life, and wherever the citizen turned he felt the irksome interference of the state.[114]

---

[113] T. Walter Wallbank and Alastair M. Taylor, Civilization: Past and Present (Chicago, Dallas, New York, Atlanta: Scot, Foresman and Company, 1942) p. 87.

[114] James Harvey Robinson, James Henry Breasted, and Emma Peters Smith, History of Civilization: Earlier Ages (Boston, New York, Chicago, Atlanta, Dallas, San Francisco, Toronto, London: Ginn and Company, 1951) p. 360.

Truly, it was a regulated life then as it will be again under the beast's rule. People will buy and sell in a completely controlled society. Thus, we see that the last government of Rome was indeed similar to the administration under the beast.

Other prophecies concerning the beast's rule strengthen this idea further. Habakkuk 2 contains a vision concerning the time when a leader arises whose desires cannot be satisfied but heaps to himself all nations and all peoples— who "ladeth himself with thick clay" (heavy rules and regulations, which in that day were written on clay tablets and baked) (Hab. 2:6). The rest of the chapter deals with lesser authorities who assist in the reign. But the chapter ends with a pronouncement of woe to the one who says to an idol, "Arise, it shall teach!" (Hab. 2:19). Are not these the words of the false prophet?

Isaiah, too, speaking of the time when Israel will be purged and refined by the "spirit of judgment, and by the spirit of burning" (Isa. 4:4), says:

> Woe unto them that join house to house, that lay field to field, till there be no place, that they may be placed alone in the midst of the earth! In mine ears, said the LORD of hosts, Of a truth many houses shall be desolate, even great and fair, without inhabitant. (Isa. 5:8–9)

The beast tries this, too, because Daniel 11:39 says that he will "divide the land for gain." But it won't work because the result will be: "Yea, ten acres of vineyard shall yield one bath [about eight gallons], and the seed of an homer shall yield an ephah" (Isa. 5:10). Since a homer is 86 gallons, harvesting 3 1/2 gallons is a mere pittance of what was sown.

Government-controlled farms fail, just as the huge collective Communistic agriculture programs of Russia failed.

It is the time of Zechariah's "flying roll" (Zech. 5:2) that judges the sins of the people. The roll shall "enter into the house of the thief, and into the house of him that sweareth falsely by my name: and it shall remain in the midst of his house, and shall consume it with the timbers thereof and the stones thereof" (Zech. 5:4).[115]

Zechariah's next vision, the ninth in a series of ten, describes "wickedness" personified in the commercial world (see Zech. 5:5–11). In this time of great wickedness and total control over the economy, how can the righteous survive? Habakkuk replies, God can supply their needs supernaturally in spite of the wickedness in commerce, for "the just shall live by his faith" (Hab. 2:4).

The Number

"And that no man might buy or sell, save he that had the mark, or the name of the beast, or the number of his name" (Rev. 13:17). The Scriptures mention this number two other times.[116] Both tell of the tribute King Solomon received for one year—666 talents of gold. It may be that the false prophet proclaims the new ruler to be Solomon's successor. He could claim that Solomon was a forerunner (the type) of the one who would rule the kingdom of God. We believe he is, except that it is Jesus, the Son of God, who rightfully holds this position as the Prince of peace.

Scripture is careful to tell us to count the numbers. In spiritual language, six is the number of man. No matter

---

[115] See Hab. 2:11.
[116] 2 Kings 10:14; 2 Chron. 9:13.

how many sixes you add, it is still only the number of a man! Many occupy themselves with speculation on the number. Suffice it to say that when the time comes, the elect will recognize it and avoid its use. One thing is noteworthy though: There seem to be three choices: the mark, the name of the beast, and the number of his name. These may be issued according to whether they are buyers or sellers. The first, the mark, may be assigned to the common consumer as a sign of his religious allegiance to the ruler. The number and name of the beast may be assigned besides the mark to license importers and sellers.

Whatever they represent, they keep strict control in the hands of the unholy trinity—the beast, the false prophet, and the dragon. These, plus all the little people of their huge bureaucracy, comprise the adversaries of God in the end times.

Chapter 20

THE RERUN

(REVELATION 14)

"And I looked, and, lo . . .," exclaims John as he reflects back on the previous scene describing God's adversaries. Having seen both armies of the conflict, God's and Satan's, he anxiously anticipates the description of the conflict itself.

Actually, what he is about to see replays the times of the trumpet judgments of Revelation 8 and 9. However, although Revelation 14 repeats the same 1,290 days, the events emphasized deal with the affairs of men rather than the

```
                        Time Line
   Seals
       1 2 3 4 5↕6 7              1 2 3 4 5 6  7  Trumpets
                  Go Through To   1 2 3 4 5 6 ▼7  Vials
   You Start Here *               Back of Scroll
```

catastrophes of nature. They fill in human provocations that precipitate the judgments. If the activities of this chapter could be dubbed into the physical background of Revelation 8 and 9 like a movie production, then they could replay together to form a more complete picture.

Before the conflict begins, John sees a wrap-up of the first half of the prophetic week.

> And I looked, and, lo, a Lamb *stood on the mount Sion,* and with him an hundred forty and four thousand, having his Father's name written in their foreheads. (14:1, emphasis added)

The last glimpse we had of the 144,000 was in the midst of the week. They were standing on Mount Moriah preaching to those faithful Jews gathered in the temple to pray for deliverance from the Russian invasion. The Jews responded to their message, and God removed the "veil" from their hearts. On this day, however, the Day of Atonement, they stand just outside the tent on Mount Zion. With their spiritual eyes open to the gospel, Jesus appears in their midst to reveal His wounds as Israel's scapegoat. This happens just before the fifth seal.

The opening of this chapter directs us to the next event, the rapture of the 144,000 Jewish witnesses. When the scene opens, the Lamb still stands in their midst. Jesus Himself will accompany them back to heaven and usher them into the Father's presence, where He acknowledges them before the throne. Before we look at this sequence, we will examine the place on which the Lamb stands—Mount Zion.

The Tabernacle of David

Much speculation surfaces today concerning the rebuilding of the Jewish temple. Rumors circulate constantly in the Christian community about it. Even religious Jews now living in the land speak longingly of the building of the "third temple."

In 1998, I visited a site in Jerusalem set up by the Temple Institute, an organization dedicated to restoring the Jewish temple with its ceremonial worship. Leaders of this group lectured about and displayed items they have prepared for use when the temple site becomes available. These items include harps, trumpets, a million-dollar golden lampstand, and instruments for sacrificial rituals. An article written in 1984 in the *Jerusalem Post* concerning a school for "the study of priestly rites in the temple" says that the school is "preparing itself for the arrival of the Messiah and construction of the Third Temple which might come at any moment."[117]

Most people, Christians and Jews alike, expect that the temple must be built on Mount Moriah where both Solomon and Herod's temples were believed to have stood. However, with the many references to Zion as the place of future blessing, we cannot help but wonder if this might be the site of an interim temple.

Paul certainly links Zion with the redemption of the nation when he states in Romans 11:26: "And so all Israel shall be saved: as it is written, There shall come out of Sion the Deliverer, and shall turn away ungodliness from Jacob" (see Isa. 59:20). This could refer to a deliverer coming out of a people, since we know that Zion has become a general

---

[117] Abraham Rabinovich, "Wary Neighbors," *Jerusalem Post*, 1–7 Jan. 1984.

term for God's devoted believers. Zionism, an inflammatory political issue among the nations, is another term to be considered.

However, Isaiah speaks of the redeemed returning with singing unto Zion (Isa. 51:11)—a place that is definitely connected with the city of Jerusalem. Since the Lamb stands on a mountain called Mount Zion with the 144,000, we wonder if this will be the place of Israel's redemption and, therefore, the site of a sanctuary.

In speaking of Israel's dispersion because of her sin, the prophet Amos declares that David's tabernacle will be rebuilt on its own site as in the days of old.

> In that day will I raise up the tabernacle of David that is fallen, and close up the breaches thereof; and I will raise up his ruins, and I will build it as in the days of old: that they may possess the remnant of Edom. (Amos 9:11–12)

This was a curious prediction to make since Solomon's temple had not yet been destroyed when Amos made it. To go back to David's tabernacle was to retrace their steps. At the time of Amos's writing, the foundation of David's tabernacle was already in ruins. It was filled with breaches perhaps caused by the earthquakes of Uzziah's day and left unrepaired. What reason would God have to return the Jews to David's original site *unless* it was His intent to return to Zion instead of Moriah? Of course, God knew that the temple mount would be occupied by the Dome of the Rock in this future time, and any attempt to build there would initiate a holy war. Nevertheless, a typical picture may be the reason for the switch.

Moriah is connected with the sacrifice of the Son. Abraham almost offered Isaac, his promised son, on this same mount as a foreshadowing type of God offering His Son Jesus.

Gordon's Calvary, located in a quarry just north of the original wall of ancient Jerusalem, was the northernmost extension of Mount Moriah. The mountain had been cut to form a dry moat north of the city wall for protection from invasion, since it was the most vulnerable approach to the city. It was beside the road to Jericho and Joppa and intersected with the road north to Samaria. Historically, the Romans always crucified their victims along a public road as a deterrent to crime. The quarry wall north of the road clearly depicts a skull, having indentations for eye sockets and a bridge for the nose, thus fulfilling the name Golgotha, the place of the skull. Here Ron Wyatt discovered squared holes chiseled out of rock that he believes held the upright posts of crosses. Then, too, the Damascus Gate was located just a few hundred feet from the rock face. Jesus, according to Hebrews 13:12, "suffered without the gate." Close by, a rich man's vineyard containing a tomb has been discovered. So surely, putting together all these factors, we can surmise that Jesus died on Mount Moriah. Thus, the spiritual significance of Moriah was fulfilled in Christ's death.

Zion, not Moriah, is the rallying place for the return of the Jews, hence, the term Zionism. Was not Amos looking far beyond the sacrifice of God's Son to the redemption of His regathered nation? And more than that, by referring to the rebuilding of David's tabernacle on its own ruins, was he not defining Zion as a specific place?

Add to this the reason Amos gives for raising the tabernacle again: "that they may possess the remnant of Edom," another event connected to their redemption. The remnant, or all that is left of Edom today, is the rock city of Petra. This may refer to the woman's flight to safety following her redemption, since most prophetic scholars agree that Petra is most likely the place of her safety.

But the most important reason for the significance of Zion may be connected with the ark of the covenant. The tabernacle of David was different from the tabernacle in the wilderness. David's tabernacle consisted only of the ark of the covenant that was recovered from the Philistines. The other pieces of furniture belonging to the tabernacle remained in Gibeon, where the tabernacle of the congregation stood. David and Solomon offered some blood sacrifices on Zion, but the people still sacrificed at Gibeon or other high places (1 Kings 3:2, 4, 15). The Levites ministered to God before the ark mostly with music—singing and playing of trumpets and cymbals. The altar David built on the threshing floor of Ornan on Mount Moriah was for saving the people from God's plague. This lends credence to the thought that Moriah is connected with sacrifice and salvation from sin but Zion with the redemption of the regathered nation where it is necessary only for Christ to show himself.

In his book *The Temples That Jerusalem Forgot*, Earnest L. Martin presents historical evidence that Herod's temple was actually built over the Gihon spring in the city of David. He maintains that "not one stone remains" of that structure, according to Jesus' words, "There shall not be left here one stone upon another" (Matt. 24:2). According to Martin, the so-called temple mount—called the Harem esh-Sharif by the Arabs—was in fact the Roman army camp. Hence, it was not destroyed. This strengthens the idea that

Jesus will not stand on Moriah but somewhere in the city of David when He reveals His wounds.

Repeatedly, Isaiah, the prophet who proclaimed Israel's glorious future, speaks of Mount Zion as the place from which God operates. The psalms resound with the same thought. David, as author of many of them, constantly refers to the blessings of God coming from Zion. Of course, they literally did in his day; as that was the site of the ark of the covenant.[118] In fact, the first mention of Zion in the Scriptures speaks of the Jebusites' fortress that was taken by David to which he later brought the ark.[119] So Zion represents God's original dwelling place in Jerusalem.

But the tabernacle of David housed the ark of the covenant only until a permanent house could be built. If Israel were somehow able to recover the ancient ark, they could set up a temporary structure on its former site and begin to worship almost immediately, since the priesthood has already prepared itself.[120] Without doubt, the priests would erect an altar for sacrifices. The return of the ark being a repeat of history, David's tabernacle site would be the most logical place to put it until a permanent house could be built. Archeologists have already uncovered the ruins of David's city, and the actual site could be utilized with some modifications. Also, this site is not in dispute but already belongs to the Jews. The question is: Does the ark of the covenant still exist?

---

[118] 1 Kings 8:1.

[119] See also 1 Chron. 11:15.

[120] In December 1970, Yeshiva Avoclas Hakodesh, a special school to train young Israelis of the tribe of Levi in the ancient rites of sacrifice, was founded by Rabbi Hirsh Ha-Cohen. Colin Deal, *Christ Returns by 1988, 101 Reasons Why* (Rutherford College, NC: Self Published 1979) p. 60

Two tenable claims contend for its existence. Ron Wyatt claimed to have found the ark of the covenant along with various other items connected with the temple, in a chamber deep under the rock quarry at Golgatha. According to his report, he searched for years through a labyrinth of passageways and excavations and found a chamber filled with stones that housed the ark. The way into the chamber was so narrow he could barely squeeze his body through. He has searched Zedachiah's cave (under the Arab quarter of the city) looking for the original passageway entrance to the cave (through which it was originally carried), only to find it blocked. He claims to have notified the authorities, but as long as the Jews look to the place where the Dome of the Rock stands as their temple site, it would create political mayhem to publicize it.

The other possibility is that faithful priests stole it away from Jerusalem during Manasseh's apostasy and carried it by stages to the headwaters of the Nile. Graham Hancock, who wrote *The Sign and the Seal,* espouses this view. Tradition stubbornly persists that the ark of Solomon's day is hidden away in a church in Aksum, Ethiopia. According to the legend of Menelik II, the supposed son of Solomon and the queen of Sheba, Menelik stole the ark of the covenant from his father and brought it to Ethiopia. Though the legend is most certainly a myth to explain its presence in Ethiopia, there is a possibility that Shishak, the Egyptian monarch who sacked the temple after Solomon's reign, may have allowed his allies, the Ethiopians, to claim the ark as part of the spoil.

Coptic Christianity of Ethiopia has a whole culture devoted to their possession of God's law. Ethiopia's claim of possession surfaced in western literature as early as A.D.

325.[121] It has continued to persist even as late as the rule of Haile Selassie. The stately "Lion of Judah" told a reporter in 1935 that Ethiopia was taking steps to preserve the ark of the covenant that was in their possession at that time.[122]

We would pass all this off as fable except for a prophecy in Isaiah that mentions Ethiopians bringing a present to Mount Zion (Isa. 18:1, 7). When this present comes to Mount Zion, it is a signal to the whole world, the lifting high of an ensign or standard signifying that God is doing something special again in Israel.

History may repeat itself. David brought up the recovered ark of the covenant and housed it in a temporary tabernacle, charging his son with the responsibility of building a permanent structure. Similarly, the Jews could bring back the ark of the covenant from Ethiopia or from its underground tomb (whichever is the real one) and set it up on the original site. Then after Jesus comes back to earth, He will build the great third temple spoken of by Ezekiel and Zechariah. The warring Captain will come as the head of the Lord's hosts to redeem Israel and destroy all the Lord's enemies. He will establish dominion just as David did by destroying and subduing the nations around him. Later, Christ will come as the Prince of peace like Solomon (whose name means "peace") and build the great millennial temple.

Therefore, we conclude that in the tribulation, the place of significance is not on Mount Moriah, the traditional site

---

[121] Taken from Kerah Negast (*Glory of Kings*), written by Yeshak of Aksum from information found in the Coptic writings discovered in A.D. 325, among the treasures of the Church of St. Sophia of Constantinople.

[122] Gordon McCreagh, "The King of Kings," *Saturday Evening Post*, 21 Sept. 1935.

of the temple, but on the original site of David's tabernacle on "old Zion." (The hill called Zion today has only been so called since the fourth century and is not the site of David's city.) Here the faithful will hear the gospel preached; here, too, the Lord "shall suddenly come to his temple" (Mal. 3:1) that the Jews may look on him "whom they have pierced" (Zech. 12:10). Here they cry, "Surely he hath borne our griefs, and carried our sorrows: yet we did esteem him stricken, smitten of God, and afflicted" (Isa. 53:4). Here, too, we see the two witnesses become invincible. Therefore, Zion becomes the holy hill superceding Moriah and anticipating the final mountain[123] to be established at the Lord's triumphal return.

But what happened to the "measured-out" court and the idol set up by the beast? Are they on Mount Zion as well? Probably not. The so-called temple mount remains a holy place in the eyes of the Jews. It is likely that the covenant with the beast includes the right to rebuild on the Harem esh-Sharif. (One of the possible sites of the original temple promoted by Asher S. Kaufman is just north of the Dome of the Rock.)[124]

At this point in the vision, building may be in progress. Isaiah, speaking of the restorations in the time of Cyrus, says: "Even saying to Jerusalem, Thou shalt be built; and to the temple, Thy foundation shall be laid" (Isa. 44:28). We know we have a double fulfillment because of the significance given to the building of the temple in the books of Haggai and Zechariah along with portions of their prophecies that are still future. Since the ultimate fulfillment of

---

[123] Isaiah 2:2.

[124] Asher S. Kaufman, "Kaufman Responds to Jacobson," *Biblical Archaeology Review*, March/April 2000, p. 61.

the rest of their messages speak of the latter-day restoration, the prominence of the foundation becomes important. In Zechariah's visions, it is the Messiah Himself who ultimately builds the third temple after He is crowned King (Zech. 6:13) but not until God confronts a religious and self-righteous nation with a revelation of Himself and His plans. Thus, they will begin to build by laying a foundation, but they will be opposed as they were in the days of Ezra and not be able to finish. In his day, an altar for the burnt offering and the daily sacrifice was set up months before the foundation itself was laid (Ezra 3:1–3, 8–11). After that, opposition hindered the building for years and finally stopped it (Ezra 4:24). God raised up two prophets to encourage the people.

Is not this a close parallel to the future restoration? Believing this, we can surmise what happens next. The Jews, possibly because they already possess their ancient ark, press for the right to rebuild a permanent house for it on Moriah as their part in the holy covenant. Upon being granted this right, they begin to build, as they did of old, by first erecting the altar. Then after the daily sacrifices are reinstituted, they begin to lay the foundation by outlining the whole structure, including the porch. Because the ark of the covenant cannot be installed in an unfinished and unconsecrated building, the activities of the feast days must be divided between the two holy places.

The 144,000 may begin to preach on Moriah where the priests weep between the porch and the altar at the Feast of Trumpets. Then they may move to Zion to complete the activities of the Day of Atonement, since this involves going behind the veil to the ark. We cannot be too specific about this, as there is little information to go on. However, we suspect that Jesus shows Himself on Mount Zion when the live goat is brought forth for a scapegoat. Following closely behind the beast sets up of the idol probably in the outer courtyard (at the corner of the altar)[125] on Mount Moriah which the angel told John not to measure. The beast halts all sacrificing, both those on Moriah and those (if any) on Zion, making the beast's new religion the only worship possible.

The beast need not sit on holy (measured-off) ground to fulfill 2 Thessalonians 2:4 which says: "So that he as God sitteth in the temple of God, shewing himself that he is God." We always assume that the temple here is that of the Jews. What if it is an another already existing building such as the Dome of the Rock? He could use it for this purpose, making it *his* temple. After all, he does not have years and years of time to build a magnificent structure. With all the warfare, earthquakes, and plagues of this period, the beast will probably utilize what is already there. Another possibility: He may sit in the temple of God, showing himself as god, during the three days when the two witnesses lie dead. Then he could sit in the measured-off foundation and unfinished temple of God, auspiciously gloating over his victory.

Looking back now to the events of the chapter 11, we fill in more details leading up to the time of the Gentile takeover.

The Scapegoat

John watches excitedly as the faithful witnesses, with the Father's name sealed on their foreheads, are finally be

---

[125] The Tanakh, an English translation of the Hebrew Bible, assigns the idol to the corner of the altar in Daniel 9:27.

vindicated before their brethren with their message confirmed. They have come to Zion to preach the Lamb's redemption. They may not be necessarily inside the tabernacle itself. Due to the precipitous location, the structure may be small and probably could not hold such a large number.

Consequently, they will probably gather outside on the steep slopes. After all, Isaiah's words say, "How beautiful *upon the mountains* (Moriah and Zion?) are the feet of him that bringeth good tidings, that publisheth peace; that bringeth good tidings of good, that publisheth salvation; that saith unto Zion, Thy God reigneth!" (Isa. 52:7, emphasis added). Suddenly, the object of their message appears in their midst. The Messiah, as the freshly slain Lamb (God's salvation for the whole world), stands with the 144,000, proving and confirming their testimony of Him.

The Messiah comes to fulfill the types concerning the Day of Atonement. He stands the door of the tabernacle, revealing His wounds as the slain first goat, yet alive as the second goat to carry away their sins. After the high priest confesses the sins of the nation, Christ carries them away when He returns to the Father. "And so all Israel shall be saved," says Paul in Romans 11:26–27, "There shall come out of Sion the Deliverer, and shall turn away ungodliness from Jacob: for this is my covenant unto them, *when I shall take away their sins*" (emphasis added).

Therefore, it is necessary for the Lamb of God to stand upon Mount Zion to fulfill this Day of Atonement, the Yom Kippur of the Jews.

The Second Rapture

> And I heard a voice from heaven, as the voice of many
> waters, and as the voice of a great thunder: and I heard

the voice of harpers harping with their harps: and they sung as it were a new song before the throne, and before the four beasts, and the elders: and no man could learn that song but the hundred and forty and four thousand, which were redeemed from the earth. These are they which were not defiled with women; for they are virgins. These are they which follow the Lamb withersoever he goeth. These were redeemed from among men, being the firstfruits unto God and to the Lamb. And in their mouth was found no guile: for they are without fault before the throne of God. (14:2–5)

The song the saints sing denotes the spontaneous worship that comes from seeing their brethren redeemed, those same brethren who had unmercifully persecuted them for turning away from Judaism. Their "new song" of praise and worship may have begun before the Father's thundering voice rumbled. Oh, what a joy to be caught away into heaven itself on the wings of praise! Their song belongs exclusively to them. No one else in heaven can sing it. Others cannot enter into the joy they experience in seeing their very own people receive the Messiah.

These saints are so pure they are called virgins, for they have not been defiled by women. This may or may not mean literal virginity. The moral evil of this awful time will be so bad that to live within the limits of God's laws will make them appear as virgins by comparison. Jesus also called them virgins, which may be the reason they are so called.

Notice also that these saints have been redeemed from *among* people. Following the Olivet Discourse in Matthew, Jesus gives a prophetic sequence of parables concerning His return to and for His people. (Remember the resurrection and/or rapture of God's people takes place "at his coming" but each person in *his or her own order* or company.) The first company called up in this sequence is the Church;[126] therefore, the first parable focuses on the plight of the unfaithful servant of the Church in the last days (Matt. 24:42–51). The parable of the ten virgins refers to the 144,000 (Matt. 25:1–13). They are God's witnesses after Christ catches away His Church . The parable of the talents (money measurements for gold and silver) follows, depicting the responsibility of Israel to increase the silver invested in them through trial (Matt. 25:14–30). The last in the sequence, the separation of the sheep from the goats, deals with Gentiles still alive on earth when Christ sets up His kingdom after His return (Matt. 25:31–46). Thus, each of the parables deals with a different set of saints.

Many have taught the rapture of the Church from the parable of the ten virgins. However, it appears that the parable can never fit the Church for two reasons: First, the Church is the Bride. The virgins are wedding attendants who wait to go with the Bridegroom's company to the marriage. To make the Church both the Bride and the virgins is to confuse the typology.

Second, the statement, "Behold, the bridegroom cometh; go ye out to meet him" (Matt. 25:6) can never apply to the Church. The time of the rapture of the Church is a secret, instantaneous event in the twinkling of an eye and does not require going anywhere. Yet the virgins can see the Bridegroom afar off and have time to trim their lamps before going to meet Him. Remember, the 144,000 had gone to "sleep." They had been cowering because of persecution

---

[126] Jesus is the firstfruits of the dead. The Church is the firstfruits of the redeemed. The 144,000 are the firstfruits of the Jews.

and must be exhorted to go to Zion and proclaim the good news to their avowed enemies, other Jews. Nevertheless, when they finally move, they go with joy because they know the Lamb, the Bridegroom comes to meet them. Having placed this parable in its setting, let us take a closer look:

> Then shall the kingdom of heaven be likened unto ten virgins, which took their lamps, and went forth to meet the bridegroom. And five of them were wise, and five were foolish. They that were foolish took their lamps, and *took no oil with them*: but the wise took oil in their vessels with their lamps. While the bridegroom tarried, they all slumbered and slept. And at midnight there was a cry made, Behold, the bridegroom cometh; *go ye out to meet him*. Then all those virgins arose, and trimmed their lamps. And the foolish said unto the wise, Give us of your oil; for our lamps are gone out. But the wise answered, saying, Not so; lest there be not enough for us and you: but go ye rather to them that sell, and buy for yourselves. And while they went to buy, the bridegroom came; and they that were ready went in with him to the marriage: and the door was shut. Afterward came also the other virgins, saying, Lord, Lord, open to us. But he answered and said, Verily I say unto you, I know you not. (Matt. 25:1–12, emphasis added)

At the startling news of His coming, those genuinely endowed with the Holy Spirit (with oil) respond to the charge. The unprepared must rush off to get what they lack.

Every group of believers has its counterfeits, and the virgins are no different. While the oil-less virgins' message contained the appearance of truth (they carried lamps, some truth concerning the kingdom), their lamps would not be used until dark; therefore, their lamps looked like those of the other virgins. Trimming a lamp means clipping off the burnt part of the wick to make it burn brighter. The wick will light and burn up without oil.

The wick speaks of the flesh[127] through which the Spirit flows to produce light. Clipping or cutting off the flesh aids burning, but it does not produce it. Curbing the flesh without any oil—the Spirit—produces darkness, not light; religion, not life. Seen this way, the difference in the wise virgins and the foolish virgins is apparent. Thus, the foolish virgins cannot respond to the charge because they are in the dark without oil. Since both groups started out in the daylight, it was not apparent that one group lacked oil. Awaking in darkness revealed the difference between the two groups.

In spiritual language, ten is the number of law, testimony, and responsibility; five is the number of grace. The fact that five were wise virgins does not mean that half the ones God called did not make it. It simply means that others were claiming the same testimony, preaching the same message of the kingdom, suffering the same persecution, but they did not have oil. They were not sealed with the Holy Spirit. God extended grace to both groups. The foolish virgins had lamps, that is, testimonies, but nothing to power them. Several "Christian cults" at large today will probably align themselves with the Jews after having vast numbers of their members left behind at the rapture of the Church. The Jehovah's Witnesses, in particular, preach the message of the kingdom and claim to be the 144,000.

---

[127] The "flesh" in spiritual language means mankind in his natural state. Curbing natural tendencies will not produce God's light. Only the Holy Spirit can do that.

However, upon examination, it can be seen that these "witnesses" have no oil in their lamps.

The wise virgins follow the Lamb wherever he goes. They have been "redeemed from the earth . . . and from among men" (14:3–4). This presupposes that others are left behind. In this case, it is the saved who are removed. Later, we will see the opposite, where the wicked are removed from among the just. The Lamb or, in another metaphor, "the Son of the woman," has been caught back to the throne and so have the virgins, the 144,000 witnesses.

They are the "firstfruits unto God and to the Lamb" (14:4). The term "firstfruits" indicates a harvest to follow. So the virgins bring in the fullness of the Gentiles, but the 144,000 themselves are the firstfruits of the Jews. Both the Jewish witnesses and their converts, the great Gentile multitude, are raptured at the same time because they are essentially the same company. Those around the world who chose to believe have accepted the message of salvation. The world is ripe for judgment. Now comes the worst. Israel has been left behind as God's witness to the beast's empire. But how much better to receive the offer of grace and escape the refiner's fire!

We pause in our discourse to mention a precedent for *two* raptures. We have two examples: Enoch, who walked with God, and He took him, and Elijah the prophet who was caught up to heaven in a whirlwind. In Enoch's case, the incident was reported after the fact. No one knew ahead of time when it would be. Enoch knew about the judgment to come because he named his son Methuselah, "man of the dart." All three uses of the word *dart* in the Bible refer to judgment. The flood came the year of Methuselah's death. (Do the math.) This is a close parallel to the secret rapture of the Church. God took Enoch out before His wrath afflicted the earth with the flood.

The other example, Elijah, not only knew God would take him alive to heaven but also knew the day. Elisha, his apprentice, knew this as well as the prophets. It was not a secret. In addition, Elijah left behind another prophet to take his place, one who performed more miracles than Elijah did. This will certainly be true of the two witnesses who can call down fire during the last half of the week as opposed to the 144,000 who had simply preached the gospel of the kingdom and judgment.

Beyond that, we recall that Malachi predicted that Elijah would come just before the great "day of the Lord" and the restoration of the kingdom (Mal. 4:5). Jesus said that John the Baptist fulfilled the place of Elijah (Matt. 11:14). However, the 144,000 fulfill the same mission as John the Baptist by preaching repentance to the nation Israel just as John did. So by extension, we might say they come in the spirit of Elijah. Both John and the 144,000 present the sacrificial Lamb to Israel. John says, "Behold the Lamb of God" (John 1:36). The sealed company stand with the Lamb in their midst. Therefore, we have two examples of believers being caught up to heaven that correspond to the catching away of the Church (a secret) and the 144,000 and their converts, the great multitude, openly in the midst of the week.

The Everlasting Gospel

And I saw another angel fly in the midst of heaven, having the everlasting gospel to preach unto them that dwell on the earth, and to every nation, and kindred, and tongue, and people, saying with a loud voice, Fear God, and give glory to him; for the hour of his judgment is come: and worship him that made heaven, and earth, and the sea, and the fountains of waters. (14:6–7)

At this point, the scene changes again. John sees another angel flying in middle heaven. (The last angel he saw flying there was the one crying, "Woe, woe, woe!") This angel carries the message of the everlasting gospel. This is not a new gospel. Actually, it is the same message; it never really changes. It is the message of the cross and the Lamb. God's mercy is everlasting to all who listen. He preaches the message again to be sure all have heard. Those who reject it will have two witnesses against them on judgment day: the virgins and the angel.

The everlasting gospel replaces the everlasting covenant. The everlasting covenant made with Noah after the flood has been broken. In that covenant, God granted people the right to govern by giving them capital punishment. He later refined the ordinances of government in the universal Ten Commandments. Speaking of the time when the earth will turn upside down (Isa. 24:1), Isaiah said

> The earth also is defiled under the inhabitants thereof; because they have transgressed the laws, changed the ordinance, broken *the everlasting covenant*. Therefore hath the curse devoured the earth, and they that dwell therein are desolate: therefore the inhabitants of the earth are burned, and few men left. (Isa. 24:5–6) emphasis added.

The earth turns over in the sixth seal after the Gentile multitude has been caught up to heaven. Few people are left who have not already heard the gospel. The Jewish remnant has been redeemed; therefore, the angel's everlasting gospel message leaves a rejecting world guilty. Luke confirms that the judgment is on those who are left worldwide.

> I tell you, in that night there shall be two men in one bed; the one shall be taken, and the other shall be left. Two women shall be grinding together; the one shall be taken, and the other left. Two men shall be in the field; the one shall be taken, and the other left. And they answered and said unto him, Where, Lord? And he said unto them, Wheresoever the body is, thither will the eagles be gathered together. (Luke 17:34–37)

Three different time zones emerge in this passage: where the men sleep, it is nighttime; where the women grind grain, it is daybreak; a little farther around the world, the men are already in the field. The separation leaves behind the unbelieving to face the judgments ahead: "Wheresoever the body is, thither will the eagles be gathered together." The everlasting gospel may separate out a few more. Nevertheless, God is perfectly just to punish the remaining world.

The Trumpet Announcements

> And there followed another angel, saying, Babylon is fallen, is fallen, that great city, because she made all nations drink of the wine of the wrath of her fornication (14:8).

Now, another angel follows, declaring the fall of Babylon. The Babylon of Revelation is that great city which is responsible for all nations having to drink the wine of God's wrath. This is because of her fornication (idolatry) learned from her prototype, ancient Babylon. We will learn about this city later in the vision (Revelation 17). The mention of it here places its fall at the right time in the sequence. The predicting of the fall of ancient Babylon contains a clue to the present time. Jeremiah says:

> Behold I am against thee, O destroying mountain, saith the LORD, which destroyeth all the earth: and I will stretch out mine hand upon thee, and roll thee down from the rocks, and will make thee a burnt mountain. (Jer. 51:25)

Did Jeremiah predict this for a city lying on a plain? Clearly, the meaning to ancient Babylon was spiritual, *mountain* being a figure of speech for a kingdom (Dan. 2:35).

It may, however, point to a literal fulfillment in spiritual Babylon; since the second angel's trumpet of Revelation 8 caused a burning mountain-like object to fall into the sea. The city of Rome, later identified as spiritual Babylon, is more likely to be rolled "down from the rocks," situated as it is on seven hills. Also, the possibility of Rome becoming the site of a volcanic mountain exists since the African and Eurasian continental plates meet down the center of Italy. The disturbance caused by the falling mountain-like meteorite plunging into the sea so close to the plate joint might easily touch off volcanic activity.

The second angel declaring in Revelation 14 the downfall of Babylon probably refers to the same event as the second angel introduced in Revelation 8. Remember, the trumpet angels were prevented from blowing their trumpets until the sealed company (144,000) and their converts were safely escorted to heaven and the believing remnant was also sealed (Rev. 7: 1). This sequence follows after the earth turns over (sixth seal), which follows the redemption of the Jewish faithful and the rapture of the witnesses (fifth seal). Therefore, the first angel here corresponds to the first trumpeter; the second angel, to the second trumpeter, and so on.

Though the numbered angels may be the same as those of Revelation 8, the point of view is different. The time sequence, viewed from heaven, shows the specific reasons for the trumpet judgments. Evidently, the second trumpeter announces his judgment for the wicked city of Rome. The third angel follows.

> And the third angel followed them, saying with a loud voice, If any man worship the beast and his image, and receive his mark in his forehead, or in his hand, the same shall drink of the wine of the wrath of God, which is poured out without mixture into the cup of his indignation; and he shall be tormented with fire and brimstone in the presence of the holy angels, and in the presence of the Lamb: and the smoke of their torment ascendeth up for ever and ever: and they have no rest day nor night, who worship the beast and his image, and whosoever receiveth the mark of his name. Here is the patience of the saints: here are they that keep the commandments of God, and the faith of Jesus. And I heard a voice from heaven saying unto me, Write, Blessed are the dead which die in the Lord from henceforth: Yea, saith the Spirit, that they may rest from their labours; and their works do follow them. (14:9–13)

Remember how the third trumpeter caused the waters to turn to wormwood? Jeremiah promised wormwood to false prophets and all those who worship false gods.[128] The angel delivers this judgment for that very reason. From this, I think we can safely conclude that this is the time that the false prophet forces the issue of worshiping the beast.

This comes after the fall of Babylon, which, in turn, follows a general judgment made in response to believers' prayers (Rev. 8:3) and possible persecution (probably caused by spiritual Babylon) mentioned at the beginning of Revelation 8.[129]

This means that the shortened day of the fourth trumpet with its greater heat falls on those who persist in their idolatry and wickedness even after the judgment of the bitter waters. Man's evil deeds wax worse and worse. The time of the last three trumpet judgments (woes) has come in the Revelation 14 sequence. Nevertheless, instead of proceeding with other details of the trumpeters, John pauses in the midst of judgment to show the endurance of the earthly saints, the Jewish remnant.

With people all around them accepting the beast's religion and following the decrees of the false prophet, the saints endure great hardship. Their patience comes from their belief that Jesus is coming shortly to set things right. They know the beast has a limited rule. Therefore, they, like Moses, refuse "the pleasures of sin for a season; esteeming the reproach of Christ greater riches" (Heb. 11:25–26). A voice from heaven confirms this when it commands John to include this in his writing: "Blessed are the dead which die in the Lord from henceforth: Yea, saith the Spirit, that

---

[128] Jer. 9:15; 23:14–16.

[129] The false church headquartered in Rome may join the Jews in persecution of the 144,000 and their converts. Later, we learn that the city will be drunk on the blood of saints.

they may rest from their labours; and their works do follow them" (14:13) Of this Isaiah says

> The righteous perisheth, and no man layeth it to heart: and the merciful men are taken away, none considering that the righteous is taken away from the evil to come. He shall enter into peace: they shall rest in their beds, each one walking in his own uprightness. (Isa. 57:1–2)

Jesus joins these with the martyrs of the first three and a half years to bring in the quota of martyrs. Both are exhorted to rest until God finishes the judgment. Both earn great rewards.

The Wine Press

The scene changes. John sees a white cloud.

> And I looked, and behold a white cloud, and upon the cloud one sat like unto the Son of man, having on his head a golden crown [divine authority] and in his hand a sharp sickle. And another angel came out of the temple, crying with a loud voice to him that sat on the cloud, Thrust in thy sickle, and reap; for the harvest of the earth is ripe. And he that sat on the cloud thrust in his sickle on the earth; and the earth was reaped. (14:14–16)

This scene reminds us of the parable of the wheat and tares. Jesus interpreted the parable thus:

> He that soweth the good seed is the Son of man; the field is the world; the good seed are the children of the kingdom; but the tares are the children of the wicked one; the enemy that sowed them is the devil; the harvest

is the end of the world; and the reapers are the angels. As therefore the tares are gathered and burned in the fire; so shall it be in the end of this world. The Son of man shall send forth *his angels*, and they shall gather out of his kingdom all things that offend, and them which do iniquity; and shall cast them into a furnace of fire: there shall be wailing and gnashing of teeth. Then shall the righteous shine forth as the sun in the kingdom of their Father. Who hath ears to hear, let him hear. (Matt. 13:37–43)

Jesus has appeared to the nation of Israel—the woman. He has made a new covenant with them. They are the good seed, the children of the kingdom He sowed in the world. Satan came along and, through the beast and the false prophet, sowed bad, idolatrous seed in the world. This parable takes place during the last half of the week. Thus, the Lord refuses to pull out the tares until both seeds mature for harvest. The saints that die in this separation are safely gathered to the "barn." Notice once again, it is the *Son's* messengers who dispense the judgment. Those who escape death give off a great light. The messengers reap the earth!

But John sees another angel come out of the temple. (These judgments that originate in the temple in heaven are connected with the vial judgments on the back of the scroll.) These are the wrath of God poured out according to the offenses committed against Him personally. Idolatry fits into that category:

And another angel came out of the temple which is in heaven, he also having a sharp sickle. And another angel came out from the altar, which had power over fire; and cried with a loud cry to him that had the sharp sickle, saying, Thrust in thy sharp sickle, and gather the clusters of the vine of the earth; for her grapes are fully ripe. And the angel thrust his sickle into the earth, and gathered the vine of the earth, and cast it into the great winepress of the wrath of God. And the winepress was trodden without the city, and blood came out of the winepress, even unto the horse bridles, by the space of a thousand and six hundred furlongs. (14:17–20)

The vine of the earth is a figure of speech that represents Israel. A prophecy in Isaiah that we mentioned earlier says:

For the vineyard of the LORD of hosts is the house of Israel, and the men of Judah his pleasant plant: and he looked for judgment, but behold oppression; for righteousness, but behold a cry. Woe unto them that join house to house, that lay field to field. (Isa. 5:7–8)

A portion of Israel has joined with the beast. Some have even accepted his kingdom. God has a special judgment for this: the second and third woes. Isaiah merely repeats what Moses said would be their latter end.

For their vine is of the vine of Sodom, and of the fields of Gomorrah: their grapes are the grapes of gall, their clusters are bitter: Their wine is the poison of dragons, and the cruel venom of asps. Is not this laid up in store with me, and sealed up among my treasures? To me belongeth vengeance, and recompense; their foot shall slide in due time: for the day of their calamity is at hand, and the things that shall come upon them make haste. For the LORD shall judge his people, and repent himself for his servants, when he seeth that their power is gone [the two witnesses of chapter 11 are killed], and there is none shut up, or left.

And he shall say, Where are their gods, their rock in whom they trusted, which did eat the fat of their sacrifices, and drank the wine of their drink offerings? let them rise up and help you, and be your protection. See now that I, even I, am he, and there is no god with me: I kill, and I make alive; I wound, and I heal: neither is there any that can deliver out of my hand. For I lift up my hand to heaven, and I say, I live for ever. If I whet my glittering sword, and mine hand take hold on judgment; I will render vengeance to mine enemies, and will reward them that hate me. I will make mine arrows drunk with blood, and my sword shall devour flesh; and that with the blood of the slain and of the captives, from the beginning of revenges upon the enemy. Rejoice, O ye nations, with his people: for he will avenge the blood of his servants, and will render vengeance to his adversaries, and will be merciful unto his land, and to his people. (Deut. 32:32–43)

The angels gather the grapes for the winepress outside the city. This involves gathering those Israelites who have opposed God and joined with the beast. These may be members of the Antichrist's army; for we know a battle is brewing because of the description of the blood rising to the horses' bridles. The conflict between Satan's forces and the Captain's forces finally comes to a head. Isaiah describes the winepress itself.

Who is this that cometh from Edom, with dyed garments from Bozrah? This that is glorious in his apparel, travelling in the greatness of his strength? [answer] I that speak in righteousness, mighty to save. Wherefore art thou red in thine apparel, and thy garments like him that treadeth in the winefat? [Answer] I have trodden the winepress alone; and of the people there was none with me: for I will tread them in mine anger, and trample them in my fury; and their blood shall be sprinkled upon my garments, and I will stain all my raiment. For the day of vengeance is in mine heart,[130] and the year of my redeemed is come.

And I looked, and there was none to help; and I wondered that there was none to uphold: therefore mine own arm brought salvation unto me; and my fury, it upheld me. And I will tread down the people in mine anger, and make them drunk in my fury, and I will bring down their strength to the earth. I will mention the lovingkindnesses of the LORD, and the praises of the LORD, according to all that the LORD hath bestowed on us, and the great goodness toward the house of Israel, which he hath bestowed on them according to his mercies, and according to the multitude of his lovingkindnesses. For he said, Surely they are my people, children that will not lie: so he was their Saviour. In all their affliction he was afflicted, and the angel of his presence saved them: in his love and in his pity he redeemed them; and he bare them, and carried them all the days of old. But they rebelled, and vexed his holy Spirit: therefore he was turned to be their enemy, and he fought against them. (Isa. 63:1–10)

---

[130] See also Isa. 61:2.

The enemy has touched the apple of God's eye, His chosen people. In wrath, with an even greater vehemence against the Israelis who side with the beast, God takes up His sword. The "vine of the earth" includes, also, Gentile nations near the Middle East with whom the apostates agree. Joel shows us some of the reasons why the Gentiles are included in this judgment.

> For, behold, in those days, and in that time, when I shall bring again the captivity of Judah and Jerusalem, I will also gather all nations, and will bring them down into the valley of Jehoshaphat, and will plead with them there for my people and for my heritage Israel, whom they have scattered among the nations, and *parted my land* [the beast's bureaucracy, or perhaps even earlier, the UN's division in 1948, or the Palestinian State?]. And they have cast lots for my people; and have given a boy for an harlot, and sold a girl[131] for wine, that they might drink. Yea, and what have ye to do with me, Tyre, and Zidon, and all the coasts of Palestine? will ye render me a recompence? and if ye recompense me, swiftly and speedily will I return your recompence upon your own head; because ye have taken my silver and my gold, and have carried into your temples my goodly pleasant things; the children also of Judah and the children of Jerusalem have ye sold unto the Grecians, that ye might remove them far from their border.

---

[131] Though many believers will be beheaded, others will be sold as slaves. Going into slavery may be God's provision against having to wear the mark of the beast.

Behold, I will raise them out of the place whither ye have sold them, and will return your recompence upon your own head: and *I will sell your sons*[132] *and your daughters* into the hand of the children of Judah, and they shall sell them to the Sabeans, to a people far off: for the LORD hath spoken it. Proclaim ye this among the Gentiles; Prepare war, wake up the mighty men, let all the men of war draw near; let them come up: Beat your plowshares into swords, and your pruninghooks into spears: let the weak say, I am strong. Assemble yourselves, and come, all ye heathen and gather yourselves together round about: thither cause thy mighty ones [Maruts, small independent comets] to come down, O LORD. [Evidently, one-third of the earth's remaining population will be gathered here since that is the quota of people destroyed in the sixth trumpet by these "terrible ones." See Rev. 9:18.] Let the heathen be wakened, and come up to the valley of Jehoshaphat: for there will I sit to judge all the heathen round about. [The Son of man commands the angels who are ready to reap:] Put ye in the sickle, for the harvest is ripe: come, get you down: for the press is full, the fats overflow; for their wickedness is great. Multitudes, multitudes in the valley of decision: for the day of the LORD is near in the valley of decision. (Joel 3:1–14, emphasis added)

The actual treading of the winepress takes place just before Christ's return to earth with His armies. We know this because His garments are already stained when He de-

---

[132] This is absolute justice and will be initiated when the kingdom is first set up. The slavery will last only until the year of jubilee whereupon they will be set free (see Lev. 25:10).

scends with the armies (Rev. 19: 13). Revelation 19 describes this and is part of the seventh-trumpet judgment. The armies in the valley of decision fight the final battle of Armageddon. The war begins, however, in the sixth-trumpet judgment with the astronomical comet army attacking first.

Then the return of Christ follows, accompanied by an earthquake and the great hail of the seventh trumpet/vial judgment. From all this destruction, "blood" will stain horses' bridles for 1,600 furlongs (a furlong is approximately 582 feet). Changed to miles, 1,600 furlongs would be a linear distance of 176 or so miles. This is the distance from the plains of Esdralon, the traditional site of Armageddon, to the city of Bozrah in the land of Edom from which Christ emerges from the winepress.

Regarding the blood reaching the height of the horses' bridles in this great distance, it is interesting to note that this long valley that contains the Jordan River, the Sea of Galilee, and the Dead Sea, sits on top of the longest crack on the surface of the earth. The fault system with its dropped center blocks reaches from 36 north latitude in Syria down the Jordan Valley, the Gulf of Aqaba, the Red Sea, and 2,500 miles into the continent of Africa forming the great Rift Valley. This equals one-third of the distance from the north pole to the south pole. Surely, the greatest earthquake the world will ever[133] know must be felt more severely here in the earth's deepest valley. Ezekiel tells us that the salt sea will be healed. It will be made fresh and filled with fish (Ezek. 47:8–12) like the great sea. That indicates an outlet to the ocean. Evidently, the earthquake will open a passage to the Red Sea, causing the entire valley to flood with wa-

---

[133] Matt. 24:7.

ter. Then, as the water rises in the battlefield to the point that the horses are forced to swim, the bloody waters will reach the bridles. Temporarily, the sea "runs" red just as the river at the Battle of Stalingrad ran red in World War II. Part of the color may be due to dust accompanying hail in the seventh-trumpet judgment.

And so we have come to the end of the scroll again. During the "rerun," we have seen the Lamb stand upon Mount Zion, the oldest holy place in Jerusalem. We have seen the virgin/witnesses raptured from among the Jewish remnant while the woman remains behind to face the refiner's fire.

We have also seen the treading of the winepress—the final battle of Armageddon. Now, we are ready to turn the scroll over and look at the back side, where the vials of wrath are being prepared. Here, we will cover this ground again for a third time, adding the final touches—the end results of the judgments.

Chapter 21

THE HOLY WRATH

(REVELATION 15)

Sickened by the bloody scene of the winepress, John is relieved to look heavenward at a new sign developing.

> And I saw another sign in heaven, great and marvellous, seven angels having the seven last plagues; for in them is filled up the wrath of God. (15:1)

The last sign he saw there was the woman giving birth. This sign, being equally wondrous, features seven angels bearing the seven last plagues. John describes this sign as "great and marvelous." The pageantry on the heavenly screen continues. This may be another reason people's hearts fail them for fear. The sky fills with omens that portend of righteous judgment. These pour out God's wrath in full measure. However, before the action begins, the scene switches.

> And I saw as it were a sea of glass mingled with fire: and them that had gotten the victory over the beast, and over his image, and over his mark, and over the number of his name, stand on the sea of glass, having the harps of God. (15:2)

God apparently wants John (and us) to know that even though the final and, therefore, most severe judgments hang precariously over the human race, He will have a faithful remnant through it all. In the end, these will emerge purified from the furnace of His wrath. Victories are won over: 1) the satanic ruler, the beast, another god; 2) his image, an idol; 3) over his mark, the seal of ownership for buying and selling; and 4) the number of his name, 666.

These four violate the Ten Commandments, especially the first four. The first commandment, "Thou shalt have no other gods before me" (Exod. 20:3), refers to the worship the beast receives as god (Rev. 13:12). The second, "Thou shalt not make unto thee any graven image" (Exod. 20:4), relates to the prompting of the false prophet for people to make an image of the beast "which had the wound by the sword and did live" (Rev. 13:14). The third commandment, "Thou shalt not take the name of the LORD thy God in vain" (Exod. 20:7) refers also to the mark. In the beast's kingdom, the name to swear by and the name that carries official authority is the symbol 666—the number of the beast's name. In contrast, God's name is blasphemed (Rev. 13:6). In the fourth commandment, "Remember the sabbath day, to keep it holy" (Exod. 20:8), all work, including buying and selling, was restricted to six days. In the beast's kingdom, the only restriction to buying and selling is the possession of his mark. Thus, we see the world system stands diametrically opposite to God's first four commandments.

Earlier, we said that the back side of the scroll is transcribed with judgments given for offenses against God personally. Now, we see that the beast's regime provokes extreme judgment. The faithful band of believers that John saw on the sea of glass had stood firm in that open affront to their God. No matter how severe the judgments are because of the extreme wickedness, the Father wants John to know that God's people have a planned, victorious end.

And they sing the song of Moses the servant of God, and the song of the Lamb, saying, Great and marvellous are thy works, Lord God Almighty; just and true are thy ways, thou King of saints. Who shall not fear thee, O Lord, and glorify thy name? For thou only art holy: for all nations shall come and worship before thee; for thy judgments are made manifest. (15:3–4)

After the plagues are poured out, the saints stand on the sea of glass in front of the throne victoriously proclaiming, "Great and marvellous are thy works, Lord God Almighty; just and true are thy ways, thou King of saints." They sing both the song of Moses and the song of the Lamb. Like Moses, they too have witnessed the mighty works of God in moving the universe against the wicked. They could sing Psalm 46, because they have lived through it.

God is our refuge and strength, a very present help in trouble. Therefore will not we fear, though the earth be removed, and though the mountains be carried into the midst of the sea. (Ps. 46:1–2)

They praise God because He is almighty, because His judgments on the wicked are just. They praise Him for fulfilling His Word. All nations will eventually come and worship, now that His mighty power has been revealed to them. The nations know the judgments to be from God. "For the earth shall be filled with the knowledge of the glory of the LORD, as the waters cover the sea" (Hab. 2:14).

Having made His point, God returns John's attention to the fulfillment of the sign he saw earlier.

And after that I looked, and, behold, the temple of the tabernacle of the testimony in heaven was opened: and the seven angels came out of the temple, having the seven plagues, clothed in pure and white linen, and having their breasts girded with golden girdles. (15:5–6)

John sees the same seven angels, portrayed in the sign, coming out of a wide-open temple in heaven. Dressed in pure, white linen, tied about the breast with golden belts, they resemble priests. Can angels be dressed as priests? Nowhere in Scripture do we see heavenly beings functioning as priests. Indeed, even Christ had to become a man before He could be a priest for mankind. The Mighty Angel who offered the prayers of saints in Revelation 8 at the golden altar surely was none other than the Lord Jesus Himself. Angels are what their name implies—messengers—delivering God's words or engaging in battles with Satan's angels to carry out God's will.

However, these angels/messengers are dressed in the likeness of Christ as He appeared to John at the beginning of the vision. They have the same type of robes and the same girdles about the breasts. The pure, white linen of their robes is the same as those of the saints returning with Christ in Revelation 19:8—fine linen, clean and white. Further, another messenger explained in that chapter that fine linen is a figure of speech describing the righteousness acts of saints. Though angels are sometimes portrayed in long, white robes (Mark 16:5), the robes are never described as linen. Linen in Scripture is generally restricted to the tabernacle, priests, and kings and only casually mentioned as a commercial product for the rich. The only reference to any being that could be construed as an angel (although the passage does not say he is so) is the man in white linen who appeared to Daniel and Ezekiel (Ezek. 9:3). However, his appearance almost certainly describes him as Jesus before His incarnation.

> Then I lifted up mine eyes, and looked, and behold a certain man clothed in linen, whose loins were girded with fine gold of Uphaz. His body also was like the beryl, and his face as the appearance of lightning, and his eyes as lamps of fire, and his arms and his feet like in colour to polished brass, and the voice of his words like the voice of a multitude. (Dan. 10:5–6)

Is not this our Lord? Therefore, these messengers, wearing the garments of priests and having the seven plagues, seem to be saints who have been assigned this task. I must confess this comes as a surprise to me. Although we identified the messengers (angels) of the seven churches as believers, it never occurred to me that saints would participate in the judgments. Could this be why the Lord wants His

Church to know about future things so they will be prepared for such tasks?

This provoked me to study the angels of the New Testament. What I discovered was this: four times "messengers" were assigned to represent certain beings, that is, as sending them on their behalf. 1) The Father has His angels (Mark 8:38; Rev. 3:5); 2) Michael, the archangel, has his angels (Rev. 12:7); 3) the dragon, Satan, has his angels (Rev. 12:7); and 4) *the Son has His angels* (Matthew 13:41).

When Jesus comes for the Church, His Father's angels accompany Him; and they are apparently present when He judges the Church. "For the Son of man shall come in the glory of his Father with his angels; and then he shall reward every man according to his works" (Matt. 16:27). Perhaps the Father's angels help gather the living saints from the four winds of heaven. Whether or not this is true, angels seem to be present for the judgment and rewarding of the Church.

> Whosoever therefore shall be ashamed of me and of my words in this adulterous and sinful generation; of him also shall the Son of man be ashamed, when cometh in the glory of his Father with the holy angels. (Mark 8:38)

And again:

> He that overcometh, the same shall be clothed in white raiment; and I will not blot out his name out of the book of life, but I will confess his name before my Father, *and before his angels.* (Rev. 3:5, emphasis added)

Later, Christ says: "And, behold, I come quickly; and my reward *is with me,* to give every man according as his work shall be" (Rev. 22:12, emphasis added). So we expect the Father's angels to be present at the judgment seat of Christ, which would probably take place soon after the rapture/resurrection of the Church. We say this because the Church, as pictured in the elders, had already have received their crowns before John was caught up to heaven. Therefore, the Father's angels serve the Son on the Father's behalf.

Since the angel/prince Michael, is especially assigned to the nation Israel (Dan. 12:1), it is appropriate, then, that he lead the battle against the dragon that seeks to destroy the woman, Israel. Being a prince, he rules over other angels in his army. Therefore, they are his to command.

Satan is known as "the prince of the power of the air" (Eph. 2:2). As a prince, He, too, commands other fallen angels.

The Son of man (Jesus), in the parable of the wheat and the tares, sends forth *His angels* to reap at the end of the world. Is not that what we see happening here?

> And one of the four beasts gave unto the seven angels seven golden vials full of the wrath of God, who liveth for ever and ever. And the temple was filled with smoke from the glory of God, and from his power; and no man was able to enter into the temple, till the seven plagues of the seven angels were fulfilled. (15:7–8)

The priestly angels serve the Son in claiming His kingdom. Truly, their garments speak of their work. They, after all, administer judgment against insulted holiness. When they emerge these already have the seven last plagues in their hands. Then, one of the living creatures (probably the eagle-like creature representing the Mighty Angel) gives each angel *an added vial* of wrath to pour on top of his plague. Whether the trumpeting angels of Revelation 8 and 9 announce the coming plagues immediately before each delivery, we cannot say for sure. Perhaps the two witnesses announcing them as the "little open book" warn some time before the plagues actually fall. Nevertheless, these angels carry both the plagues and the vials, pouring them out at the time appointed. Although the contents of the vials have been written on the back of the scroll, this merely serves to demonstrate the separation of offenses—those against men versus those against God. Nevertheless, the plagues spoken of here are exactly what was announced by the trumpets. Since they have already been described in Revelation chapters 8 and 9, no further explanation is necessary.

The vials are the heavenly side of the picture. We know they actually occur close together (each vial following each plague), because we are told in chapter 10 that when the voice of the seventh angel sounds, the mystery of God will be finished. However, the added vials of wrath poured on top of each plague are yet to be enumerated in the text. Each plague will grow to a fullness of wrath as its vial completes the judgment. We will see this demonstrated as we watch the vials being poured out in the next chapter.

After the angels received the vials, the temple was filled with the "smoke from the glory of God, and from his power" (15:8). No one can enter into the temple until the seven plagues are fulfilled. That means for the entire period of the last half of the week—the time of His wrath, "the great tribulation," no one can intercede to deter God from performing justice. The closed temple makes it clear that the time for mercy has ended. It is a time of holy wrath.

The prophecy in Habakkuk concerning the beast's rule ends thus: "But the LORD is in his holy temple: let all the earth keep silence before him" (Hab. 2:20). The trumpet and subsequent vial judgments cover the same 1,290 days as the beast's rule. We look at the trumpet judgments to see this:

> And the seventh angel sounded; . . . and the temple of God was opened in heaven, and there was seen in his temple the ark of his testament; and there were *lightnings*, and *voices*, and t*hunderings*, and an *earthquake*, and *great hail*. (Rev. 11:15, 19, emphasis added)

The plague of the seventh trumpet destroys the armies gathered at Armageddon and southward in the winepress. This same set of circumstances match the vial.

> And the seventh angel poured out his vial into the air. And there were *voices*, and *thunders*, and *lightnings*; and there was a *great earthquake*. . . . And there fell upon men a *great hail* out of heaven. (Rev. 16:17–18, 21, emphasis added)

Notice the seventh trumpet and the seventh vial seem to be combined. They contain the same outpouring of wrath—the same thunder, lightning, voices, earthquake, and great hail (meteorites). No wonder the voice declared to John earlier that when the seventh angel sounded, the mystery would be ended. Therefore, with the judgments completed, God opens the temple to the point that all can see the ark of His testament.

The sign John sees at the beginning of this chapter can also be seen from the earth. The believers' outcome and the seven angels leaving the smoke-filled temple show us the events as seen behind the scenes in heaven. In the next chapter, we will see the effects of the poured-out vials on the earth.

Chapter 22

THE FULL MEASURE

(REVELATION 16)

And I heard a great voice out of the temple saying to the seven angels, Go your ways, and pour out the vials of the wrath of God upon the earth. (16:1)

As the angels exit, a voice thunders out of the glory cloud filling the temple, the Father's voice directs specifically, "Go your ways," indicating that the judgments are aimed at individual targets.

The First Vial

The first angel pours his vial down on idolatry that is once again in vogue. Idol worship began when the image of the beast was set up in the temple area just before the invasion by Russia, but God has allowed it to mature to its fullness. Since this violates the first commandment, God's judicious answer falls specifically on the idol worshipers.

And the first went, and poured out his vial upon the earth; and there fell a noisome and grievous sore upon the men which had the mark of the beast, and upon them which worshipped his image. (16:2)

Although the first angel poured his vial on the earth generally, its result is an individual application. This vial, poured on top of the trumpet judgment that announced falling hail and fire rain mixed with dust, inflicts the ongoing wrath from these initial ingredients. When this type of plague fell on Egypt in Moses' day, both humans and beasts developed boils breaking out in blisters (Exod. 9:10). Ancient Jewish sources[134] state that the naptha (crude oil) together with hot stones poured down on Egypt. "The Egyptians refused to let the Israelites go, and he poured out naptha over them burning blisters." It was "a stream of hot naptha." Psalm 105:32 speaks of God giving them "hail for rain, and flaming fire in their land." Can it be that the same thing happens here?

Probably the same rain of hot crude oil, some of it still burning, falls on the people of the beast's kingdom. Flaming oil burns deeply into the skin, leaving wounds that are difficult to heal. This is particularly to be expected if, because of the disruption of the earth's magnetic field, excessive radiation from space is allowed to reach the ground. Skin subjected to radiation resists healing. At first, the burn appears not to amount to much more than a blister. Nevertheless, it proves increasingly hurtful as it refuses to heal, spreading into a putrid, open ulcer.

Believers heeding the warning of the two witnesses, who are faithfully prophesying God's plans, stay under cover.

---

[134] Midrash Tanhuma, Midrash Psekta Rabatis, Midrash Wa-Yosha.

Thus they escape both the plague and the sores that result. At first, the idol worshipers will scoff at them, but then, irritated by discomfort and envy, their hatred will rage. The difference God puts between His own people and the idol worshipers will make the fires of persecution burn even hotter.

The Second Vial

> And the second angel poured out his vial upon the sea; and it became as the blood of a dead man: and every living soul died in the sea. (16:3)

Food supplies dwindle as the sea, one of the few sources of food left, ruins. The crops of the great combined farms had failed miserably. In addition, even that which did survive the drought has been destroyed by the fire-rain. Food rationing has become necessary, perhaps this is another reason the government requires a mark for purchasing.

The second angel pours his vial on top of the plague that had dropped the burning, mountainous object into the Mediterranean Sea. This caused the sea to turn red from the dissolved ferruginous dust accompanying the "mountain." Only one-third of the sea was initially affected by the trumpet judgment. With the pouring out of the vial, however, the conditions change and spread to the rest of the sea.

The whole sea becomes as the blood of a dead man. A dead person's blood differs from living blood because of the lack of circulation. The nearly clear plasma separates from the hemoglobin when blood ceases to flow, creating patches of concentrated red blood cells. Thus, the picture gradually changes from a sea of brilliant red to a sea floating with dark, decaying debris. Broken ships, dead marine life, and dead bodies drift on the surface. The descriptive term "blood of a dead man" is apropos.

The burning mountain warms the sea, making ideal conditions for decay. A rotting stench drives the population from the coasts as each wave dumps its load on the beaches. The breeding of flies and other vermin that result make a total clean up nearly impossible. Disease from bacteria flourishing in the decaying organic matter, make people sick.

The death of the sea creatures is partly due to the bitter dust and the impact of the falling "mountain"; but the ongoing effect is probably due to a condition known as "Red Tide."

Red tide is a natural phenomenon, where certain algae color the sea surface with a brownish red sheen that gives off a neurotoxin. The toxic water proves lethal to fish and to other marine creatures when in great concentration. Recently it has been blamed for the deaths of hundreds of whales, dolphins and manatees in North American waters. Wind and waves release the toxin into the air forming an irritating gas that affects humans near the shore. They experience a burning sensation in the eyes and nose, and a dry, choking cough.

Red tides are caused by several species of microscopic marine phytoplankton, microscopic plantlike cells that produce potent chemical neurotoxins. Normally they inhabit seawater without harm, but when conditions are conductive to a "bloom," they can increase to several million cells to one liter of seawater bringing devastation to as much as several hundred square miles of ocean.

Because Florida suffers frequently from "blooms," much research has been done to understand the cause. According to a 2001 study released by NASA News they found that iron in the Sahara dust clouds deposited in the waters west of Florida and the Gulf of Mexico set the stage. They tracked the dust clouds produced by storm activity using satellites and ground-based instruments. They found that when the clouds reached the Florida waters the iron content in seawater increased by 300%. When this happens, a bacteria, Trichodesmium, uses the iron to convert the nitrogen in the water into a more usable form for other sea life. The phytoplankton, being a primitive plant uses the nitrogen to multiply speedily giving off deadly toxins in its wake.[135]

They further believe that the plankton enter a dormant stage at some point in their life cycle, forming cysts that sink to the bottom sediments forming a "seed bed effect." Any disturbance of the ocean floor would send them to the surface, positioning them for their next stage of growth.

When the burning mountain falls into the sea turning the water red from a ferruginous dust[136] and churning up the sediments of the sea floor, not to mention adding the necessary heat to warm up the water, we would have conditions for a gigantic bloom of red tide, especially if a "seed bed" lies dormant.

Whether red tide is involved or not once the balance of life is broken, creatures dependent on those destroyed will also die. Eventually, the whole sea would become one giant cesspool.

With the scarcity of food in view, we are ready to look at the next vision in Zechariah's sequence. This vision

---

[135] NASA News, "Dust from Africa Leads to Large Toxic Algae Blooms in Gulf of Mexico, Study Finds," Release #01-85, August 28< 2001 Can be found on the web under red tide.
[136] Iron

follows the one of the flying roll (the unrolled scroll), a document unleashing judgments announced in the "open book."

> Then the angel that talked with me went forth, and said unto me, Lift up now thine eyes, and see what is this that goeth forth. And I said, What is it? And he said, This is an ephah that goeth forth. He said moreover, This is their resemblance through all the earth. And, behold, there was lifted up a talent of lead: and this is a woman that sitteth in the midst of the ephah. And he said, This is wickedness. And he cast it into the midst the ephah; and he cast the weight of lead upon the mouth thereof. Then lifted I up mine eyes, and looked, and, behold, there came out two women, and the wind was in their wings; for they had wings like the wings of a stork: and they lifted up the ephah between the earth and the heaven. Then said I to the angel that talked with me, Whither do these bear the ephah? And he said unto me, To it an house in the land of Shinar: and it shall be established, and set *there upon her own base*. (Zech. 5:5–11, emphasis added)

In this vision, an angel shows Zechariah an ephah, a measurement similar to a bushel basket. Actually, Josephus says that an ephah was comparable to the Attic Medimnus, which is about one and one-twelfth of an English bushel.[137] It was used to measure wheat, barley, or other grains. Notice the measurement was the same for the whole earth,

---

[137] William Wilson, *Old Testament Word Studies* (Grand Rapids: Kregal Publications, 1978, 1979) p. 147.

indicating the whole world is on the same standard. A woman personifies this system by her name "wickedness." The angel slams down the lid and shuts the woman in the basket so it can be moved. The economic system symbolized here evidently began elsewhere but will finally be established in ancient Babylon upon "her own base."

As food becomes the number-one commodity of the business world, opportunity for gain creates the temptation to cheat. Greedy business men take advantage of the situation. Wickedness permeates the commercial scene, forcing the government to act. Here the government of the kingdom seizes the opportunity to completely control society. Therefore, because of the scarcity of food and the wicked, unfair merchants, the beast makes the mark mandatory for buying and selling. The mark may be introduced initially as a convenience and a sign of allegiance to the new ruler, setting apart a new elite. However, in the emergency, the beast takes the opportunity to gain more power. With only marked purchasers able to buy or sell, all undesirables of the kingdom can now be eliminated by starvation or execution.

Concerning the new location of the headquarters, "a house in the land of Shinar," the US News & World Report said in 1977[138] that the Iraqi Ba'athist regime held an almost mystical belief that Iraq is destined to lead a radical socialist revolution. At that time, they were erecting a huge headquarter's building in Baghdad. They also channeled their national spending toward developing the nation's 29 million acres of arable land. Reason? "When the oil runs out, we'll be ready to export food, and that is the next boom

---

[138] Dennis Mullin, Iraq: Determined to Upset U.S. Plan for Mideast Peace US News & World Report May 16 1977, p. 94

commodity." The Persian Gulf, called the greatest artery of shipping in the world because of the oil industry, could also be used to import food from the unspoiled eastern seas to feed the kingdom's empty stomachs. "And his mouth [was] as the mouth of a lion" (Rev. 13:2). Will Babylon, symbolized by the lion, become the feeding mouth of the kingdom?

The part of Zechariah's vision concerning commerce returning to its own base places spiritual Babylon back on literal Babylon—the ancient city. For centuries the importance of Babylon has been insignificant, but in these last years, political events and economic pressures have brought her back into prominence. The *New York Times* (20 March 1979) reported that Iraq is working feverishly to restore the ancient city of Babylon. Work began in 1978. The leadership of Iraq may not take too kindly to the beast taking over their dreams for the city. Nevertheless, the necessity of importing food for the kingdom overshadows any jealousies that exist. Babylon will come back into a brief existence. It is no longer outside the realm of possibility that the commercial activity of the end times may center around ancient Babylon. Therefore, the second vial will finalize the wrath against the spiritual Babylonian system, forcing a relocation of its capitol. It will also unveil its true idolatrous nature, which we examine in detail in Revelation 17 and 18.

The Third Vial

The third angel poured out his vial upon the rivers and fountains of waters, and they became blood. The initating cause of the bloody water comes from the detonating meteor of the third-trumpet judgment that sprayed with meteoric iron. The ferruginous dust from the broken meteor[139] dyes the waters red. The dust will make the waters bitter also. so that many people will die. Looking at the third angel's words, we see the provocation behind this judgment. The saints are being persecuted.

> And the third angel poured out his vial upon the rivers and fountains of waters; and they became blood. And I heard the angel of the waters say, Thou art righteous, O Lord, which art, and wast, and shall be, because thou hast judged thus. For they have shed the blood of saints and prophets, and thou hast given them blood to drink; for they are worthy. And I heard another out of the altar say, Even so, Lord God Almighty, true and righteous are thy judgments. (16:4–7)

The third vial is being poured out when the economic crisis requires that all receive the mark of the beast. Those who receive it agree with the blasphemous policies of the Antichrist. Those who refuse will incur his wrath. As a result, he evidently will declare all-out war against the saints.

Blood will flow like a river from saints and prophets alike. God's justice in judgment renders like for like, "You like blood? Have some to drink!" John hears the angel's approval: "Even so, Lord God Almighty, true and righteous are thy judgments" (16:7).

Now we know which third of the world's rivers will be affected—those in the Middle East centered around the beast's headquarters.

---

[139] Most meteorites striking the earth will belong to the bloody dragon's original tail. Therefore, they can be expected to deliver the same red dust..

The Fourth Vial

> And the fourth angel poured out his vial upon the sun; and power was given unto him to scorch men with fire. And men were scorched with great heat, and blasphemed the name of God, which hath power over these plagues: and they repented not to give him glory. (16:8–9)

In this plague (the fourth trumpet), the daylight was diminished to one-third of its shiningas a result of a more rapid rotation. The vial adds heat. Remember, the fourth trumpet judgment had shortened the day to sixteen hours to protect the elect. Isaiah mentions a possible reason the day will need to be shortened.

> Moreover the light of the moon shall be as the light of the sun, and the light of the sun shall be sevenfold, as the light of seven days, in the day the LORD bindeth up the breach of his people, and healeth the stroke of their wound. (Isa. 30:26)

A light seven times more intense will bring proportional heat because it denotes proximity. The quick turning may keep the oceans from getting hot enough to boil. No wonder all humans would perish if the days were not shortened!

God mentions the sun as an instrument of judgment when speaking with Job. He says, "Hast thou commanded the morning since thy days; and caused the dayspring to know his place; that it might take hold of the ends of the earth, that the wicked might be shaken out of it?"[140] The

---

[140] Job 38:12–13.

conflict involving the passing comet may alter the earth's orbit to the point that its closest approach to the sun will be much nearer. The moon, too, may be nearer. That would mean that, at least for a season, the light and heat would be intense. The sun taking hold of the ends of the earth (the magnetic poles) implies the earth will be near enough to have its magnetic field unusually affected. Perhaps a wobble in its revolution causes the sun's rays to strike at a more direct angle.

The closer sun was also a condition in the past when a great comet threatened the earth. The Indians of the Chewkee tribe on the Gulf Coast say, "It was too hot. The sun was put a hand 'breadth' higher in the air, but it was still too hot. Seven times the sun was lifted higher and higher under the sky arch, until it became cooler."[141] The Kasha tribe in the interior of British Columbia relate: "The sky was pushed up and the weather changed."[142]

Reports from the Skylab experiments (1973-74) revealed a solar wind that directly affects our weather on earth. It is defined in an article by Jack B. Zirker, director of the Skylab workshop on Coronal Holes. He says that this solar wind boils off the sun's corona in a "wild expansion of gasses and tears through the solar system in all directions at enormous speeds." Up close, this energy might have an even greater affect on the weather.[143]

---

[141] Alexander, *North American Mythology*, p. 60 as quoted in Immanuel Velikovsky, *Worlds in Collision* (New York: Doubleday, 1950), p. 189. This may correspond to the many times the shadow on the sundial changed in Ahaz's reign.

[142] Ibid.

[143] Jack B. Zirker, "The Sun's Expanding Halo," *Science Year 1980* The World Book Science Annual (Chicago: World Book—Childcraft International, Inc. 1980) p. 13

Mankind has taken for granted the comfort of the earth's temperature. A narrow band of fluctuating temperatures supports life on this planet and, apparently, no other in our solar system. Now they will blaspheme God for changing that band. In their discomfort, their anger will increase.

How can people get back at God? By gnashing against His followers. Yet every attempt to deal with the two witnesses, the lampstands of Revelation 11 (whom the people blame for the plagues), ends in failure. The deaths of those attempting to hurt the witnesses will inflame the populous even more.

Still, God provides a cover from the physical heat for His own. Isaiah mentions a praise offered to God for this mighty provision: "For thou hast been a strength to the poor, a strength to the needy in his distress, a refuge from the storm, *a shadow from the heat*" (Isa. 25:4, emphasis added).

The heat is for the wicked. "For, behold, the day cometh, that shall burn as an oven; and all the proud, yea, and all that do wickedly, shall be stubble: and the day that cometh shall burn them up, saith the LORD of hosts, that it shall leave them neither root nor branch" (Mal. 4:1). Malachi prophesied to the remnant that returned from Babylon, so he could not possibly have spoken about the physical disasters that were last on the earth in the eighth century B.C. This day of burning is yet to come!

The Fifth Vial

And the fifth angel poured out his vial upon the seat of the beast; and his kingdom was full of darkness; and they gnawed their tongues for pain, and blasphemed the

God of heaven because of their pains and their sores, and repented not of their deeds. (16:10–11)

The fifth angel poured his vial on top of the plague where the falling star had opened the bottomless pit. Black smoke had rolled out to darken the sun and fill the air with ash and dangerous creatures. This confirms that the opened pit is nearby. It is the beast's kingdom that receives the greatest concentration of ash. The pains people suffer probably come from the locust-like creatures with the power to torment for five months. Pain may result from the creatures' stings, but sores most likely come from their flesh-tearing teeth. Remember, they were commanded to feed on wicked people instead of vegetation. If they are anything like regular locusts, they will have voracious appetites.

All God's blessings, taken for granted by an ungrateful world, are being removed one by one: Food, water, healing power, temperature control, and now light. So far during these judgments the plagues have scourge mankind's natural senses to the limit. Their noses have been stopped by the stench of the destroyed Russian army and rotting fish and marine life. Their ears have been made deaf by explosions of detonating meteors and groaning earth strata. Their mouths have been galled by the taste of bitter waters. Their skin has been burned, "boiled," and bitten. Now dense darkness, in the form of ashes, irritates their eyes and extinguish all light, even that held as close as arm's length. It will be a pure dose of hell on earth! Thus ends one woe.

The Sixth Vial

And the sixth angel poured out his vial upon the great river Euphrates; and the water thereof was dried up, that the way of the kings of the east might be prepared. (16:12)

The sixth angel poured out his vial on the plague that released the angels bound at the Euphrates River. A great earthquake had occurred (Rev. 11:13) after the two witnesses had been resurrected and had ascended. This earthquake completed the second woe. This had occurred along the earth fracture discovered by astronaut Vance D. Brand.[144] This system of fractures belongs to the southern Arabian plate believed to be rotating away from the African plate.

The "star" that had penetrated to the soft interior of the earth had set the interior molten sea to churning. As a result, an earthquake felt along the plate may have cut off the headwaters of the Euphrates and at the same time caused a tenth of the city of Jerusalem to fall. Isaiah mentions another area that was affected. "And the LORD shall utterly destroy the tongue of the Egyptian sea [the Gulf of Suez]; and with his mighty wind, shall he shake his hand over the river, and shall smite it in the seven streams, and make men go over dry shod" (Isa. 12:15). Since all these areas belong to the same fracture system, the drying up of the river and the fall of the city probably had occurred simultaneously. The destruction of the gulf follows shortly after, during the seventh trumpet and vial.

The Clay War

The earthquake marks the end of the 1,260 days of the woman's and the two witnesses' protection. Only thirty days

---

[144] He photographed three hitherto unknown fractures extending from a center in Lebanon, one of which extends into the headwaters of the Euphrates River.

of the beast's 1,290-day rule remain. It is the time of the end spoken of by Daniel. He reports on the political scene:

> And at the time of the end shall the king of the south [Egypt] push at him [the beast]: and the king of the north [Iraq or newly re-formed Assyria] shall come against him [the beast] like a whirlwind, with chariots, and with horsemen, and with many ships; and he [the beast] shall enter into the countries and shall overflow and pass over. He shall enter also into the glorious land, and many countries shall be overthrown: but these shall escape out of his hand, even Edom, and Moab, and the chief of the children of Ammon. He shall stretch forth his hand also upon the countries: and the land of Egypt shall not escape. But he shall have power over the treasures of gold and of silver, and over all the precious things of Egypt: and the Libyans and the Ethiopians shall be at his steps. But tidings out of the east and out of the north shall trouble him: therefore he shall go forth with great fury to destroy, and utterly to make away many. (Dan. 11:40–44)

The three kings (Egypt, Israel, and Iraq/Assyria?), that the beast subdued when he rose to power, rebel. In Daniel's description of the image seen by Nebuchadnezzer, ten toes of iron mixed with clay symbolize the final kingdom that rules the territory. Of these he says, "The kingdom shall be partly strong, and partly broken" (Dan. 2:42). The clay, not the iron, is what breaks. Therefore, the beast will succeed against the governors of the rebellious to the point of taking away their finances. But before he can totally put down the insurrection, he will hear pressing news of another threatening invasion of peoples from the east and north.

Israel's guerrilla army (the woman), now out of hiding since her 1,260 days of protection are up, will escape. She has been active in the rebellion, and the beast will probably be pursuing her when the bad news arrives. The beast will rush home to mobilize his forces against the new invaders. John views the call to action:

> And I saw three unclean spirits like frogs come out of the mouth of the dragon, and out of the mouth of the beast, and out of the mouth of the false prophet. For they are the spirits of devils, working miracles, which go forth unto the kings of the earth and of the whole world, to gather them to the battle of that great day of God Almighty. (16:13–14)

The satanic trinity dispatches its messengers. The beast maintains his spell he over the west and the south by spiritual deception, the working of demonic miracles. The deceived nations will come with their armies as though hypnotized.

Here we pause to fit in Zechariah's tenth vision, the one following the removal of the economic center to Babylon:

> And I turned, and lifted up mine eyes, and looked, and, behold, there came four chariots out from between two mountains; and the mountains were mountains of brass. In the first chariot were red horses; and in the second chariot black horses; and in the third chariot white horses; and in the fourth chariot grisled and bay horses. Then I answered and said unto the angel that talked with me, What are these, my lord? And the angel answered and said unto me, These are the four spirits of the heavens, which go forth from standing before the Lord of all the earth. The black horses which are therein go forth

into the north country; and the white go forth after them; and the grisled [spotted] go forth toward the south country. And the bay [vigorous] went forth, and sought to go that they might walk to and fro through the earth: and he said, Get you hence, walk to and fro through the earth. So they walked to and fro through the earth. Then cried he upon me, and spake unto me, saying, Behold, these that go toward the north country have quieted my spirit in the north country. (Zech. 6:1–8)

Zechariah gives us another view of Armageddon. This prophecy presents a curious picture filled with meaning. The brass mountains are rather obvious in the spiritual language: mountains equal kingdoms and brass stands for judgment. The kingdoms could refer to the beast's kingdom and those of the invaders, but we have no knowledge of an eastern kingdom. Rather what we have is a description of a spiritual war between the forces of evil versus the forces of God that will spell out judgment for *both* armies on the ground. The beast has just sent out a supernatural appeal to the nations of the West (Europe?). Now God calls for His army—the astronomical army from heaven. He has already loosed the angels in the Euphrates, making way for the eastern hoards. However, He is not on their side. His purpose is simply to gather them to the winepress.

In Zechariah's vision, two other features define the circumstances: chariots and horses. The chariots are the four spirits of the heavens standing before the Lord of all the earth. The horses define the direction of the war. East meets west, and the clash affects the north and the south. Black horses spilling to the north tell of hunger, while spotted horses attack the south. The vigorous horses affect the whole earth. Since the victorious white horses also go north, the angel comments that the spirit (of anger) is satisfied in the north country. The vigorous (bay) horses that attack the whole earth are probably those we saw in the sixth trumpet—God's army, the independent comets striking from the sky.

Somehow, the Far East has escaped the beast's authority. The allied kings may represent a regrouping of the political "one worlders" of spiritual Babylon or simply eastern kings who consider the beast's kingdom easy prey because of the devastation it has undergone. On the other hand, perhaps the "clay toes" will call for help for their cause, but whatever the reason for the kings coming, God is over it all, arranging a surprise supper at Armageddon.

Jesus breaks into the scene where John is recording and says:

> Behold, I come as a thief. Blessed is he that watcheth, and keepeth his garments, lest he walk naked, and they see his shame. And he gathered them together into a place called in the Hebrew tongue Armageddon. (16:15–16)

It will become increasingly difficult to walk in righteousness (keeping one's garments). As the beast conscripts troops for his army, the refusal to fight brings more persecution. The importance for knowing the times is clear: "And they that understand among the people shall instruct many," says Daniel 11:33, "yet they shall fall." Just before giving the details of Armageddon in chapter 14, we noted that the Lord gave a similar blessing: "Blessed are the dead which die in the Lord from henceforth: Yea, saith the Spirit, that they may rest from their labours; and their works do follow them" (Rev. 14:13).

It is the same time. Some will die for their faith. The temptation to give in to the beast will be strong. The day of the Lord will come as a thief on the unsuspecting and those weak in the faith. Believers have the Word of God, prewritten history coming to pass in their day. They also have the sure promise of the Lord's return. Those who endure to the end will be saved through the whole outpouring of wrath. Others will be victims of the conflict. Those caught unprepared when Christ comes "as a thief" will lose precious rewards that could have been theirs. Later, at the judgment, there will be no glorious outer garments to cover the undergarments of righteousness, which Christ gives. They will be embarrassed by their lack. They should have kept their garments (remained faithful).

The Seventh Vial

> The seventh angel poured out his vial into the air; and there came a great voice out of the temple of heaven, from the throne, saying, It is done. And there were voices, and thunders, and lightnings; and there was a great earthquake, such as was not since men were upon the earth, so mighty an earthquake, and so great. (16:17–18)

Of this time Isaiah says:

> The earth is utterly broken [at all the plates], the earth is rent asunder, the earth is shaken violently. (Isa. 24:19 AMP)

> The earth shall reel to and fro like a drunkard, and shall be removed like a cottage;[145] and the transgression

---

[145] Cottage = a shed for the watchman looking after the fruit at harvest.

thereof shall be heavy upon it; and it shall fall, and not rise again. (Isa. 24:20)

All this final action of the globe will bring about an entirely new surface to the earth. The plates will move under such stress. John says, "And every island fled away, and the mountains were not found" (Rev. 16:20).

The heavens, too, will be new because the earth "shall fall and not rise again." This means it will roll on its axis and come to rest in its permanent position. (I understand from those who study[146] the motions of the earth that to shift the equator to the position of a pole and vice versa requires a greater force than turning the earth upside down.) We were just told that the earth has never experienced a greater earthquake since people have been on the earth. Not since the ice ages have there been such changes implied as these when heaven and earth are rearranged.

The stars will appear in different places, because of the changed axis. But the most startling change in the heavens will be the descent of the heavenly city that becomes the most brilliant light in the sky. (Rev. 21:24)

Jerusalem receives the final effects of the sixth vial.

And the great city was divided into three parts, and the cities of the nations fell: and great Babylon came in remembrance before God, to give unto her the cup of the wine of the fierceness of his wrath. And every island fled away, and the mountains were not found. And there

---

[146] Immanuel Velikovsky, *Earth in Upheaval* (New York: Doubleday, 1955), p. 129.

fell upon men a great hail out of heaven, every stone about the weight of a talent: and men blasphemed God because of the plague of the hail; for the plague thereof was exceeding great. (16:19–21)

The last great earthquake will divide Jerusalem into three parts, knock down the remaining cities of the world, and separate Babylon for special attention.

I have commanded my sanctified ones, I have also called my mighty ones for mine anger, even them that rejoice in my highness. The noise of a multitude in the mountains, like as of a great people; a tumultuous noise of the kingdoms of nations gathered together: the LORD of hosts mustereth the host of the battle. They come from a far country, from the end of heaven, even the LORD, and the weapons of his indignation, to destroy the whole land . . . Therefore I will shake the heavens, and the earth shall remove out of her place, in the wrath of the LORD of hosts, and in the day of his fierce anger. And it shall be as the chased roe, and as a sheep that no man taketh up: they shall every man turn to his own people, and flee every one into his own land. Every one that is found shall be thrust through; and every one that is joined unto them shall fall by the sword. Their children also shall be dashed to pieces before their eyes; their houses shall be spoiled, and their wives ravished. (Isa. 13:3–5, 13–16)

The "sanctified ones" are the Son's angels. The "mighty ones" are the natural agents under their command. The natural weapons will rain a shower of great hail, weighing a hundred pounds apiece, on people. But before God sends this astronomical army against His enemies, Jerusalem comes under attack, stirring up His anger!

> For I will gather all nations against Jerusalem to battle; and the city shall be taken, and the houses rifled, and the women ravished; and half of the city shall go forth into captivity, and the residue of the people shall not be cut off from the city. Then shall the LORD go forth, and fight against those nations, as when he fought in the day of battle. And his feet shall stand in that day upon the mount of Olives, which is before Jerusalem on the east, and the mount of Olives shall cleave in the midst thereof toward the east and toward the west, and there shall be a very great valley; and half of the mountain shall remove toward the north, and half of it toward the south. And ye shall flee to the valley of the mountains; for the valley of the mountains shall reach unto Azal: yea, ye shall flee, like as ye fled before the earthquake in the days of Uzziah king of Judah: and the LORD my God shall come, and all the saints with thee. And it shall come to pass in that day, that the light shall not be clear, nor dark. (Zech. 14:2–6)

So the weapons of God's indignation, the hailstones (meteorites) will fight against the nations, causing people to flee for home as Isaiah said. Finally, Jesus Himself will appear in the twilight with all the saints. He describes this event in Matthew:

> Immediately after the tribulation of those days shall the sun be darkened, and the moon shall not give her light, and the stars shall fall from heaven, and the powers of the heavens shall be shaken: and there shall appear the sign of the Son of man in heaven: and then shall all the tribes

of the earth mourn, and they shall see the Son of man coming in the clouds of heaven with power and great glory. (Matt. 24:29–30)

In the dimness of the twilight (brought about by all the volcanic ash still in the atmosphere), the glory clouds will stand out as the last rays of the sun after sunset reflecting off a very high cloud. Every eye shall see Him! Jesus will return with His army of saints! We will see more about this in chapter 19.

Haggai speaks of the last shaking, which is also mentioned in Hebrews.

Yet once, it is a little while, and I will shake the heavens, and the earth, and the sea, and the dry land; and I will shake all nations, and the desire of nations shall come. (Hag. 2:6–7)

Joel echos:

The sun and the moon shall be darkened, and the stars shall withdraw their shining. The LORD also shall roar out of Zion, and utter his voice from Jerusalem; and the heavens and the earth shall shake. (Joel 3:15–16)

Peter summarizes:

But the day of the Lord will come as a thief in the night; in which the heavens shall pass away with a great noise, and the elements shall melt with fervent heat, the earth also and the works that are therein shall be burned up. Seeing then that all these things shall be dissolved, what manner of persons ought ye to be in all holy conversation and godliness, looking for and hasting unto the coming of the day of God, wherein the heavens being on fire shall be dissolved, and the elements shall melt with fervent heat? Nevertheless we, according to his promise, look for new heavens and a new earth, wherein dwelleth righteousness. (2 Pet. 3:10–13)

The seventh angel has poured his vial into the air, the space between heaven and earth. Both have been affected. The natural hail sent through the air has added to the volcanic ash already there. Great clouds block the light. Into this darkness "shall the Sun of righteousness arise" (Mal. 4:2).

And so we have come to the end of the scroll again, revealing completely the back side. Truly, it is a full measure of wrath!

Chapter 23

THE GREAT WHORE

(REVELATION 17)

John has seen the decrees from the throne pronounced and prosecuted. Both sides of the document in the Father's hand are completed. Since He has fully executed the edicts against the guilty, it is time for the Lord of glory to return to the earth and receive His kingdom. Yet we see a pause in the sequence once more. John has yet to see some aspects of the doomed. He has seen the Antichrist with his idolatrous religion and its final collapse. He has not seen the unfaithful Church and her cohorts that Jesus left behind at the rapture. Now one of the angels (a saintly messenger who comes out of the temple having the seven last plagues) invites John to see the whore in yet another flashback, revealing one of the main characters under judgment. Perhaps this angel is the one with the plague and vial that eventually destroys her.

> And there came one of the seven angels which had the seven vials, and talked with me, saying unto me, Come hither; I will shew unto thee the judgment [sentence][147] of the great whore that sitteth upon many waters: with whom the kings of the earth have committed fornication, and the inhabitants of the earth have been made drunk with the wine of her fornication. So he carried me away in the spirit into the wilderness: and I saw a woman sit upon a scarlet coloured beast, full of names of blasphemy, having seven heads and ten horns. (17:1–3)

The angel's words and subsequent revelation appear to be a mixed metaphor. He tells John he will show him the great whore that sits on "many waters." Then he transports John to a wilderness—presumably dry—where a woman sits, not on waters at all but on a great beast instead. The angel tells John, en route, that this woman has intercourse with kings, and the people are drunk from the "wine" of this intercourse. Thus, we have symbols of mixed imagery since the woman cannot commit fornication with the beast while riding him in the wilderness and make people drunk!

Sorting out the hodgepodge in these figures of speech, let us deduce the picture intended. The angel tells John later in the passage, "The waters which thou sawest, where the whore sitteth, are peoples, and multitudes, and nations,

---

[147] George Ricker Berry, *The Interlinear Greek–English New Testament* (Grand Rapids: Zondervan, 1973), p. 655. Berry translates the word "judgment" as "sentence."

and tongues" (v. 15). John neglected to tell us that he saw the woman on the waters. Perhaps he thought the angel's reference was sufficient to imply that detail; or maybe he wondered at the woman with such wonder that he simply forgot to mention it. In any case, the sea of people clearly represents the Gentiles, for that is the figure of speech used in spiritual language to denote Gentiles.

John had witnessed this scene before when he saw the beast rise up out of the sea. However, the woman was not present with the beast then. In addition, the horns of the beast already had their crowns in that scene. The angel tells John later in this chapter that the horns have not received their kingdoms as yet (v. 12). Therefore, the present scene appears to have taken place earlier, since the horns are crownless here. Evidently, the earlier scene began at the time of the beast's rule after disposing of the woman.

The present scene may have happened like this. The angel deposits John in a wilderness, perhaps similar to the Sinai that lies between Israel and Egypt along the coast. He sees a woman who appears to be sitting on the waters of the Mediterranean. Suddenly, a several-headed beast rears its heads from beneath the waters. Then it rises out of the waters and parades onto the beach, carrying the woman on its back. Evidently, the cavorting of the woman with the beast under the waters has been going on for some time. Finally, she brazenly rides him out into the open. She expects to continue her ride on the beast indefinitely, but of course, we know the beast has other plans. He will emerge a second time from the "sea" of Gentiles with the authority in his hands.

Royal Robes?

Returning to the rest of the scene, John describes the whore:

And the woman was arrayed in purple and scarlet colour, and decked with gold and precious stones and pearls, having a golden cup in her hand full of the abominations and filthiness of her fornication. And upon her forehead, was a name written, MYSTERY, BABYLON THE GREAT, THE MOTHER OF HARLOTS AND ABOMINATIONS OF THE EARTH. And I saw the woman drunken with the blood of the saints, and with the blood of the martyrs of Jesus: and when I saw her, I wondered with great admiration [wonder]. (17:4–6)

There she sat, regally arrayed in purple and scarlet. Her colors and the encrustation of jewels on her vestments indicate royalty dressed for a coronation. Her attire is similar, except for the color of gown, to that of Queen Elizabeth II when she was crowned queen of England. Queen Elizabeth II wore a purple velvet cape trimmed with ermine, the imperial robe of state[148] (see color plate) over her dress of white satin entirely encrusted with precious and semiprecious stones. Surely, nothing short of a coronation requires such splendor!

Although the British sovereign wears the crimson robe of a peer of Parliament at the beginning of the coronation ceremony, she divests herself of it when she sits in the coronation chair. Therefore, she never wears the red with the purple. Since the woman seen by John wore the purple over the red, the red of the whore's gown suggests the coronation gown itself rather than another vestment. Actually, a pure white gown is out of character for her. Her coronation gown matches her steed, the scarlet beast, and blends with his nature and body. Red usually signifies blood in Scripture. In

[148] *The Crown Jewels and Coronation Ritual* (London: Pitkin Pictorals London Ltd. 1953) p. 21

this case, the color may signify a bloodthirsty nature, since verse 6 shows her drunk with the blood of the saints.

Expositors of Revelation tend to identify the woman as the false church. Post-Reformation Christians identified her as the Roman Catholic Church, probably because of her blood purges. The color of the hierarchy of the church, the cardinals, who dress in red vestments, must have seemed to them like a positive identification. Later expositors saw her as the super church, Rome reunited with the professing Protestants left behind at the rapture. The church's preoccupation with power and desire to rule over people and nations certainly matches the picture of one dressed in anticipation of a coronation. Although all the above is true, is this enough for positive identification?

Coronation Regalia

Coronations have much regalia connected with the ritual. Queen Elizabeth II wore the imperial state crown on her head and carried in her right hand the scepter of the cross (see color plate). In her left hand, she held the sovereign's orb, a golden ball encrusted with jewels and pearls and topped with a cross. The orb supposedly symbolizes the dominion of the Christian religion over the world. *The Crown Jewels and Coronation Ritual* lists the orb as the most sacred of the coronation regalia. The Queen handled various other pieces before the ceremony was complete.

The woman before John also possesses coronation regalia. However, she has not yet received her sovereign's crown. Nevertheless, we know from the purple robe that she expects to receive it. Instead of a crown, she wears the stamp of ownership on her forehead, which says: MYSTERY, BABYLON THE GREAT, THE MOTHER OF HARLOTS AND ABOMINATIONS OF THE EARTH.

Her Majesty Queen Elizabeth II, photographed by Cecil Beaton on Coronation Day, 2nd June 1953. She wears the Imperial Crown of State. In her right hand she holds the Sceptre with the Cross; in her left hand the Sovereign's Orb. On her wrists are the gold 'Bracelets of sincerity and wisdom,' and on her right hand the Coronation Ring is seen. Her Majesty is arrayed in the purple velvet Imperial Robe of State. Her coronation gown of white satin is **entirely encrusted with stones, both precious and semiprecious.**

The woman does, however, have a golden cup, the symbol of her religious leanings. Even older than the orb as part of the coronation regalia, the cup dates back to the original Babylon. Jeremiah speaks of Babylon herself as being a "golden cup," making the whole world drunk.[149] Thus, he refers to the religion that originated in her. The cup appears to have been part of the ritual in crowning kings in primitive Babylon and later in Assyria.[150]

Like her mother, the original Babylon, this aspiring queen will serve her initiates an intoxicating brew from her cup. With abominable doctrines, made more palatable by the wine, she induces a drunken state in her would-be subjects by political intercourse—mixing religion with politics. The outcome of this mixture promises peace to the world.

The "wine" of peace will dull people's minds, hypnotizing them to accept the abominations necessary to achieve peace. Paul says: "For when they shall say, Peace and safety; then sudden destruction cometh upon them" (1 Thess. 5:3). Crimes committed to achieve this peace will bring down the judgments of God.

The Woman's Character

The "great whore" speaks of the woman's character, not her name. Like the "Jezebel" of the church of Thyatira, she will call herself a Christian, even though her doctrines are of the world. She also will mix in sorceries from the occult (Rev. 18:23). Like Jezebel, she will lust for power over the population. She expects to rule over the heads of the political beast after riding him to power.

---

[149] Jer. 51:7.

[150] Alexander Hislop, The Two Babylons, (Neptune, NJ: Loizeau Brothers, 1916, 1943, 1959) see illustration p. 5.

Actually, the historical Jezebel was herself a product of Babylon, the ancient system of religio-political authority. Drawing from her religious inclinations, she ruled the land through her weak husband Ahab. The woman John sees intends to do the same, prompted by the same system. Therefore, before we assign an identity to this present-day whore, we would do well to investigate the system that has stamped its character upon her and after whom she is named.

Babylon, a city built on the plains of Shinar several years after the flood, established itself on the foundations of rebellion. Genesis 11 says:

> And it came to pass, as they journeyed from the east, that they found a plain in the land of Shinar; and they dwelt there . . . And they said, Go to, let us build us a city and a tower, whose top may reach unto heaven; and let us make us a name, lest we be scattered abroad upon the face of the whole earth. (Gen. 11:2, 4)

God had told Noah to be fruitful, multiply, and replenish the earth—implying the whole earth. Instead, these people said, "Let us build us a city and a tower, whose top may reach unto heaven; and let us make us a name, lest we be scattered." The word city used here carries the idea of "fortification" in the Hebrew. The tower also carries the same idea. A tower was for overlooking the surrounding territory so no enemy, man or beast, could slip up and take them by surprise.

They had a problem with wild beasts in those days. We know this because Nimrod, "the mighty hunter," was famous for his protection against wild beasts, especially leopards. So building a city and a tower for their own name and protection, though a natural response, shows rebellion and independence from God. They no longer had to trust Him; they could do it themselves. This was probably the first organized attempt at humanism, a banding together for mutual protection. The coming together included the whole earth. God said of their plans:

> Behold, the people is one, and they have all one language; and this they begin to do: and now nothing will be restrained from them, which they have imagine to do. (Gen. 11:6)

"Let us make us a name, lest we be scattered," they said. But cooperation was not the end of their coming together. In making a name, some began to rule over others—lifting up a human ruler instead of God.

> And Cush begat Nimrod:[151] he began to be a mighty one in the earth. He was a mighty hunter before the LORD: wherefore it is said, Even as Nimrod the mighty hunter before the LORD. And the *beginning of his kingdom* was Babel. (Gen. 10:8–10, emphasis added)

Nimrod perverted the intentions of God by gathering the whole population to himself. He introduced the lust for power on earth. God had given men the right to govern through allowing capitol punishment for the sake of justice (Gen. 9:5–6). Nevertheless, the king of Babel went

---

[151] Nimrod was known in history by the name of Ninus. *Nineveh* means "habitation of Ninus." Nimrod is the name given for his hunting prowess, Nimrod from *Nimr*, a "leopard," and *rada* or *rad*, "to subdue." Hislop, *Two Babylons*, p. 44.

beyond punishment for murder. He lusted after power to rule over people.

Babel or Babylon, as the city was later called, was also the beginning of pagan idolatry. God as Lord was replaced by many gods and served by priests and priestesses who were no more than ceremonial prostitutes: hence, the name "mother of harlots." Alexander Hislop, in his book *The Two Babylons*, traces this pagan politico-religious system through all the nations of the ancient world, proving beyond all doubt that Babylon was their mother.

Hislop shows that the woman John sees, along with the title on her forehead, fits exactly with the character of the ancient city. He brings to light that this system began as secret societies called "mysteries" in which only the initiates were taught the deep doctrines. Discussing the importance of the golden cup in the woman's hand, he says:

> To drink of "mysterious beverages," says Salvarte was indispensable on the part of all who sought initiation in these Mysteries. These "mysterious beverages" were composed of wine, honey, water, and flour. From the Ingredients avowedly used, and from the nature of others not avowed, but certainly used, there can be no doubt that they were of an intoxicating nature; and till the aspirants had come under their power, till their understandings had been dimmed, and their passions excited by the medicated draught, they were not duly prepared for what they were either to hear or to see.[152]

---

[152] Hislop, *Two Babylons*, p. 4.

The cup introduced the secret knowledge of the mysteries and bound them not to divulge such things on pain of death.[153] The mysteries appealed to the bodies, souls, and spirits of flesh-oriented people. Concerning the appeal to the lust of the body, Hislop says:

> The Chaldean Mysteries can be traced up to the days of Semiramis, who lived only a few centuries after the flood, and who is known to have impressed upon them the image of her own depraved and polluted mind. That beautiful but abandoned queen of Babylon was not only herself a paragon of unbridaled lust and licentiousness, but in the mysteries, which she had a chief hand in forming, she was worshiped as Rhea, the great "Mother" of the gods, with such atrocious rites as identified her with Venus,[154] the mother of all impurity, and raised the city where she had reigned to bad eminence among the nations, as the grand seat at once of idolatry and consecrated prostitution.[155]

They excited the human spirit by the exclusiveness of the order—the elevation they experienced in power over those of lesser knowledge, not to mention the spiritual contact with the demonic spirit world in their secret goings on. Occult power is bound to have been at work then as it is now in idolatrous systems. Summed up, the Babylonian mysteries were the embodiment of everything that belongs to the world—the lust

---

[153] Free Masonry and Mormanism also bind their initiates of the higher, most secret knowledge by the same oath. Both are children of Babylon.

[154] Since the planet Venus is of much later appearance (the time of the exodus), it would be an addition to earlier teachings.

[155] Hislop, *Two Babylons*, p. 5.

of the flesh, the lust of the eyes, and the pride of life (which is really a lust for power over others).

Babylon, then, is a title of a system that began after the flood and continues with us today. It began as a city and spread to the entire world, but its seat finally settled in Rome, along with the empire.

In discussing the various religions that developed through the history of the Roman Empire, the *Encyclopedia Britannica* states that the worship of the great mother of the gods, Cybele, along with the mystery religions, was imported from Hellenism into Roman society in 199 B.C. Hislop identifies Cybele as the mother of the Babylonian messiah. He wrote:

> Before our Lord was either conceived or born, that very day now set down in the Popish calendar for the "Annunciation of the Virgin" was observed in pagan Rome in honor of Cybele, the Mother of the Babylonian Messiah.[156]

So we see yet another reason to call Babylon "mother." The whole religious system embodied in the Eluesinian mysteries has been in the world since the fifteenth century B.C., but it ended in the fourth century A.D. when it was absorbed into the church. It is Satan's alternative to God's way. It has been present all along, but it comes forth in the last days in its modern dress with the emphasis on power.

The Mystery of the Woman and the Beast

After viewing the present-day woman in her splendor, John sees her drunk with power. Her intoxicated state comes from the satisfaction of disposing of the saints. Martyrs'

---

[156] Hislop, *Two Babylons*, p. 102.

blood poured out on her altars in the name of peace and unity will satiate her bloodthirsty nature.

From the beginning, unity provided the excuse to persecute dissidents. The Roman ruler Constantine had conquered in the name of Christianity and used the church as a means to establish and preserve his power in the empire. At about the same time and resorting to allegorical interpretation, Augustine discarded the teaching that Christ would return to set up his kingdom on earth. Instead, he believed that Christ would return *after* the church established the kingdom on earth. For this, the church needed to have political power; therefore, he welcomed the joining of church and state. This inexorably led to the idea of one unified church to which all had to conform. Thus, the establishment of the state church confirmed the "fornication" of the "kings of the earth" with the church, whose flirtation with the world had begun nearly a hundred years before.

This future revival also will seek complete control over the population. As we shall see in the next chapter, other idealists will join the church in an attempt to bring in a Utopia on earth. Now that most of the world's societies will lie in ruins, little needs to be torn down to make way for the new society. It will be the perfect opportunity to start afresh with the right government. Since the universal church can reach all the way to the grass roots of the nations, she will be the logical partner to recycle Plato's *Republic* and Augustine's *City of God* into a new society.

The new state church will not tolerate competition from religious deviates, such as Jews preaching about some Lamb of God and His coming kingdom. Since they refuse to join the unified religion, Babylon/Rome will viciously attack the 144,000 Jewish witnesses and their converts worldwide. The martyrs' blood of true believers will cry out from under the altar, pleading for justice. But they will have to wait. It is her hour for the moment. The government, the head which she drives, will go along with her blood lust (his body is also a bloodthirsty red). The Islamic kings, who rule over the leopard-like beast, hate the true believers as well. She rides confidently over the beast's heads, not realizing her inebriated state clouds her judgment.

John marvels with great perplexity.

> And the angel said unto me, Wherefore didst thou marvel? I will tell thee the mystery of the woman and of the beast that carrieth her, which hath the seven heads and ten horns. The beast that thou sawest was, and is not; and shall ascend out of the bottomless pit, and shall go into perdition: and they that dwell on the earth shall wonder, whose names were not written in the book of life from the foundation of the world, when they behold the beast that was, and is not, and yet is. And here is the mind which hath wisdom. The seven heads are seven mountains, on which the woman sitteth. And there are seven kings: five are fallen, and one is, and the other is not yet come; and when he cometh, he must continue a short space. And the beast that was, and is not, even he is the eighth, and is of the seven, and goeth into perdition. (17:7–11)

John has no trouble identifying the city of which the angel speaks. It is Rome, without a doubt—the city famous for sitting on seven mountains. The glorious city from which Roman law emanated, where all power at that time was invested in the Caesars, the very same power that had exiled John to Patmos. Yes, he knew exactly who the woman/city was.

The angel explains that the seven mountains are not just literal mountains but also figures of speech denoting kingdom power. In other words, there are seven heads of government. (Remember, the Lord used a mountain as a symbol of His future rule in the Book of Daniel. In Nebuchadnezzar's dream, the stone that broke the image became a great mountain [Dan. 2:35]). So the interpretation of the seven mountains is double—literal and a figure of speech.

Looking at the seven mountains as seven different forms of kingdom rule, let us test the interpretation against history. Did Rome, the city that sits on seven literal hills, pass through seven changes of government rule? To this, history answers a decided yes. With brief periods of transition from one form to another, they were: 1) the Etruscan kings; 2) the republic (senate of the upper class); 3) the democracy (senate joined by lower-class representation of ten tribunes); 4) two military dictatorships; 5) two military triumvirates; 6) the empire (Caesars 31); 7) the bureaucracy (coemperors of the east and the west divisions with extensive organization). History also testifies that the rule of the city over the kingdom ceased when the barbarians conquered Rome. Therefore, history confirms that the last head of the beast died.

The angel told John that of these seven forms of government, "Five are past, one is in power [in John's day], and one more will develop and rule for a while. Then it will die only to be revived again at a later time." John lived under the sixth form, the empire. The bureaucracy was yet to come. The eighth form, as the angel said, was of the seven. The only form that died was the last. Therefore, the beast will revive the bureaucracy, as we have already seen in an earlier chapter. Nevertheless, for a time the woman called Babylon holdwill the reins of the kingdom.

The angel told John, "I tell you the mystery of the woman and the beast that carries her." At the end of the chapter, the angel reveals that the woman *is* that city that rules over the kings of the earth (Rev. 17:18). She is also the city that sits on seven hills. (King James says mountains but the word means "a rise—mountain, hill, etc. vs. 9.) Rome is known throughout history as the city that sits on seven hills. Therefore, the mystery of the woman seems to be wholly with the heads of the beast. She also sat on many waters—peoples, multitudes, nations and tongues (Rev. 17:15). That makes her a universal influence.

But the mystery of the beast is different. Yes, his heads are "under" the woman and connected to Rome (the city not the empire) but his horns and his body come from a different source.

> The beast that thou sawest was, and is not: and shall ascend out of the bottomless pit, and go into perdition: and they that dwell on the earth shall wonder, whose names were not written in the book of life from the foundation of the world, when they behold the beast that was, and is not, and yet is. (17:8)

This empire comes straight from the pit, that is its founding comes from the enemy. It existed before but now it has come back. The Roman empire is not the only one to last for hundreds of years. While the woman was gaining power over the people and kings through the Papacy, Satan initiated his counterfeit kingdom of God in a militant religion that was to conquer as much or more territory than the Romans did. He picked an Arab named Muhammad and showed him the vision of an angel. He told him he was to become the prophet of God (Allah). As he wrote the words that he received, he began also to preach to the people. He preached a doctrine of good works. Islam has five pillars of the faith: 1) There is no God but God; Muhammad is the prophet of God, 2) Five daily congregational prayers, 3) The zakāt, an oblicatory tax paid once a year. (The payment that makes the rest of one's wealth religiously and legally pure.) 4) Fasting during the month of Ramadān. 5) The hajj, a trip to Mecca at least once in their lifetime. Each of these is defined with laws governing them. They deny the trinity believed by Christians and denigrate Jesus to a mere prophet. One's entrance into paradise is determined by his works. It is a religion straight up from the pit. Consequently, any empire built upon it comes from the same source.

A great empire did come from it. By Muhammad's death the new religion was firmly established among the Arabs. The most prominent ruler to succeed Muhammad was his father-in-law who founded the Umayyad dynasty. He began to expand the empire and conquered most of the nations surrounding Arabia. Through the centuries that followed their conquest included all of the Persian Empire, the northern rim of Africa, half of Spain, Turkey and across the Bosporous into lower Eastern Europe. This empire began to decline when the Mongols invaded from the east. But even then the conquerors of the Persian borders succumbed to their religion. Passing through many changes in leadership and various amounts of territories this empire lasted until the Ottomans were defeated by the Allied armies of World War I and the land split up by the League of Nations in 1920. The empire having begun in A.D. 634 with the first Umayyad ruler, basically lasted 1286 years, 57 years longer than the Roman Empire. (753 B.C.-A.D. 476).

Thus the Woman and the Beast both began to rise in power about the same time. Both have declined. Both will be revived. The leader of this revived empire, a horn on one of the heads, is of Greek descent (Dan. 8:23). He evidently comes to power through the heads. However, he defers to the other horns to consolidate his power. The powerful body behind him (the leopard's body—the territory), follow the horns who are their kings. With the rise of Muslim fundamentalism and the renewed use of Jihad, we may be seeing the revival of this empire.

> And the ten horns which thou sawest are ten kings, which have received no kingdom as yet; but receive power as kings one hour with the beast. (17:12)

> And the ten horns which thou sawest upon the beast, these shall hate the whore, and shall make her desolate and naked, and shall eat her flesh, and burn her with fire. For God hath put it in their hearts to fulfill his will, and to agree, and give their kingdom unto the beast, until the words of God shall be fulfilled. And the woman which thou sawest is that great city, which reigneth over the kings of the earth. (17:16–18)

The ten kings will not be compatible with the city and its ambitions. In an earlier chapter, we suggested that these kings will come from the Moslem world in the Middle East. These will believe the beast is their great Mahdi.

The woman, in her drunken state, will fail to assess the true nature of the beast she rides. Being intent on the destruction of saints and having the cooperation of the kings in this endeavor, she will fail to notice that their goal is not the same as hers.

We set the destruction of the city of Rome at the second trumpet judgment. If we are right, that will give the beast dominant power through the remaining five judgments. The Moslem monarchs will unseat the city, destroy her, and raise the beast to his full power.

Looking at our contemporary world and the modern city of Rome, does this mysterious woman still exist? Will she be only the reunited worldwide super church under the direction of the Pope, as many expositors suppose? Or will she extend influence far beyond the religious aspect with a view toward total world domination? In the next chapter, we will seek to answer these questions.

Chapter 24

THE GREAT CONSPIRACY

(REVELATION 18)

As John ponders the mysteries of the whore and the beast, a great and glorious angel descends, illuminating the earth beneath with his splendor.

And he cried mightily with a strong voice, saying, Babylon the great is fallen, is fallen, and is become the habitation of devils, and the hold of every foul spirit, and a cage of every unclean and hateful bird. (18:2)

Babylon arose from a primitive local politico-religious system on the plains of Shinar to a vast politico-religious system ruling over the world. Her center of political power moved with each conquering empire, ending finally in Rome. The intoxication of her idolatrous religion poured out of her cup to all peoples. Hence the words: "The inhabitants of the earth have been made drunk with the wine of her fornication" (Rev. 17:2). Consequently, though her beginning was small, in the end she will influence the whole world politically and religiously.

Babylon Enters the Church

The original "doctrines of demons" taught to the religious initiates of the mysteries in Shinar counterfeited God's salvation. The teachings included a counterfeit redemption through the woman's seed[157] conceived miraculously. They also had a trinitarian godhead that elevated the mother of god as an equal to the father and son. Under them were many lesser gods. The character of the gods, and indeed the whole system, was licentious and immoral, but it masqueraded as God's plan.

When the empire was established in Rome, they made Babylon's doctrines the valid religion of the state and later added emperor worship. However, its official status changed when Constantine became emperor of Rome. He adopted Christianity as his personal religion and ended the domination of idolatry. He liberated the people to freedom of religion in A.D. 313 with the Edict of Toleration. Then Christianity took an upswing. Churches rejoiced in their new freedom, and the two religions coexisted in the empire. Things changed, however, when Theodosius came to power in A.D. 323, because he abolished idolatry altogether, making Christianity the state religion.

---

[157] Satan knew God would send His Savior through the "woman's seed" because of the prediction given in Genesis 3. So he counterfeited it from the beginning.

Church membership became compulsory, and the church lost its purity. A conglomeration of believers and unbelievers resulted when thousands of heathen were forced into the Church. Heathen doctrines and practices entered along with them. The immoral aspect of the pagan religion fell out of favor, but because the teachings and symbols were similar, they gradually mixed. Few protested. After all, it had been years since the state persecuted the Church. Her zeal for the truth had dulled when she let down her guard. Augustine's teaching that the Church, not Christ, should establish righteous rule in the world took root. To gain the power she needed, the Church went to bed with the world.

Corrupted Christianity plunged the world into the Dark Ages as she let religious ceremonies and sacramentalism[158] replace the Word of God to obscure the light of the pure gospel as preached by the apostles. The amalgamated doctrines gradually became Roman Catholic dogma. Nevertheless, it did lift up Babylon, this world's system, to a higher and broader influence in the name of righteousness. It did serve to mold all life under a unified Church, even though the Church mixed truth with Babylonian doctrines. Her goal changed from converting the world to ruling over it.

To say that Babylon has fallen and become the habitation of demons and every foul spirit is to say she will return to her original spiritual state. We have already seen that the commercial side of Babylon will be taken out of Rome and put back in Shinar. Now we see that the Christianity that is

---

[158] Sacramentalism substitutes ritual for faith in salvation. For instance, infant baptism replaced believer's baptism (which identified the believer with Christ's death and resurrection), in effect birthing the child into the kingdom of God without faith. The Lord's Supper became a literal sacrifice of Christ's body, etc. A recognized priest had to administer all of these.

in her will be stripped out as well. She will return to the idolatrous worship of demons, in fact, to the worship of Satan himself under the rule of the beast.

The city of Rome, the woman of Revelation 17, will wear the title of Babylon. She will be the harlot who pretends to the world's throne. However, the Babylon spoken of here is the system itself. The woman will be destroyed, not Babylon. "Babylon is fallen, is fallen and become . . ." Babylon will return to her original base, to her demonic extravaganza, full of occult phenomenon; while Babylonic Rome, the city, will face judgment.

How will this future Rome gain power to grasp at world rule in the first place? In the last chapter, we raised the question: Is there a system in the world today that could invest such power in this city? This next verse in chapter eighteen gives us a clue:

> For all nations have drunk of the wine of the wrath of her fornication, and the kings of the earth have committed fornication with her, and *the merchants of the earth* are waxed rich through the abundance of her delicacies. (18:3, emphasis added)

The clue: kings and merchants collaborating with religion have more power in their hands than armies. All attempts to reunite the Roman Empire and rule the world by military force have failed. Charlemagne managed to capture only part of the western branch. The Holy Roman Empire of Otto I ruled over even less. Napoleon captured but a portion. Hitler and Mussolini also tried, but it was not to be restored by military power.

Merchant power will put the empire back together. Later on in chapter 18, we are told that Babylon's "merchants were the great men of the earth" (18:23), that is, the richest and most powerful, the ones behind the scenes that rule governments with their control over finances. Therefore, great merchant power will restore the empire to Rome.

Our modern world saw this power begin to form with the dream of one man, John Ruskin. Ruskin (1819–1900) was born in London, England, the son of a wealthy wine merchant. He was educated in art, literature, architecture, mathematics, Latin, and Greek. He traveled widely after his graduation from Oxford but returned in 1870 to become the Slade Professor of Art. In this position, he began to have a profound influence over his students.

Art, however, was not his primary interest; it simply served as a platform for his preaching. His dream of using socialism as a tool to subject the world to responsible leadership electrified his students. "He was obsessed with the ideas and inspirations derived from Plato's *Republic*, which he read almost every day."[159] Engaging his students in community experiments—building roads, designing socialistic projects of various kinds—he planted his ideas and dreams of a new world firmly in their aristocratic minds. He proclaimed "they were possessors of a magnificent tradition of education, beauty, rule of law, freedom, decency, and self-discipline, but that this tradition could not be saved, and did not deserve to be saved, unless it could be extended to the lower classes in England itself and to the non-English masses throughout the world."[160]

Cecil Rhodes, one of Ruskin's students, picked up the challenge and made it his life's goal. He copied Ruskin's

---

[159] Kenneth Clark, *Ruskin Today* (New York: Holt, Rinehart and Winston, 1965, c1964) p. 269.

[160] Carroll Quigley, *Tragedy and Hope*, (New York: Macmillan and Company, 1966, 1974) p. 130.

inaugural lecture in longhand and kept it with him for thirty years. Becoming highly successful in business, he used his vast fortune to further his goal. With financial help from Lord Rothchild and Alford Beit, Rhodes exploited the gold fields and diamond mines of South Africa. After monopolizing both industries, he set out to claim a strip of Africa from the Cape to Egypt so he could build a railway for the empire. And he almost did it. His income rose to about five million pounds sterling a year, but due to his earnest desire to federate the English-speaking peoples and bring all the inhabitable world under their control, his accounts were usually overdrawn.

Nevertheless, the tremendous power of the merchants really began in 1891 when Rhodes met with several other former students and associates of Ruskin to form a secret society. At that time, they dedicated themselves to Ruskin's goal of socialistic rule. The society consisted of wealthy and influential aristocrats of Europe. Rhodes himself led the meeting. William T. Snead, Lord Alford Milner, and Lord Esher became an executive committee, while Lord Balfour, Sir Henry Johnston, Lord Rothchild, Lord Alfred Grey, and others formed the "circle of initiates."[161] Still others put together an outer circle known as an "association of helpers." The outer circle, however, was not formed until the period of 1909–1913.

If organizing was a big step in developing their power, combining their money boosted it even more. Rhodes donated his vast fortune to finance their activities. He set up a

---

[161] Forming a secret society protected their alms and paved the way for the combining of philosophic and humanistic religious leanings. Plato drew much meaning from the "circles" of nature and formed much of his idealistic theory of an ideal state from the mathematical circle.

trust, partly to be used as Rhodes scholarships to spread his ideas and the rest to be at the disposal of the organization after his death. Others followed his example, putting their monies into protected tax-exempt foundations set apart for their special causes. With their monies secure, they moved on to gain the power to control governments. Country boundaries offered no barriers. They installed their secret "roundtable" initiates from the super rich of the whole world but particularly the banking enterprises. Today they collectively control trade, set interest rates, and make or break economies through centralized banking, having first obtained the legislation to control banking to their advantage.

The "establishment," a name they call themselves, has been working behind the scenes in political affairs until this present day, gaining more and more power. Having abandoned the idea of confederating the world under the British Empire, they are currently working to bring the world together under one-world government—*their government*. They instigated both the League of Nations and the United Nations. They financed the Bolshevik revolution and the Communist government from its inception. The outcome of the summit meetings with Russia—Yalta, Potsdam, and other negotiations following World War II—show the effects of the establishment's manipulation of governments. After the war, they allowed Russia to absorb most of Eastern Europe. Their purpose: Consolidate as much of the world under one large block of socialism so it may be combined with other large blocks under a central world government.

Later, the establishment made efforts to consolidate Europe into a block. In 1948, they signed the Treaty of Rome,[162] combining six nations in the Common Market, at that time a purely commercial endeavor. On January 1, 1973, it was expanded to nine countries. Greece was added in 1980, bringing the number to ten. When the commercial cooperation among them became a success, they moved on toward a politically united Europe. It is still developing today with a central government and their own currency.

Nor has the elite crowd overlooked the United States government. Rather, they gradually steal freedoms with each new administration. The Council of Foreign Relations, a kind of political club run by the establishment, controls many of the international moves of the United States. Their work, as the name indicates, focuses on foreign policy. It has almost become a prerequisite for State Department officials to be appointed from the CFR. Nor does it matter which party is in power, since the council dominates them both. Between their appointees and the Rhodes scholars, the public officials elected by the people have little opportunity to direct America's foreign affairs to her own advantage. The CFR has been behind the scenes maneuvering our government toward surrendering to a world community for the past several decades. It seems obvious when we look at the events of the vision that the power and influence of the United States are missing. This is another reason to believe that America's political power will disappear sometime during the future world war.

Only two remaining power bases will struggle to control what is left of civilization—the kings of the earth allied with

---

[162] Thus, we have the first mention of the city of Rome in the modern establishment of Babylon.

the woman and the ten kings allied with the beast. Expositors have sometimes obscured this passage by making the beast a leader of Europe and combining the "ten kings" with "the kings of the earth." The passage, however, distinguishes between the two, showing them in conflict. The ten kings hate the whore (Rev. 17:16), but the kings of the earth are her lovers. This is but another of Revelation's divisions.

After the war described in the four horsemen of the seals, with the strength of the superpowers broken, Europe will be free to unite with the socialistic nations that remain, with the establishment ruling at the top. Ostensibly, the consolidation will be for peace, to put an end to all war. Actually, the goal of the elite is power to rule over a perfect society.

One block of humanity, however, stands relatively aloof to its socialistic doctrines. Islamic people do not lend themselves toward socialistic thinking, being fanatical, independent, and fiercely religious. Consequently, the politico-religious whore will never totally convince them to be part of *her* one world.

Even though the ideology of socialism has not affected the Arab world, they will, however, make a covenant with the woman, as we have said. The Arab community of the Middle East is important to Europe because of its oil supply. Europe is important to the Middle East for trade and security.

Looking back at the vision and the known outcome of all this, we can see that the establishment's efforts will be frustrated when the starving Russian hoards take matters into their own hands and invade the flourishing Middle East. Then the establishment's negotiations with the Arabs will be jeopardized. Europe will be forced to say in Ezekiel's words: "Art thou come to take a spoil?"

Sheba, and Dedan [the Arabs], and the *merchants* of Tarshish, with *all the young lions* thereof [the establishment], shall say unto thee [Russia], Art thou come to take a spoil? hast thou gathered thy company to take a prey? to carry away silver and gold, to take away cattle and goods, to take a great spoil? (Ezek. 38:13, emphasis added)

Meanwhile, the beast will have his own ideas as to how to handle the situation and soon will find himself in conflict with Rome.

The Powerful Horns

For the ships of Chittim [Cyprus—Greek shipping empires?] shall come against him: therefore he shall be grieved, and return, and have indignation against the holy covenant: so shall he do; he shall even return, and have intelligence with them [the ten kings?] that forsake the holy covenant. And arms shall stand on his part, and they shall pollute the sanctuary of strength, and shall take away the daily sacrifice, and they [the beast and his followers] shall place the abomination that maketh desolate. (Dan. 11:30–31)

This scripture belongs in Daniel's passage listing those Gentile powers that will rule over Israel until the "end." It begins with the end of the Persian kings and the rise of Alexander the Great. It continues through the struggles of Alexander's successors, the prominent ones being the Ptolmaic Dynasty in Egypt (the king of the south) and the Seluecid Dynasty in Syria (the king of the north). Tracing the kings of Daniel 11 through history, we find that verse

20 refers to Julius Caesar. "Then shall stand up in his estate a raiser of taxes in the glory of the kingdom: but within few days he shall be destroyed, neither in anger, nor in battle."

Roman interference in Asia Minor had already been evident during the latter rule of the Seluecids. Julius Caesar stood up in the "estate" of the former ruler when he made himself undisputed master of Greece, Asia Minor, and Egypt. While emperor, he changed "the vicious system of taxing the provinces. He did this by permitting each town to collect its own share of taxes in its own way,"[163] a significant reform in favor of the poor people. He brought much glory to Rome and made great plans for building and reform. But his days were few—48–44 B.C.—only four years. He was put to death "neither in anger, nor in battle" by a jealous senate who feared his power.

This brings Daniel's list of Gentile rulers to within forty-four years of the birth of Christ. Passing over the age of grace, just as we did with Daniel's seventy weeks prophecy, verse 21 shows us the rising of the "little horn," the one predicted to take away the daily sacrifice.[164] He will rise up in the estate of Roman power, but the rest of the passage makes it clear that he must establish himself among Middle Eastern powers, not European. That is why we assign the horns to Arab rulers rather than any ten nations of the European union.

The territory of the beast's kingdom will be more like Alexander's. The mouth of the kingdom will be Babylon,

---

[163] Henry W. Elson, *Modern Times and the Living Past*, (New York, Boston, Chicago, Cincinnati, Atlanta: American Book Company, 1933) p. 179.

[164] Many assign this portion to Antiochus IV, however verse 20 separates the rulers. Verse 19 refers to Antiochus III, the Great.

the same as intended by Alexander to rule his empire. All the activity of Daniel's chapter pertaining to the kingdom's future ruler deals with the kings and armies of this territory. The king of the north (Syria, Assyria/Babylon), the king of the south (Egypt), and Israel will be the clay toes of the kingdom, not mixing well with the rest. These will reluctantly agree to give the beast the kingdom. They eventually will rise in rebellion at the beginning of the last thirty days before Christ returns. We mentioned this in the chapter 16, naming the rebellion the "clay war." Therefore, the beast will be in a continuous struggle to maintain his power and authority to the end. Perhaps this is why the kings, the horns, will only have power with the beast for one hour—the hour it takes to destroy the whore.

Looking back to the conflict with Rome, we see that the covenant the beast will have "indignation against" is called "holy." This makes us suspect that the religious forces in Rome will have brought it about. Ecumenical Protestantism, united with Roman Catholicism and cemented together with humanism, will bring about an agreement with Islamic Arabs and Judaism. The beast will break this covenant, at least the part that has to do with Judaism, in the middle of the week. Then he will begin his bid for absolute power. The horns, powerful Middle-Eastern kings on the revived head of the empire, will yield to religious fanaticism under a strong delusion,[165] supported by their subjects. They will collaborate with the beast in his rebellion against the harlot. Thus, Babylon, the whore of Rome, will ride the empire during the first half of the week but will be unseated and destroyed early in the second half of the week,

---

[165] 2 Thess. 2:11–12.

leaving the beast struggling to maintain his grip over the remaining territory. Thus, the beast will rise to power under the direction of Rome. Hence, it can be said that he will stand up in his estate.[166]

The Religious Aspect of Babylon

This chapter presents a sketchy description of the establishment that we believe will finally consolidate its power in the city of Rome. Professor Carroll Quigley, a sympathizer and companion to the establishment, has written a history of its development in his book *Tragedy and Hope*. In the book, he clearly holds up the establishment's philosophy as the hope of the world. He says:

> I know of the operations of this network because I have studied it for twenty years and was permitted for two years, in the early 1960s, to examine its papers and secret records. I have no aversion to it or to most of its aims and have, for much of my life, been close to it and to many of its instruments. I have objected, both in the past and recently, to a few of its policies . . . but in general my chief difference of opinion is that it wishes to remain unknown, and I believe its role in history is significant enough to be known.[167]

The professor's religious views are especially interesting. He calls for a return to the "tradition of the West, as clearly established in the Christian religion and in medieval philosophy . . . that man must use rationality to the degree it is

---

[166] Dan. 11:21.

[167] Gary Allen, *None Dare Call It Conspiracy*, (Rossmoor, CA: Concord Press, 1971, 1972) p. 12, quoted from Carroll Quigley. Note the humanistic rationality throughout.

possible in handling a universe that is well beyond man's present rational capacity to grasp. . . . And in recognizing it, we must return to the tradition, so carelessly discarded in the fifteenth century" (p. 1277). The fifteenth century is the time of the Reformation. So, in effect, the professor calls for a return to the mother Church.

Ten pages later, talking about the different organizations being formed in the European Community, he says: "All this is very relevant in the last chapter on the disintegration of the modern, unified sovereign state and redistribution of its powers to multi-level hierarchial structures remotely resembling the structure of the Holy Roman Empire in the late Medieval period" (p. 1287). (The Holy Roman Empire was heavily Church dominated.) Earlier in the book in discussing various controversies of the Church over doctrine, he includes both Luther and Calvin as promoters of heresy along with the Arians, the Manicheans and the Jansenists (p. 1239). This leads us to assume that the religious forces at work to reunite with the Catholic Church and return to the philosophies of the Church before the Reformation will also bring back the persecution of true Bible believers for their lack of conformity.

The importance of religion to the establishment lies in the need to develop a world community that can agree about the truth and live in peace. According to globalist educator Mortimer J. Adler, the problem concerns the kind and degree of cultural unity required for world community as a basis for world government and world peace. He says diverging philosophies and religions will have to come to a "unity of truth." He goes on to say we have no problem with Eastern religions—only the Western religions which claim to be based on supernatural revelation "that promise supernatural help in achieving salvation." These "dogmatic religious differences will not yield to adjudication by any of the logical means."[168] Therefore, the inference is that Christianity, Judaism, and Islam stand in the way of a unity of the truth. If we can't agree with other religions, we can't really have peace.

The wine in the whore's cup is the promise of world peace brought about by the establishment's unity of truth. The Jewish witnesses and their converts will not conform, hence, the blood bath. The persecution will grow fierce during the first half of the week. The world drunk from the "wine of peace" and already conditioned by end-time violence will support the globalists in the hope of peace. Rome will be chosen as the headquarters, probably because it is centrally located but also for its ancient glory. The world will wonder as she is restored to magnificence, even surpassing her past. The Vatican, too, will restore its pomp and ceremony, taking on more authority as politics and religion mix.

Malachi Martin sets forth in his book *The Keys of This Blood* his understanding of Pope John Paul II's goals for globalization and the role of the Catholic Church with himself as head. The Pope's assessment of the players divides them into several provincial globalists. The first, Islamic peoples with their laws and faith. He sees them as ultimately redeemable as they receive the illumination that they need. (This shows his misunderstanding of the Islamic religion and its passion.)

The second is the Christians, (Evangelical sects) and non-Christians (the so called Christian Cults). These he calls "minimalists" because they expect to be least in the

---

[168] "Persecution Nearing?" *The Christian Enquirer*, May 1985, p. 11.

world's population until the "end-times." Each has deep-rooted opposition to the Catholic church.

The third group consists of the Orthodox religions (Greek, Russian, Armenian. etc.), who are anti-papal.

The fourth are the non-Christian religions of animism, Shintoism, Hinduism, and Buddhaism, antiquated religions that are soon to be overcome by modern civilization.

The fifth are "apartment" groups—the Japanese, Chinese, and Jews. They have no desire to join with the world but rejoice in their "apartness." He lists Russian Communism separately and was openly suspicious of Gorbachev and other leaders.

Beyond these various groups (mainly religionists), he lists certain individual groups that he calls "piggy-back globalists," namely the humanists, the megareligionists, and the New Agers. Out of these groups, one stands out in sheer numbers. While the humanists have "sixty or so groups around the world, the megareligionists have around five hundred."[169] This group seeks to combine all religions into a megareligion to unite the world in peace. All political systems will be combined also under one world government. It is this group that has a mysterious "Brotherhood" (the conspiracy we mentioned earlier). However, the avowed purpose of this group is to make the world safe for *commerce*. It is reported that Bill Moyers, television commentator, followed David Rockefeller on a globe-trotting trip and discovered that "just about a dozen or fifteen individuals made day-to-day decisions that regulated the capital and goods throughout the whole world."[170]

---

[169] Malachi Martin, *The Keys of This Blood*, (New York, London, Singapore, Sydney, Tokyo, Toronto: Simon and Schuster, 1990) p. 297.
[170] Ibid., p. 326.

Pope John Paul II recognizes all these groups, but he is convinced that the only way the world can truly become one is to unite under the Roman Catholic Christianity.[171] Catholicism reaches nearly every corner of the earth. Its leaders alone could turn the tide. Believing he has a part in this, the Pope waits for a sign from the Lord—"the woman highlighted by the sun," which he saw in a vision declaring his destiny to lead such a revival in the Church. Probably his age and infirmity will interfere. However, he may pass this vision on to the next pope whose efforts would involve the "kings of the earth," making Rome the capitol of the remaining world. With the merchants' embellishments, Rome truly will become the world's jewel of a city.

Thus, we conclude that chapter 17's whore, temporarily wearing the title of Babylon, is Rome. It will house the establishment of merchants, kings, and priests who will strive to control the reunited empire from the continent of Europe. The horns,[172] the strength of the empire, on the other hand, will be leaders in the consolidated Arab confederation who agree to give their allegiance to the beast (the little horn of Daniel 8). They will break with Rome after the great victory over the Russian invaders, a victory claimed in the name of the dragon, the "god of forces." When the beast and his allies destroy the city, all pretense of morality or vestiges of Christianity will go, and idolatry will become the religion of the world. Lucifer will replace Allah and be openly worshiped. Babylon, the system, will be reinstated in her own land, in her own city. The "kings of the earth"

---

[171] Ibid., p. 492.

[172] Their strength probably lies in their control of the world's oil. Most if not all of the rest of the world's supply has been destroyed. This could be the reason for the invasion from the east.

will succumb to the beast's supernatural summons at the end, drawing them to the winepress of God's wrath.

A Brief Spiritual History of the Church

Here might be a good place to look back at Christ's letters to the seven churches, reviewing the Church's spiritual progress through time. First, the Ephesian church stood as a bulwark against many heresies trying to enter the early Church. Even the apostle John wrote of this in 2 John. Then Polycarp, the bishop of Smyrna, mentions two heretical sects led by Valenticus and Marcion. The faithful martyrs of the Smyrna church stood firmly on the Word delivered by the apostles, but even then, the Church was plagued by men wanting to inject their own ideas into the gospel. Irenaeus, a pupil of Polycarp, wrote a book entitled *Against Heresies*.

After that came the attack on Christ's deity, which was settled at the Council of Nicea in A.D. 325. By this time, Constantine was constantly interfering with Church affairs. The letter to the church at Pergamos reveals that the Church was living with the world at Satan's seat—the seat of world government. Evidently, this was the beginning of collaboration between the Church and the state.

During the next century, Augustine strengthened this union with his dependence on the state to bring down the heresies of Donatism and Pelagianism. His writings influenced the Church from then on. In the *City of God*, Augustine outlined his ideas on grace and predestination, possibly in answer to the insistence of the "free will" of man taught by heretical groups such as Pelagianism. He also brought in an allegorical interpretation of Scripture, while previously the Church had followed a literal understanding of Scripture.

The next several centuries saw the Church in the grip of Thyratiran "Jezebelism," the infusion of Babylon into Catholic dogma and salvation by works. The rule of the Church over earthly kings resulted in power that totally corrupted it. It was the licentiousness and greediness of clerics in Rome that prompted Luther to launch his great protest. He was not the first to suggest reform, since many had preceded him in the two hundred years before his day. Yet he was perhaps the loudest and was a thorn in the Roman Church's side. John Calvin joined Luther and others. However, Calvin revived Augustine's doctrine of grace and predestination. These pure reasonings of human philosophies replaced the simple doctrine of grace taught in Scripture and deadened the Church in "reformed" theology. The reformed churches also retained their "state" status persecuting those who refused their teachings and remained outside their church. Thus, the letter to the Sardis church: "Thou hast a few names even in Sardis which have not defiled their garments" (Rev. 3:4).

The 1800s brought forth a movement in the Church away from state and clerical oppression. The Scriptures came alive again, and Augustine's theory of the Church ruling before Christ comes was discarded by many. The "coming again of Christ," along with prophetic Scriptures, was studied and systematized under the dispensationalists. The lack of the Sardian church (of not knowing about the Lord's coming) was overcome.

Following hard upon that was the revival of the power gifts, the "charismata," in the great Pentecostal movements and the Charismatic renewal. This was the challenge set before the Philadelphian church. So we come at last to today's Laodicean church that is without zeal.

This is but a brief and sketchy outline of the history of the Church. Yet it is only the story of the *visible* Church. Christ's *invisible* Church will tell the real story at the judgment seat of Christ. Although we have reached the last stage of growth through time, vestiges of every stage still exist in the world, all the way from the Ephesian church to the Laodicean.

God Remembers Babylon

Returning now to the vision, John hears a voice from heaven saying,

> Come out of her, my people, that ye be not partakers of her sins, and that ye receive not of her plagues. For her sins have reached unto heaven, and God hath remembered her iniquities. Reward her even as she rewarded you, and double unto her double according to her works: in the cup which she hath filled fill to her double. How much she hath glorified herself, and lived deliciously, so much torment and sorrow give her: for she saith in her heart, I sit a queen, and am no widow, and shall see no sorrow. Therefore shall her plagues come in one day, death, and mourning, and famine; and she shall be utterly burned with fire: for strong is the Lord God who judgeth her. (18:4–8)

A companion passage in Isaiah describes Rome's future downfall with a few more details.

> And thou saidst, I shall be a lady for ever: so that thou didst not lay these things to thy heart, neither didst remember the latter end of it. Therefore hear now hear, thou that art given to pleasures, that dwellest carelessly, that sayest in thine heart, I am, and none else beside me; I shall not sit as a widow, neither shall I know the loss of

children: but these two things shall come to thee in a moment in one day, the loss of children, and widowhood: they shall come upon thee in their perfection for the multitude of thy sorceries, and for the great abundance of thine enchantment For thou hast trusted in thy wickedness: thou hast said, None seeth me. Thy wisdom and thy knowledge [power], it hath perverted thee; and thou hast said in thine heart, I am, and none else beside me. Therefore shall evil come upon thee; thou shalt not know from whence it riseth [missiles?]: and mischief shall fall upon thee; thou shalt not be able to put it off: and desolation shall come upon thee suddenly, which thou shalt not know. Stand now with thine enchantments, and with the multitude of thy sorceries, wherein thou hast laboured from thine youth; if so be thou shalt be able to profit, if so be thou mayest prevail. Thou art wearied in the multitude of thy counsels. Let now the astrologers, the stargazers, the monthly prognasticators, stand up, and save thee from these things that shall come upon thee. (Isa. 47:7–13)

One would think God is talking to ancient Babylon from the mention of astrologers, etc. But occult doctrines will permeate the Church more and more as it moves toward apostacy. It seems clear that Pope John Paul II has passed on, since he would not condone what will happen to his Catholic church.

The beginning verse of this prophecy makes it clear He speaks to a daughter of Babylon.

Come down, and sit in the dust, O virgin daughter of Babylon, sit on the ground: there is no throne, O daughter of the Chaldeans. (Isa. 47:1)

This daughter seeks a throne (world rule) and thinks she has finally achieved her goal. She will be queen; there will be no other. Man will accomplish his greatest feats. Drunk with power, she exalts herself. Little does she know that under her very nose the beast and the ten kings plot against her. Instead of reigning, she will sit in the dust! Her destruction comes without warning. Those "with whom thou hast laboured, even thy merchants, from thy youth: they shall wander every one to his quarter; none shall save thee," says Isaiah, as he closes out the prophecy (Isa. 47:15).

Turning back now to the voice John hears from heaven, we hear first the lament of kings. These, however, are not the kings of the horns but unified world leaders such as the United Nations who supported the whorish Rome.

> And the kings of the earth, who have committed fornication and lived deliciously with her, shall bewail her, and lament for her, when they shall see the smoke of her burning, standing afar off for the fear of her torment, saying, Alas, alas that great city Babylon, that mighty city! for in one hour is thy judgment come. (18:9–10)

In Revelation 17, the angel told John that the horns will "hate the whore, and shall make her desolate and naked, and shall eat her flesh, and burn her with fire" (17:16). Thus, the Arabs, through unexpected terrorist activities, will destroy the landscape ("make her desolate"), possibly by exploding a nuclear device. They will make her naked by taking away her royal vestments, that is, stripping her of all authority. She will be partly consumed ("her flesh eaten") by radiation, and all that will remain of this once glorious city will be ruin and devastation.

This is only the initial action, however, because we are told later in Revelation 19 that her "smoke rose up for ever and ever" (19:3). Putting together some events that we know come after this in the trumpet judgments, we may surmise the following sequence: Suddenly and without warning, the beast and his ten allies will victimize Rome in a terrorist attack. A mushroom cloud may even ascend over the city.

Merchant ships, seeing the cloud and knowing exactly what has happened, lament as they watch. At that moment, the second angel pours out his plague, and a great mountainous-sized meteorite falls into the sea, destroying one-third of the ships. The waves displaced by the falling mountain rush over the shorelines, reaching perhaps even to the site of the city. Still later, after the sea has deadened and the fifth trumpet sounds, the star with the power to open the bottomless pit falls on the city site. This not only forms a giant volcano but also smothers everything east of it with smoke and ash, darkening the beast's kingdom.

After the air clears (Jesus will remove the veil that covers the earth when He returns [Isa. 25:7].), the smoke of the new volcano continues to rise. The column of smoke remains even in the new earth as a testimony to the righteousness of God over the wicked city (Rev. 19:3).

The Lament of the Merchants

> And the merchants of the earth shall weep and mourn over her; for no man buyeth their merchandise any more: the merchandice of gold, and silver, and precious stones, and of pearls, and fine linen, and purple, and silk, and scarlet, and all thyine wood, and all manner vessels of ivory, and all manner vessels of most precious wood, and of brass,

and iron, and marble, and cinnamon, and odours, and oint-
ments, and frankincense, and wine, and oil, and fine flour,
and wheat, and beasts, and sheep, and horses, and chariots, and slaves, and the souls of men. (18:11–13)

Pausing in the midst of this passage to consider these
luxuries, we find that the list reads in order of their worth
in the empire: gold being the top and the souls of men the
least important. The second least important, slaves, will
most likely be made up of the very poor who have been
sold because of debt. Many could also be believers who
will not accept the establishment's religion. Earlier, God
will call for His own to come out of Babylon to avoid the
destruction. He may have been referring to such.

The luxuries, in the order of their listing, possess the
ingredients to satisfy all that is in the world. Gold through
purple speaks of wealth and authority, satisfying the lust for
power. Silk through marble speak of finery, fulfilling the lust
of the eyes. Cinnamon through sheep speak of sensuous delights to satisfy the lust of the flesh. The army, slaves, and
religious philosophies will provide the means to gain power
over the masses. Continuing now with the list:

And the fruits that thy soul lusted after are departed from
thee, and all things which were dainty and goodly are
departed from thee, and thou shalt find them no more
at all. The merchants of these things, which were made
rich by her, shall stand afar off for the fear of her torment, weeping and wailing, and saying, Alas, alas that
great city, that was clothed in fine linen, and purple, and
scarlet, and decked with gold, and precious stones, and
pearls! For in one hour so great riches is come to nought.

And every shipmaster, and all the company in ships, and
sailors, and as many as trade by sea, stood afar off, and
cried when they saw the smoke of her burning,[173] saying, What city is like unto this great city! And they cast
dust on their heads, and cried, weeping and wailing, saying, Alas, alas that great city, wherein were made rich all
that had ships in the sea by reason of her costliness! for
in one hour is she made desolate. (18:14–19)

The profitable business of open world trade and especially transporting costly goods to the revived Rome ends.
Just when the supremely confident whore, surrounded by
innumerable luxuries, reaches for the crown, the dream—
the long sought-after goal—turns to ashes. It appears that
the elite have lavished all their wealth on this city with the
intent that all other imperial cities would seem dim by comparison. In one hour, God crumbles it.

Heaven's Response

Rejoice over her, thou heaven, and ye holy apostles and
prophets; for God hath avenged you on her. And a mighty
angel took up a stone like a great millstone, and cast it
into the sea, saying, Thus with violence shall that great
city Babylon be thrown down, and shall be found no
more at all. And the voice of harpers, and musicians,
and of pipers, and trumpeters, shall be heard no more at
all in thee; and no craftsman, of whatsoever craft he be,
shall be found any more in thee; and the sound of a

---

[173] Being land locked, smoke from original Babylon could not be seen
at sea.

millstone shall be heard no more at all in thee; and the light of a candle shall shine no more at all in thee; and the voice of the bridgroom and of the bride shall be heard no more at all in thee: *for thy merchants were the great men of the earth*; for by thy sorceries were all nations deceived. And in her was found the *blood of prophets*, and *of saints*, and of all that were slain upon the earth. (18:20–24, emphasis added)

Long oppressed by this powerful city, the Church will rejoice in her judgment. Great joy will burst forth among the saints, who hear the report of her fall. Countless lives have been ruined by the insidious system residing there. Ruined lives, however, are not the worst of her crimes. Murder and massacre fill her cup with bloodguiltiness. From the time of the early apostles, the ancient capitol of Rome directed the persecution against the Church. Even later, when the Babylonian doctrines mixed with Christianity, the Church, itself, with headquarters in Rome, persecuted true believers. Having regained this power after the rapture of true believers, Babylon is responsible for the saints' blood "under the altar" mentioned in the fifth seal. This one city is directly responsible for much bloodshed in the Church.

Indirectly, by her connection with the elite, she will be also responsible for other bloodshed in various parts of the world. Many a martyr in the heavenly company, rejoicing over Babylon's fall, lost his life through Communist brutality. Since the elite, working to set up their socialistic rule, financed these various Communist regimes, they must accept responsibility for their actions.

Then, too, there are the world wars also instigated by their manipulation of economies and governments. The deaths on the battlefields, as well as the deaths by starvation and disease, must be added to her account. Joseph J. Carr, author of *The Twisted Cross*, thinks Hitler may have been initially influenced by the secret organization in Europe to hate Jews. If so, then, we must add the deaths of six million Jews to her account as well.

In the final analysis, the system culminating its power in this city represents the restored and surpassed splendor of the ancient empire. This one city has been Satan's single most effective force against the earth. No wonder God devotes what amounts to two full chapters of the vision to Babylon's exposure and downfall.

All deception and pretense will be put aside. The dragon will fill in the religious void left by Babylon's fall. From then on, mankind's choice will clearly be between the god of this world embodied in the dragon or the Lord God Almighty of heaven. Hallelujah! Babylon is fallen!

Chapter 25

THE TRIUMPHANT RETURN

(REVELATION 19)

Hallelujah! Hallelujah! The rejoicing continues. Judging Babylon is a great triumph! John hears a tumultuous round of praise from the multitude present. The multitude includes the true Church, persecuted by imperial Rome as well as by the Roman Catholic church during the Reformation. Also present are the Jewish witnesses with their Gentile converts, who know the most recent wrath of religious Babylon. Firsthand experience with the power-hungry whore prompts their joy over the righteous retribution. They celebrate with shouts.

> Alleluia; Salvation, and glory, and honour, and power, unto the Lord our God: for true and righteous are his judgments: for he hath judged the great whore, which did corrupt the

earth with her fornication, and hath avenged the blood of his servants at her hand. And again they said, Alleluia. And her smoke rose up for ever and ever. (19:1–3)

Excitement works its way through the crowd to the center of the throne. The elders fall down to worship again, this time joined on the floor by the four living creatures, saying: "Amen; Alleluia" (v. 4).

A command rings out from the throne, "Praise our God, all ye his servants, and ye that fear him, both small and great" (v. 5). In response to this call to worship, John hears a great multitude (the redeemed plus the angelic hosts) and a voice as the sound of many waters (Christ's priestly voice), and the voice of mighty thunderings (the Father's voice) all saying in unison: "Alleluia: for the Lord God omnipotent reigneth" (v. 6).

The Bride

Now with the pretender to the throne judged, the true princess—the intended one espoused to the rightful heir—will come forth. She will come to Him without spot or wrinkle because she has made herself ready. She will be ready by His wishes through her obedience, whereas the whore aspired to the throne by *her own* wishes. Invited to the side of the rightful ruler of the earth, the Bride will come dressed in the genuine splendor of righteousness. The Lord Jesus Christ Himself will present the glorious daughter of Almighty God to Himself, thus fulfilling the second portion of the eastern marriage tradition.

Confusion exists in some circles as to just which of God's people will make up the Bride. We know the Church is included; but is she only the Church? Some contend that the Bride will consist of all the redeemed from all time. The next sequence before John clears up the problem.

> Let us be glad and rejoice, and give honour to him: for the marriage of the Lamb is come, and his wife hath made herself ready. And to her was granted that she should be arrayed in fine linen, clean and white: for the fine linen is the righteousness [es] of saints. And he saith unto me, Write, Blessed are they which are called unto the marriage supper of the Lamb. And he saith unto me, These are the true sayings of God. (19:7–9)

The announcement suggests an eastern-style wedding that consists of three parts: The espousal, the presentation of the bride, and the marriage supper. The espousal or engagement of the couple, usually arranged between their families, announces the pledge of their intent to come together later as man and wife. The presentation takes place the day of the wedding when someone, usually the bridegroom's father, presents the bride to the bridegroom. After they exchange vows, the wedding party and their invited guests sit down to the wedding supper.

Looking at the marriage of the Lamb in this light, we see from the action in the above passage that the presentation is in progress. We know this because it speaks of the Bride's wedding garment. It also anticipates the wedding supper when it speaks of the blessedness of those invited. Thus, the Bride in this passage has already been espoused to the Lamb. The espousal took place on earth earlier when the Holy Spirit, sent by the Father, invited and sealed those who believed in Christ and espoused them to Him as a chaste virgin.[174] Neither Old Testament saints nor tribulation saints are involved in this. Therefore, they could not be part of the espousal.

Besides that, the second phase of the wedding, the presentation, is before us; and most of the saints in the aforementioned groups are not yet resurrected.[175] Resurrection surely must be a prerequisite for entering into so intimate a relationship as marriage with the Lamb.

Furthermore, the ones present are called the "wife" of the Lamb, that is, those who have already entered the first phase of the marriage procedure. According to Jewish custom, the espoused one was called "wife" even though the couple had not yet come together. For example, the angel Gabriel's words to Joseph, "Fear not to take unto thee Mary thy wife" (Matt. 1:20). So having not been resurrected yet nor involved in the espousal earlier, Old Testament saints and the tribulation saints of the last half of the prophetic week will not be present for these portions of the wedding.

Our text presents another consideration. It says, "His wife hath made herself ready" (19:7). As we mentioned earlier, part of the reward gained by individuals who overcome is to be clothed in the measure of glory they have obtained through obedience to Christ. Here in this passage it says, "And to her was granted that she should be arrayed in fine linen, clean and white: for the fine linen is the righteousness [es] of saints" (19:8).

---

[174] 1 Cor. 11:2.

[175] The wedding presentation follows the fall of spiritual Babylon at the second-trumpet judgment. Old Testament saints will not be resurrected until the sixth-trumpet judgment and the tribulation saints after the seventh-trumpet judgment.

The Bible mentions fine linen, the clothing of kings and priests, for the first time when Joseph, son of Jacob, was "arrayed in vestures of fine linen" as a symbol of his authority to reign in Egypt.[176] Paul says that Christ "loved the church and gave himself for it; that he might sanctify and cleanse it with the washing of water by the word that he might *present it to himself* a glorious church not having spot or wrinkle" (Eph. 5:25–27). Cleansing will be a prerequisite to overcoming. The overcoming will clothe the Church in righteousness and give her the right or authority to reign.

Finally, if all the redeemed make up the Bride, who will come to the wedding supper, the third portion of the wedding? The angel announcing the marriage commissions John to make out the invitations. "Write," he says. "Blessed are they which are called unto the marriage supper of the Lamb" (19:9). From this we conclude that, if we have a bride and bridegroom celebrating a wedding supper, then we must also have friends and associates with whom to celebrate it. Isaiah tells about a time when the Lord will make a "feast of fat things" and of wine and will destroy the veil that covers the earth (Isa. 25:6–7, the wedding supper?).

Naming the various groups of believers, we pause to sort out the allegory. Christ as the Lamb is the Bridegroom. The Church, defined in Revelation 2 and 3, is the Bride. The 144,000 sealed company are the virgins whom the Bridegroom takes with him to the marriage. Their Gentile converts will also be invited guests. These rejoice to follow the Bride and Bridegroom to the wedding supper on earth that will take place after the coronation of the King.

---

[176] Gen. 41:42.

Others will join them as they leave. Old Testament saints will rise just in time for the procession. John the Baptist, the last of the old covenant prophets, referred to himself as the "friend of the bridegroom." Jesus said that although John was the greatest of the prophets born of women, "he that is least in the kingdom of God is greater than he" (Luke 7:28). John is not part of the Church. Jesus also said that Abraham, Isaac, and Jacob will sit down in the kingdom, presumably, to eat the wedding supper. People belong to their own orders and, therefore, will have their own places in the kingdom to come. The Church's function appears to be mainly administrative—both politically and spiritually. This fits the picture of the bride of a sovereign ruler. Psalm 45 describes prophetically the coronation of the king and the presentation of His bride.

> She shall be brought unto the king in raiment of needlework: the virgins her companions *that follow her* shall be brought unto thee. With gladness and rejoicing shall they be brought: they shall enter into the king's palace. (Ps. 45:14–15, emphasis added)

So we see that the virgins are also companions of the Bride. Although they will live in the palace, they will not rule. They appear to be special servants to assist the Bride and Bridegroom (perhaps like the relationship of the Levites to the priests in the Old Testament tabernacle). The Lamb has "virgins" that follow him wherever he goes (Rev. 14:4), and the Bride has "virgins her companions that follow her" (Ps. 45:14). These are separate from the tribulation saints who will be resurrected after Christ's return to earth. They are separate, also, from those charitable Gentiles of Matthew

25 who are still alive after the judgments. Nevertheless, they will all be invited guests to the wedding supper of the Lamb.

Thus, we conclude that only the blood-bought throng that began at Pentecost and ended at the rapture before the tribulation will make up the Church. All the rest of the redeemed belong to other groups and will have other functions in the kingdom.

> And I fell at his feet to worship him. And he said unto me, See thou do it not: I am thy fellowservant, and of thy brethren that have the testimony of Jesus: worship God: for the testimony of Jesus is the spirit of prophecy. (19:10)

Meanwhile, getting back to the vision, John watches the troops of believers assemble as they prepare to depart for the earth. He becomes so overwhelmed by the truth that he is receiving from the angel that he falls down to worship him. Rebuked by the messenger for worshiping, John learns about the spirit of prophecy that we explained earlier (chapter 1). The one speaking is *John's fellowservant* and *of the prophets* (in other words, only a man) who merely speaks words from God. Again the messenger confirms that he is a saint—a fellow believer of John's brethren. He has the spirit of prophecy that enables him to give the testimony of Jesus, that is, to speak God's words to John.

We really cannot blame John for being confused, because when we look back in the passage to find where this particular "angel" is first mentioned, we see him described as a mighty angel (but obviously not *the* Mighty Angel). It is the same angel who took the millstone and cast it into the sea, then prophesied, "Thus with violence shall that great city Babylon be thrown down, and shall be found no more at all" (18:21).

He is not even a heavenly angel. John has no time to dwell on his mistake, because the action of the vision resumes.

Invasion from Above

> And I saw heaven opened, and behold a white horse; and he that sat upon him was called Faithful and True, and in righteousness he doth judge and make war. His eyes were as a flame of fire, and on his head were many crowns; and he had a name written, that no man knew, but he himself. And he was clothed with a vesture dipped in blood: and his name is called The Word of God. And the armies which were in heaven followed him upon white horses, clothed in fine linen, white and clean. And out of his mouth goeth a sharp sword, that with it he should smite the nations: and he shall rule them with a rod of iron: and he treadeth the winepress of the fierceness and the wrath of Almighty God. And he hath on his vesture and on his thigh a name written, KING OF KINGS, AND LORD OF LORDS. (19:11–16)

Heaven suddenly opens. The Captain of the army rides His victorious white war horse. He is called Faithful and True because in righteousness He judges and makes war. His eyes burn as they search out His foes. On His head rests many crowns (diadems). Although we are not told the number of crowns, we can be sure they are equal to or more than the ten crowns connected to the beast's kingdom, more than adequate authority to wage His war.

Besides the name Faithful and True, Christ moves in the authority of a secret name known only to Him. It may refer to the task at hand, judging the enemies of God, or it may be the same new name promised to the overcomers of the Philadelphian church: "And I will write upon him my new name" (3:12), perhaps a name connected with power since their problem was weakness. It may be that some over-comers are saints being used as messengers of wrath like the "mighty angel" John tried to worship. He certainly used the power gift of prophecy. Thus, their new names may be identified with His and refer to judgment.

Christ's clothes, premarked with red stains, symbolizes His work as well as His right to perform it. He shed His *own blood* on the cross for their sakes, but the nations have rejected it. Consequently, He stained His garment by treading the winepress alone, pressing out *their own blood.*

In connection with this task, John mentions his favorite name for Christ—the Word of God, not simply "Logos" but with the definite article, "the" Word of God. "The expression of God" in all His mercy will be forced to satisfy His holy nature by righteously judging the wicked.

Behind Him will stream the armies—the Bride followed by the virgins and others that also will ride victorious white steeds. The Bride will prepare to assume her position of authority. She will be dressed the part, clothed in white linen, clean and white—a contrast to those who are under judgment.

The sharp two-edged sword of utterance, the spoken word with which He will fight those remaining, will be in Christ's mouth. He will speak the word, and it will happen exactly as He says, like the cursing of the fig tree void of fruit (Matt. 21:19). His spoken word will never fail, and the nations will come to regard it as a rod of inflexible iron.

A fourth name, stamped on His vesture and the His flesh of His thigh, will read, "KING OF KINGS AND LORD OF LORDS." As clothes in Scripture often stand for the works and/or character of an individual and since the linen that will clothe the saints stands for the same, surely His garment will be like theirs.[177] This will be another expression of His authority to execute the laws of God. The title written on His thigh may speak of a personal oath to the Father to fulfill the title. The touch of God on Jacob's thigh changed his name to Israel—a soldier of God. The touch of God the Father on Jesus the Son conferred the supreme title over all. Instead of carrying a sword on His thigh as any ordinary soldier, He will carry the written authority along with the power to execute it in His mouth.

As John finishes with the description of the armies, the scene changes. An angel stands silhouetted against the sun. He cries with a loud voice to all the birds of prey.

> And I saw an angel standing in the sun; and he cried with a loud voice, saying to all the fowls that fly in the midst of heaven, Come and gather yourselves together unto the supper of the great God; that ye may eat the flesh of kings, and the flesh of captains, and the flesh of mighty men, and the flesh of horses, and of them that sit on them, and the flesh of all men, both free and bond, both small and great. And I saw the beast, and the kings of the earth, and their armies, gathered together to make war against him that sat on the horse, and against his army. And the beast was taken, and with him the false prophet that wrought miracles before him, with which he deceived them that had received the mark of the beast, and them that worshipped his image. These both were cast alive into a lake

---

[177] Linen clothed kings and priests. Linen also depicts works done apart from the flesh. Other garments mentioned in Scripture, wool and animal skins, are produced by the flesh.

of fire burning with brimstone. And the remnant were slain with the sword of him that sat upon the horse, which sword proceeded out of his mouth: and all the fowls were filled with their flesh. (19:17–21)

Middle heaven, the second heaven, is the realm of the unseen satanic hosts. The angel announces special permission for unclean fowl to feed on the armies on the battlefield. Diabolic appetites of hatred, murder, torture, and savage brutality receive an invitation to sup at will on the emotions and minds of the gathered armies.

Their natural counterparts, physical eagles, hawks, and other birds of prey, live close by. God has bequeathed Idumea, southeastern Israel, the very place of destruction of the Russian army, to the wild beasts and unclean birds as a perpetual dwelling place (Isa. 34:15–17). These scavengers, having an abundance of dead men and animals to feed on during the judgments, will steadily increase in number. Their increase is a good thing, too, since so great a slaughter would be practically impossible to dispose of otherwise. This will possibly be the last time meat is available to beasts and birds of prey on earth, because we know the animals of the kingdom are herbivorous (Isa. 11:6–9). However, God may intend to keep this area for the judgment of those who transgress His laws during the kingdom. Isaiah speaks of such a place that people can visit to remind themselves that His laws must be obeyed.

And they shall go forth, and look upon the carcases of the men that have transgressed against me: for their worm shall not die, neither shall their fire be quenched; and they shall be an abhorring unto all flesh. (Isa. 66:24)

Here, also, may be a lake of fire created during the destruction of the Russian army (Isa. 34:9–10). If God does intend to keep this fearful place of judgment, then the ravenous beasts that dwell here during the kingdom age will be confined to this one area.

John does not see the fowls gather; he only hears the invitation. Instead, he sees the "entree." The menu includes a variety of tastes. No distinction between "the small" and "the great," for all are offered. The beast with his armies and the kings of the earth with their armies (gathered initially to fight against the eastern hoards) join together to fight Christ and his army descending from above.

It is a gloomy day, not entirely dark, yet not light either. The maruts, the terrible ones (small independent comets of the sixth trumpet), fill the sky with dust and debris. The upper atmosphere also carries the load of volcanic ash left over from the fifth trumpet and vial. Because of these two conditions, the sun and the moon cannot be distinguished. Therefore, when the armies of heaven penetrate this gloom, every eye can see them, for the glory of God lights up the clouds (Joel 3:15; Zech. 14:6–7; Matt. 24:29–30).

Actually, the Lord does not interfere with the battle in progress (the beast against the kings of the East) until Jerusalem falls.

> For I will gather all nations against Jerusalem to battle; and the city shall be taken, and the houses rifled, and the women ravished; and half of the city shall go forth into captivity, and the residue of the people shall not be cut off from the city. *Then shall the LORD go forth*, and fight against those nations, as when he fought in the day of battle. (Zech. 14:2–3, emphasis added)

The kings of the East appear to be winning. (Jerusalem will have been occupied by the beast since the midst of the prophetic week.) The timing is right. The glorious procession comes into view. All have heard of Christ's coming. They understand perfectly what they see. The beast and his generals, inspired by the devil and his demons, being rebellious and audacious enough to contend directly with the Lord of Glory, aim their weapons at Him.

Abandoning His horse, Christ descends to the Mount of Olives just as the angel promised at His ascension. Suddenly, the greatest earthquake of all time rips the mountain in half, forming a great valley extending eastward from Jerusalem. Those who escape capture in Jerusalem can flee through the newly formed valley. Water bursts forth from a new mountain in the north and divides the flow between east and west, emptying its streams into both seas. One or both flow through Jerusalem[178] depending upon where they divide. The eastern half will flow into the Dead Sea Valley that extends along the great fault line. Besides that, the Red Sea will pour into the valley also.

Zechariah describes the plague that kills the armies.

> And this shall be the plague wherewith the LORD will smite all the people that have fought against Jerusalem; their flesh shall consume away while they stand upon their feet, and their eyes shall consume away in their holes, and their tongue shall consume away in their mouth. And it shall come to pass in that day, that a great tumult [noisy commotion] from the LORD shall be among them; and they shall lay hold every one on the

---

[178] Isa. 33:21; Ezek. 47:1–12; Zech. 14:4–5.

hand of his neighbor, and his hand shall rise up against the hand of his neighbor. (Zech. 14:12–13)

In the tumult and uproar of the natural catastrophe, the fighting forces destroy each other. The terror, intensified by the horrendous sound emanating from the scraping earth strata, unleashes irritation, confusion, and anger. Uncontrolled passions lead to murder. It's every man for himself, even against his fellow soldiers.

Isaiah describes this scene in its final fulfillment:

> Behold, the name of the LORD cometh from far, burning with his anger, and the burden thereof is heavy: his lips are full of indignation, and his tongue as a devouring fire: and his breath, as an overflowing stream, shall reach to the midst of the neck, to sift the nations with the sieve of vanity: and there shall be a bridle in the jaws of the people [see 2 Thess. 2:11–12], causing them to err. . . . And the LORD shall cause his glorious voice to be heard [part of the tumult], and shall shew the lighting down of his arm [that is, the lowering of his arm, Christ], with the indignation of his anger, and with the flame of a devouring fire, with scattering, and tempest, and hailstones (of the weight of a talent, seventh vial). For through the voice of the LORD shall the Assyrian[179]

---

[179] The last great entanglement of the heavens with the earth was in Isaiah's day (8th century B.C.). It directly caused the death of Sennacherub's army, the commotion and great earthquake in Uzziah's day (Amos 1:1; Zech. 14:5), and the changing of the shadow of the sundial in Ahaz and Hezekiah's reigns (2 Kings 20:9–11; Isa 38:7–8). All these brief mentions show a great disturbance in the solar system. But it is also clear that Isaiah saw a time of even greater destruction at the end of the age.

be beaten down, which smote with a rod. . . . For Tophet is ordained of old; yes, for the king it is prepared; he hath made it deep and large: the pile thereof is fire and much wood; the breath of the LORD, like a stream of brimstone, doth kindle it. (Isa. 30:27–28, 30–33)

Tophet means burning. Perhaps this is the fearful place mentioned earlier rather than the local garbage dump called by that name in Jesus' day. Nevertheless, this Tophet is prepared especially for the beast. Before the destruction of the armies, John sees the beast and the false prophet cast alive into a lake of fire. "And the remnant were slain with the sword of him that sat upon the horse, which sword proceeded out of his mouth: and all the fowls were filled with their flesh" (Rev. 19:21).

The consuming of the flesh, eyes, and tongues of the armies comes as the result of a spoken command. The battle is over. The Lord has won! A great voice thunders out of the temple in heaven, "It is done." The birds of prey begin the cleanup. The waters wash out the valley, healing even the great salt sea. It is the beginning of a new earth!

Chapter 26

THE LAST AGE

(REVELATION 20)

Yes, the battle is over. Now begins the judging of war crimes. But before people stand before the Judge, the leadership of the rebellion must receive retribution. We were told in the last chapter that the beast and false prophet were cast alive into a lake of fire (19:20).

These two, along with their armies, had actively fought against the Lord. The King's quick action in dealing with them confirms Proverbs 29:4: "The king by judgment establisheth the land." The guilt of the beast and the false prophet is unquestionable: not subject to trial. So great are their crimes, they are ushered into the place of eternal punishment a full thousand years before anyone else, even before the third member of the satanic trinity—Satan. God has further use of Satan, as we will soon see. However, the armies that fought against the Lord and died on the battlefield, will be reserved for judgment of the dead after the thousand years. He will retain the living kings in prisons (Isa. 24:21–22) until their turn in the judgment of the living.

Daniel supplies a small detail concerning this time. Speaking of the beast and the length of his reign, he says,

> And from the time that the daily sacrifice shall be taken away, and the abomination that maketh desolate set up, there shall be a thousand two hundred and ninety days. Blessed is he that waiteth, and cometh to the thousand three hundred and five and thirty days. (Dan. 12:11–12)

Using Daniel's figures, 1,335 days minus 1,290 days equals 45 days. Evidently, this is the time set aside for judging those left alive on the earth. Unbelieving Gentile nations or individuals who out of compassion hid God's people during the persecutions receive grace and are permitted to enter the kingdom. Of course, by this time they will have believed. How could they not after all that has happened (see Matt. 25:31–46)? Blessed indeed is the person who survives this judgment!

> And I saw an angel come down from heaven, having the key of the bottomless pit and a great chain in his hand. (20:1)

Returning to the vision, John watches as a mighty Angel comes down from heaven, having the key to the bottomless pit and a great chain in His hand. Although we have no clue to the identity of this mighty angel other than the possession of the key, we suspect He is the Mighty Angel, the Alpha and the Omega who has the keys of death and hades. It is most appropriate for Jesus, the archenemy of Satan, to lock him up. He takes the dragon, Satan, binds him with chains, and locks him in the bottomless pit. Satan's time has run out. The Angel, acting on orders from the Father; sets an official seal on Satan, who offers no resistance. He knows it is useless.

Satan's restraint will last for one thousand years, and then he will be released for a short while again to deceive the nations.

> And he laid hold on the dragon, that old serpent, which is the Devil, and Satan, and bound him a thousand years, and cast him into the bottomless pit, and shut him up, and set a seal upon him, that he should deceive the nations no more, till the thousand years should be fulfilled: and after that he must be loosed a little season. (20:2–3)

In this passage, there can be no doubt as to who is being restrained, because all names for the enemy are used except one—Lucifer. "Morning star" no longer suits him. The "dragon" appeared in Revelation, but the "old serpent" was in the Garden of Eden. Using all the names points to the fact we are not looking at a spiritual or physical representation here but the saints' spiritual archenemy in person.

Satan's work of deception and independence from God had flourished throughout all the former historical periods. By such means, he had gained control of a vast kingdom of darkness. Now this rule ends; a new age begins.

In the new age, God will try people's hearts in an ideal environment distinguished not only by its multiplied blessings but also by those things that are absent from it. Such things that belong to the curse will be overcome, since the Lord of Righteousness will control all negative forces. The world will flourish without sickness,[180] without death,[181] without material lack, without fear, without war, without darkness, and without a devil and demons to deceive. People will live under a world government that will maintain international peace and social and economic order with absolute justice.

Only the sinful hearts of men will still be out of order. In this perfect environment, God will prove that, even under ideal conditions, sinful hearts are unredeemable except by the blood of Jesus. At the end of the age, Satan will be loosed just long enough to incite a rebellious uprising. He will deceive people into thinking they can oppose God and win. But before we get into that, let us return to the vision. Now that the present rebellion has been put down, we see another picture. The Ancient of Days installs a new government. Daniel describes the transition of power prophetically:

> I beheld till the thrones were cast down [that is, of the old world order], and the Ancient of days did sit, whose garment was white as snow, and the hair of his head like the pure wool: his throne was like the fiery flame, and his wheels as burning fire. (Dan. 7:9)

---

[180] Sin and rebellion still produce sickness, but when the nations learn to abide by spiritual laws, it will disappear. Isaiah says that the "inhabitant shall not say, I am sick: the people that dwell therein shall be forgiven their iniquity" (Isa. 33:24). Also Zechariah says, "There shall be the plague wherewith the LORD will smite the heathen that come not up to the feast of tabernacles." So sickness or physical disaster will attend disobedience and rebellion, at least until repentance.

[181] The wages of sin is still death. So the sinner who persists in his sin will still die, either by plague or by judicial order if his crime calls for it. But because of the cleansed earth (no more curse), a fuller revelation of spiritual laws, and freedom from satanic forces, men may attain great ages.

The evil Empire has lost its leaders, the beast and the false prophet, and its inspiration, Satan. Jesus will now judge the nations according to their treatment of the Jews. The death sentence is already decreed on those wearing the mark of the beast.

God the Father[182] will come to earth in His chariot throne to witness the trial and the coronation of His Son. Daniel continues:

> A fiery stream issued and came forth before him: thousand thousands ministered unto him, and ten thousand times ten thousand stood before him: the judgment was set, and the books were opened. I beheld then because of the voice of the great words which the horn [the beast—the little horn of verse 8] spake: I beheld even till the beast [the Empire, having the ten horns] was slain, and his body [the subjects] destroyed, and given to the burning flame. . . . I saw in the night visions, and, behold, one like the Son of man came with the clouds of heaven, and came to the Ancient of days, and they brought him near before him. And there was given him dominion, and glory, and a kingdom, that all people, nations, and languages, should serve him: his dominion is an everlasting dominion. which shall not pass away, and his kingdom that which shall not be destroyed. . . . But the saints of the most High shall take the kingdom, and possess the kingdom for ever, even for ever and ever. (Dan. 7:10–11, 13–14, 18)

---

[182] This is a confusing passage. Does God the Father have a separate body besides Christ's, or are these two seen together as two separate manifestations of the Son seen from different perspectives? We cannot tell.

Isaiah also describes the transition of authority, beginning with the cause of the last earthquake:

> The earth shall reel to and fro like a drunkard, and shall be removed like a cottage; and the transgression thereof shall be heavy upon it; and it shall fall, and not rise again. And it shall come to pass in that day, that the LORD shall punish *the host of the high ones* [Satan and his angels] that are on high, and *the kings of the earth upon the earth.* And they shall be gathered together, as prisoners are gathered in the pit, and shall be shut up in the prison, and after many days they shall be visited. Then the moon shall be confounded, and the sun ashamed, when the LORD of hosts shall reign in mount Zion, and in Jerusalem, and before his ancients gloriously. (Isa. 24:20–23, emphasis added)

Apparently, God will restrain the fallen angels along with Satan, their jurisdictions turned over to the saints, as Daniel said. After the thousand years, they will be visited and turned loose with their leader.

Until that time, the glory of the kingdom will outshine both the sun and the moon. The moon will blush with embarrassment, while the sun will shrink in shame. The glorious reign of the Lord will fulfill all His promises to the ancient patriarchs of old.

The Final Company of the First Resurrection Rises

> And I saw thrones, and they sat upon them, and *judgment* was given unto them. [Notice John makes a scene change here, which means these thrones are not necessarily the same as that which the Church already occu-

pies, i.e., Christ's throne. These thrones may well be on
the earth.] (20:4, emphasis added)

The tendency in interpreting this passage is to assume
that the thrones belong to the saints being resurrected in the
next verse. However, to prevent this misassumption, we have
a scene divider—"and I saw." Therefore, the thrones given at
this time[183] fulfill the positions already promised. As the kingdom rule begins shortly, the new King appoints those who
will rule in His government to their specific positions. For
example, Jesus promised his disciples they would sit on twelve
thrones judging the twelve tribes of Israel.

> *And I saw* the souls of them that were beheaded for the
> witness of Jesus, and for the word of God, and which had
> not worshipped the beast, neither his image, neither had
> received his mark upon their foreheads, or in their hands;
> and they lived and reigned with Christ a thousand years.
> But the rest of the dead lived not again until the thousand
> years were finished. This is the first resurrection. Blessed
> and holy is he that hath part in the first resurrection: on
> such the second death hath no power, but they shall be
> priests of God and of Christ, and shall reign with him a
> thousand years. (20:4–6, emphasis added)

John watches as the beheaded martyrs of the beast's rule
rise from the dead. These are the last of the first resurrection.
Six companies of resurrected beings belong to this category.
He saw the resurrected Jesus in His glory at the beginning of
the vision. That counts as the first resurrection. Since then,

---

[183] The judgment of the living should have already transpired, probably along with the angels and kings mentioned earlier.

he had witnessed the resurrection of two companies—the 144,000 with their converts and the two witnesses—plus the assumed resurrection of the Church after seeing the crowned elders. These are resurrections two, three, and four. The fifth comes at the end of the second woe (Rev. 11) where John heard the time announced for the resurrection of the Old Testament saints. Now he sees the sixth company rise. These refused the mark of the beast. Upon rising, they will receive high rewards and reign in some capacity with Christ a thousand years. This last order of saints completes the first resurrection, that of the just.

The second resurrection (the seventh in number counting Christ's resurrection) is not to life but rather to condemnation and eternal death. It takes place at the end of the thousand-year reign so that all the unsaved are present at the same judgment. Those who will reject Christ during the millennium are not yet born. These will be the rebels of the last uprising mentioned earlier plus any who commit capital crimes during the thousand-year reign. All these will be sentenced to the second death, that is, permanent separation from God. Only the degree of torment remains to be decided.

However, first the rebels of that judgment have to die, which is what John sees next.

The Last Uprising

And when the thousand years are expired, Satan shall be loosed out of his prison, and shall go out to deceive the nations which are in the four quarters of the earth, Gog and Magog, to gather them together to battle: the number of whom is as the sand of the sea. And they went up on the breadth of the earth, and compassed the camp of the saints about, and the beloved city: and fire came down from God out of heaven, and devoured *them*. (20:7–9, emphasis added)

With the curse abolished, the population explodes during the thousand years. The life span of mankind has increased, complicating the matter. Isaiah says, "A little one shall become a thousand, and a small one a strong nation: I the LORD will hasten it in his time" (Isa. 60:22). Again, he says, "There shall be no more thence an infant of days, nor an old man that hath not filled his days: for the child shall die an hundred years old; but the sinner being an hundred years old shall be accursed . . . for as the days of a tree are the days of my people" (Isa. 66:20, 22). Isaiah speaks of the sinner that dies judicially for sin as being only a child though he be one hundred years old. With the increased age of people and death only by accident[184] or by execution for an infraction of the law, the population reaches a crowded state.

Even so, the heavenly government maintains perfect order. Nevertheless, the perfect conditions are not enough to quell sinful human desires. People long to overthrow the authority that keeps them from doing as they please without consequences. The strain of being forced to live moral, decent lives proves to be too great. When released, Satan will stir these rebellious hearts to hope. His deception: Satan's power can overcome God's.[185] The rebellious rally around their leader. Whole nations fall prey to his deception, as many as the sand of the sea.

---

[184] If that death is even possible since the Bible does not mention any other resurrections. But then what about the case of murder? Will the King restore all such victims with life immediately?

[185] Apparently these rebels are as ignorant of God's Word as the rebels of our day.

Convinced in their cause, the rebellious march against the city. The saints who live near the beloved city, Jerusalem, do not resist. No army rises to the defense. No person fearfully shrinks in retreat at this display of human power. The saints know their God and His Word. There is no contest whatever; God simply drops fire from heaven and consumes the lot. Whooosh! It is finished! The physical earth remains intact as fire cleanses the last vestige of the curse—unredeemed, rebellious mankind. Suspended in death, they await their eternal sentence that will be issued at their resurrection. Satan, the inspiration of this final rebellious action, receives his doom first.

> And the devil that deceived them was cast into the lake of fire and brimstone, where the beast and the false prophet are, and shall be tormented day and night for ever and ever. (20:10)

Joining the rest of his "trinity of evil," Satin's torment begins. How blessed is the universe with Satan gone! All strife ceases.

The new earth, now totally pure, contains only born-again believers washed in the blood of Christ. Paul said Jesus would reign until He put all enemies under His feet.

The last enemy left to conquer is death itself. The sin problem has been entirely cleared up; therefore, its wages—death—can be eliminated. With no reason or inspiration to sin, the law of sin and death can be repealed. The born-again believers who are left had remained faithful to God when the rebellion swept the earth. Their faith held true. Now they are ready and worthy to receive their eternal state. Since they are alive, this may involve a change similar to that affected on living saints at the rapture. As Paul said of the Church, "We shall not all sleep [die], but we shall all be changed" (1 Cor. 15:51). With death destroyed, the purified earth enters the eternal state.

Purification by Fire—A Doctrinal Error?

Here we interrupt the sequence of this chapter to discuss a popular doctrine that seems to be in error. The doctrine states that after the millennium, God will destroy the heavens and the earth by fire and remake them for eternity. This teaching totally ignores the great changes that have already occurred during the judgment week. A careful study of the following verses will show that this doctrine contradicts several passages of Scripture.

Haggai, a prophet who lived after the last great catastrophes of the days of Amos, Isaiah, and the Greek poet Homer, tells us under inspiration:

> For thus saith the LORD of hosts; *Yet once*, it is a little while, and I will shake the heavens, and the earth, and the sea, and the dry land; and I will shake all nations, and the desire of all nations shall come: and I will fill this house with glory, saith the LORD of hosts. (Hag. 2:6–7, emphasis added)

This has already happened in the great tribulation and the millennium. The shaking came during the judgments and the glory came during the millennium. The writer of the book of Hebrews quotes this passage and adds:

> And this word, Yet once more, signifieth the removing of those things that are shaken, as of *things that are made*, that those things which cannot be shaken may remain. (Heb. 12:27, emphasis added)

From this, we understand there can be only one more great destruction of the heavens and the earth. This has just occurred in the vision John saw. Also, Jesus, speaking of the tribulation in the Olivet Discourse, tells us in Matthew 24:21 and Mark 13:19 that destruction like this has not been since the creation *nor ever will be again*. Why then do the proponents of this doctrine say that the whole earth will be burned again?

The changes of the earth's surface that occur during the tribulation period have already made a new earth. Several permanent changes are mentioned, most of them near Israel.

> And it shall come to pass in the last days, that the mountain of the LORD's house shall be established in the top of the mountains, and shall be exalted above the hills; and all nations shall flow unto it. (Isa. 2:2)

This mountain rises during the earthquake when Christ touches down on the Mount of Olives. And at the same time:

> All the land shall be turned as a plain from Geba to Rimmon south of Jerusalem: and it shall be lifted up, and inhabited in her place, from Benjamin's gate unto the place of the first gate, unto the corner gate, and from the tower of Hananeel unto the king's winepresses. And men shall dwell in it, and there shall *be no more utter destruction; but Jerusalem* shall be safely inhabited. (Zech. 14:10–11, emphasis added)

This passage follows the description of the armies that are destroyed at Christ's return. Evidently, the upheaval contributes to their demise. Another passage concerning the lay of the land around Jerusalem says:

> Behold, the days come, saith the LORD, that the city
> shall be built to the LORD from the tower of Hananeel
> unto the gate of the corner. And the measuring line shall
> yet go forth over against it upon the hill Gareb, and shall
> compass about to Goath. And the whole valley of the
> dead bodies, and of the ashes, and all the fields unto the
> brook of Kidron, unto the corner of the horse gate to-
> ward the east, shall be holy unto the LORD; it *shall not
> be plucked up, nor thrown down any more for ever.* (Jer.
> 31:38–40, emphasis added)

The city built on the uplifted ground shall not be destroyed ever again. Not only are there changes in the land
but also of the waters.

> And it shall be in that day, that living waters shall go out
> from Jerusalem; half of them toward the former sea, and
> half of them toward the hinder sea: in summer and in
> winter shall it be. (Zech. 14:8)

Ezekiel tells of the source of the waters. They come out
of the new millennial temple that will evidently be built
over the fountain.

> Behold, waters issued out from under the threshold of
> the house eastward: . . . and the waters came down from
> under from the right side of the house, at the south side
> of the altar. (Ezek. 47:1)

These waters will issue out of the right side of the eastern gate of the millennial temple (described in Ezekiel 40–
44). A little more than thirteen miles from this point, the
waters will become a river men cannot ford.

> These waters issue out toward the east country, and go down
> into the desert, and go into the sea: which being brought
> forth into the sea, the waters shall be healed. (Ezek. 47:8)

The healing of the Dead Sea waters means that, now it
has an outlet. We have already been told that the "tongue
of the Egyptian sea" (Gulf of Suez) will be destroyed (Isa.
11:15). Evidently, the huge crack underlying the whole Rift
Valley will widen, opening it up to the Red Sea. This deep
channel will provide waters for ocean-going vessels barely
twenty miles from Jerusalem. Since the city itself is built
on a plain, however, none of these ships will sail the rivers
of Jerusalem because Isaiah says:

> Your eyes will see Jerusalem, a peaceful abode, a tent that
> will not be moved; its *stakes will never be pulled up*, nor any
> of its ropes broken. There the LORD will be our Mighty
> One. It [Jerusalem] will be like a place of broad rivers and
> streams. No galley with oars will ride them, no mighty ship
> will sail them. (Isa. 33:20–21 NIV, emphasis added)

Joel says:

> And all the rivers of Judah shall flow with waters, and a
> fountain shall come forth of the house of the LORD,
> and shall water the valley of Shittim. (Joel 3:18)

Here is yet another reference to the permanency of the
work accomplished in the judgments on the earth.

The healing waters pouring forth from the altar in the
temple will flow toward the east country until they reach the
newly formed sea in the Jordan Valley. From there, the blessing, which the living waters symbolize, flow out to the whole

world just as waters of the seas flow one to the other, as ocean touches ocean today. The waters from Jerusalem will wash every shoreline of the earth with healing and regeneration.

With the land regenerated, the waters regenerated, and the people regenerated who remain after the cleansing fire destroys the rebels, what further purpose is there for purging the earth with more fire? Could this doctrine of purification and remaking the heavens and the earth simply be an attempt to explain Peter's solemn warning of destruction by fire? Could it not be that because we have failed to understand the physical side of the judgments, we have not seen that the purging by fire had been going on all along? Let us examine Peter's words and see:

> But the day of the Lord will come as a thief in the night; in the which the heavens shall pass away with a great noise, and the elements shall melt with fervent heat, and the earth also and the works that are therein shall be burned up. Looking for and hasting unto the coming of the day of God, wherein the heavens being on fire shall be dissolved, and the elements shall melt with fervent heat? Nevertheless we, according to his promise, look for new heavens and a new earth, wherein dwelleth righteousness. (2 Pet. 3:12–13)

Looking at the first phrase in this passage, we find Peter talking about a physical situation: "The heavens shall pass away with a great noise." And yet in this physical description, the translators have assumed a metaphorical translation for the Greek word *parerchomai*, translating it "pass away" meaning "to perish" instead of its literal meaning "to pass by." What's wrong with its literal meaning?

The heavens shall pass by with a great noise. Put in the context of what we know of the judgments, this makes perfect sense. A heavenly body passing close to the earth, dropping debris from its tail in the form of exploding meteorites certainly would be noisy!

Now taking the second phrase of this verse, "And the elements shall melt with fervent heat," how else can this be translated in a more literal manner? The Greek word *idstoicherion*, translated "elements" in the King James Version, literally means "something orderly in arrangement, i.e., (by implication) a serial (basal, fundamental, initial) constituent."[186] Today we think the word *elements* refers to such matters as hydrogen or oxygen, but suppose the Spirit of God meant the basic arrangement of the tectonic plates of the earth's crust? Add to this thought the literal meaning of the Greek word *luo*, which does not mean "melt," as translated in the KJV but rather "loosen" or "dissolve." Putting these together, Peter may be saying something like: "The basic tectonic plates that make up the earth's surface will loosen with fervent heat."

The last phrase is, "And the earth also and the works that are therein shall be burned up." How can we match this with the two former phrases? Beginning with the Greek word for "earth," *ge*, we find its primary meaning is "soil." However, by extension, it may mean "a region or the solid part or the whole of the terrene globe (including the occupants of each application)." Ironically, the phrase "burned up" means literally "to burn down (to the ground)." The Greek word *katakoai* comes from *kaoi*, "to set fire to," and *kata* meaning "down." By selecting from these meanings that which best fits the judgments, we could say, "And the

---

[186] Strong's Concordance

soil also or the solid part or region (of said continental plates) and the works of the inhabitants therein will be burned down to the ground."

Looking at verse 12, we find we can translate it more specifically also. For the words "being on fire," we could put "the heavens glowing with the heat of fire" because this is what the Greek word *puroomai* means. The verse would then read: "Wherein the heavens glowing with the heat of fire shall be loosened or broken apart and their constituent parts melted down (*teko*) in fervent heat." Thus, the destruction described by Peter probably refers to the burning from inflammable falling naptha, the scraping continental plates causing volcanoes and volcanic intrusions and the fiery falling meteorites. Just as Peter said, most of the earth's surface will be new from the upheavals caused by the clash with the heavenly body.

Whole land masses sink, while others rise. New mountains form while others are carried into the sea (Ps. 46:2). The landscape is pockmarked by falling meteorites. Changes in the rotation of the earth cause whole continents to slide over the inner layers of the earth, bringing them to rest in new locations. This is especially to be expected when the geographical poles reverse themselves, and the earth turns upside down. They may even break apart at the plates, forming new seas or closing old ones. The earth will have to be remapped.

When the earth turns over, the animal kingdom that survives will be subjected to massive doses of radiation, as will people, because the magnetic network of the protective Van Allen belts will be broken up and reformed. This will probably affect a change in their genes. We know the lion's offspring will no longer eat meat but the luscious herbage that shall replenish the new earth.[187] There may even be some new species. (Who would dare to argue these are not created by God?) The life span of humans will increase.

Every detail of the destruction of the old earth has a planned end in the new. Hallelujah! Thus, the very thing that works destruction in the old earth will bring about a re-creation in the new earth.

Yes, Peter, we truly look forward to a new earth, and in the process, a new heaven. The new location of the earth's orbit and rotation will rearrange the stars as viewed from the earth's surface, making them appear in different positions. That which survives from the passing body will add to the new arrangement as it finds its place in the heavens. The sky, too, will have to be remapped. Therefore, we conclude that the doctrine of fire destroying the heavens and the earth after the millenium is based on a misunderstanding of the nature and magnitude of the physical judgments. Hitherto, we have not begun to imagine what mighty works God intends to display when He accomplishes His will and fulfills His Word. This truly is the missing message of Revelation.[188]

The Last Resurrection

> And I saw a great white throne, and him that sat on it, from whose face the earth and the heaven fled away; and there was found no place for them. (20:11)

The final judgment has come. The throne, the only object set in this scene, occupies the center. It would seem

---

[187] Isa. 65:25.

[188] *The Missing Message of Revelation, Natural Catastrophes Ordained By God* is the former title of this book in its first edition.

that God intends to emphasize the lordship of Jesus, who surely must be the one on the throne, since all judgment is committed to the Son. He alone has the keys to death and hell. Besides, Jesus said that every knee would bow to Him, declaring Him Lord. The look of condemnation registered on His face for evildoers repels heaven and earth by reason of incompatibility. Heaven and earth are already totally cleansed by His blood and, therefore, not under condemnation. Their escape will spare them from viewing His face in this attitude. The unsaved, on the other hand, will stand to face Him and further acknowledge Him Lord of all. The fear of God permeates the atmosphere around the throne. Dread hangs heavy as the unredeemed stand to receive their final doom, especially since they have already received a taste of hell while awaiting the judgment.

> And I saw the dead, small and great, stand before God; and the books were opened: and another book was opened, which is the book of life: and the dead were judged out of those things which were written in the books, according to their works. And the sea gave up the dead which were in it; and death and hell delivered up the dead which were in them; and they were judged every man according to their works. And death and hell [Hades] were cast into the lake of fire. This is the second death. And whosoever was not found written in the book of life was cast into the lake of fire. (20:12–15)

John marvels as he watches the small and the great stand before God. Equal at last, their standing among others is of no consequence now. The justice brought forth is based on the laws of God extant for the day in which they lived. The books are opened, revealing each person's life, all precisely kept. The book of life is open also as a double witness. None of their names appear there, but that offers a confirmation that these have refused God's grace. Now they must face the consequences and take the judgment themselves. The great man cannot bribe this judge nor can the small man offer excuses. The Judge levels them both on the charge of unbelief. The sentence will pronounce the punishment commensurate with the evils they have performed.

The Prisons of the Damned

The sea gave up the dead in it, as well as hades and death. This is curious, because we tend to think that all the unredeemed dead as being confined to hades (The KJV translates hades as hell). No doubt, these terms represent three different types of prisons for them where they are held until the judgment. They will enter hell, the eternal place of retribution, *after* the judgment.

We usually believe hades to be a place of burning and darkness located somewhere in the interior of the earth. Those who have seen glimpses beyond physical life, either by clinical death or by visions, seem to agree about this region. The children of the Adullam Rescue Mission in China were carried to hades in visions during an outpouring of the Holy Spirit. They all testified of the darkness and the burning with smoke.

Unsaved people who are revived from clinical-death experiences also see these fiery regions. Betty Malz tells of a man who called after seeing her testimony on television. (She had reported her death experience and subsequent visit to heaven). He disagreed with her about the existence of heaven, for his clinical death experience took him through caves of fire. He was still having nightmares about it.

Dr. Maurice Rawlings prayed for a man experiencing a trip to hell as he revived him several times during a heart attack. The patient cried out that he was burning in hell. After prayers of repentance and for salvation, he experienced heaven but in the end survived. From this incident, Dr. Rawlings began a research into the reality of spiritual existence after death. He has written a book, *Beyond Death's Door*, about his research on this subject.

Death may be a temporary prison for spirits who eventually drop into the darker regions. These spirits may be separated from their bodies but not yet established in their levels of existence to await the resurrection. Concerning this, the Indian Christian mystic Sahu Sundar Singh was told: "After death the soul of every human being will enter the world of spirits, and everyone according to the stage of his spiritual growth, will dwell with spirits like in mind and nature to himself, either in the darkness or in the light of glory."[189]

A numberless multitude have been killed because of the rebellion. They need not establish a plain of existence, since the judgment of the white throne follows immediately. Therefore, they are called out of death instead of hades.

The Sea and God's Judgment

An explanation of the sea being a prison for the dead may refer to the many people who have perished in the sea by divine judgment. First, we have the flood and its connection with the rebel angels. Then, we have Pharaoh and his army, strong rebels against God. Many wicked cities have perished suddenly by sinking beneath the sea.

---

[189] Sundar Singh, *Visions of Sundar Singh of India,* (Minneapolis: Anker G. Dahle, 1926) p. 10

Isaiah says the wicked are like a troubled sea. Great numbers will perish in the sea during the overturning of the earth. The great armies of Armageddon will perish in the inflowing waters of the Red Sea. This could explain why the sea is a prison because these people will not simply die; God will kill them in judgment. Will He keep them in a separate place? We don't know. Returning to the vision, we find that only death and hades are cast into the lake of fire spoken of as the second death. John does not mention the sea again.

Jesus told John in the beginning of the vision that He held the keys to death and hades. We deduce from this that He has the power to unlock the hold of death over those held therein. In other words, He is the resurrection and the life. This will empty the temporary prisons, since it will be the final judgment. His powerful keys will have already resurrected all others who were entitled to life.

John finishes the scene with this statement: "And whosoever [the same "whosoever" who could have come to Jesus or offered a faith sacrifice in the Old Testament] was not found written in the book of life was cast into the lake of fire" (v. 15).

Chapter 27

THE NEW JERUSALEM

(REVELATION 21)

Depression must have gripped John as he watched the unsaved dead receive their final judgment. His descriptive pen is almost stripped of detail as he tells about it in five short verses (20:11–15). It says something about John's nature—and God's—when he lavishly spends what amounts to thirty-five verses to tell of the blessedness of the saints in chapters Revelation 21 and 22. Looking now at this blessedness, may the Lord fill us with anticipation and deep gratitude at having escaped this final judgment through His mercy.

The New Heaven and the New Earth

> And I saw a new heaven and a new earth: for the first
> heaven and the first earth were passed away; and there
> was no more sea. (21:1)

The doom of the previous scene dissipates as the splendor of the new scene replaces it. John's despair vanishes. He views the renewed earth cleansed from the twenty-first century's rebellion, recovered from its chastisement, and relocated in its permanent position in the solar system. What a glorious place it is, too!

The earth had moved traumatically during the last trumpet and vial when Christ returned. We recall this moment, remembering Isaiah's words: "The earth is utterly broken down, the earth is clean dissolved, the earth is moved exceedingly. The earth shall reel to and fro like a drunkard, and shall be removed like a cottage; and the transgression thereof shall be heavy upon it; and it shall fall, and not rise again" (Isa. 24:19–20).

> Then the moon shall blush, and the sun shall be
> ashamed; for the LORD of hosts shall be king on Mt.
> Zion, and in Jerusalem His glory shall be before His el-
> ders. (Isa. 24:23 MLB)

Because of the many changes, the heavens have taken on a new look. The moon has been left a blushing pink from the red dust of the sixth seal. The light reflecting from its surface is no longer significant. People will never again sing songs about its silvery hue. Future generations may wonder about the color blindness of their ancients. They may say, as we do today about lost information, "Everybody knows the moon *has always* been pink."

Perhaps another factor in the moon's diminished light is the new location of the sun in respect to the earth. The sun, too, will be ashamed—because of distance? No longer the large bright orb adored by idolatrous people of the earth, the sun is greatly outshined by the glory of the reigning King. Therefore, the source of light comes from Him and not the sun, which is probably not as close to the earth as it once was. The starry heavens (if they can be seen at all), are different too, because of the new polar axis established when the earth fell, never to rise again.

However, the greatest change in the heavens will be the appearance of the city of God. John will describe the city in detail later, but we mention it here because of the tremendous influence its light has in making the heavens new. Suspended over the earth, it will light one hemisphere continuously so there will be no night. We know this because Jerusalem, surely located directly below, will never be without its light. No wonder the sun is ashamed and the moon blushes!

We have already covered much of the description of the new earth in the previous chapter; however, there is one point mentioned here by John we have not covered: he saw "no more sea." We could assume that he refers to the Mediterranean Sea, since it was the only great sea known to John personally. Yet we know from Ezekiel 47:20 that at least a portion of the Mediterranean remains since it forms the western border of the land during the millennium. Therefore, we must understand his statement to have a broader application.

No More Sea

John saw an overview of the earth several times in the course of his vision. Consequently, he must have become familiar with the general geography of it with its distribution of four-fifths water to one-fifth land mass. So when he viewed the new earth, the outstanding thing he noticed was the change in the proportion of land to water.

Redistribution and relocation of the land mass has occurred. In addition to the one hundred tons of space debris added to the earth in normal times, we will have additions from the judgment. Remember, the judgments have slightly increased the total mass of the earth. First, great numbers of meteorites fell in the sixth seal and the first trumpet along with their dust. These probably are insignificant, but then we have the mountainous chunk that fell into the sea during the second trumpet. More debris peppered one-third of the earth when the detonating meteor sprayed the rivers. Add to this the hundred-pound hail that fell in the seventh vial. All of this describes what fell in the vicinity of the Middle East. Who is to say that is all that fell on the earth.

However, the earth-changing mass that makes the most difference is the "star" of the fifth trumpet that penetrated the earth's crust. The shock waves from the impact may have weakened or even cracked some tectonic plates. The stress of the seventh trumpet, when the earth ran helter skelter off its orbit and rolled a quarter turn on its axis, could have fractured large continental plates and caused a more even distribution of land to water. This would have left large islands surrounded by smaller seas instead of huge continental divisions and even larger oceans.

The continents have been fractured before. Geologists now believe that the forerunner of our present continents was one super continent that they named Pangaea. They speculate that Pangaea originally was formed by isolated land masses "ramming together." (In times when the earth's motions are disturbed, the surface crust can fracture, and these blocks can move around.) Such individual blocks of crust are called *terranes*. Many locations today give evidence of relocated terranes which have jammed together to form a new unit. Pangaea, itself, has since split into the various continents that we now see and drifted apart during the last *"few million years,"* according to geologists.

Geologists already predict what the Bible says will be in the new earth in part, except they project it millions of years into the future. (Scientists need millions of years to accomplish these things because they expect everything to progress at its present speed. However, when God interrupts the natural processes and supercedes them, changes can occur very suddenly.) The continents we now see will fracture radically again, as they did in the past. The Bible makes reference to one such time when it says: "And unto Eber were born two sons: the name of one was Peleg; for in his days *was the earth divided*" (Gen. 10:25, emphasis added). *Peleg* means "division." The word for *earth* in this passage means "dry land."

Besides the breaking and spreading of continental plates to admit the invading oceans, new land masses may be forming. The Mid-Atlantic Ridge, a mountain range under the Atlantic Ocean between the continents, and similar underwater ranges in the Indian Ocean may have risen above the surface through the outpouring of lava generated in the earth's convulsions. The South Pacific and its "hot spots"[190] have probably also been generating new crust by pouring lava to the surface. Add to this, broken pieces of the North and South American continents that may crowd into the surface space now occupied by the Pacific Ocean. Hot spots under the oceans where the crust is thin will make new

---

[190] Hot spots are thin places in the crust where lava spasmodically invades the upper crust.

islands as lava cones surface. In such an upheaval (as bad as the one in Genesis 1:2),[191] all great oceans could become small connecting seas.

Of course, we can only speculate about these changes worldwide, but in the vicinity of the Middle East, the prophets of God spell it out specifically. Ezekiel tells us of a river which will flow from Jerusalem into the Dead Sea and will heal its waters (Ezek. 47:8). Isaiah tells us that Jerusalem at the time of the Messiah will become a place of broad rivers and streams[192] that is definitely not so today. Perhaps Jerusalem's raised plain will make for broad, shallow rivers. Isaiah also talks of the tongue of the Egyptian sea being destroyed.[193] Zechariah tells us that the Mount of Olives will split in half, forming a great valley reaching to the east (Zech. 14:4–5). All of these speak of changes in Jordan's Rift Valley.

Putting together a composite of these facts, we can deduce the overall picture. The healed waters of the Dead Sea that contain "the fish of the great sea" (Ezek. 47:10) can only mean one thing: it now has an outlet to the world's oceans. That means that all the land in the Jordan Valley or joining valleys that are below sea level will be filled with ocean water. (Though we lament the loss of these beautiful agricultural centers, we must remember that the entire earth during the millennium will become a well-watered garden.) The broad rivers of Jerusa-

---

[191] Jesus said that this upheaval will be greater than all upheavals since the beginning of the world. (The word translated *world* here means the whole world, in other words, since the creation. That means it will be greater than the flood, greater than the fall of the tower of Babel, greater than the exodus, and greater than the upheaval in the days of the prophets.

[192] Isa. 33:21.

[193] Isa. 11:15.

lem flow as a result of the newly opened fountains on the ridges (Ps. 65:9–10) to eventually gather in the many ravines that stretch eastward toward the Judean Desert. The invading sea will join them at sea level, skirting the plain some distance from where the city itself rests.

The destruction of the tongue of the Egyptian sea and the splitting of the Mount of Olives tell a broader story. Evidently, the effects of the last trumpet moved the huge crack under the Rift Valley exceedingly. It is entirely possible that the African plate has suddenly rotated away from the Arabian plate, widening the Rift Valley and shoving up more mountains against the European plate, at the same time raising some of the bottom of the Mediterranean Sea. As the Gulf of Aqaba widens, the Gulf of Suez closes, putting horizontal stress on the upper reaches of the Rift Valley because of the rotation. Although there is a known fault line already near Jerusalem, the great earthquake of the second woe (that will fell a tenth of the city) is bound to have weaken the area even more. Thus, the mountain range will snap at its weakest point, which happens to be the Mount of Olives. Farther away and yet part of this same picture, the horn of East Africa will tear away from the continent, opening the Red Sea and the Indian Ocean into the interior of Africa.

Besides this being a geologically active spot even now, Isaiah says that the headwaters of the Nile will be turned away, the river will dry up along its canals and even the sea to the north will dry up,[194] possibly because of the raised bottom of the Mediterranean. This may or may not be permanent. This means that Egypt, the spiritual symbol of the "world," may be as dependent on rain as the rest of the

---

[194] Isa. 19:5–6.

Middle East. It almost never rains in Egypt today. (Rain is the blessing of God. See Zech. 14:7–9) Presently, Egypt's sole dependence for existence is on the waters of the Nile River. So included in the broader picture of the revised waterways of the earth are the revised weather patterns.

The redistribution of the seas will change the weather so that the moisture rising into the atmosphere will be even. That will most likely eliminate deserts on the earth. Add to that the difference in the heat distribution. This will change the winds. The closer heavenly city will probably not emit the tremendous heat that boils off the sun, and if the sun is farther away, even the equator may become a temperate zone. In fact, the whole earth's weather may become more like the present temperate zones of the earth. The seasons will still exist but not in violent extremes.

Yes, it truly is a new earth. Isaiah says it best: "For, behold, I create new heavens and a new earth: and the former shall not be remembered, nor come into mind" (Isa. 65:17).

With the burnt and barren surface sporting jagged new mountains, roving seaways, rivers, fountains, and perhaps even new continents, the surface will renew itself and bear no resemblance to the old earth. Truly, it will become a lush green, populous paradise well able to support the generations to come.

The New Jerusalem

Returning now to the vision, John, unlike us, is not so impressed with the new earth. He merely states the fact and goes on to describe the outstanding feature of this new heaven and earth—the New Jerusalem. Perhaps for fear that the wonder of his description will not be believed, John phrases his next scene divider in the form of an oath. Then as he watches the city approach, the Lord speaks out of heaven:

> I, John, saw the holy city, new Jerusalem, coming down from God out of heaven, prepared as a bride adorned for her husband. And I heard a great voice out of heaven saying, Behold, the tabernacle of God is with men, and he will dwell with them, and they shall be his people, and God himself shall be with them, and be their God. And God shall wipe away all tears from their eyes; and there shall be no more death, neither sorrow, nor crying, neither shall there be any more pain: for the former things are passed away. And he that sat upon the throne said, Behold, I make all things new. (21:2–5)

John can plainly see the glory of the Bride, but God Himself has to reveal what makes her glorious. When the redeemed move into their new home with the Bridegroom; His eternal purpose is realized—to live with His people. His glory, shining out of their consummated union, causes John to wonder at its splendor. Separated from all earthly hindrances (sin and all its ramifications), the Bride revels in the fullness of joy found in His resident presence. This joy, which evidently translates into an adornment John can see, sparkles in its descent.

The Lord is so anxious that all the earth should enter into the blessedness of this relationship that He says to John:

> Write: for these words are true and faithful. And he said unto me, It is done. I am Alpha and Omega, the beginning and the end. I will give unto him that is athirst of the fountain of the water of life freely. He that overcometh shall inherit all things; and I will be his God, and he shall be my son. (21:6–7)

God has already accomplish all that is necessary for the new earth to enter into the joy of the Lord and the abundant life. The example of those who enter in is on display (those in the city). The gospel invitation extends to the unsaved generations to come. Will they receive the water of life so aptly pictured in the fountain pouring out from under the altar of the temple?[195] Or will they reject it? The gospel remains a choice, palatable only to the thirsty.

The rebellion of the last chapter shows that many will reject it. Therefore, mankind will face a consequence if they reject this spiritual water. The Lord goes on to say:

> But the fearful, and unbelieving, and the abominable, and murderers, and whoremongers, and sorcerers, and idolaters, and all liars, shall have *their part* in the lake which burneth with fire and brimstone: which is the second death. (21:8, emphasis added)

Of course, this is true for all ages, because the gospel never really changes and neither do the consequences of rejecting it. Nor does faith, the means to apprehend the gospel, change. The Old Testament saints looked forward to the fulfillment of God's promise of salvation in Christ. We of the Church look back. Nevertheless, both ages saw a measure of God's working in their own time, but these of the millennial age will be more accountable. They will have the *fulfillment* of God's prophetic Word charged to their accounts along with the ever-present evidence of the New Jerusalem. Even so, some will never lay hold of faith.

---

[195] Ezek. 47:1.

Looking at the list of rejections, we find they will represent varying degrees of sin. Furthermore, these varying degrees of sin occupy their own part in the lake of fire. No doubt, unbelievers of all ages are included. The Lord files each condemned person according to the degree and category of sin, because the sins mentioned are common to every age. Besides, they seem to increase in degradation as the list progresses.

The first category, the fearful, are those timid souls who fail to make decisions for Christ. They are never quite sure of anything, so they neglect to exercise faith. In their world of self-protection and self-sufficiency, they simply ignore God.

The second group, the unbelievers, go a step further. They have made definite choices. They decided against Christ in favor of the world. They are guilty of greater sin than the fearful.

The abominable are yet a step lower than the unbelieving. They are not content with unbelief but provoke and ridicule the faithful. These scorners take pleasure in persecuting Christians, whether by words or deeds. Jesus pointed out the seriousness of this when He said it was better for a man to be thrown into the sea with a millstone tied to his neck than to offend one of His little ones (Matt. 18:6).

The murderers categorize those whose lives are taken over by anger, bitterness, and resentment. Jesus opened His kingdom laws by cautioning His disciples against the effects of anger (Matt. 5:21-26). Anger unchecked leads to murder. Murder far exceeds ridicule. This is the first of the five commandments regarding our fellowmen. It was, also, the first sin committed by man against man. Cain was a murderer.

Whoremongers, the next category, express the ultimate depth of degradation in moral impurity. The word itself taken from the Greek word *pornos* comes from the same root as "pornography." It means male prostitution. Other sins leading to this part of hell probably include fornication, adultery, harlotry, and other acts originating in lust. Jesus warned of this danger with His law covering moral impurity (Matt. 5:27-30).

The sorcerers, *pharmakos* in the Greek, means those devoted to the magical arts—especially those who use drugs, potions, spells, enchantments, or who traffic in the spirit world. All dealings of the occult characterize this group of sinners.

Idolaters worship other gods and fall before images for the purpose of gain. They appeased the demon spirits in the idols for the sake of prosperity and fertility (gain). That is why the New Testament continually equates covetousness and greed with idolatry. The kingdom law exhorted, "Seek ye first the kingdom of God, and his righteousness; and all these things shall be added unto you" (Matt. 6:33); but the "lust of the eyes" consumes idolaters. Therefore, all extortion and thieving for gain also fall under this category.

Lastly, we come to liars. This includes all fakes, bearers of false witness, teachers of false doctrines, and (by implication) all hypocrites—the worst of the lot. Hypocrites make a pretense of being good people, elevating themselves in pride while indulging in all manner of evil secretly. Jesus called them a generation of vipers.

Looking closer at this compartment for liars in the lake of fire, we find that Jesus confirmed its existence. In reference to the evil servant of Matthew 24:48 who was appointed ruler over His household (the Church), Jesus says He will "appoint him his portion with the hypocrites." The Greek word *meros* translated "portion" in this parable is the same word translated "part" in Revelation. It is the same place as the "part" for all liars.

Having obeyed the voice to write what he heard, John turns his attention back to the glorious city still descending from heaven.

> And there came unto me one of the seven angels which had the seven vials full of the seven last plagues, and talked with me, saying, Come hither, I will shew thee the bride, the Lamb's wife. (21:9)

Again, the angel advises John as one who already knew the plans of God. This is the second time one of the messengers having the seven last vials shows John a city. Whereas the first messenger showed him the whore that was a city, this messenger shows John the pure chaste Bride, also a city. When John tries to worship this same "angel" in the next chapter, the messenger describes himself as a "fellowservant, and of thy brethren the prophets." Since he was a brother of John and of the contemporary prophets, this refers to the Church. He further says that he was "of them which keep the sayings of this book" (22:9). The Father gave the Book of Revelation only to the Church, not to heavenly beings. Therefore, this messenger is a saint who has been blessed by reading, hearing, and keeping the words of God's final Revelation. Who else among the saints knows God's plans but those who study this book? Who else will understand what God asks them to do? This messenger also uses the power gifts of the Holy Spirit, because he speaks forth the word of Christ in prophecy.

Earlier in the vision, John tried to worship another of the seven messengers (Rev. 19:10). His words also were, "See thou do it not: I am thy fellowservant, and *of thy brethren* that have the testimony of Jesus: worship God: for the testimony of Jesus is the spirit of prophecy" (19:10, emphasis added). Thus, we have further proof that saints will dispense judgment and know God's revealed plans. This knowledge not only brings joy to their hearts but also much blessing. The blessing comes from participating in the judgment. Jesus had entrusted to this particular "angel" the responsibility of pouring out one of the seven plagues and its vial of wrath.

Returning now to the vision with the invitation, the angel carries John from his vantage point (probably from outer space, since he could see both an overview of the new earth and heaven as well) to a great high mountain, presumably on the new earth.

The angel shows him a scene whose placement in events falls much earlier. Even though John has just seen the judgment of the unsaved dead that follows the millennium, the city had come down to hover over the earth at the beginning of the thousand-year reign. We know this because Isaiah speaks of the light from the Lord as already functioning in the millennial age (Isa. 60:19–20). Because this light originates in the city, John sees the descent in a flashback just as he has many other events during the viewing of the Revelation. By placing the city's description here, God effectively ends the vision on a positive note, saving the best for last.

The Physical Description of the City

The city is slowly moving down through space. It descends from another plane. (Those who have visited heaven always speak of passing through the starry heavens before reaching the third heaven where God resides.) John watches the glorious descent, fascinated with the sparkling light display. He had seen the light before. The same jasper light that surrounded the Father at the throne bursts forth from the jeweled city, clear as crystal, flashing a light yellow green.

As it came closer, John is able to distinguish the city's shape. John's "angelic" companion, who had a golden reed, measured the length, breadth, and height of it. They were equal—all twelve thousand furlongs (1,500 miles). But we cannot tell if the height was measured from the edge of the city or the center. Because of this, interpreters differ over the shape of the city, whether it will form a cube or a pyramid. Some believe the Holy of Holies, being a cube, describes the dwelling place of God. Others argue that the picture of the Church as a spiritual temple resting upon a foundation of prophets and apostles and topped with the capstone of Christ fits a pyramid rather than a cube.

Testimony corroborates the latter view. Both Marvin Ford and the Adullam Orphanage[196] children saw the city as actually three cities, one suspended above another, in a pyramidal shape. According to their testimony, each ascending city appeared smaller than the one below, with the throne in the top city. Each level of ascendancy was more glorious than the one beneath.

Looking now at the size of the city, we find we can compare it to the size of our moon. If the shape will be pyramidal, the combined size of "the three cities in one" would be between $1/3$ to $1/2$ the size of the moon, which is 2,160 miles in diameter. If the moon were set upon the surface of the earth, it would reach from San Francisco to Cleveland.

If the city happens to be a cube set inside the dimensions of a cubed moon, it would look something like this:

---

[196] Though the Adullam children had their glimpse of heaven in the early 1900s, Marvin Ford testifies he saw the same thing in the early 1970s.

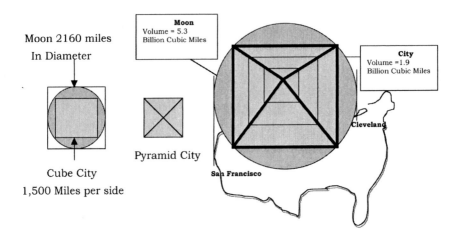

Moon 2160 miles In Diameter

Moon
Volume = 5.3
Billion Cubic Miles

City
Volume =1.9
Billion Cubic Miles

Cube City
1,500 Miles per side

Pyramid City

Cleveland

San Francisco

Seen at close range, it will appear very large—so large that it can never rest on the earth, whatever its shape. Fifteen hundred miles would be the distance from New York City to Bismarck, North Dakota, and again as high. The height may cause a problem. (Mount Everest is just 5.5 miles high.) A mass reaching 1,500 miles high on the earth's surface might disrupt the earth's balance, causing a wobble in rotation. In addition, its ground level alone would obliterate the land area of Israel. In the last chapter, we looked at the permanent changes around Jerusalem. They could not be if the city will be located there. Also, since the nations of the saved will walk in its light (Rev. 21:24), surely it will shine from overhead.

The city has a wall, great and high and entered by gates. John counted twelve gates, each with its own angelic guard. The gates have titles just as old Jerusalem's gates. Their names are the same as those of the sons of Jacob—the nation Israel—through whom came the one who said, "I am the door." Symbolically, this states that salvation is of the Jews. Three gates open on the east side; three on the north; three, on the south and three, on the west; thus the wall can be penetrated from all directions, speaking of universal access. "Whosoeverwill" can come from any direction. The only prerequisite, to enter each person must come through Christ.

The angel measured the wall to be 144 cubits (216 ft. to 289 ft., depending on which cubit measure[197] was intended). John does not say whether this refers to the height or width of it. However, he did say that the city has a wall great and high. It is doubtful if 216 feet would be considered high since the city is so tall. Still he may be speaking of it compared to a man standing at ground level. In that case, it would compare to the height of a sixteen-to-twenty-story building, again depending upon the size of the cubit. Such tall walls would require great thickness just to stand up. Ancient Babylon's walls were reported to be over 200 feet high and 86 feet thick.

Spiritually speaking, 144, the square of twelve, speaks of perfect authority or administration. Thus, it speaks of the law of righteousness that surrounds the city.

The great walls rest on twelve stones. We are not told how large they are, but they must be considerable to even be noticed under such great walls. We doubt if they are supportive since the city is most likely suspended in space. Therefore, their only apparent purpose is adornment and instruction. Remember, the Church is built on a foundation of the apostles and prophets. Therefore, the names of the twelve apostles are written on the stones.

Also, the foundation stones are garnished with precious and semiprecious stones. Recall the shining stones and glowing

---

[197] Cubit = 18" to 20.65"

colors John saw at the throne. If those stones conveyed underlying truth, perhaps these do, too. Therefore, their purpose could be more than just decoration. The description of the millennial Jerusalem on earth suggests a clue.

> O thou afflicted, tossed with tempest, and not comforted, behold, 1 will lay thy stones with fair colours, and lay thy foundations with sapphires. And I will make thy windows of agates, and thy gates of carbuncles, and all thy borders of pleasant stones. And all thy children shall be taught of the LORD; and great shall be the peace of thy children. In righteousness shalt thou be established: thou shalt be far from oppression; for thou shalt not fear: and from terror; for it shall not come near thee. Behold, they shall surely gather together, but not by me: whosoever shall gather together against thee shall fall for thy sake. Behold, I have created the smith that bloweth the coals in the fire, and that bringeth forth an instrument for his work; and I have created the waster to destroy. No weapon that is formed against thee shall prosper. (Isa. 54:11–17)

After writing about the glorious stones that will adorn the foundations and borders of Israel during the time of her restoration, the prophet draws a seemingly unrelated conclusion. He seems to say that because of the stones, the children will be taught of the Lord and live in peace and safety. On the other hand, it may be that the two are related.

Perhaps these fair stones, besides being ornamental, use light to communicate instruction to the redeemed as well as to provide protection. Knowing the value of crystals in communication today, this is not really too far out. Even in ancient days, God used the urim and thumin ("lights" and "perfections") to communicate with the children of Israel in the wilderness. Many believe that the urim and thumin referred to the stones set in the high priest's breastplate.

In Psalm 36, the psalmist says: "For with thee is the fountain of life: *in thy light shall we see light*" (Ps. 36:9, emphasis added). In His light is their instruction. And again in Psalm 37: "And he shall bring forth thy righteousness as the light, and thy judgment as the noonday" (Ps. 37:6).

Using light as a vehicle to carry out law and justice in the kingdom may be referred to in an earlier passage of Isaiah.

> For the LORD shall comfort Zion: he will comfort all her waste places; and he will make her wilderness like Eden, and her desert like the garden of the LORD; joy and gladness shall be found therein, thanksgiving, and the voice of melody. Hearken unto me, my people; and give ear unto me, O my nation: for a law shall proceed from me, and I will make *my judgment to rest for a light of the people*. (Isa. 51:3–4, emphasis added)

In telling the Jewish witnesses (the 144,000) His plans for Israel's restoration; God mentions that His law and judgment become "a light of the people." We know that the preceding verse is to be taken literally because we have already seen that the Judean desert will abound with broad rivers. It is not hard to imagine the rolling hills becoming like Eden. Therefore, we are dealing with a literal blessing here. Why should we see the "light" of the law as a spiritual simile only? It may literally transmit judgment or even punishment against Israel's would-be enemies.

Furthermore, besides power to transmit the law as "light," the power may also destroy as a weapon. In 1960, man made his first laser, using a synthetic ruby crystal to excite light and direct it with intense force. Great laser-type beams are the weapons of the future. Even today, we hear talk of concentrating waves, light, or other electromagnetic waves and directing them against an enemy. This might well be the purpose of the pleasant stones on Israel's borders, rather than embellishment—especially if the power source originates in the heavenly city. Could this be the source of the fire that falls on the last rebellion?

Looking back at the heavenly city, we may be able to ascribe the same significance here. If the foundation stones of the wall are communicative and protective, they are the ultimate in satellite communication. It might even explain why the city sparkles so because light waves are continuously emitted.

Jesus told the twelve apostles they would sit on twelve thrones judging Israel. Since the names of the apostles are engraved on the foundation stones, there may be a connection. Although the stones are located in the heavenly city, they may transmit decisions to earth via light beams. Of course, this is speculative, but all too often we do not take God as literally as we should.

Nevertheless, walls are for separation as well as protection. Jesus tells John after the description of the city

> Happy is he who has washed his robes so he can have a right to the tree of life and may enter through the gates into the city, because outside are dogs ["apostates," 2 Pet. 2:21–22], sorcerers, whoremongers, murderers, idolaters, and hypocrites. (Rev. 22:14–15, my paraphrase)

Sin still prevails in the hearts of those shut up in the outer darkness, but the city is a fortress of righteousness. Those who enter here are separate forever from the presence of sin and all its consequences. The principles of the separation are laid down by the teaching of the apostles, hence, another reason for their names being on the stones. All sound doctrine teaches that sinners are separated from God. Walls around God are protective because entering His holy presence without first dealing with the sin question means certain death.

Seen as a type, the teachings of the apostles hold up the wall and the gates, making the only way into God's presence through Jesus, who is "the door."

Leaving the wall, John describes the gates. The twelve gates are twelve pearls: each gate is one pearl. When Marvin Ford was carried over the city during his death experience, he estimated the round pearlized gates to be about a hundred miles in diameter. We would think this a bit thick for a gate, especially since the walls may not be more than 200 feet thick themselves. This seeming discrepancy, however, adds more to the description of the gates.

Once again, we look to the millennial pattern on earth for our clue. Although their shape is different, a tunnel-like structure instead of a sphere, the gates to the millennial temple measure from 37–43 feet wide by 75–86 feet deep (depending upon the size of the cubit used). On entering the temple, one will have a distance to go and six gatekeepers (three on each side) to pass before he emerges into the outer courtyard. These may well be diminutive copies of the gates in the heavenly city because they both serve the same purpose. They will bring the redeemed into the presence of God.

Besides that, we know the gates in the other temples were not deep like these. So if they are alike, then the heavenly city gates will be much deeper than 216-foot deep walls. Of course, Marvin Ford only guessed at the size of the pearly gates, but for the sake of figuring, let us say he was right. Using these figures, it would be possible to cut a tunnel through the giant pearl as large as eighty miles through and again that high. With such an enormous opening, we might have provision for a space vehicle shuttle port to transport government officials back and forth to earth.[198] A large port would be necessary to accommodate the flow of traffic, both of men and angels, from a mere three openings per side. If the gates were located equidistant from each other, they would still be 500 miles from center to center.

The spiritual picture portrayed in the gates is that of the "pearl of great price." Surely, no other pearls in the universe can equal these gates. Thus, we have a clear picture of the man who sold all that he had to purchase this great pearl. As this pearl represents the entrance to *the kingdom of God,* what he has purchased is the right to enter directly into the city. This shows, by type, that entering into the kingdom of God is not a momentary passing but an extended effort on the part of the believer. While salvation is acquired in a moment by faith, entering into the kingdom requires passing through a period of restricting the flesh (the narrow way) before one comes under the full government of the King.

Stretching inward like an enclosed mall whose sides, ceiling, and floor gleam with pearly light, the passageway opens directly to the main street of the city. With such a difference between the gate and the wall, it might pass through the outer rim of the city in order to reach the street directly, especially if the gate is several miles deep. This would be the region where the unrewarded saints live. We say this because

---

[198] Space vehicles will be unnecessary for resurrected saints or angels, but the kings of the earth may not all be the resurrected Church but also include saved mortals in these position as the population increases.

of Jesus's words to John: "Blessed are they that do his commandments, that they might have right to the tree of life and may enter in through the gates into the city" (22:14).

Remember, the overcomers' reward for the Ephesian church was the right "to eat of the tree of life, which is in the midst of the paradise of God" (2:7). These trees grow along the city's main streets (22:2). Of course, the possibility exists that the gates provide access to both the outer region and the central section. Perhaps this is why an angelic guard is stationed at each gate to direct traffic according to rights. Another reason for the angels could be that the base of the city is accessible to the redeemed on earth, not for residency but to conduct official business. The kings that represent the nations bring their "glory and honour" into the city (21:24–27).

Looking into the city, John says, "The street of the city was pure gold, as it were transparent glass" (21:21). John first viewed the city from a point outside as it descended from above. As it approached, the walls and foundations came into view first. Now he appears to be ascending over the city where he can see the streets. His first glimpse of the city from a distance had been the sparkling light. Seeing the light pass right through the solid gold streets caused him to look for the source of the light. John had seen Jesus glorified on the Mount of Transfiguration. He was also familiar with the Old Testament history of the Shekinah glory dwelling in the Holy of Holies in the tabernacle and temple. Naturally, he looks for the temple to be the source of light. But after looking the entire city over, he comes to this conclusion: All of it is equally lighted by God and the Lamb; therefore, their very presence in the city takes the place of a temple.

Gone from view is the temple John saw earlier in the vision from which the vial judgments were dispensed. It has been replaced by this beautiful city with room for all the redeemed to dwell with their God. Remember the great proclamation, "Behold, the tabernacle of God is with men!" (21:3) The whole city is a temple. The whole city is the Bride, with foundations of the apostles and the capstone of Christ.

Looking back to the nature of the street, John does not say it was gold surfaced with glass[199] but pure gold with light passing through it. The nature of gold has not changed, but the light passing through it has more power. The Shekinah glory of God lightens every millimeter of the city, right down to the spaces between the molecules.

Here we make a deductive observation: This city is not something that can be seen only on a spiritual plane. People can see it from earth or at least its light. Also, kings of earth can enter it. Saints from the city commute back and forth to their posts. Therefore, it is a hybrid—a cross between heaven and earth. It is a cross between the natural and the spiritual, the material and the etherial. In that sense, it is like the resurrected Christ who was truly man and truly God, truly human and truly divine and in possession of all power, the natural and the spiritual. The saints who have been made like Him in resurrection are also a cross between the two worlds. They can go back and forth from the city to the earth and fit in comfortably in both worlds.

The city provides a complete blend of God meeting and fellowshiping with people—God living with people between heaven and earth. Therefore, the pattern of the former tabernacles carries through in the city, since they

---

[199] Those who have walked these streets in visions say that the surface is not hard like glass but soft like carpet.

were but foreshadows of God's eternal purpose—to tabernacle with His people.

The throne of God has come to rest in it with all of its authority. However, the ark, its type, has disappeared forever. A temple is unnecessary because temples are places to meet with and worship God. Christ is at home, in residence. He will receive worship as the Bridegroom. Worshipers will have no need to go anywhere. His people will live with Him in constant communion and worship in His presence, for the whole city will be a temple. The Lord God Almighty will fill the whole of it with His glory! There we shall literally "walk in the light, as he is in the light" (1 John 1:7).

The streets, then, will mostly be for fellowship rather than travel. Those who have seen heaven tell us that travel is instant with no time involved. If we want to be at a certain place, we will be there instantly. The streets and paths will be for leisurely strolling with Christ or fellow believers.

The Light of the World

> And the city had no need of the sun, neither of the moon, to shine in it: for the glory of God did lighten it, and the Lamb is the light thereof. And the nations of them which are saved shall walk in the light of it. (21:23–24)

Light will fill the whole city so completely that neither the light of the sun nor the moon will be discernable. These will not be done away, however, because they represent proof that God is keeping His covenant with Israel.

> Thus saith the LORD, which giveth the sun for a light by day, and the ordinances of the moon and of the stars for a light by night . . . .If those ordinances depart from before

521

me, saith the LORD, then the seed of Israel also shall cease
from being a nation before me for ever. (Jer. 31:35–36)

Again, in Genesis, we are told: "While the earth
remaineth, seedtime and harvest, and cold and heat, and
summer and winter, and day and night shall not cease" (Gen.
8:22). From the conditions of God's promise, we see that
the change in the earth's position will not have eliminated
the seasons. Therefore, the earth will remain tilted at an
angle to the sun.

Nor will it have eliminated the rotation, because night
and day still exist, at least in part of the earth. The nations of
the saved, however, will be exempt from night, walking continually in the light of the city. Isaiah confirms this. He says:

The sun shall be no more thy light by day; neither for
brightness shall the moon give light unto thee: but the
LORD shall be unto thee an everlasting light, and thy
God thy glory. Thy sun shall no more go down; neither
shall thy moon withdraw itself: for the LORD shall be
thine everlasting light. (Isa. 60:19–20)

Since the earthly Jerusalem will constantly be bathed in
God's light, it is always in view of the heavenly city. Three
possibilities present themselves in order for this to be true.

One, the earth will revolve around the city with the same
face always turned toward the city, like the moon which
turns the same face to the earth or the planet Venus which
always turns the same side toward the sun.

Two, the city will revolve around the earth at a point in
space (22,300 miles out) called by scientists geostationary,
which will allow the satellite to match the earth's speed of
rotation. Hence, the heavenly city will remain stationary

over earthly Jerusalem. This second possibility, by defining the distance involved, will mean that the city, a third of the size of the moon or larger, will be eleven times closer than the present moon.

Three, the earth will turn that quarter turn on its axis, and the earthly Jerusalem will be the north pole with the New Jerusalem revolving above it and traveling with the earth around the sun.

We tend to favor the latter because of the connection the "north parts" has with the throne of God. Lucifer tried to sit on the mount in "the sides of the north" (Isa. 14:13). Ezekiel saw the great whirlwind cloud of the glory of God come out of the north (Ezek. 1:4). Judgment armies were always sent from the north.

If the city will be located over the north pole, the natural ordinances will continue as usual. The city will turn at the same rate as the earth, and the gates on the four sides will always face the same direction. Day and night will go on undisturbed in the southern hemisphere. The western hemisphere, which has basked in gospel light for years, will end up underneath as the hemisphere subject to night, hidden from the supernatural light. Isaiah says that messages will have to be sent to some in the kingdom who have not seen the glory of God that they may come and see (Isa. 66:18–19). Therefore, a place will exist where the city cannot be observed.

Coming to Jerusalem in its glorious light will be a requirement in the millennium. Isaiah says that *all flesh will come* from new moon to new moon and from Sabbath to Sabbath to worship in Jerusalem and behold God's glory (Isa. 66:23). All will come to the light, the expression of His glory! Just think what that shows in the advancement of transportation.

Light seems to be the single most important subject of Revelation 21. John's first glimpse of the heavenly city was this light. Now at the end of the chapter, we find that the nations of the redeemed will walk in the light of the glory of God and bring their glory into it as well.

> And the nations of them which are saved shall walk in the light of it: and the kings of the earth *do bring their glory and honour* into it. And the gates of it shall not be shut at all by day: for there shall be no night there. (21:24–26, emphasis added)

The gates will remain open because of the constant stream of activity between the heavenly city and the earth, a regular Jacob's ladder. Divinely appointed rulers will bring God's "glory" into the city, glory that they have worked out in their lives. Revelation 22 speaks of the Lord giving His servants light "and they shall reign for ever and ever" (22:5). Therefore, the glory and the authority that they have will manifest itself visibly as light in the heavenly city. All who possess this light may enter. By contrast: "And there shall in no wise enter into it anything that defileth, neither whatsoever worketh abomination, or maketh a lie: but they which are written in the Lamb's book of life" (21:27).

Those who foster evil cannot enter, not even under the cover of night. Earthly gates shut to protect against nighttime marauders. Without the cover of night, no cloak for evil exists. Therefore, the works of darkness will have no hiding place in the city. Light, which manifests truth, makes no provision for lies or evil.

The lampstand of His perfect light will fully manifest itself in this final tabernacle. No longer confined to the throne, it will fill the entire city, clothe its subjects, and reach beyond to the nations on earth. Jesus is the light of the world!

Chapter 28

THE LIVING WATERS

(REVELATION 22)

After finishing the discussion on the light, the darkness, and who may enter the city of light, the angel takes John up to the throne and shows him the other outstanding feature of the city—the water.

The Living Water

And he shewed me a pure river of water of life, clear as crystal, proceeding out of the throne of God and of the Lamb. In the midst of the street of it, and on either side of the river, was there the tree of life, which bare twelve manner of fruits, and yielded her fruit every month: and the leaves of the tree were for the healing of the nations. And there shall be no more curse: but the throne of God and of the Lamb shall be in it. (22:1–3)

The river of life reveals the presence of the third member of the trinity. In His Almighty power, God the Father thunders orders from the throne; God the Son shines forth the effulgence[200] of that power at the throne; but God the Holy Spirit flows from the throne carrying the means to translate that energy into eternal life forever and ever. Water in the natural is the carrier for all the essentials of life. The Bible as the Word of God is solid and tangible, but the truth it contains is fluid, cleansing away the curse and bringing life in its place. This pure water originating in the Spirit brings forth just that—pure uncorrupted life.

The Replaced Altar of Incense

The river, the street, and the trees will replace the old shadow of the altar of incense in the new tabernacle. In the first tabernacle, this altar and its censor typified Christ's work as the mediator High Priest who interceded on behalf of His people before the Father in heaven, while the Spirit interceded on earth (Rom. 8:26).

In our eternal state, we no longer will need a mediator (being in God's presence all the time), the altar of incense—an intermediate means of communication with God—will not be necessary. Formerly, it anticipated Christ's work through the Spirit in the Church and later in redeemed Israel. The Spirit began this work in us when "the truth," as waters of life (a *rhema* from God), convicted us and after we repented and believed brought about our spiritual rebirth. As we continued to receive the truth of His Word, a river collected and began to flow out of our innermost beings. It was the mighty Spirit ministering life to those around us.

---

[200] Heb. 1:3

Nevertheless, the flow only continued by staying in "the way." This way was searched out by prayer as we learned to walk in God's will by faith. We became "trees of righteousness, the planting of the LORD" (Isa. 61:3) as we drew life from these waters and produced the fruit of the Spirit. Christ became "the way, the truth and the life" (John 14:6) to us as we approached the throne of grace for all our needs.

Now the fact of this work is on permanent display. In this final tabernacle, "the way" is a beautiful street that begins at each gate and ultimately leads to the throne. "The truth" is a crystal clear river of the water of life flowing from the throne and supplying gardens on every level as it flows in the middle of the divided street. "The life" is in the tree of life, multiplied many times over from the one in the original garden on earth. The city, Christ's well-beloved, His Bride, will be a "garden enclosed,"[201] yielding "pleasant fruits" for the taste of the Bridegroom. In short, the Bride will be a delight to her husband, His glory (revealed in her) will be her dowry to Him. Thus, the design of the city shows that the culmination of Christ's work as intercessor is a Bride adorned by her fruitful "ways."

The Ark of the Covenant

We equated the ark in the former tabernacles to the throne, the dwelling place of God the Father. The ark, with its limited access, was hidden behind the veil and surrounded by cherubim. Its inaccessibility portrayed the holiness of God. The veil and cherubim protected His unholy people from destruction, by keeping them out of range. Jesus

---

[201] Song of Sol. 4:12–16.

opened "the way" to the throne and the Father's presence by sprinkling the blood on the mercy seat.

The mercy seat was the lid to the box (*ark* means "box"). Originally,[202] in the ark were three marvelous types: 1) the righteousness of God as revealed by the tablets; 2) the power to resurrect the dead as seen in Aaron's dead rod that sprouted; and 3) the bread sent from heaven as seen in the pot of hidden manna. After His blood was sprinkled on the heavenly mercy seat, Christ became all these things to the Church. The design of the city portrays this by showing the throne to be the source of the living waters, life-giving power found in Him who is "the resurrection and the life."

The message of Romans 6 demonstrates that these waters are filled with resurrection power. Paul said that when we were baptized into Jesus' death, we were buried in Him (v. 3). Though we were submerged in ordinary water, it typified this river of resurrection life. Paul says that we came out of these waters to walk in "newness of life" found in the resurrection (vv. 4–5). He further says that we reckon ourselves dead to sin (v. 11) by obeying the doctrine (v. 17, the truth of the river?). In doing so, we became servants of God, yielding fruit unto holiness (the trees of life drawing from the river to produce the fruit of the Spirit?) and, in the end, life everlasting (v. 22). Having looked at the spiritual types found in the crystal river, let us turn now and look at its natural and tangible delights as found in its productivity.

The Trees of Life

Innumerable trees line both sides of the river inside the divided street. These trees produce fruit perpetually because

---

[202] Later in history, only the tablets remained inside.

of the constant water supply. Since the city is pure crystal-line gold, the nutrients for the trees are wholly in the water, bypassing the need for soil. The whole city is like a gigantic hydroponic greenhouse without the possibility of blight or disease, since the curse has been eliminated. Hydroponic greenhouses on earth need constant maintenance to keep viruses and plant diseases under control. Soil and insects must be eliminated, as these are the sources of disease. How-ever, in the New Jerusalem, disease will not exist because of the purity and power of the water. The beauty of plants, grown to perfection, will delight the eyes. The trees will produce twelve crops of fruit, a different crop each month, perhaps even different varieties.

The monthly fruits will mark time on the calendar of the New Jerusalem and the city below. With a continuous day, it would be difficult to keep track, otherwise. If one needs to know what month it is, he may check the fruit and see what is in season.

Although the fruit will provide food, the leaves will be "for the healing of the nations." Since those who live in the city will have no need of healing because sorrow, crying, and pain have been eliminated, the healing will be for those on earth. In fact, Ezekiel tells us that these same trees will grow on earth and line the sides of the river flowing from the temple.

> Now when I had returned, behold, at the bank of the river were very many trees on the one side and on the other. . . . And by the river upon the bank thereof, on this side and on that side, shall grow all trees for meat, whose leaf shall not fade, neither shall the fruit thereof be consumed: it shall bring forth new fruit according to his months, because their waters they issued out of the

> sanctuary: and the fruit thereof shall be for meat, and
> the leaf thereof for medicine. (Ezek. 47:7, 12)

Healthy, non-fading (evergreen) leaves will provide an eternal remedy for ill health. They are perpetually available. Like the fruit, people cannot use them up. The one condition seems to be their location. They will only be available in the middle of "the way" along the river of life. This is a spiritual picture; nevertheless, it will work out in reality on earth.

The nations need healing for a reason. Sickness, at this time, can only come as a result of disobedience[203] (being out of "the way"). Nations that refuse to come up to the Feast of Tabernacles will display an open affront to God. As a result, the blessing of water (rain) will be withheld. Those of the Bride in charge of nations, who will also have power over the weather, will cut it off at a first offense. If the nations persist, however, a plague will develop in their people. Restoration, pictured in the leaves, will come when they repent and come back to "the way."

The Waters Cleanse Away the Curse

> And there shall be no more curse: but the throne of God
> and of the Lamb shall be in it. (22:3)

Another aspect of the river will be the "washing of water by the word" (Eph. 5:26). Yes, the curse will end, but this will not alleviate the authority of the throne over nature. Rather, it will enforce the authority; because the rest of the verse following the "but" says "the throne of God

---

[203] Zech. 14:17–19.

and of the Lamb shall be *in it.*" "It" refers to the subject of this discussion, the river. Earlier, John spoke of the street of it, also referring to the river. (All the "its" at the end of chapter 21 refer to the city.) Therefore, life-giving words filled with authority will flow from the throne and carry with them the responsibility of conforming to God's standards. Thus, the cleansing power of the water will come from the authority in it.

Being out of "the way" brought the curse in the first place. Adam and Eve were thrust out of the garden after their disobedience. As long as the waters from the fountains flowed past the tree of life and they walked in God's instruction, all went well; but when they turned from God's authority and yielded to another, the curse overtook them.

The same was true of Israel. Moses gave them a choice of blessing or cursing, according to whether they would obey God's words. Later, Moses sang it to them in the form of a song:

> Give ear, O ye heavens, and I will speak; and hear, O earth, the words of my mouth. My doctrine shall drop as the rain, my speech shall distil as the dew, as the small rain upon the tender herb, and as the showers upon the grass. (Deut. 32:1–2)

The words of the Lord's mouth came forth to the earth as the water of life, the same water Jesus offered the woman at the well. The water was available in Moses' day, Jesus' day, and on through history into the millennium. In the new earth, God pictures the restoration of these powerful waters in the natural realm by healing the Dead Sea, where the "healed" waters will bring forth life to the whole earth (Ezek. 47:8–9).

In the pure atmosphere of the New Jerusalem, living water will pour out of the crystal sea (the cleansing laver and sea of brass in the former tabernacles) on which the throne rests. From there, it will wind through the city like a sprawling vine, carrying the life force to fruit-producing trees. This shows the power of God's Word to cleanse from the curse and to reproduce the fruit of the Spirit. Thus, we have displayed yet another aspect of the water, showing Christ's work as the vine, replacing the cleansing power of the Old Testament laver.

The Showbread of the Heavenly City

> And his servants shall serve him: and they shall see his face; and his name shall be in their foreheads. (22:3–4)

With the authority of God's name written on their foreheads, believers will serve Him. This will constitute fellowship, communion, and authority—face-to-face with God the Father in complete oneness. One with the Father, one with the Son, and one with each other in the unity of the Spirit, they will express the power in this unity—the showbread of His presence in His people.

Unity with Himself and the Father was something Jesus promised His disciples. In John 14, Jesus told Philip that to see Him (Jesus) was to see the Father, because the Father was in Him. He further promised that "because I live, ye shall live also. At that day ye shall know that I am in my Father, and ye in me, and I in you" (John 14:19–20). Jesus was talking about the union that takes place when communing with Him. Partaking of one bread makes us all one loaf in Him. Jesus said this in regard to preparing a place in His Father's house for them. The function of the showbread in the old tabernacles was to display God's union and communion with His people who were always in His presence. The elders will have the same place of unity with the Father that Jesus prepared for them. Paul said that the process of becoming one with Him has to do with being changed to be like Him.

> But we all, with open face beholding as in a glass the glory of the Lord, are changed into the same image from glory to glory, even as by the Spirit of the Lord. (2 Cor. 3:18)

The elders seated on the thrones surrounding the Father's throne will receive the highest measure of His glory. They, above all others, will be the most conformed to His image. They have earned that right by allowing their lives to be changed. They may sit in His presence—face-to-face. From their seats of authority to their crowns of authority to the authority of His name written on them, they will be vested with His authority. That will be glory! This was the answer to Jesus' prayer.

> That they all may be one; as thou, Father, art in me, and I in thee, that they also may *be one in us*: that the world may believe that thou hast sent me. . . . And the glory which thou gavest me I have given them; that they may be one, even as we are one: I in them, and thou in me, that they *may be made perfect in one*; . . . and I have declared unto them thy name. . . (John 17:21, 23, 26, emphasis added)

So we see that the glory all comes from being in Him. When this is accomplished in the Church, the world recognizes the authority. Paul defined the "riches of the glory of this mystery among the Gentiles" as "Christ in you, the hope of glory: whom we preach, warning every man in all wisdom, that we may present every man perfect in Christ Jesus" (Col. 1:27). Paul warned repeatedly that the flesh cannot help God out. It is only in the measure of our union with Him that any glory comes.

The elders, the "bread of faces," the "showbread" will declare the work of Christ's union with His people. These seats in His presence will always be occupied by various ones who display this glory. He was the bread that came down from heaven and gave people life. He entered into their lives as they partook of Him until He had worked in them "a far more exceeding and eternal weight of glory" (2 Cor. 4:17). They show the ultimate of what God can do with a person who yields all. Therefore, the elders always sitting before Him will replace the showbread of the other tabernacles. The table of showbread will have its place in the final tabernacle. It is an example (even in the millennium) of where God desires to bring all of His people.

And Again the Light

> And there shall be no night there; and they need no candle, neither light of the sun; for the *Lord God giveth them light*: and they shall reign for ever and ever. (22:5, emphasis added)

We have seen how the light of the Lamb will illuminate the whole city and shine down on the earth below, putting the sun and moon to shame. Nevertheless, here we see the light in respect to its effect on the saints. The light speaks spiritually of the light of the lampstand, Jesus, the light of the world, who gives forth truth for understanding. As the saints in the city bask in this light, they will continue to grow in spiritual understanding.

Many saints over the years have testified to having seen the heavenly realms in visions. Though these reports can never carry the weight of Scripture, they may add some insight to it. H. A. Baker reports what the Adullam children saw. He says the angels showed them the inside of one of the houses that lined the street opposite the river. They saw a room furnished with a golden table on which was a Bible, a flower vase, a pen, and a book. The pages of the Bible, which were bound with gold, emitted a glorious light that lit up the whole room. Looking at this report, it would seem that instruction is included in this part of the city.

Marietta Davis also testifies concerning learning in heaven. Caught up for nine days during an illness, she saw the infants' paradise. She says, "Children and infants are taught about the redemption and introduced to Christ's sacrifice by the angels." Perhaps this is why we are not shown the antitype of the brazen altar in the New Jerusalem. However, according to testimony, it is on this level that the cross is prominent. John was not shown the lower portions of the city. Here is the most likely place to learn more about the cross, since it is basic to both salvation and sanctification. The Bible, book, and pen seen by the orphans will offer opportunity for more understanding of God and His ways.

Much of the Church is ignorant of God's ways. Christians have been filled with the traditions and doctrines of men. Only truth from God's Word revealed by the Holy Spirit is eternal. Therefore, many saints will be starting with the infants and children to learn the ABCs of spiritual maturity.

Paul's ambition was to know Christ, to experience victory over the circumstances of life, and to obtain a good resurrection. When we learn all about people, we get to know them. Those who have failed to overcome the tests on the earth because of their lack of knowing Christ will be placed in paradise according to their development.

Therefore, we would expect to find the rewards for overcomers connected with their residency in the city. Marietta Davis was told that "these floral plains and warbling melodies are but the lower order of the habitation of the sanctified." [204] Sadhu Sundar Singh says regarding his visions: "In it [heaven] are innumerable planes of existance, and the soul is conducted to that plane for which its progress in the world has fitted it." He was told by one recently taken to heaven: "In nearby houses, saints like-minded to himself lived in happy fellowship." [205] H.A. Baker mentions that others visiting heaven report that there are arrangements of sevens in the heavenly order—a series of ascending plains, as well as a series of arrangements on each plain. Sundar Singh talked to souls in heaven before the resurrection. We would expect this to be true of the permanent dwelling in the New Jerusalem also, since the earning of rewards comes from life on earth, and the prizes will not be given out until after the resurrection. From all this, we believe the saints will have their own particular places where they will fit in and find their greatest joy.

We may speculate that if, indeed, there exist three ascending cities, those who fail to overcome dead religious works, unfaithfulness, and worldliness (the first three prob-

---

[204] Gordon Lindsay, *Scenes Beyond the Grave* (Dallas: Christ For the Nations, 1976) p. 22.

[205] Sundar Singh, *Visions of Sadhu Sundar Singh of India*, (Minneapolis: Anker G. Dahle, 1926) p. 27.

lems to overcome) will live in the first city along with the infants and children. Those who overcame worldliness or false teaching will reside in the second city, leaving the top city for those choice ones who will enjoy personal nearness to Christ. They will have overcome dead formalism, weakness in the things of the Spirit, and complacency.

Some will obtain enough personal glory to see Christ unveiled in all His splendor. While communication will be possible with all saints at all times, those who have visited heaven tell us that, in His presence, His glory must be toned down to the degree that the saints are prepared to look upon Him. Since glory translates into light energy, we understand why this must be so.

Looking back over the opportunities to overcome difficulties and develop glory, we can see how the appropriation of His work in believers' lives will create degrees of glory. Those who take advantage of the Lord's work as "the door of the sheepfold" will overcome the outer darkness. They will make it through the gate but not all the way to the street. They will be clothed only in the undergarment—the barest covering of light. They will have no developed glory. The more of Christ's work appropriated into the life, the more accumulation of His glory will be realized, and the greater capacity to behold His glory.

Since the furnishing of the tabernacles have a specific distance from the ark or throne in their relationship to it, we believe saints will reside near the last work of Christ they appropriated into their lives. The top overcomers will enjoy the fullness of Him who fills all in all. "And this is life eternal, that they might *know thee* the only true God, and Jesus Christ, whom thou hast sent" (John 17:3, emphasis added). The greatest thing, then, is to know God! Jeremiah says:

Thus saith the LORD, Let not the wise man glory in his wisdom, neither let the mighty man glory in his might, let not the rich man glory in his riches: but let him that glorieth glory in this, that he understandeth and knoweth me. (Jer. 9:23–24)

Yes, God will give His servants light, and they will reign forever and ever. Eternal life will continue to grow, ever expanding in the knowledge of God in the ages to come. Those beginning their ABCs in the lower city will mature and take on more authority. All His servants will serve Him.

Terrestrial people will continue to increase after death is abolished. Therefore, the administrators will have to assume greater responsibilities. Nothing will remain static because of the light. Therefore, those learning their ABCs will continue growing. After all, those in the heavenly city will have an ever-expanding universe to rule over.

The Conclusion of the Vision

Evidently, the "angel" showed John the inside of the top city that other testimonies say contains the throne. The water originates in the cloud over the throne where the Spirit "broods" over the waters, but they probably pour out of the sea of glass. After that, they flow to every level and plain right down to the infants' paradise. Later, they will surface on earth, flowing out of the holy mountain where the new temple will be built and then to the whole earth. The throne of heaven reaches to earth, God's footstool, and He will make the place of His feet glorious (Isa. 60:13).

After showing John the pure water, the angel finally spoke and said:

> These sayings are faithful and true: and the Lord God of
> the holy prophets sent his angel to shew unto his ser-
> vants the things which must shortly be done. (22:6)

The Lord God has revealed to us His servants His plans concerning the future of the world. They are not tentative. He will do these things! His integrity depends on it.[206] John has been the instrument that the Mighty Angel used to record the message to us all. Now the angel prophesies the Bridegroom's words to us as the Church, saying: "Behold, I come quickly: blessed is he that keepeth the sayings of the prophecy of this book" (22:7). John began this book of his vision, promising blessing to all who would read, hear, and keep the words of this prophecy. The Lord repeats the blessing again. It is here that John swears to the veracity of these things which he has seen and heard. The vision is complete.

Overwhelmed by the total message, John forgets that it is a mere messenger of God who has shown him the city. He falls down before the feet of the "angel." Again, he receives a reprimand. "Don't!" exclaims the angel. "I am a servant like you, the prophets, and those keeping the words of this scroll. Worship God!" By this he confirms his manhood. Actually, John had confirmed it earlier when he watched him measure the walls.[207] Then the angel begins to prophesy:

> Seal not the sayings of the prophecy of this book: for the
> time is at hand. He that is unjust, let him be unjust still:
> and he which is filthy, let him be filthy still: and he that
> is righteous, let him be righteous still: and he that is

---

[206] The reader must understand I refer to John's vision, not my interpretation of it.
[207] Rev. 21:17.

holy, let him be holy still. And, behold, I come quickly; and my reward is with me, to give every man according as his work shall be. (22:10–12)

The day of the Lord will come like a thief to try the hearts of people. Two classes of sinners and two classes of saints will be tried. The unjust person is simply the unjustified person whose sins were never covered by the blood. On the other hand, the filthy person loved to wallow in sin. Both are condemned. Both will receive just retribution for their works. The same is true of the redeemed. The righteous person has been cleansed by the blood, but the holy person has developed Christ's glory. Their rewards, too, will be different. Marietta Davis, viewing people in the process of dying, was told: "The departure of a spirit from its unsettled and shattered habitation below, worketh no change in its nature."[208]

The Alpha and Omega

I am Alpha and Omega, the beginning and the end, the first and the last. Blessed are they that do his commandments. (22:13–14)

This is the final mention of the Alpha and Omega, the first and last letters of the Greek alphabet. Three times now, Jesus has declared that He is these two letters. The first time John heard it was when he turned to see "the voice that spoke with him" who said, "I am Alpha and Omega . . . .What thou seest write in a book" (1:11). The title is new to John. We know this because John does not mention it in any his previ-

---

[208] Gordon Lindsay, *Scenes Beyond the Grave* (Dallas: Christ for the Nations), p. 19.

ous writings. In this mention, it reveals authority in a command intimating, "This is who I am, therefore write."

Jesus stated it again as John saw the heavenly city descending. This time, it was sandwiched in between the "true and faithful" words: "Behold, I make all things new" and "I will give to him the waters of life freely." The last mention comes after the promise to reward faithful work. From these three applications, we conclude that the Alpha and Omega conveys the authority in a language that can instruct, make things new, give life, and reward faithful service.

In short, Jesus says in effect, "I am the language by which the Godhead communicates with people and with all nature." In the past, we have understood His statement to mean He is the whole alphabet, the first letter and the last and everyone in between.

But this is not necessarily so. Electronics experts have devised a way to store volumes of information in computer banks using only two numbers, one and zero. From these two numbers, used in a myriad of combinations, every bit of information can be translated back into words via the electronic circuitry. Alpha and Omega are not just letters but numbers also. The Greeks had no separate number system but used each letter to represent a number. Neither did they have a number for zero. Alpha equaled one and Omega equaled eight hundred. If one and zero offer myriads of combinations for computer programmers, just think what combinations are available to 1/800. Consequently, we could understand Jesus to mean that He is the computer language that, by the power source of the Holy Spirit, enables people to tap into God's computer bank—the unlimited and infinite wisdom and knowledge of the Father (Col. 2:2–3) for in Him these things are hidden.

A careful study of the Bible indicates that everything that happens is the result of some "word." Jesus told the devil that "man shall not live by bread alone, but by every word that proceedeth out of the mouth of God" (Matt. 4:4). It was so from the beginning. Words carry authority. "God said . . . and there was." The author of the Book of Hebrews says that Jesus is "the author" of our faith. He writes our progress with words. A careful look at the list of the heroes of faith in Hebrews 11 shows that each acted upon some "word" from God.

Even the natural life on earth is activated by words. Biochemists have discovered that the life force of every living species, whether plant or animal, is carried on by words. DNA and RNA, nucleic acids in the cells that build the proteins of life, do so by a four-letter [209] language code. This code forms instruction to the cells as to which proteins to make—how and when. The code gives the orders in sentences punctuated by extra bits of protein at the end of each set of instructions. Biochemists have broken the code and can duplicate the instructions.

Since all life, whether spiritual or natural, proceeds from words, we see the importance of the Lord's statement. He is everything the world needs—the Word of life. All God's authority is transmitted through the Word. As the Bread of Life, He is the Logos, the solid expression of the thoughts of the Father. As the water of life (as found in the vine), He becomes a "rhema," a moving, fluid truth that develops faith. As the Alpha and Omega, He is the language from which both the Logos and the rhema are derived. Hebrews says that He is "upholding all things by the word of his power" (Heb. 1:3). Nothing in the universe can equal the power of the Word!

---

[209] Four is the spiritual number that speaks of the natural world.

Even God places more importance on His Word than His name.

> I will worship toward thy holy temple, and praise thy name for thy lovingkindness and for thy truth: for thou hast magnified thy word above all thy name. (Ps. 138:2)

The Alpha and Omega works all the works of God!

The Outsiders

> For without are dogs, and sorcerers, and whoremongers, and murderers, and idolaters, and whosoever loveth and maketh a lie. (22:15)

We have defined all these accursed ones except the dogs when we discussed the divisions of hell. According to Peter, two kinds of people reject the gospel after they have once embraced it: dogs and pigs.

> But it is happened unto them according to the true proverb, The dog is turned to his own vomit again; and the sow that was washed to her wallowing in the mire. (2 Pet. 2:22)

In Scripture, swine are always classified as unclean, so washing will not change their natures. This is a simile of a professor of the faith—one who walks among Christians, embracing the doctrine for a while but who never had a genuine experience with the Lord to change his heart. Eventually, he will obey his natural ways and return to his sin.

But the dog is of a different class. The dog in Scripture inspires contempt, being classified as the lowest of creatures. For instance, Deuteronomy says:

Thou shalt not bring the hire of a whore, or the price of
a dog, into the house of the LORD thy God for any vow:
for even both these are abomination unto the LORD thy
God. (Deut. 23:18)

Dogs typify persons who received the Lord into their
lives, even tasting of the power gifts. Like Balaam, they can
prophesy God's words [210] and lead others, but they love the
wages of unrighteousness. These "allure through the lusts
of the flesh, through much wantonness," says Peter (2 Pet.
2:18). Eventually, in pursuing their sin, they are overcome
and, finally, renounce the Holy Spirit, becoming apostates.
Like dogs, they will try to return to the Christ who was once
inside them. Nevertheless, they will not be able to receive
Him again because they are guilty of trampling the blood of
their salvation[211] underfoot. The writer of the Book of Hebrews says that a worse punishment (than physical death for
the broken law of the Old Testament) awaits them. Peter
also says they would have been better off never to have known
righteousness than to have turned from the holy commandments. The sad thing about these "dogs" is that many may

---

[210] Not that Balaam was ever a believer, but he is an example of greedy,
power-seeking people.

[211] Once the Holy Spirit is insulted by being renounced and expelled,
He cannot enter back into a person's spirit again. The Scripture says
that it is given unto men once to die. It also says that Jesus came to
taste death for every man—each man, one death. These had received
the Holy Spirit as a result of their initial faith in Christ's death for
them. But upon expulsion of the Holy Spirit, there is no legal way that
Christ can die again for them so that the Spirit can re-enter. Hebrews
6:4–6 says, "For it is impossible for those who were once enlightened,
if they shall fall away [apostatize], to renew them again unto repentance; seeing they crucify to themselves the Son of God afresh, and
put him to an open shame."

have been former servants of the Lord—pastors and teachers. Satan takes special pleasure in destroying them.

Thus, Jesus separates forever two classes of people—the righteous and the unrighteous. The righteous are blessed beyond measure in His presence. The unrighteous are relegated to the trash incinerator forever.

The Branch and the Morning Star

Jesus, still prophesying through His "angel/messenger," swears with an oath:

> I Jesus have sent mine angel to testify unto you these things in the churches. I am the root and offspring of David, and the bright and morning star. (22:16)

Here, the Lord declares the fact that He and His "angel" have the same voice by announcing, "I Jesus . . . am the root and offspring of David [the Branch], the bright and morning star." Isaiah originally prophesied the coming of David's offspring: "And there shall come forth a rod out of the stem of Jesse, a Branch shall grow out of his roots" (Isa. 11:1).

We know Isaiah speaks of a king springing out of the loins of David because of the mention of the ruler's "rod." Besides that, the rest of the chapter refers to the rule in the millennium. Jeremiah elaborates on the Branch more fully:

> Behold, the days come, saith the LORD, that I will raise unto David a righteous Branch, and a King shall reign and prosper, and shall execute judgment and justice in the earth. In his days Judah shall be saved, and Israel shall dwell safely: and this is his name whereby he shall be called, THE LORD OUR RIGHTEOUSNESS. Therefore,

behold, the days come saith the LORD, that they shall no more say, The LORD liveth, which brought up the children of Israel out of the land of Egypt; but, The LORD liveth, which brought up and which led the seed of the house of Israel out of the north country, and from all countries whither I had driven them; and they shall dwell in their own land. (Jer. 23:6–8)

This righteous Branch was revealed to Israel in the midst of the week (Zech. 3:8). Later in Zechariah's vision, He directs the building of the temple on earth. The title, the Branch, refers to the present work of the Mighty Angel fulfilling God's promises to Israel, i.e., returning them to their land, redeeming them, and purifying them in the "finer's pot" like silver.

The rest of the title that Jesus applies to Himself, the "Bright and Morning Star," refers to His past work as the Mighty Angel when He called Israel out of Egypt. At that time, He called the morning star, the planet Venus, into existence. (Ancient historical sources indicate that the planet Venus was originally a comet.) Velikovsky believed it was the visible cloud that led the children of Israel through the wilderness.

Paul tells us that the rock that followed Israel in the wilderness was Christ (1 Cor. 10:4). The rock Paul referred to is spoken of in Deuteronomy where Moses declares that Israel's rock is the God of truth and justice (Deut. 32:4). The psalmist called God "their rock, and the high God, their redeemer" (Ps. 78:35). Moses saw God as the "solid rock," their salvation, behind the comet of old.

The glorious things accomplished through this natural agent redeemed Israel from Egypt. Jesus, acting as their personal Angel directing the heavenly hosts, inflicted injury on the enemies of Israel. Pharaoh and his army perished in the Red Sea. Egypt's dragon (crocodile god) Rahab (the writhing serpentine tail of the comet which appeared to fight against the head with thunderbolts) also perished in the Red Sea in a mighty physical display of God's power.

Later, Israel was prevented from worshiping the morning star, itself, when Moses returned from the mountain. The golden calf was an attempt to form an image to the comet in the sky. Velikovsky says:

> The comet Venus, of which it is said that "horns grew out of her head," or Astarte of the horns, Venus coranata, looked like the head of a horned animal; and since it moved the earth out of its place, like a bull with its horns, the planet Venus was pictured as a bull. The worship of a bullock was introduced by Aaron at the foot of Mt. Sinai.[212]

Aaron's defense, when confronted by an angry Moses, was, "I put gold into the fire, and out came this calf." This must have appeared as strong supernatural evidence for a bull god, since the comet in the sky also took on this form at one time. Evidently, the image in the fire was Satan's handiwork, a craft to support the delusion.

Although Moses squelched the initial attempt to set up the worship of a star god openly, the movement went underground. Israel evidently continued to worship the star secretly, because God accused them of it later through the prophet Amos (5:26). Those who trusted in only that which they could see made images to represent the "star of [their]

---

[212] Immanuel Velikovsky, *Worlds in Collision* (New York: Doubleday, 1950), p. 180. Scriptures that may indicate the cloud as a comet are: Ps. 74:13–14; 78:23–25; 89:10 (Egypt's name for the dragon of the exodus was Rahab); Isa. 51:9; Amos 5:25–26.

god." This might explain why they lacked faith even in view of the mighty works of God on their behalf.

The other nations worshiped the bull openly. Satan, as Lucifer—the morning star—appropriated this power to himself (just as he does in this vision) and was worshiped by the other nations under the symbol of a bull or cow. The sacred cow of India could be a remnant of this ancient time.

Jesus came as the Morning Star. He was not the comet; He was the Captain over the hosts of God. The comet was one of the hosts. Jesus was the authority behind the natural agent. However, the star was all that was visible. It was only symbolic of the one directing it all. Thus, Christ, as the mighty Captain, came first as Israel's Morning Star. This second time, He will come as the Branch of Righteousness, the LORD OUR RIGHTEOUSNESS, the Sun of righteousness (Mal. 4:2) who follows behind the morning star.

The Final Invitation

And the Spirit and the Bride say, Come. (22:17)

The Spirit of God works alone or through the Church to persuade people. If they turn from their sin and choose God's mercy, they will escape the judgments of this book. Now is the time. Now is the hour of salvation. Come now while there is still mercy. Come before the angels bring forth the plagues and no one can enter His temple to intercede and stay His hand. Come, you sons of Abraham, be purified. Come now before the "fining pot" is fired. Come out of her, all you who are part of Babylon, all you who are chasing rainbows or seeking to be gods yourselves. Come, all you who carry a faltering lantern of Jehovah's witness. Come, be a part of the chaste virgin who is the Bride!

The Final Warning

After the final invitation, Jesus, still speaking a word of prophecy through His angel/messenger, closes the vision with a warning.

> For I testitfy unto every man that heareth the words of the prophecy of this book, If any man shall add unto these things, God shall add unto him the plagues that are written in this book. And if any man shall take away from the words of the book of this prophecy, God shall take away *his part* out of the book [tree][213] of life, and out of the holy city, and from the things which are written in this book. (22:18–19, emphasis added)

The two things He warns about are adding and subtracting from the prophecy. Since the consequences are severe, we would all do well to confirm our interpretation before we attempt to teach it to others. First, we must not add. That word in the Greek (according to Vine) is *epitithemi* which means literally "to put upon" (*epi*= superimposition (of time, place, order, etc) plus *tithemi*= "to place." To put any meaning to the words or the symbols other than what God intends or to draw from any source other than the Spirit of God who inspired them, brings destruction both to the teacher and the student of such an interpretation. Therefore, the first prerequisite must be to know the source of the interpretation so we will not add.

Teaching comes from three sources: the Spirit of God, that is, the spirit of truth; the spirit of man—reasoning in his own mind; and a demonic spirit who deliberately teaches lies. Human teaching will always be a mixture of at least

---

[213] King James says "book," but it is a wrong translation.

two of these sources. To find the interpretation of the Spirit of God, one must look to the teaching of godly people whose lives prove the Spirit's control and whose doctrines follow the orthodox, fundamental truths of Scripture. Out of this must be sifted that which comes from the teachers' own human spirits. This is possible when comparing teachers with each other and the Scriptures. One person's darkness[214] is covered by another person's light. The Spirit of Truth is our guide.

On the other hand, the mixture of the human spirit with a demonic spirit will add false meaning to the prophecy. These efforts lead students away from traditional salvation, causing them to bypass the blood of the cross. The following is a good example of this. The New Age SUN newsletter, a publication of the Spiritual Unity of Nations which is "dedicated to the spiritual unity of religions, nations and peoples," claims that

> No one can create divine order—it is already there—what we do is harmonize ourselves with this divine order.
>
> The Book of Revelation is written as a revelation—an unveiling of something. It is not the book of doom but rather a book of realization, an illumination. The theme of the book is the theme of our lives—to estab-

---

[214] Darkness is simply a lack of light, a failure to see because all the facts are not available. God does not intend this warning for earnest teachers who have put forth their best explanations. They meant no perversion. They simply suffered a lack of light. History and circumstances have shed much light in our time that the saints of other centuries could not even imagine. Think how the present civilization has advanced in the last fifty years both in social and technical fields. God is not warning those who missed the interpretation for lack of understanding but rather those who, through using the symbolism to develop false teaching, led others away from God.

lish divine order within our minds and hearts. In order to understand this book, we need the same spirit that John had—filled with illumination and understanding. John used imagery, i.e., a seven-headed beast 666, to portray states of consciousness. Thoughts put into form. A new heaven and a new earth mean new thoughts—a new order of life in Aramaic. The Book of Revelation is about the revelation of Christ within every individual Jesus revealed the Christ within himself which started a chain reaction to reveal it within all humanity.[215]

Notice the perversion: we do not need a Christ who is Savior. We all have a christ within us. To say that Revelation is not a book of doom is to remove its power because those who believe this teaching can render any meaning they like to "portray states of consciousness." We can agree with one statement; however, we do need the same spirit John had—the Holy Spirit. This teaching leaves its disciples to face the plagues. Therefore, adding would be false interpretation, humanistic or demonic.

Second, we must not take away from the "words . . . of this prophecy." Subtracting is taken from the Greek word *aphaireo* which means "to remove." It is translated "cut off" in Mark 14:47 and Luke 22:50, where Peter cut off the soldier's ear.

This portrays chopping pieces from the whole. By example, teachers who subtract from the full meaning of the prophecy. This could involve selecting certain passages for worth and discarding others, failing to see the literal interpretation, taking away its proper placement in time, or

[215] "New Age Apostasy," *Prophecy Newsletter.* International Christian Communications, Vol. 1,#7, quoted from S. U. N. (a New Age Newsletter) 1985 Back page.

removing its relevance to the Christian. To do so does not jeopardize the teachers or their disciples' salvation (provided it is based on sound doctrine), but it greatly hinders their knowledge of God's purposes. Worse, it obscures it for others—cutting them off from the blessing that comes from reading, hearing, and keeping the words of this book.

God is looking for those who will take enough interest in His plans for this earth that they will be helpful in organizing His future kingdom. Not only will they be helpful, but in learning about His providential unalterable plan for this earth, they will discover His wisdom, almighty power, and begin to know God's mind. If Christians understood the letters to the churches and grew to maturity, they would not be "cut off from the privileges of the tree of life and other such rewards promised to overcomers. However, to say that the Book of Revelation is relevant only to the past or has some vague allegorical meaning is to remove importance from the prophecy. Consequently, God may say in effect, "You don't believe I can do what I say I will do? *You* are not worthy to behold My glory at close range."

Other warnings of this nature are found in the Law (Deut. 4:2) and the historical writings (Prov. 30:6), which, coupled with this in the prophetic writings, make it clear that God expects us to believe what He says. Proverbs says to add to His words makes us liars. Deuteronomy says to add not nor diminish. God's heart cries: "O that they had such a [mind and] heart in them always, (reverently) to fear Me, and keep all My commandments, that it might go well with them, and with their children for ever!" (Deut. 5:29 AMP). To do this requires faith in His Word.

Continuing now with the remainder of the warning, Jesus says:

He which testifieth these things saith, Surely I come
quickly. Amen. [and John comments] Even so, come,
Lord Jesus. The grace of our Lord Jesus Christ be with
you all. Amen. (22:20–21)

Whether Christ comes tomorrow or a thousand years
from now, as finite short-lived creatures, we have only brief
spans of life to heed His warning. He *will* come quickly!

We add our agreement to John's words. Even so, Come!
Come with Your glory that we may see You. Come, adopt
us as full adult children that we may serve You. Come, oh
beloved Bridegroom, come. Take us to Your final tabernacle.

Conclusion

Our civilization ripens for judgment, so surely the end
is near. In the light of all this, is it not time the Church
grew up and made herself ready for the responsibilities
ahead? It seems obvious that most schisms and in-house
fighting over doctrine in the true Church result from immaturity. Let us understand this: God gives ministry for
one purpose only, that "we *all* come in the *unity of the faith,*
and *of the knowledge of the Son of God,* unto a perfect man,
unto the *measure* of the stature of the fulness of Christ"
(Eph. 4:13, emphasis added). Therefore, let us quit our bick-
ering, lay down our jealousies, move out of our exclusiveness, and get on with developing the kingdom of God within
the whole Church so the Bride will be ready to reign! Let
the Bride cry, "Draw me. Sanctify and cleanse me! Make me
fit to dwell in the palace of the King!"

To order additional copies of

RIGHTLY DIVIDING
THE
BOOK OF
REVELATION

Have your credit card ready and call
Toll free: (877) 421-READ (7323)
Or send $25.00* each plus $5.95 S&H** to

WinePress Publishing
P.O. Box 428
Enumclaw, WA 98022

Or order online at: *www.winepresspub.com*

*Washington residents, add 8.4% sales tax
**Add $1.50 S&H for each additional book ordered